March On !

Dorset's cap badge perpetuated on stone – Landi Kotal, Khyber – photographed by Sybil Graham in 1992.

March On!

An Infantry Battalion in England, India and Burma 1941 – 1945

Norman Havers

A SQUARE ONE PUBLICATION

First published in 1992 by
Square One Publications, Saga House
Sansome Place, Worcester WR1 1UA

British Library Cataloguing in Publication Data
Havers, Norman

March On!: Infantry Battalion in England,
India and Burma,
1941 – 1945
I. Title
940.54

ISBN: 1 872017 54 1

Typeset by Direct Design, 73 Cavendish Street, Worcester. (0905) 359856
Printed by Billings & Son, Worcester.

Dedicated to
The 2nd Battalion
The Dorset Regiment

Acknowledgments.

Readers of this book will become familiar with an exceptional personality—Dr Joe Chamberlin, our Medical Officer. His love for the battalion was matched by our affection for him. Now I am further indebted and record my gratitude for the help and encouragement, so characteristically and freely given throughout four years of writing. Similar debts are owed to Harold Jones, Andrew MacKenzie and Harry Newcombe, their memories of the great days when we were Dorsets, have been invaluable. All four have provided a stimulus without which I would have faltered. Jock Murrills has kindly donated the notes taken at the 'A' Company 'O' Group, on 27th April they, like himself, a miraculous survival of the subsequent battle. Ben Bazeley, one of those who built the Imphal to Tamu road, has also contributed his time and I am indebted to him for maps and the item on Kangpokpi. A valued addition to the text is Mr Niketu Iralu's account of the arrival of the Japanese, also the action as a guide, performed by his brother Savino.

The War Diary and Lieutenant-Colonel White's book 'Straight on for Tokyo' have been spines on which to build, as has my outline account so laboriously written in longhand by Eileen in 1947. She, as with so many wives of authors, bore the brunt of years when, the writing of 'March on' dominated all else, and drafts needed vetting and constructive criticism. Jane, our daughter, also donated long hours to the correction of my manuscript.

Tony Bridge, who reluctantly departed for the job of Brigade Major to 5 Brigade, is another whose praise and encouragement kept me going. As did Sybil Graham and Glyn and Vivian Partos, their belief in the value of this undertaking came when most needed. To them I express my thanks.

The following books have added to my knowledge of the operations throughout Burma:

Fergusson, Bernard, Beyond the Chindwin, Collins, 1945.
Brett-James, Anthony, Report my Signals, Hennel Locke, 1948.
Slim, Field Marshal Sir William, Defeat into Victory, Cassell, 1956.
Allen, Louis, Burma The Longest War 1941-1945, Dent, 1984.
Seaman, Harry, The Battle at Sangshak, Leo Cooper, 1989.

My knowledge of the battle at and around Kohima has been revived by reading, yet again: Swinson, Arthur, Kohima, Cassell, 1966.

My understanding of that remote world in which we were, has been furthered by: Williams, J.H, Elephant Bill, Hart-Davis, 1955.
Wheeler, Tony, BURMA - a travel survival kit, Lonely Planet, 1985.

I am grateful to Collins for the quotation from The Turn of the Tide 1939–43, by Arthur Bryant, in which General Sir Alan Brooke describes a visit to the 2nd Division in Yorkshire. I also acknowledge the kind permission of the British Library to make use of the map Burma 93 C/l.

I acknowledge my debt to the Imperial War Museum for their photographs of Dorsets at the Irrawaddy and Ywathit and of the Ava Bridge. Those of the Grant tank and Shenam Ridge are included by Courtesy of the Director, National Army Museum, London. The photograph of the Dorsets arrival at Southampton is included thanks to the kindness of the Editor of the Evening Echo, Bournemouth. Special thanks are due to Rosemary Hill, for finding the splendid one of the Reina del Pacifico. The remainder have been in my possession since the days when they were taken.

The generosity of Colonel R Wheatley DSO, in letting me have a copy of Popham, Hugh, The Dorset Regiment, Leo Cooper, 1970, enabled me to conclude the history of our regiment.

That Major General Walker CBE was prepared to read my manuscript and write the Foreword, is a compliment to all who served under the Dorset cap badge. They, like me, will be grateful to him.

My publisher, Mary Wilkinson, deserves a special mention for tolerance when faced by my manuscript. Her advice and guidance has made the book possible and for that I am properly appreciative.

Contents

List of Maps

With the exception of the map on page 68 these were drawn by the author.

FOREWORD

Major General M.J.D. Walker CBE
General Officer Commanding 2nd Infantry Division

A Regiment's history is made by those who serve with it; every member of a Regiment contributes in some measure and deeds of valour, demanding courage and steadfastness are performed daily - many of them going unnoticed. But that does not alter the fact that they have been performed.

It is only those who were there, who know the stark realities of the Dorset's contribution to the War in Burma – the hostility of the environment and the enemy, the risks of death, the tragic loss of friends, the comradeship of shared adversity and the hardihood of the dangerous months during which body and soul fight the enemy, the elements and fatigue. Others can only guess what it was all like.

Field Marshal The Viscount Slim describes the war in Burma as a Soldiers' War and how victory came, not from the work of any one man, but from the sum of the efforts of the men in the ranks and their regimental officers.

In this book, Norman Havers describes in vivid and remarkable detail both the nature of the war years and this 'Soldiers' War' from the perspective of a regimental officer in 2nd Battalion The Dorset Regiment. It is a tribute to those who served with such distinction in the battalion and a graphic portrayal to those who did not, of five years in the battalion's life. I commend it to all.

1st March 1992
Imphal Barracks

York

Michael Walker

The 39th and the 54th Regiments, which in 1881 amalgamated to become the 1st and 2nd Battalions, The Dorsetshire Regiment, shared the honours and distinctions that followed service throughout the world. Thus when the 2nd Battalion on June 23rd 1944, were at milestone 100 on the road outside Imphal, it was the following greetings that were received by Lieutenant-General Montagu Stopford:

> Lieutenant-Colonel O.G.W.White and all ranks 2nd Battalion, The Dorset Regiment pay their humble duty to their Corps Commander on this ONE HUNDRED & EIGHTY SEVENTH Anniversary of the BATTLE of PLASSEY. They assure him that this battalion continues to pursue the enemy with that same indomitable will and energy which inspired MAJOR EYRE COOTE and our illustrious forebears to meet, defeat and rout the NABOBS Hordes on that memorable field. "Primus in Indis".

The motto "Primus in Indis" (First in India) and the battle honour "Plassey", were unique to the 39th Regiment. They had been awarded following the victory of three thousand men under Clive of India, at Plassey, near Calcutta, on June 23rd 1757. There they had faced an army numbering fifty-five thousand under Surajah Dowlah, Nabob of Bengal, and routed them in an overwhelming victory. Three years earlier the 39th had been the first British regiment to land in India and at Plassey, with conspicuous valour, it took the lead in the centre of the line of attack. Thus the motto bears a double meaning, for it not only records that the Regiment was the first of the King's regiments to serve in India, but was first in courage in the battles of those days.

Introduction

Sunday 3rd September 1939

A day so well remembered, not only as the first day of a war that was to change our lives, but as one of warm, serene and unbroken sunshine, so much in contrast to the cold reality of a European War; following the German invasion of Poland, two days before. That sun also in striking contrast to the grim and sombre broadcast by Prime Minister Neville Chamberlain, advising us, as we had anticipated he would, that we too were at war with Germany. And yet afterwards, as we turned away from our wireless sets and in some cases returned to the sunshine, perhaps to complete our air-raid shelter, there was a profound sense of relief. Indeed there was almost a lightening of hearts in the ending of the years in which we as a nation had abjectly compromised with the dictators - Hitler and Mussolini, in unworthy endeavours to maintain peace. Now we and our Empire, together with our Allies, would take up arms and cleanse the world of the evil of the more formidable of the two (the Italian could wait) and, as before on such momentous occasions we were supremeley confident in our ability to do so, no matter how great the odds.

On that day the 2nd Battalion The Dorsetshire Regiment was stationed at Aldershot, being one of the three infantry battalions within the 5th Infantry Brigade of the 2nd Infantry Division. Three weeks later they were en route to France, with the division as a whole, to take up a defensive position on the Franco-Belgian border.

This was to be the first leg of a long pilgrimage to distant places, far beyond contemplation at a time when there were no expectations other than action in Europe alongside the French Army. Both facing our common enemy - the Germans.

The winter was not only bitterly cold for ill-housed men striving to establish defences in waterlogged or frozen ground, but demoralising in its lack of action against the enemy. Thus it would have been with a sense of relief and feelings such as those held on 3rd September when, in the early hours of 11th May 1940 the division and the Dorsets with them, moved forward into Belgium to counter the invasion of that country by the Germans. But by the 16th, they were in danger of being overwhelmed and, with the front line breaking around them, their withdrawal commenced. Continuing clashes with the ever advancing enemy and brave rearguard actions were to no avail. Still within their brigade and division the Dorsets after fourteen harrowing days reached Dunkerque, their strength then less than three hundred, about one third of what it had been. There they embarked on a most unlikely troop-carrying vessel, a Thames dredger, but which eventually and safely put them ashore at Margate.

By the end of June the 2nd Dorsets (as we were generally known) were operational and seemingly recovered from the disasters in France. They were happy to be established in their new and more agreeable role of defending some six miles of the Yorkshire coast, centred on the seaside town of Hornsea.

It was there that I, newly commissioned and with so much to learn about soldiering, joined them at the beginning of January, 1941, destined to take command of 8 Platoon in 'A' Company.

CHAPTER ONE

The Making of a Battalion

1941

The anxieties of 1941, as Britain adjusted to the defeat of the French and of its own near defeat and continuing vulnerability, did not impinge too much on us in Yorkshire, a county then only marginally affected by the war and, having an abundance of open spaces, ideal for the training of soldiers. We remember the bitter cold of winter on the moors and the snow driven into face and body by the winds of those exposed places. How we cursed them at the time and thought ourselves hard done by, but no country could have been better for the toughening of our 'new blood'.

My first days with the 2nd Dorsets would have been no different to those of other, similar, new arrivals – trying hard to appear nonchalant in the execution of duties for which we had had little preparation. Almost immediately, one was Battalion Orderly Officer and thus visiting strange bodies of men in strange places, as part of the routine of attending Company meals and enquiring as to whether there were "any complaints", doing so in a manner to deter (one hoped) expressions of dissatisfaction. I was there on a bad day – there was a shortage of meat and the complaints were many. Later one proceeded to 'turn out the guard' at Battalion Headquarters; established at Wassand Hall, a house within grounds inland of the town of Hornsea. Having turned out and inspected the guard, a call was made at the detention room to see the prisoners. Blackouts had to be inspected and the guard disturbed a second time in the small hours of a night spent sleeping in the orderly room, where one prayed for peace and quiet. A breakfast inspection at 0730 hrs ended the assignment.

Six months of service had achieved much in an impossibly short time (see Appendix A), but the real learning was starting now. How fortunate I was to be where I was! Doing things, even the tricky supervision of grenade throwing by the ham-handed, who could cast grenades to the rear as well as to the front, was easy. Not easy was formal routine, when one so much feared doing or saying the wrong thing. How we envied the self-assurance of the regulars, seemingly so sure of themselves in this, their accustomed habitat.

I was allowed to settle down in the Battalion as a temporary member of 'R' Company (the Reserve Company) prior to taking up my allotted platoon. A stay lengthened by a bout of 'flu but in due course I was interviewed by our C.O., Lieutenant-Colonel E.L. Stephenson DSO., MC., wished well and was on my way to 'A' Company ensconced in the village of Withernwick, in splendid isolation and nicely back from the coast. A place remembered for kind hospitality, its farmhouses lit by oil lamps (the mess was in one and I in digs in another) and for the snow which enveloped us for much of January.

8 Platoon would have looked askance at this raw subaltern with whom they had

been saddled and, by expecting the worst, would have tried to shield themselves from the consequences. I had been told that they were a good platoon and once I recovered from the full realisation of the heavy responsibility thrust upon me and these strangers became familiar personalities, life settled into an agreeable routine. We consisted of the Platoon Sergeant, a Lance-Sergeant*, a Corporal, three Lance-Corporals and 32 men in the customary three Sections and Platoon HQ. Most were from London or the big cities and able to accept this interlude of soldiering with an inbuilt toughness behind a wisecracking unflappability, which supported me as it did them. I remember them with admiration and affection.

Within a few days I was able to write home: 'I think I can honestly say that I am enjoying life as never before'.

As was customary for our newly commissioned officers, I was soon off to the Infantry Training Centre at Lincoln, and taking a toughening course at the Platoon Commanders' School, established by 1st Corps. For two weeks, much as at our Officer Cadets Training Unit, or OCTU for short, we fulfilled the roles of men in an infantry platoon.

I vividly recall the first morning, we had hardly moved off before we were wading through a river, so cold that it would have been frozen solid had it not been fast moving. Then to continue almost non-stop across an open landscape until 1530 hrs, by which time we had made a couple of bayonet charges across ploughed fields (can there be anything more exhausting?) and surprised to be still on our feet which, being encased in mud, were like lead weights. But the food we ate that evening, like a pack of wolves wearing service dress, was excellent and included lashings of butter and cream. Subsequent days included two designated as 'Wet', during which we could be up to our waists in water and we had the misfortune of a couple when there was an over-generous fall of snow. They and a final endurance test in which, when caught by enemy fire in a ploughed field, we were made to lie flat in half-frozen mud while awaiting a smoke screen, added much to our earlier training and we departed better soldiers.

**On 24th and 25th February our routine was interrupted by a 2nd Division exercise, one of a series to which our reaction, favourable or otherwise, was generally determined by the weather and the amount of marching. In this we had to repel German forces of an infantry division which, together with an armoured division, had overrun the defences situated between Atwick and Bridlington – an extent of sandy beach. We Dorsets had the initial task of defending the town of Great Driffield. Then, rejoining our brigade and together with 4 Brigade and in conjunction with the 8th Armoured Division, we attacked the enemy and recovered Bridlington. Stirring stuff! The second day was watched by General Sir Alan Brooke, C in C Home Forces, who wrote:

> "to Bridlington to watch exercise by 2nd Division. Very cold and whole country covered with snow" ... "Under such conditions it is hard to maintain the enthusiasm of troops in training. And yet those winter Exercises were essential and I have the most vivid recollection of that heartening enthusiasm displayed by all ranks under the most trying conditions."

* *Sergeant Gwilliam and Lance-Sergeant Oliver.*

** *See Appendix B*

In March, for greater mobility, we moved inland to the town of Selby and, when our Company Commander, Captain Donald Baynes, announced where we were going and described its vital statistics of three cinemas and a multitude of pubs, the cheers were loud and long. And as those cinemas charged us half price, the best seats were only nine pence. Easily affordable, even for us.

Another Divisional exercise followed, one in which I was Column Commander to the main body – three miles of vehicles. With a pre-dawn start and snow falling, I was map reading like never before and learning the job the hard way – and physically hard too, for our trucks were without windscreens. Their absence had the advantage of allowing better vision forward so that, with eyes half closed against the bitter cold, you peered beyond the patch of light from the masked headlamps into a dim world of vague shapes, one that was sensed as much as seen, and we longed for the dawn.

A day or two later I was an umpire in a two-day Divisional signals exercise in The Wolds. Umpiring was popular as one was able to shed one's pack, wear a white arm-band, with luck you had a vehicle and, using just a modicum of discretion, 'killed' senior officers.

This 'learning by doing' kept subalterns busy within a demanding routine in which, as we crept up the ladder of seniority, and leave or courses meant that other officers were absent, we could find ourselves acting as company commander. The Friday afternoon Pay Parade, taken by all officers in turn, was an occasion when subalterns were in contact with all the 130 or so men, and learned names, and also improved their arithmetic! The withdrawal from the bank of what seemed to us a large quantity of cash, and dispensing it knowing that any deficiency at the end of the day was our responsibility, was something of a headache – great would be our relief when all balanced! Every few days there was the unwelcome job of Company Orderly Officer – a 24 hour duty, and always someone had to look after the messing. Church parades, when we were expected to look and be smart, became numerous.

From time to time junior officers would arrive, some to stay, others to go on elsewhere. With other ranks also coming and going we were something of a changing society, but slowly and surely becoming a cohesive whole with an identity. Many of those in transit were rejects from other battalions, and I remember well the arrival of a corporal and three or four privates of the Welch Regiment and the terrible blight they cast upon 8 Platoon until, to our delight, they were shifted on...

During 27th, 28th and 29th of March, the Dorsets were a small element within a major exercise involving, it was said, 100,000 troops whose great responsibility it was to defend that part of Britain. The size of the operation was apparent during the first night as we moved in our column of vehicles towards the supposed enemy landing; sharing a road with many other units that were new to us and in which artillery was most evident, they pulling back to reform in our rear. A recipe for chaos, as every type of military vehicle from tanks downwards jostled for road space in darkness, so that they might progress in opposite directions along a winding road. That we managed to move unscathed and at high speed as often as we did, between the frequent periods of little or no progress, was something of a miracle.

At 0400 hrs we descended from our vehicles so that we might continue our advance on foot, and doing so along a minor road from the A614 at Moor End. Later, when south of Market Weighton, we struck due east across country; very probably those inhabitants looking out upon this scene of great activity were drawing consolation, if nothing else, from the sight of so many troops for their defence should the Germans really come. We then crossed that part of The Wolds lying between the villages of Sancton and Bishop Burton, before returning to the lower ground and continuing across country to Molescroft and beyond, stopping only when we were north of Beverley. Rest within the shelter of a garage, preceded the midnight crossing by 'A' Company, of the more than bank high River Hull and the adjacent canal. This, our first experience of such 'messing about in boats', was done in a near gale with rain and sleet. Those who were there will remember the paralysing cold of that second night, made worse by the approach to the river across a field under two inches of water and over which the assault boats had to be carried. With wet feet, following the crossing, we covered another mile, passing through Tickton and finally turning north towards Eske Wood. We halted to await the dawn, sheltered by no more than the hedge of a field, having no greatcoats, for they could not be brought forward to us. At pre-dawn, huddled groups could be seen seeking warmth around forbidden fires. The gathering light disclosed a dreary world of wet snow and slush, and Donald hurried off to find shelter, where we remained until 1300 hrs when the scheme was abandoned. It being a Saturday we were more than delighted to be back in Selby at 1630 hrs, in good time for the opening of pubs, which must have enjoyed a roaring trade!

In a letter to my mother I wrote: "one thing about these schemes is that they make so enjoyable the simple pleasures of eating and sleeping". Indeed they did! Demanding exercises were essential, for they not only helped to toughen amateur soldiers who had not experienced France, but they enabled those commanding at Brigade, Division and Corps levels to practice the art of moving large bodies of men and their appendages under realistic conditions.

A week later we started a four-day Corps scheme.

So much activity played havoc with the issue socks which, at foot inspections, I found so full of holes as to be beyond repair. Five weeks earlier, my mother had started marshalling ladies at her church to knit socks and they were arriving, together with scarves, gloves and mittens.

At about that time I received my Government issue camp kit, consisting of a folding bed and chair (still in occasional use), canvas bucket, bath and basin, all rolled up in a valise, which doubled as an outer sleeping-bag.

Under the more temperate conditions of early May, but still described by me as 'two pullover weather', we were doing cross-country runs in the manner of those units commanded by General Montgomery, who had decreed that all under the age of forty – and from which there were no exceptions – did a seven mile run each week. This was partly to eliminate the 'dead wood' among majors and above. I doubt that 2 Div. had many useless senior officers after France and the running, which we disliked, was soon dropped and forgotten.

Then there was an Inter-Brigade Stunt, of which we expected the worst and which fulfilled our expectations. After an afternoon march of nine miles, which was easy enough, we were kept hanging about until 0230 hrs; then to set off fast-marching across country for ten and a half hours and battle for and capture our objective. A combination of cold, dampness and just too much hard going wrecked our feet, sufficiently for the 20 mile march home having to be cancelled, and we were given transport.

We were not sorry on 17th May to be boarding a train back to Hornsea – if only to rest our feet in the static role of coastal defence. For such a move each company marched to a collecting area, on this occasion Selby Football Ground. Having assembled and reported ourselves as present and correct, we marched as a battalion behind our Corps of Drums, to the railway station – there to board a 'special'. At our destination we would enter the town, again formally marching in what we hoped was a reasonable display of military precision and smartness – sufficient to impress our hosts and ignoring, as best we could, the inevitable flanking escort of small boys. As we progressed the companies departed their separate ways to their designated areas, guided by a member of the advance party that had been busy in preparation for our arrival.

No Withernwick for 'A' Company this time but a front line position, 8 Platoon finding itself not only on the left of the company, but on the extreme left of the Dorsets' front and just within a line of cliffs extending northwards to the right flank of our friends – the Camerons, a mile away. The 1st Battalion The Queen's Own Cameron Highlanders and the Territorial Army Battalion – The 7th Worcestershire Regiment, were our opposite numbers in 5 Brigade and our lives were to be intertwined throughout the war, as they were, but less directly, with the infantry battalions in the two other brigades within the 2nd Division, they being:-

4th Brigade	1st Battalion Royal Scots
	2nd Battalion Royal Norfolk Regiment
	1st/8th Battalion Lancashire Fusiliers
6th Brigade	1st Battalion Royal Berkshire Regiment
	1st Battalion Royal Welch Fusiliers
	2nd Battalion Durham Light Infantry.

On that cliff, 8 Platoon settled into slit trenches dug into the front edge, poor shallow things which we were only able to improve marginally, due to the unstable nature of the gravelly soil. We were well aware that if we had to fight the Germans from them, a few shell bursts and they would be no more than a heap of loose earth on the beach, and we with them! As instructed, we manned them at dusk and dawn which, in early summer, allowed us less than three hours in bed, but that could be supplemented during the day.

Morning stand-down was when visibility to sea attained ten miles as advised by the coastguards, just down the road. On a dull day that could be noon or after. I have happy memories of mornings spent below those cliffs, strolling in solitude along my deserted beach to which civilian access was prohibited; made fascinating by the jetsam of ship's timbers, life-belts, some bearing strange names (what I wonder was the Graslin, its house flag two blue vertical stripes on a white ground?) and other bits and pieces in amazing variety. Once, I had, until they were dealt with by the Navy, six conical

German mines. Mines coming ashore and having to be detonated were a frequent reminder of the war at sea, as was a drifting lifeboat a mile out, appearing and disappearing within the waves of an angry sea. Using binoculars, three men could be seen within it and, as we watched, they fired verey lights. Our coastguards guided the Bridlington RNLI lifeboat to their rescue.

Much of this record of those distant days comes from letters to my mother, their contents a constant surprise. One in May mentions a run of success I had at cards, against the six other officers in our company mess – Donald Baynes, Captain Thomas our second-in-command (soon to depart), Second-Lieutenants Rolfe and Holder, a new arrival which must have been Clive Chettle and an attached gunner. Such had been my success that it was suggested I must have 'worked' the shipping lines in peace time as a professional gambler, probably under the alias of 'Fat Joe'. It is that word 'fat' that surprises me – after so much exercise!

So topsy-turvy was our routine that I started a letter dated 1st June at 0345 hours, having returned from an inspection of my Section posts – incidentally in pouring rain. The Platoon's fishing had been something of a wash-out for the weather had been so bad, with high winds making storm seas, that a 'trot' (a long baited line) all 60 feet of it, laid a week earlier had remained beyond our reach.

In mid-June, after a lot of farewells with the locals seemingly very sorry to see us go, we left Hornsea for good, aware that we had more important tasks ahead.

We returned to Selby for a tougher regime under a new commanding officer, for we also said farewell to Lieutenant-Colonel P.G. (Peggy) Boon who had succeeded Colonel 'Steve' and who had ruled over us with a light hand. We had become slack, it was said, and were in need of a shake-up, and that we got.

Our new C.O. was 43 years old Lieutenant-Colonel G.N. Wood OBE, MC, a much respected Dorset officer with a good World War 1 record and service in India between the wars, which included two years in the Khyber, when he was a Brigade-Major; but he was soon to be described by me, in one of those letters, as a 'Terror'. Among his failings, when viewed from the level of a subaltern (no man is perfect), was his expectation that officers worked seven days a week; thus one's presence in York on a Saturday was not easy to justify. But we survived and became a better unit. George Wood is remembered for galvanizing the battalion through its officers, the junior ones in particular. And in particular also for his obsession with messing and his insistence that every mess (each company had its own) must have a Duty Officer present at every meal. He had instigated a weekly Officers' Conference, held in the evening so as to not interfere with routine, and at which our shortcomings of the past week were made clear. At one, following his discovery that his order regarding messing was not being fully implemented, he ordered that, until he decided otherwise, all officers would attend all meals unless prevented by duty. The subsequent weeks remain clear in the memory, we think of them with a mixture of horror and wry amusement and of the strange sights as officers left their beds on Sunday mornings and hurried through the streets. And of Headquarters Company, so flush with officers that a dozen could be watching half that number of men eating their Saturday supper.

The return to Selby saw a change from the frost and rain which had so bedevilled life at Hornsea to quite a heat-wave. Thus an 'A' Company anti-invasion exercise, during which we battled the 16 miles from near Wetwang, east of Driffield to Rudston near Bridlington, had us sweating. On such occasions Yorkshire hospitality proved itself when we sought night billets, the need of our HQ being for a room with a light, where plans could be made and orders given. And what a splendid variety we had, as on this occasion – first night the kitchen of a small pub, second the attic of a vicarage.

Part of our training was concerned with the theory and application of clearing built-up areas, as would be needed were the Germans to take possession of villages. A drill was evolved so that the approach to and searching of occupied buildings was done under covering fire, mainly from our light machine-guns and movement in the open was by short dashes to cover. During a morning at the end of June, 'A' Company carried out a Village Fighting Exercise in the village of Church Fenton, and while the cooks prepared lunch we officers looked-in at the pub. There we met the Chief Instructor at the nearby airfield and Flight-Lieutenant Nicholson VC., who still showed the scars from the aerial battle, for which he had been decorated. At a time when the army was not held in high regard by the RAF, it was exhilarating that these two, who had been watching our advance down the street, should shower us with compliments on our morning's work.

The outcome was an invitation to the Company to see the airfield and have tea there as their guests and that we five officers would fly. On reaching Church Fenton Airfield, all but we five went off with guides. Rolfe and I were paired to go up in an Airspeed Oxford and had a wonderful 75 minutes, during which we were able to take the controls. It was my first flight and I marvelled at the beauty of the world below and of the clouds when we broke through to the unbroken sunshine above them.

On that day, the temperature being high and our exercise a strenuous one, we were in shirt sleeve order, ie – in shirts and trousers, not dress for formal visiting. On approaching the officers' mess for tea, there were objections from RAF officers who were not of our party, to our lack of jackets and our exposed braces. Some pacifying was necessary before we were reluctantly allowed in, much to the embarrassment of our hosts and ourselves.

In August we were off by train for 'field firing' on the eastern slopes of the Pennines at Wharton Camp, from the village of that name, a few miles to the north of Richmond. There, in open country, we fired our weapons for two days, using live ammunition under as near to war conditions as was possible and enjoyed the excitement that resulted from an element of danger. Having done that we were to march back the 70 miles, and of these we eliminated ten during the evening of that second day. That gave us an easy 15 miles on the next day, to an arranged night at a cricket field; with the men in marquees and the officers in the pavilion. Our optimistic cooks thought that our vehicle camouflage nets could be used to catch trout in the adjacent river; needless to say they couldn't.

Donald Baynes, by then a major, had moved on and had been succeeded by Captain Dick Purser, a regular officer and a Dorset who had only recently joined us. Knowing Dick's love of shooting, I think it probable that it was his idea that we should try for rabbits on the adjoining estate. Armed with rifles and my pistol, we had bagged two when we fell foul of the irate owner and had to withdraw.

Next day we marched to Wetherby, en route fighting off an agreed attack by our

Bren-gun carriers, who attacked us again in the night – a wet one. However on the last day, after a mid-day battle in a village, we were home and dry by early evening.

Leave, which meant so much to everybody, had consisted of eight days and a 48 hours' break every three months, the latter little used as we were so far from home. Now they were combined to give a clear eight days at destination, a material improvement. I noted that one could catch the train at Kings Cross at 1600 hrs and be at Selby four and a half hours later.

On 19th August we changed base again in a move north of 30 miles to the small market town of Boroughbridge. With a population of only 800 it was a fraction the size of Selby but, with open country almost at our back doors and forgetting all those pubs and the cinemas, it was an infinitely preferable base for a very active battalion. Desirable also in its location, on the major north and south road the A1, at the crossing of the River Ure, 50 miles inland of Bridlington Bay, with that tempting beach for an enemy landing. Of necessity companies were widely distributed, but we in 'A' were fortunate in being allocated the house and grounds of Boroughbridge Hall, near the town centre. There the men lived in huts and company headquarters occupied the house, a building only remarkable for its state of chronic decay. It was comfortably near the Three Greyhounds Hotel, requisitioned as the officers' mess and where most officers lived. Those who did not were married and chose to have their wives living in or near the town, in the manner of camp-followers in earlier campaigns. This was much to the disapproval of George Wood, who would have been delighted to order them home, because they flouted the Army policy that, where possible, southern units were in the north and vice versa. Thus in the event of invasion, distance would reduce the stress of divided loyalty between family and unit. To fully enjoy a war, and strangely there was much that could be enjoyed, one had to be single, which thankfully I was.

Not being in billets we received a Field Allowance of 14s. 0d. a week, the equivalent of what had been paid for our digs. My recollection is that Second-Lieutenants were in receipt of a 12s. 6d. a day (62 1/2p), from which there were, as always in the services, deductions – no wonder our favourite tipple was beer!

For three weeks the battalion was host to a trio of Polish officers, whose heel clicking and stiff formality in the mess when our Colonel was present put us to shame. We were sorry for them in their loneliness. What, I wonder happened to them?

During this period 'A' Company had an unexpected addition to its strength, in the arrival of Private Chichester-Constable. A veteran of World War 1, the scars of which showed in his twisted face, he was a recently cashiered officer, having – it was said – knocked down a senior officer who had made a derogatory remark about a lady. We who knew him could well imagine him doing so. All ranks liked and admired him and he seemed to like us, for he chose to remain in the battalion after he had regained his commission.

We then entered a particularly busy routine of night exercises, ranging from 'digging-in' in front of an enemy position, to attacks on actual airfields of which there was an ample supply in that part of Yorkshire. Human nature being what it is, those acts of hostility against another service, were always popular. On one occasion in which 8 Platoon was to the fore we not only attacked under cover of smoke and cut their periphery wire fencing but advanced through the gap in a full-blooded charge on the defending RAF personnel, our bayonets fixed and ready for use – real inter-service warfare!! These were encouraged by the RAF as an effective way of testing their ground attack defences and, I imagine, for the way in which they enlivened a dull routine in need of excitement, as did ours.

During the closing months of 1940, The Chiefs of Staff whose wartime role was the direction of the Fighting Services, appreciating the futility of a linear defence along some two thousand miles of coast, nearly half of which was assailable, adopted a policy of mobile defence behind an outer screen. In the summer of 1941 the 2nd Division was an important element in that striking force. Situated so ideally as we were, we could move rapidly north or south to counter a German landing on the east coast; as in September, on the most memorable of schemes. Then the enemy had 'landed' at Skegness, sufficiently distant for the dash south of 100 miles or so to generate a momentum of its own. This was a fast moving exercise in which we had priority over other traffic and in the manner of fire-engines, dashed at maximum speed towards our objective; having the added bonus of the Home Guard on duty at road junctions to ensure our unrestricted right of way. Great fun!

At such times when the Army remained woefully deficient in troop carrying vehicles, rifle platoons travelled in the upholstered comfort of single deck buses which had been conscripted into 'companies' and whose civilian drivers shared our enjoyment in driving with such a wild abandon.

A few days later we travelled north to the vicinity of Hadrian's Wall, near Hexham, a scheme I remember only for my failure to see The Wall and for kind hospitality after a cold night in the open, when I was invited to enjoy the comfort of a bathroom.

Soccer above all games, then and later, was the most popular. At Boroughbridge weekly inter-platoon matches, in which platoon commanders had to play as part of the policy of moulding our lives into the lives of those for whom we were responsible, were taken very seriously. Long suffering 8 Platoon was sorely tried by my poor efforts at right-back yet, in spite of that handicap, we were only losing one game in four, an example of their excellence.

We were good at stacking stooks, as we discovered when we went to the aid of a local farmer, desperately short of labour. While there we tackled all the allied jobs associated with a harvest, from building a rick to driving the tractor, and performed them with zeal. Such work helped to give a purpose to life so seldom apparent in training, much of which, for the poor bloody infantryman, consisted of the perpetual foot slogging from A to B and having reached B, returning to A. Those fast moving exercises were the 'icing on the cake' and civilians seeing them and army vehicles perpetually dashing hither and thither, were convinced that their wonderfully mechanised army of which they read and heard so much, seldom marched. That may well have been so with the gunners, for example, but we infantry seldom rode and one sacrosanct item in the weekly programme was the 25 mile route march, wearing packs and carrying weapons.

If by some strange quirk of fate you led an efficient rifle platoon, ie. not a specialist platoon with its mortars or carriers or whatever, but an ordinary rifle company platoon (there were 12 in an infantry battalion) which in action would man the front line trench, you could in later life congratulate yourself on having achieved something as psychologically difficult as life can provide. That it was possible was due to the remarkable tolerance of the men and their ability to see through your veneer and those many failings to the inner man who was doing his best and who anyway, was almost as much in the 'excrement' as they.

Clive Chettle was one such platoon commander, a good mixer and games player, robust and unaffected by the minor injuries that beset us in our somewhat violent lives and which I found so difficult to ignore. He and I now shared a room in the mess for which we 'found' a gas fire. Thus, following our after dinner stroll to the pub at Langthorpe, (George Wood had put the pub which adjoined the mess out of bounds) we could return to something approaching home comforts, to our great satisfaction, being firm believers that in our uncertain lives, we should aim for comfort whenever circumstances permitted.

It was Clive and I who, at the end of October, went to York to collect our new company commander, Major Oliver Geoffry Woodhouse White, known by the regulars as 'Knocker' White but to us as Geoffry. We took the opportunity to have a good lunch, see a film and visit a pub, before arriving at the railway station. Geoffry was returning to the battalion in which his father had been an officer and he was thus virtually born and reared in it. Now he was to shake up 'A' Company much as George Wood had shaken up the battalion instigating, of all things, an hour of PT immediately after breakfast. Even being duty officer allowed no remission from this torment. In his red track-suit and known as the 'scarlet runner' Geoffry was in his element, for he had come to us after being on the staff of the Army Physical Training School. His exceptional abilities as an athlete (he had been a hurdler of international standing) caused him to have far too high an expectation of our potential which, in spite of his best endeavours, only marginally improved.

Looking back on those distant days, with a mixture of admiration for our enthusiasms and tolerance for our failings, one realises that we 'temporary soldiers' – the junior officers, existed in a kind of limbo. The present did not relate to our past, neither did it relate to what we hoped would be our future, when we returned to a continuation of our past. Unlike the professionals who we increasingly outnumbered but who, as our senior officers, ruled our lives, there was no relationship between what we were so energetically doing and our careers – so abruptly halted. In the case of some recently arrived subalterns and of these, Harold 'Jonah' Jones and Lintorn 'Snagger' Highett were two, their careers had yet to start. Our rigidly regimented lives released us from the inherited constraints of family and home, but we were sustained by the behaviour expected of us as members of a regular battalion and were able to develop qualities of which we were unaware. Thus when we eventually returned to our civilian lives, we did so as different and generally better persons.

More or less coinciding with the arrival of Geoffry, we found ourselves preparing for 'foreign parts' and being issued with tropical kit. The weather had made a decided change for the worse at the end of October when we had high winds, rain, sleet and snow and by mid-November after almost two weeks of rain, our company lines were a sea of mud and could only be crossed on duck-boards. Such was the setting when we paraded by platoons in our tropical kit, doing so at the rear of Boroughbridge Hall, where it was hoped we would not be seen by the locals, from whom these strange happenings were to be concealed.

When Churchill took the salute at the march past of the victorious troops in Tripoli, he described them as 'the flower of British manhood'. Had he seen 8 Platoon that day, he would have been hard pressed to have been so complimentary. We were good soldiers, in fact damned good ones, but seldom looked the part and certainly not then, when rows of ill-fitting shorts were displayed over white, knobbly knees and faces devoid of tan below Wolsey helmets; so completely incongruous on a dismal autumn day. The wisecracks flowed and we laughed at ourselves as our way of concealing feelings of dismay and embarrassment at being made to look so foolish. Not for the first time I envied the Germans with their clothing fit for warriors.

With embarkation leave of ten days removing chaps in shoals, those who remained were occupied with planning and packing, and a hundred other tasks necessary to launch us overseas. Conventional routine, apart from PT and country runs, virtually disappeared. We must have been excited or otherwise emotionally affected by the prospect of a more active war, but for many it was the substitute of tropical sunshine for the fast-approaching winter that appealed most. Clive and I went to Harrogate to make arrangements for our tropical kit and towards the end of the month I left for my home leave in Dorset. When I returned in early December I found that we were no longer going abroad but to Banbury, of all places, and that 'A' Company was already there.

It was during our last days in Boroughbridge that the Japanese, to whom we as a battalion had paid little attention, commenced hostilities by landing in Malaya, and with the attack on Pearl Harbour during the evening of Sunday 7th December, our time. By mid-February 1942 they captured Singapore, Malaya fell and in June they were to hold the whole of Burma up to the Chindwin, traumatic events that were directly to change our lives.

Banbury is a place of happy memories, a pleasant town with friendly people who made us welcome, just as had our Yorkshire friends, and one could not ask for more. Clive and I were particularly lucky, for we found ourselves in quarters normally reserved for majors and above. Mr and Mrs Fortescue, in their Edwardian home with two resident maids, were generous in their hospitality to us and to our batmen (who were often found in the kitchen and who spent many an afternoon asleep by the fire) and we made the most of what was to be our last billet. We were there for four months and, as 2 Div. was no longer part of the mobile reserve, we had no more of the big exercises. What we did have was Geoffry's fearsome 'jungle' assault course in the garden of the officers' mess, the climax of which was many tens of yards of swaying chestnut fencing among the branches of the tallest trees, thus providing a suicidal 'walkway'. Also remembered with no affection are the bridges spanning the Banbury canal, which when hinged open provided a ramp from the top edge of which we were expected to take a mighty leap for the far bank. Excessive casualties brought this to an early end.

I took part in a similar leap from a wooden ramp on the first day of a four weeks course at the Southern Command Weapon Training School, at Woolacombe. A heavy fall sprained an ankle necessitating my return to Banbury, to my eternal gratitude, for the course was Commando training and beyond my capabilities. Just as we had used airfields as objectives for our aggression in Yorkshire, so did this course in a great 24-hour finale, but in Devon the approach march was one of sixty miles.

1942

Early in January, we in 8 Platoon were designated 5th Columnists and, starting one evening, were allocated that night and the following day in which to sabotage the battalion, all personnel having been forewarned and ordered to carry weapons at all times. We had a wonderful evening and night and so great was our success that George Wood had to call it off after breakfast; with officers captured and offices occupied by us they just couldn't function. Today we are all too familiar with urban warfare and of how a few infiltrators can make life impossible for many. Then we were learning.

At that time Geoffry had the bright idea that 'A' Company would re-enact the Civil War battle of 1644 known as Cropredy Bridge, Clive being Cromwell and I – King Charles 1st. On the day our two forces assembled in isolation a mile from the bridge, which I had to defend but, unfortunately, lose. We were given a wirelessed order to start and I set off with a dozen fast sprinters to ensure that we had a nucleus in position ahead of the enemy, which we achieved; taking possession of a well concealed ditch from which we could dominate open ground adjoining the bridge and were soon joined by the other 'Royalists'. With the arrival of Clive and his men the battle opened, fire being exchanged in a positive fusillade of blank shot, terminating in a shouted exchange of insults. The latter expressed our outrage at being unfairly overrun by Cromwell and his mob, who had been killed by us when they made a suicidal advance over the open ground. This so incensed me that in the heat of the moment I climbed out of our position and standing face to face with Clive, drew my fighting knife, whereupon he, as might be expected, drew his. An extremely angry King Charles had to retire, doing so purple faced and in an advanced state of huff, taking his undefeated company with him. There was a lot of laughter including from the umpiring Geoffry. That this 'battle' did not take place at the actual bridge and that the scenario was largely a figment of Geoffry's imagination did not prevent everybody saying that they had seldom enjoyed themselves so much, and why could not all exercises be like that one? Why indeed? By chance it was a rare January day when the sun shone from a blue sky and one thought of spring. By coincidence, in mid-February, Clive and I were with a party dining in the 15th century White Hart Hotel at Moreton-in-Marsh where, in 1644, King Charles was a guest.

The spring-like weather was replaced by snow through to late February, when I had to visit a farmer who, for six weeks, had been unable to get his horse and cart to the road. I was therefore more than ready to be acting Assistant Adjutant for two weeks in late January and be able to view the snow-covered landscape from a room with a coal fire. Tasks ranged from running the officers' leave roster to the censoring of prisoners' letters. There were generally a few men in detention, boredom or an inability to conform being the downfall of most.

When we were abroad officers censored the letters of the men for whom they were responsible, a regular and time-consuming task. It was anything but agreeable, but we became accustomed to just another duty and one that could be done effectively with no more than a cursory glance. Occasionally we were approached by a man with letter in hand, to be asked if we would sign it as censored without looking at it and did so, being well aware of the many domestic crises during so long an absence.

To my surprise I was asked to defend a man who was to be tried by a Court Martial for desertion, an unexpected display of trust by someone unknown to me and especially so for such a serious charge. In preparation I was able to call on the help of Mr Fortescue, a practising solicitor who had specialised in this work during World War 1. A sad tale unfolded of debt and how the defendant had not returned from leave in a desperate but vain attempt to raise money to repay borrowings which in the main, resulted from his call-up. I don't recall the verdict, but his plight was considered with genuine compassion. Earlier, in Yorkshire, I had attended a court 'under instruction', hearing the tragic story of the attempted suicide of one of our sergeants. All too often married men facing an overseas posting had problems enough to cause such despair.

In March we had a visit from the Commander-in-Chief Home Forces and the Secretary of State for War, during which, as might be expected, 'A' Company gave an exhibition of P.T. Ordinary leave had ceased but embarkation leaves were being slotted in, all of which was a sure pointer that our time at Banbury was ending.

Then quite suddenly, Dick Castle, our Motor Transport Officer and I found ourselves appointed to take the brigade's wheeled vehicles (mainly 15 and 30-cwt and 3-ton trucks) to Glasgow where they were to be loaded on the ships that were to convey them to our unknown destination. I was to lead the convoy, and Dick with his fitters would bring up the rear to be available to deal with the stragglers and breakdowns from some 400 miscellaneous vehicles. At the statutory vehicle spacing of 100 yards, our column had the remarkable length of 22 miles. Thus when we started, I in Geoffry's 'PU' (the 8-cwt truck then allocated to company commanders), it was with an awareness of the dire consequences should I go adrift and we find ourselves in something of a tangle. There was nothing to indicate the names of towns and villages, for all name, directional and other road signs had been removed as one of the defences against invaders. Fortunately our scheduled speed was only 20 miles per hour so, with reasonable luck, there was time to relate what I was seeing to what was on the map and, in theory, there was no justification for getting lost. Our traffic control motor-cycle dispatch riders were not always up at the front as intended, where they could recce ahead and extend my vision but, at difficult road junctions the police and sometimes the Home Guard, who had been notified of our coming, could generally be relied upon to guide us through. The first night was spent near Birmingham after which we resumed our journey at 0730 hrs, in fog. That was succeeded by sunshine as we bore north west and crossed Cannock Chase, where I took a right fork instead of a left. An early blunder, but the map showed a lane linking where I was, to where I ought to be, and when it proved to be the private drive to a large house, there was no turning back. Resolutely pressing on, we cleverly negotiated their stable yard, after which the back lane was easy and, with a right turn onto the public highway, we were on the right road again, leaving behind no doubt, some head-scratching by furious occupants of the invaded property!

Wigan was the only town we passed through en route as obviously towns were to be avoided whenever possible. Soon we were among the bare hills south of the border, that majestic windswept land so different from our cushy south, and then we were into Scotland and its southern uplands, splendid in spring sunshine. Before long we had reached Glasgow, handing over an unexpectedly intact convoy; then accompanied by the drivers and fitters we stayed for eleven days at the staging camp in Bellahouston Park. Days which apart from a not too early in the morning run/walk within the park, were free for us to enjoy as we wished, and the Scottish hospitality exemplified on the trams, where the lady conductors refused payment of our fares.

We had known that the King and Mr Churchill were making separate visits to the battalion whilst we were away, but we had not expected to see a cinema newsreel of His Majesty watching the long suffering 'A' Company on that suspended chestnut fencing...

On 10th April we were up at 0400 hrs and away by train for an undivulged destination which proved to be Liverpool Docks. There we rejoined our units and prepared to embark.

If, as we believed, our destination was Egypt and the fighting in Libya, we had to travel via the Cape of Good Hope and circumnavigate Africa – a thrilling prospect for those who had dreamed the dreams of boyhood.

We were keen to get on board, as we stood lined-up on the quay below the towering hull of the vessel that was to be our home for many weeks. Despite the drab grey wartime paint, her sleek lines were very evident under a pair of squat funnels, so much a part of her modern looks. His Majesty's Troopship K9, was the *Reina del Pacifico*, a 580ft motor vessel of 17,700 gross tons, with quadruple screws and a speed of 19 knots. She had been built in 1931 by Harland and Wolff, for The Pacific Steam Navigation Company, to run a fast mail and passenger service between Liverpool and the west coast of South America. We were to sail on a lucky ship, one that was to complete a hazardous trooping service without damage. From late 1939 she visited India, Ceylon and Singapore, countries to which she would return, India in particular. 1940 saw her landing troops in Norway and then helping in their evacuation. Convoys to Suez via The Cape followed and then ones to Cape Town. Prior to our convoy the *Reina* crossed the Atlantic to Halifax and New York, from where she brought U.S troops to Liverpool. Our convoy was followed by her conversion to an LSI(L) – Landing Ship Infantry (Large), and putting 7,000 men ashore at Oran and later, in July 1943, she landed men of the Highland Division in Sicily. A busy 1944 ended by taking U.S troops home for Christmas from Iceland. Transport to and from the Far East kept the ship sailing to 1946 and a final release from Government service over some 350,000 miles.

When our Colonel took his battalion aboard it would have been with a justifiable pride and in the knowledge that we were as ready for war, physically and mentally, as could be any motley collection of individuals. Presumably we were at full strength and thus about 900 strong, of whom 40 were commissioned officers; just two of the latter – George Wood and his Second-in-Command, Major Tom Molloy, being veterans of the previous war. His confidence would have been reinforced by the knowledge that throughout the unblooded majority, there was that immeasurable stiffening provided by a core of veterans from France in 1940. Truly one is not a real soldier until shot at. More than ever he would have considered, as fully warranted, his recent rejection of promotion to brigadier and the command of a brigade.

For those fortunate enough to have a sense of history, this was a moment when all that had been forsaken and all that had been endured was made worthwhile. As had our predecessors in the 39th and 54th Regiments, gone overseas to fight for King and Country, so we too were doing likewise and our blood coursed a little faster at the thought.

But few would have embarked without concern for the well-being and the lives of family and friends, left behind in a country under continuing threat from the German bombers. Nobody was safe and for those from the cities of the south and midlands, and most of the battalion were, there was a real possibility of the loss of home and family. The blitz had extended north to Hull, Manchester, Liverpool, Belfast and the Clyde. It was only the threat of invasion that lessened with the passage of time.

CHAPTER TWO

The Voyage

At last we were on board and seeing our men to their quarters, below deck and seemingly below the water line, they were so far down, in hot and claustrophic conditions that we considered pretty awful. Clive and I, with two other subalterns, were sharing what had been a two-berth First Class cabin, now stripped to accommodate four bunks. While delighted at this taste of luxury and meals in the splendid dining saloon, we were profoundly embarrassed at the contrast between our quarters and those of the men for whom we were responsible.

After two days we headed north to the mouth of the Clyde, where our convoy assembled and we adjusted to a very different life, happy in the knowledge that, whatever happened, it was unlikely to entail marching! But that thought was of much concern to our senior officers, who very rightly desired that we should not only complete the long voyage reasonably fit, but with feet accustomed to boots. Because of this, and with the reluctant agreement of the ship's captain, we wore boots until lunch time.

Also on board were the Worcesters, the 10th Field Regiment RA and Brigade Headquarters, a total of about three and a half thousand men including ourselves, and therefore a lot of feet! With such numbers, parades were restricted to two hours in the morning and afternoon, half that time below, and the remainder on our allotted deck. This was a situation purpose made for Geoffry, soon appointed Ship's Physical Training Officer, who saw the vessel as a floating gym, with spars, rigging, davits and the like as apparatus for climbing. We took great care however when climbing anything which projected over the sea since we were aware that all ships had been instructed not to stop for any reason, not even a floating Dorset. Such an unfortunate would almost certainly float on the surface, since we had exchanged gas masks for lifebelts which had to be worn ready for use should we have to take to the boats.

Five days after embarkation our convoy was assembled and in the evening of the 15th of April 1942, the long journey started, the Reina underway with the unhurried steadiness of a great ship at slow speed in the confined waters of the Firth of Clyde, vibrant with suppressed power. A moment never to be forgotten and one made so very special in that they were the final hours of a beautiful day in beautiful and placid waters. Being one of the hundreds on deck and amongst those leaning on the starboard rails and thus facing towards the Isle of Arran and the setting sun going down in a blaze of glory, I was able to look down onto an approaching ferry from that island, making for the harbour at Ardrossan on the Ayrshire coast. To avoid crossing our bows, this small sea-going vessel swung to port and traversed our length, before passing astern and resuming course. She too was crowded and the sight and sound of her passengers, lining her rails, cheering and waving to us, provided a very emotional last link with home. Many who received this unexpected display of affection, or call it what you will, experienced a misting of their eyes – as I did. Our emotions at that moment were intensified by the knowledge that for some and possibly for many, this was the final glimpse of home. And I wondered as to the future of 8 Platoon and my ability to lead them as they deserved.

The Reina del Pacifico *in her peacetime livery.*

Soon we were changing course and passing the Mull of Kintyre as, with increasing speed, we made for the Atlantic, across which we had to travel 2,000 miles to penetrate beyond the range of the German Focke-Wulf Condor planes. Operating out of Brest and Bordeaux, they were able to bomb shipping over a wide area of the Atlantic, but of greater menace was their observation of ships and convoys to which they directed U-Boats, stationed at sea ready to strike. Always of special interest were the other members of the convoy, dispersed so that none was close, doggedly maintaining the same course and speed, the only variation being the occasional naval escort craft, busy gathering and cajoling the inevitable stray like a sheep-dog. Being one of so many ships, extending as far as the eye could see, made us feel we were truly engaged in a great undertaking.

After clearing the land, we pitched sufficiently to cause some seasickness, but it was not until the night of the 21st that it blew hard, and there followed a great deal of sickness. Soon after that, George Wood issued the first of two never to be forgotten (on ship) orders; 'Seasickness will cease forthwith.' It had been, until then, thought proper justification for absence from parades, but from then on it was more than ever rotten luck to suffer, because you had to carry on regardless, or at least try to.

When off duty we had the run of all the decks, which was where most of us preferred to be even if only to contemplate the ship's wake, so straight behind us, or its bow wave. After ten days the sea had changed, through shades of green and blue to a deep cobalt, and the humidity which followed the early chill winds became a dry semi-tropical heat sufficient for us to change to our tropical kit. Except for the first wash of the day, all washing was in sea-water, necessitating the use of the ineffective 'sea soap'. Although we were often very hot and sticky, we were seldom troubled with having to wash as a result of being actually filthy.

Each evening following the mounting of the guard, our drums and fifes performed, marking in army fashion the close of another day, and one without mishap. As we moved out of the North Atlantic it became less likely that we would be torpedoed, but boat drills continued to be held at least every other day.

Contact with the outer world was restricted to the contents of a daily news bulletin, wireless sets being forbidden. Such news related to home and the situation there and in North Africa, little mention would have been made of Burma; there the exodus of troops and civilians retreating before the Japs, was reaching unknown places – Kalewa, Tamu and Imphal.

Our passage south had not only brought higher temperatures but calm seas, described by me as like the waters of Poole Harbour. Conditions were ideal for sleeping on deck which men had done throughout the ages, teak planking in the fresh air being infinitely preferable to the claustrophobic conditions below. The extremes of temperature were very much a product of the rigorous blackout and sealed portholes.

By the 25th we knew that we were only a few days away from our first port of call from where letters could be sent home. Thus letter writing and the resultant censoring became part of routine – one day I cleared nearly 200. Our destination was Freetown, capital of Sierra Leone and part of British West Africa, where we dropped anchor at noon on 29th April. As we passed the first headlands we became flanked by a riot of tropical vegetation having a lushness and colour unknown at home and which, but for a few sandy beaches, extended to the water and exuded elusive whiffs of the smell of Africa. Our progress for the four miles up river was flanked by natives, spinning their canoe paddles in the air in welcome. This was the Africa of our adventure books and dreams, under the intense heat of a tropical sun, illuminating the whole with the brightness of a colour film. As we lost way we became surrounded by canoes, their occupants eager for trade or, if young, to dive for coins; all non-stop as was the babble of shouted sales talk, in which a four letter word was used with a freedom and a frequency to which even we were unaccustomed.

Whilst at anchor we were wisely confined to ship, later there were to be ample opportunities for the catching of tropical diseases. We observed an animated scene from our vantage point and local craft, ranging from fast sailing canoes to trading boats some 40 to 50 feet in length. Some of the latter were propelled by four to six oarsmen standing grouped in the bows, ahead of the piled cargo and, sitting aloft in the stern – the helmsman. Up river was a very different craft, a battleship long past its prime and seemingly sitting in the mud as a floating fort. Perhaps one of the aged heavy-weights from our Eastern Fleet and so great a liability, that Admiral Somerville ordered them to sail to the safety of African ports.

We were each allocated a cable home of three phrases selected from a short list. I chose LETTERS SENT / ALL WELL AND SAFE / ALL MY LOVE. Four weeks later this was delivered from the local post office, a security delay giving us time to reach our destination.

The evenings were enjoyed on deck when a piano was brought up and the old favourites were heard again. Sung with gusto was – 'If I should be left in this world all alone' and others like it.

When, at 0900 hrs on Sunday 3rd May, we up-anchored and slowly made our way down stream between those rich panoramas of jungle, we were ready to go and get on with the job, encouraged, if that were necessary, by news that Bath and Norwich had been bombed in air-raids. It was good to be in deep waters and sailing south amongst the flying-fish, shoals of which would shoot out from the bow wave as they sought to escape from our hull, as they did from predators. An added interest was the occasional shark's fin cleaving the surface and, if close, its body visible in the translucent water. We crossed the equator without ceremony and learned that our next stop would be on the 15th, when we would go ashore for the first time in five weeks.

Life within the confines of Freetown Harbour had been pretty grim for sweat saturated our clothing even when sitting. At sea there was the induced breeze of our passage and each day brought a slightly lower temperature.

On the 8th we learned of the British landing on the French island of Madagascar, forestalling the Japs from this potential submarine base. It was of special interest to us, due as we were to sail up the Mozambique Channel, between that island and Africa.

Four days later we were enjoying the warmth and sunshine of an English summer and saw our first albatross. Both were indications of our approach to South Africa and in late morning on the appointed day we sailed into Cape Town harbour, mooring alongside a quay much as at home. But how very different when we went ashore that evening, among the bright lights of a country not under attack from aircraft. For four of us our destination was the highly recommended Del Monica Restaurant. There we enjoyed a six course dinner which included a huge basket of fruit, among diners relaxing under the stars seen through the open sliding roof.

Next morning, a reluctant battalion took the train for a tented transit camp 18 miles away, only to cheer up on arrival, for this was a camp superior to anything we had, or would, experience, the tents white and brilliant at night under high level lighting. For two nights we were refreshed by an evening temperature that was low enough for us to don our greatcoats. The opportunity was taken to exercise our leg muscles and, on that first afternoon, 8 Platoon was off on a light-hearted march. Although encumbered by unfamiliar battledress and equipment we reached a lower peak, there to admire a view of mountains and sea. Next day we did much the same as a company. Most clearly remembered is the food which was of a quality seldom seen even before the war. A bunch of grapes for each individual was rare in war-time and for many, rare at any time.

Three days after disembarking we were back on board and preparing for a final afternoon and evening ashore. Clive and I had an 'A' Company pay parade to manage and it was 1530 hrs before we were on the quay, by then empty of troops and the many residents who would gather them up and give so generously of their hospitality. Thus alone we set off by taxi to see 'The Cape', first crossing the city and climbing a mountain road within baboon-inhabited scrub, then a change of direction into vineyards and to the small coast resort of Muizenberg. There we settled into a hotel for dinner and to talk and drink the hours away, in the firm belief that this was the last such opportunity before going into action. I was on my feet when we left the hotel, but perhaps it was that chill night air that was my undoing, for our return and boarding the ship remain a blank, that I reached my bunk was due to Clive and others, to whom I am greatly indebted.

Next morning we sailed out into the bay and away on the last lap of our great journey, passing the Cape of Good Hope in the beautiful weather we had enjoyed ashore. So large was our convoy, that only half had called at Cape Town, the remainder doing so at Durban. On 23rd we were dashing for that port to disembark someone in urgent need of surgery, then to continue alone and at high speed. We had moved into waters infested not by the Germans but the Japanese, their prime threat to us and others like us, being from their mine-laying submarines. Those who had preceded us to Durban fell foul of mines, losing one cargo ship sunk and a naval one damaged. Later there was to be more of the same in the Mozambique Channel, one victim being the boat carrying our vehicles, which was fortunately able to limp into harbour for off-loading.

A letter dated the 26th was permitted to name Cape Town as visited and that we were pressing on into higher latitudes and expected to complete the voyage on our own. That top speed of 19 knots was proving invaluable. It being a Sunday, I was reclining on the upper deck, under a hot sun tempered by the breeze resulting from our speed. Time did not hang heavily for officers; on working days we had at least two hours of lectures and discussions, outside of parades. All this and the physical activities, of which boxing played a part, had maintained a mental and physical fitness, so that we were much as we had been when we embarked so many weeks before.

No account of troopship life can be complete without mention of the lectures inflicted on captive audiences, talks that were often valued more for filling gaps in a daily programme than their ability to instruct or entertain. Officers were detailed to hold forth willy-nilly and our battalion would have been about average in having two who were able to do this tiresome job with brilliance, Captain Pryke Howard and Lieutenant Richard Dupont, who performed so well and entertainingly that they are still remembered. Pryke could look back over more years than most and use to the full a rare ability to converse, doing so on a multitude of subjects. Richard, a pupil and disciple of the artist Alfred

Munnings, was a natural performer and could 'bring the house down' when recounting a generously embroidered account of his life as an art student. Later that year, when on duty at Ahmadnagar Fort, using charcoal and colour, he decorated the walls of the Officers Mess with sketches of thoroughbred horses with a skill that brought to life their spirit and beauty.

Towards the end of May we were informed that we were not on our way to North Africa, but to India! This shattering news caused great despondency and feelings of having been cheated. There we were, as prepared a body of men as any could be to fight the Germans, only to find at the last moment that it was not to be.

George Wood, ever mindful of the temptations presented to his junior officers by the abundance of inexpensive alcohol (one favourite was brandy and dry ginger), had instigated a daily Dorset officers conference, timed to coincide with the opening of the bar at noon. At one of these, he issued the second of those never to be forgotten on ship orders – "Gentlemen, you will like India, that is an order". We ruefully smiled, and since then many a time have laughed, doing so, however, with due appreciation of the attitude of a regular soldier, who had done his stint on the North West Frontier and who had an understandable affection for the country and its people.

Lecturers, of a different ilk, did their best to prepare us for India, its customs and peoples. We were advised on the martial and non-martial races, of coolies and bearers, the need to avoid striking Indians, to 'watch' the Chinese, that ice must not be used in drinks and that we must never go outside without wearing a topee.

Weapons, respirators (as our gas masks were known), steel helmets and kitbags, that had not been seen for weeks, had to be made available at mess decks level. Equipment had to be scrubbed and blancoed. Sunbathing became compulsory within set hours. Library books had to be returned, and officers were advised on the tipping of the ship's stewards – at rates according to our rank.

In North Africa a massacre of our infantry was in progress as the German Army under General Rommel routed the Eighth Army, prior to their retreat to El Alamein.

And, in the jungle clad mountains of northern Burma and in Assam, the diseased and starving remnants of the civilian refugees from Burma and the survivors of the Burma Army, retreating north ahead of the victorious Japanese, were reaching sanctuary at the end of their long trek.

CHAPTER THREE

India

At mid-day on 2nd June, 1942, having crossed the wide and busy waters of Bombay Harbour, alive with local craft and great ships, *Reina del Pacifico* – her rails as crowded as when we sailed from home arrived in Bombay, 53 days out from Liverpool.

That afternoon 'A' Company went ashore and indulged in a short march. Life was returning to normal. And later, Clive and I sampled the splendours of The Taj, as we and others chose to call the Taj Mahal Hotel. Reputedly one of the world's great hotels, its charges we thought taking it into that category, if nothing else.

We remained on board until the 5th, thus having an easy initial introduction to India during which, amongst other leisure activities, we bathed and made a sight-seeing coach trip. It was at 0430 hrs that we finally disembarked and took the train for Kirkee, in the vicinity of Poona, a journey of 100 miles which took us up the Western Ghats and on to the central plateau, at an average height of 3,000 feet. But even at that altitude, the heat of the mid-day sun was quite something, and it was unfortunate that our native guide from train to camp marched us there by a less than direct route. It was said later, in justification, that he thought that we would have liked the opportunity to see something of the scenery. How little he knew! Never was 8 Platoon so exhausted, and I was not alone among the platoon commanders in carrying a couple of rifles in order to keep us all going. And then we saw our destination – Pashan Camp, a collection of newly erected tents standing forlorn within sun-baked mud flats. We had indeed arrived in India.

A photograph taken a few days later is of Clive and me sitting on a scrubby hill with the white tents of our camp away in the distance, behind a flat expanse of agricultural land, the bare rectangular areas of which are defined by their shades of grey. We wear the uniform of that period – Wolsey helmets, open necked shirts, shorts, hose-tops above short putties and boots. Some temporary relief from the harshness of our dreary surroundings, made so difficult to bear under a sun that seemed to us unrelenting and brutal, could be found as on that day. We and the photographer were returning from an oasis, half a mile from camp – a small village complete with fort and temple. A new world to us and one within luxurious vegetation, fed from an elaborate system of irrigation channels, distributing water from a vast well. A place so different in our English eyes, which noted the elaborate carving of humble dwellings.

In preparation for the impending monsoon which we were warned would commence with torrential rain, as indeed it did, drainage ditches were being dug so that every tent had one to take the run-off from the roof. Sharing our communal tents, which were of the small marquee variety, were flies beyond count, scorpions, lizards and snakes, in that descending order of numbers. The occasional chameleon decorated the inner roof – an eater of flies and ants. The ants were white and kept themselves out of sight but, as we soon discovered, were in sufficient numbers to ruin in one night any clothing in contact with the mud floor.

Supplementing my letters home is a small note book containing odd entries made at the time. One on the 18th reports:

> Monsoon broke six days ago. One bad night in which a number of tents collapsed. Weather much cooler. About 25% of men down with some form of fever. One attempted suicide. In bed with slight temperature. Did 21 mile march day before yesterday.

The unwanted and unexpected arrival of a British infantry division had not been welcomed by the Indian Army, which looked upon us as intruders, as indeed we were; an unhappy situation which we unconsciously aggravated by our air of superiority. Local attitudes were dominated by the very recent debacle at Singapore and the retreats in Malaya and Burma. The incompetence which had preceded those disasters and the dearth of resources in men, their training and equipment, was understandably blamed on us, the British.

Troops leaving Britain at that time considered themselves as the new post-Dunkerque breed and their commanders were determined to demonstrate that the future would be different. The British 2nd Division had to be representative of that future and able to demonstrate a toughness and fighting efficiency to match that of the Japanese. Twenty-mile marches were a bagatelle at home, but never at Pashan Camp under debilitating conditions, and in the absence of a considered policy of acclimatization and advancement by easy stages. What at home had been almost jolly affairs with song and ribaldry, as we did our regular 25 miles, changed beyond recognition. In those early weeks, during which so many went down with 'gippy tummies' or worse, to march a lesser distance became a grim endeavour.

When on the 29th 'A' Company set out on a four day exercise in the hills, we did so in non-stop torrential rain and more became sick or aggravated the diarrhoea which for many had already become an accepted part of life. So bad were the conditions that the scheme was abandoned after three days. Having a temperature of 102° I, with others, was sent back by ambulance, a blessed relief, but not the way to command a platoon.

Those weeks at Pashan Camp spoiled India for us, but having started so badly, life could only get better and generally it did. Even at the peak of the monsoon there were quite reasonable days; one such being Plassey Day, a day of some importance and, by tradition, marked by a ceremonial parade. George Wood should have known better than to attempt one under hopeless conditions, but that tradition must have swamped his good sense. At its conclusion, Clive and I went to Poona Races, which I remember not for the horses, but the colourful saris.

We junior officers recall that ridiculous parade as the one when John O'Driscoll (of happy memory) had overlooked the need to secure his hose-tops, and by the time he marched past the saluting base and our Commanding Officer he was bare-legged, the hose-tops having collapsed on to his boots... His punishment for shaming the battalion was to be forbidden entry to the mess tent for a set period during which he took all his meals in his own tent, to which, after dinner, his card-playing friends adjourned.

Pashan Camp is remembered for the all-prevailing mud which made life a misery. I would not be alone in saying that it is the latrines that I recollect most clearly; often visited after dark, in the rain and by the light of a hurricane lamp. There, deep slit trenches over which we squatted, our thighs supported on a timber rail, provided the essentials and overhead, a lean-to roof mercifully kept one dry. This was no place for quiet contemplation, being also a rendezvous for scorpions on which we kept a wary eye as they criss-crossed the ground, stings arched over their backs in constant readiness.

Our weekday routine commenced with an 0600 hrs – bugle blown – reveille, a first parade at 0645 hrs and breakfast at 0730 hrs. Morning parades were from 0900 hrs until lunch at 1300 hrs. In the early days, because of the extreme heat, an afternoon rest period found most of us lying on our charpoys (the Indian bed with a rope mattress) until tea at 1600 hrs, final parades then keeping us busy until supper at 1900 hrs. Thus the hours of daylight, which these were, were determined by a set routine. After a few weeks the siesta was dropped, as being no longer necessary in the cooler monsoon conditions.

Most training was done in the adjacent hills, away from the mud and where we had a freedom to move on gravel and amongst scrub, a place free from the constraints of cultivation. There we adjusted to an environment so different from anything at home and learned to operate within it. Developing, for example, the ability to descend quite steep slopes in a series of short, feet together, jumps, alternating to the left and the right to maintain a downward rather than an inclining, progression. And we were looking more like soldiers, our skins tanned and our tropical kit no longer so ill fitting.

Around us the grass was growing and our world the better for it.

The first items of long awaited home mail were coming through by 27th June, in my case an airgraph posted a month earlier. But it was not until 9th July that we had our first real delivery; then a great burst of cheering resounded throughout the camp following the sounding of the bugle call – Letters from Blighty. An indication of their wide ranging dates is obtained from my five letters – date stamped between between the 11th and 29th April, one birthday card (a month late) and a parcel of laundry, posted by my mother when I was in Glasgow.

A number of us were putting up our second 'pips', after completing the statutory eighteen months as Second-Lieutenant. Later the period was reduced to six, making that promotion virtually meaningless.

In early July, we became aware that our days at Pashan were drawing to a close and that we, together with the remainder of 5 Brigade, were destined for a place called Secunderabad, a prospect welcomed with cautious optimism and a belief that anywhere would be better than where we were. Some found solace in Poona, just six miles away and in those days of Empire, famous for its association with the Indian Army. For me it was just a place with an indifferent club, producing indifferent food and where you could get tight – which I did.

When, at 1745 hrs on 13th July, we paraded and then departed for Kirkee Station, there were no backward glances and no regrets. This was the start of what was, for India, a short rail journey being about 350 miles; yet only completed at 0500 hrs on the 15th. A gentle pace indeed, in part resulting from the need to halt for meals, which had to be prepared and cooked before they could be eaten.

Gough Barracks, Trimulgherry, Secunderabad, where to our delight we found ourselves, was one element of a permanent army cantonment. There we were to live in spacious stone buildings, dispersed within an expanse of grass and trees and playing fields. At last we had accommodation designed for the tropics and where there was a supporting cast of Indian bearers, dherzis for tailoring, dhobis for the laundry and more too, ranging down to fortune tellers. In the manner of a holiday after illness, Gough Barracks helped us to recover from the earlier horrors and the standard of life rose for everyone. All could be clean and smart in such an environment, one where willing dhobi-wallahs produced a bundle of washed and ironed clothing in a 24 hour service. With a dherzi making shorts to measure for what today would be 40 pence, and a pair of made-to-order leather shoes available for little more than twice that sum, we began to appreciate some of the advantages of life in India.

Officers changed their issue helmets for the pith variety (Bombay Bowlers) which, with their compact shape and better insulation, were another boost to morale, as were the helmet's distinctive Dorset pagris which incorporated two lines of green material. And we wore the green and gold cloth badge of our regiment, together with the black and white divisional badge. Our regimental green was also displayed by our dark green hose-tops, making a bold splash of colour above the khaki of short putties or gaiters.

There was little need to travel to the bazaar, for it came to us in a steady stream of locals, bearing just about anything that they thought might tempt us. And, in residence, was the ubiquitous char-wallah with his steaming urn, ready to produce a brown liquid at any hour.

An important bonus, and one that was to be as rare for us as the barracks, was that we were adjacent to the busy world of an Indian city – Hyderabad, the capital of the nizam's dominion of that name, in which we now were. Founded 200 years earlier, this native state of 15 millions occupied an area, centrally on the Deccan plateau, the equivalent of England and Scotland. Secunderabad, a mile or two to the north of Hyderabad City, with its half a million people, had a population of ten thousand and was one of the largest cantonments in India. Thus we were seeing the India of teeming streets, with a sound and a life quite unlike our own. The product of a multitude of cycles and bullock carts, overcrowded buses and many tongas – light two wheeled traps, very ready to convey two of us at a trot, by a seemingly overworked and underfed pony. People on foot predominated and we watched in admiration the graceful walk of sari clad women, with brass or copper cooking or water pots on their heads. Lower caste women would also pass, in single file under loaded baskets. Once I watched, in amazement, as six coolies moving at a slow trot conveyed a piano, of the upright variety on its back, so that their heads could be distributed within the area of that back.

Further local colour came from visiting snake charmers, ready to demonstrate their skills at producing snakes from wicker baskets. An ancient turbanned figure performed on a bulbous flute, a small boy in attendance.

A Secunderabad temple.

Hyderabad Aug '43. One of the main streets leading up to the Char Minar. Note the typical open-fronted shops on the left, and the rickshaws.

Such a place required a flag and I found myself designing and drawing one. We decided on a red upper half, separated from a lower one in green by a band of yellow. Superimposed on the red was our Sphinx, commemorating great deeds in Egypt in 1801 when the 54th played their part in the defeat of Napoleon's army and in the capture of Alexandria.

Our salubrious quarters had not enabled all who suffered from 'the squitters', to regain their health. Even Joe Chamberlin our Medical Officer extraordinary, with all his wizardry, including 50 monster tablets, swallowed en masse (with difficulty) as a congealing agent, had no effect*.

I must have been looking the worse for wear when George Wood packed me off for a few days at the Secunderabad Club. There, within a bungalow in the grounds, I had a lounge, bedroom and bathroom and the first ample supply of hot water since leaving blighty. To be woken by a bearer with a chota hazari, the small breakfast – banana, biscuits and tea, was a fair start to any day and enabled one to keep going while bathing and dressing. The days that followed were enjoyed with books from an excellent library, visits to the billiard room and swimming pool and a game or two of squash. On the second evening I shared a dinner table with Tom Molloy, remembered so well as unassuming, considerate and truly a gentlemen. Typically, he did not mention that he was assuming command of us next day, George Wood having been promoted brigadier and the command of 4 Brigade. The wings sometimes seen above Tom's medal ribbons were a reminder that he had been a fighter pilot in the First War, but shot down over German lines and their prisoner for two years. We found a common interest in books and the hours passed all too quickly.

Back at the battalion I found that Geoffry had taken over as 2 I/C and that, for the moment, our company was commanded by David Harris. Subalterns were now two to a room, Clive and I (the 'Heavenly Twins' according to Geoffry) sharing as usual. We were missing Rolfe. On our departure from Banbury, one officer had to remain, to his distress it was he. Rolfe was foolish enough to question decisions made by George Wood and suffered accordingly, thus we lost a good officer.

A feature of any Indian establishment is the Chokidar – the caretaker/night watchman. Our bungalow had one, and it amused us to think of him as the local burglar whom you paid not to steal from you and to see that his friends went elsewhere. When returning after dark, a feeble 'salaam sahib' enabled his prostrate form to be discerned in some unlikely corner. My archives include a letter dated 16.9.42, obviously penned by a professional letter writer. It is addressed to: Most Respected Masters and, cutting short a long epistle, it advised us that our most obedient servant the Chowickidar and family had worked for eleven masters last month and had only been paid by six, and with four children and an aged father and provisions very dear – could we do something about it? That we were able, I doubt.

The cry, soon to be so familiar, "Sahib! Sahib! Cobra, Burra Cobra", took us into the garden with a rush. There Clive and I joined an excited crowd of Indians, materialised from goodness knows where, and with them prodded an overgrown flower bed, to dispatch a snake as long as myself. We were also finding gigantic rats in residence, and of the two we preferred the snakes.

**Joe, who would have been a father-figure had he not looked so young, describes his attachment to us – "I was with the 5th Field Ambulance in France and greatly enjoyed two spells as locum for the Dorset's R.M.O. Then Padre Gus and I found ourselves trying to get a small convoy of ambulances, mostly 5 Brigade casualties, to Dunkerque. In Yorkshire the Dorsets were so strung out that I was detached to look after 'B' Company. I persuaded their M.O. Bob Richards that we should exchange jobs and the transfer was rubber stamped without difficulty."*

From August we had settled into an agreeable weather pattern of overcast skies. Thus a reasonable temperature which was made more so by a 24 hour breeze and a monsoon reduced to a daily rain storm of an hour or so and often in the evening. However when the skies cleared, as they did from time to time, we reverted to the intense heat which, when coinciding with a route march or two day exercise, made life difficult.

In Dick Purser, whom I had first met at OCTU where he was one of the instructors, I found a fellow small boat enthusiast and for a time he and I were able to sail both '16 footers' and 'Snipes' on a lake, two miles beyond the town, where was established the sailing section of the Secunderabad Club. One evening we actually managed to come in second in a race and were hoping to do better when civilian unrest put it out of bounds.

Our mess dinner was at 1945 hrs and when there were no guests we reckoned to be finished at 2030 hrs. Then some, of whom I was one, would settle down to cards at a time when the game was not bridge, as later, but 'vingt-et-un' and the like which we had played since those days in Yorkshire. Having played so much we must have been experts, certainly it gave us a great deal of light hearted fun.

Soft drinks were being increasingly favoured, not because we were reforming but due to our dislike of the local beer.

On 3rd August we had heard that we on our ship and those on another troop carrier – *Empress of Japan*, were about the last to pass through the Mozambique Channel before Japanese 2-men midget submarines sank three ships and that it was to Diego-Suarez, on the tip of Madagascar, that our vehicle carrying freighter had off-loaded.

Somebody decided that troops could not effectively protect themselves against the dive-bomber until they were experienced in that form of attack. When a plane was obtained for the improvement of 'A' Company, I was delighted when my voluntary services were accepted to accompany and direct the pilot. So one morning I climbed into a Leopard Moth (high-wing monoplane) acting as a pretend dive-bomber, its deficiencies offset by what seemed to me to be a completely crazy Sikh pilot. My first job was to find the company and eventually there they were, marching in columns of platoons through scrub and down we went, pulling out at the bottom of the dive with sufficient force for my face to crack down onto my knees. Somewhat bleary-eyed I observed the proceedings as we dived and swept over them 20 times. Clive, who was in command, reckoned we went as low as 20 feet, certainly low enough for me to glimpse everyone throwing themselves flat on the ground. What with dodging the hillocks and stunted trees and the, in our language 'shite-hawks', large scavengers flying around in anticipation of flesh and blood, it was quite a flight and I was thankful to complete it without being sick.

Life could be said to be full of variety for, a couple of days later I was President of a Court of Enquiry.

On 14th August we were standing-by as a result of widespread riots following the imprisonment of Gandhi and then, five days later, David being on a course and Clive in Poona in connection with some vehicles, I was in charge of the company.

I expressed surprise in a letter that India had sparrows just as at home and how much tamer the birds were, for they thought nothing of flying inside our rooms and perching on the furniture, doubtless after the insects as were our other visitors – frogs, toads and lizards. In the same letter I mentioned that the electricity supply station switched off the lighting for one second at 2100 hrs each evening, as a simple time check.

As might be expected, Secunderabad provided ample opportunities for soccer – that most popular of games for players and spectators. I had no personal regrets that the platoon matches of the Yorkshire days had languished; now, most were very serious affairs at battalion level and respected as such by a goodly number of spectators. Our char-wallahs with their shouts of "Come on the Dorsets" displayed a partisanship that remained undiminished even when the opposition was Indian and we were in receipt of a demonstration of superb bare-foot ball control.

During my temporary stewardship of 'A' Company – I avoid the repeated use of the word 'charge', when it was the Company Sergeant-Major who (fortunately) was in charge – I had the initiative to contact an Indian regiment and was able to arrange that they would attack us in a defensive position, with their twelve armoured-cars. We dug-in amongst scrub within an agreed area and camouflaged ourselves with such success that I had to stand up and wave my arms before they could spot us. They then swept over in repeated charges to our mutual satisfaction, all under the watchful eye of our CO. It may have been this company scheme that encouraged Tom Molloy to select 8 Platoon for a demonstration before our Divisional Commander, the formidable Major-General John Grover MC, whose personality was such that the very air around him was said to quiver with nervous excitement and apprehension. He certainly had that effect on subalterns but all ranks respected him and he did for the division what George Wood had done for us. Our task was to portray an advance-guard of carriers, 3-inch mortars in carriers and an infantry platoon in trucks, bumping an enemy which shot-up the leading carrier. We infantry then scattered into cover from where, after I had been whisked forward on a motor-cycle to recce the enemy, we made an outflanking movement with all the élan we could muster during a hot mid-day, and which we terminated in a victorious assault with the bayonet. 'Going-in' with the bayonet always went down extremely well with senior officers, but we were less keen. All this took place in a natural amphitheatre below an escarpment on which were our visitors and the remainder of the battalion. General Grover, as well as saying well done, commented on my Vyella shirt being conspicuous, which was the last thing any leader of a charge wished to be. Prior to leaving home George Wood had ordered a supply for his officers on the grounds that they were excellent at absorbing perspiration, as of course they were. They lasted well too, for I was wearing one when photographed on the Ava Bridge, near Mandalay in March 1945.

On the following day the battalion, less 275 men and four officers of whom

I was one, departed for Kharakvasla near Poona, a place with a large lake. There they commenced training in Combined Operations, we having been designated an Assault Division, therefore in a landing on a hostile shore the British 2nd Division would be, or would form part of, the 'First Wave'.

To our dismay the battalion was leaving Secunderabad and we who remained behind were to prepare a tented camp not far away. We had to get it into being and shift about 900 beds, kit boxes and bags, to which were added general stores, tables, benches and a hundred other things. Then, having done all that, we were told that we were going elsewhere and to take it all down again.

Trees were scarce within the arid wastes in which we trained and there was the often laughed about occasion when one of our regulars, Major 'Molly' Molyneux, was organising a battalion exercise, in which he was to command one of the two contending sides. He chose to have his preparatory 'O' Group after lunch, in a mess annex and, having a loud voice, his opposite number was able to listen-in and jot down the map reference of Molly's H.Q. and its situation beneath a lone palm, in that open country. A party was organised and set forth to cut down and remove it, only to be frustrated by the toughness of what was found to be a very mature toddy-palm. Not to be defeated they substituted a Bren gunner within the tree's foliage. Molly was a very delightful person but commanding infantry was not his forte and no one was surprised when he left for another appointment.

Before our departure I, like many others, posted home a food parcel to help with the food rationing. It consisted of 1 lb each of butter (which thankfully was in a tin), cheese, sugar and tea, plus candied peel as a make-weight.

At the beginning of October, on the return of the Kharakvasla party, we were ready to depart for Ahmadnagar, which was to be our future base, 300 miles distant as the crow flies and 150 miles inland from Bombay. We were to move as part of 5 Brigade and under a new commander – Brigadier Victor Hawkins, the son of a Dorset officer. At the far end of our journey was to be 4 Brigade opposing our advance, thus the move became an inter-brigade exercise of attack and defence; one in which our new brigadier was determined to display his abilities. To our great satisfaction we found that we were being pushed forward in trucks, as fast and as far as their carrying capacity and an apology of a road permitted. These were tactics associated with the Germans under Rommel, in North Africa; with us striving to get at the enemy so fast that we had the advantage of surprise. Once when the umpires, in an endeavour to check our speed to nearer that for which they had planned, blocked a mountain pass for 24-hours, Victor Hawkins set the sappers to build an outflanking road which they did in eight hours. On one night he put the whole of our battalion's Brens into 'A' Company and set us to strike straight into the heart of the opposition. Right or wrong, this was a refreshing boldness. We had eight days of living on hard rations – basically a tin of 'bully', three packets of biscuits, one and a half sausages and a handful of raisins or dates, per day. These were discreetly supplemented, as we were soon damned hungry. Because of the speed of our progress and a congestion to our rear, we had blankets for only one night, this when it could be unexpectedly cold after dark. For half the eight days we were in agreeably mountainous country, where there were streams for washing and bathing. The road, as might be expected, was no more than a gravelled track and one that was bone dry after three weeks without rain, so that our passage caused dust clouds – said to be visible for ten miles. One night when we covered about 80 miles through a remote area, we passed through a town and one or two villages, the inhabitants of which lined their streets, to watch in silence an inexplicable happening. Then in daylight, a bunch of vehicles including mine strayed from the route and found ourselves in a dead-end village, remembered for its enclosing high stone walls with castellated parapets. There we had to turn about in a crowded bazaar, a manoeuvre only completed with the help of the Indian police, who charged the crowd, wielding their long cane lathees.

All this had an unfamiliar freshness and we were much impressed, and probably 4 Brigade too, having been at the receiving end of so much.

It was 11th October when we reached Ahmadnagar and the Indian quarters known as Stud Farm. We knew that the last place was special and that the discomforts of rough hutments within an arid plain had to be endured. Feelings probably shared by the British soldier and his wife, stationed here in 1918, when they became the parents of Spike Milligan.

There was talk of leave and that I would soon depart for a course at a Battle School. Outside our lines there were only two places of interest, the garrison cinema and the town bazaar. The latter was described as 'lousy' but with nowhere else to shop a place visited of necessity and, if possible, by bicycle. If arriving on wheels, almost before becoming stationary, children of all sizes would unceremoniously remove the machine for 'safe' keeping. Returning later with your purchases, and with a quick cast of a coin into the roadway you would shoot into the saddle and away.

Our mess was well supplied with fruit, mainly oranges and bananas, and sometimes we had tangerines. But it is the introduction to the mango that is best remembered – that rich juicy flesh on a hot day, with that strange hint of paraffin within its flavour. One of life's compensations. Limes were plentiful but largely ignored through ignorance, and I seem to remember pomegranates as fruits of little interest. We were very conservative in our eating, for the pronounced change in climate did little to lessen our enjoyment of a traditional stew with potatoes and green vegetables.

We in 'A' Company welcomed a new Company Commander in the person of Captain Tony Bridge, one of our regulars. In France he had been in charge of the battalion's transport and then in Yorkshire he was appointed Adjutant. A demanding office during periods of change in policies and personnel and when preparing to do battle, but one accomplished to perfection. I like to think that he was glad to join us.

The period 19th to 29th October saw Lieutenants Halahan, Turner and myself at the 2nd Division Battle School, which to my profound relief was easy when compared with the one at Woolacombe. Assault Course No 3 was the toughest of a wide ranging series of exercises designed to improve our skills and test our fitness. It occupied one of the final days, away in the hills 20 miles from base.

There we advanced up a two mile long valley of rough going through tangled vegetation, rocks and dry watercourses, doing so against an imaginary enemy. Then up a hill which steepened into 40 feet of rock face, up which we scrambled thankful to find that we could manage the finger and foot-holds, and it was with much relief that we finally cleared the crest. The culminating bayonet charge over 200 yards of open ground was almost easy. All that happened in the afternoon of a day in which we started out at 0815 hrs and were back near midnight. The course included three periods of battle inoculation with live ammunition, something always welcomed after so much firing of blanks. The third was very much of a grand finale, one in which the pupils were in trenches that were subjected to a full-scale attack. Artillery opened the proceedings by putting down a three minute 'crash shoot' with high explosive, the shells dropping short and over, while sappers detonated mines set amongst the trenches. This was immediately followed by machine-gun fire and by a platoon of carriers surging over us with their Brens firing and bringing up the rear, a company of infantry, also banging away with their weapons. Quite a party! No wonder I did my best to keep a cigar going in a display of bravado, as we three sat laughing in the bottom of our trench.

A week later I was in charge of a brigade leave party of 135 chaps, our destination being the leave camp on the Secunderabad racecourse. Two special rail coaches were attached to various trains and we set forth at 1700 hrs on a two and a quarter hours first lap, after which we had to wait until 0400 hrs the next day before proceeding.

We had two cooks and by 2030 hrs all were tucking into a most welcome 'bully' stew, with lashings of hot tea by courtesy of the steam engine, a ready source of boiling water. It was my doubtful privilege to have a meal in the station dining room ordered, as was the custom, by the guard 'phoning ahead before we started. When our second train arrived I joined a compartment containing another officer and was then within the civilian section of the train. There I watched at close quarters, the lower class Indian who seemed to spend so much of his life on station platforms, often asleep or at least lying prone until the arrival of a train. With the 3rd Class coaches invariably packed there would be a struggle between the newcomers and the occupants who would do their best to discourage or repel the boarders. On the train starting some would fall back to await another, those more hardy clung to the closed doors or scrambled head first through the windows.

I was able to get out my sleeping bag and sleep until 0730 hrs, when we stopped for 30 minutes and issued rations and obtained more hot water. Then another change of trains at midday and again hot water, our journey ending at 1800 hrs, 25 hours after it had started.

I then learned that the party I was to have taken back had departed and that the prisoner I was to have escorted had escaped, so somewhat relieved I accompanied the others to the camp. A morning of shopping and the great find of six Penguin books, preceded the return at 1730 hrs with the two cooks and an empty handed prisoner's escort.

At that time we had an issue of free air mail letter cards for Christmas, with a picture of holly on the front. They travelled via the Karachi Air mail.

November 14th saw 'A' Company, made up to full strength by an infusion from 'D', departing on foot to take up duty as the outer guard at Ahmadnagar Fort, within which was the political prisoner Pandit Jawaharlal Nehru – the future first prime minister of a free India at the start of a long family dynasty. We made no contact with him for he was confined within the central portion of living quarters, isolated by an inner ring formed by a guard of the Indian Army. This large stone built fort a few miles outside the town, within an enclosing ditch was not unlike some of the defensive castles in Britain, but without the advantages so often enjoyed by them, escarpments and water. Here that outer ditch was effective because of its great width and depth and, in earlier years, the wild beasts free to roam within it. I remember the pleasure of reclining in a camp-chair and doing so in weather that matched an English summer at its best. From that elevation I could look down on the traffic generated by a town of 50,000 inhabitants, much of which was that unchanging bullock cart, convoys of which would pass in a leisurely progression to the sound of creaking axles, much shouting, whip cracking and bell jangling. We were one small chapter in a long history, a major part of which was the capture of this place by the great Duke of Wellington. More recently, during the 1914–918 war, Germans had been interned within its walls, as had been Boers during the South African War. My happy static life lasted a miserably few days, for on the evening of the 16th Clive and I were told that we were going on leave, not in ten days as planned – but tomorrow.

Officially, leave was for seven days plus a maximum of two days for travel. And there was a free travel warrant for 600 miles, each way.

Knowing of the delights of Ootacamund, that little England in the Nilgiri hills, at a height of 7,000 ft and not far from the southern tip of India, we had arranged to go there. After an initial train journey to the main line we obtained the last two-berth compartment on the air-conditioned Madras Express, the comforts of which were ours for 23 hours, that time broken only by meals. After a three-hour wait at a station near Madras, we boarded the well named Blue Mountains Express at 2130 hrs, taking to our bunks, as we had dined while waiting. After that second night of travel we awoke to the sight of lush green vegetation, of palms and banana and orange groves with, in the far distance, the Nilgiri Hills, blue in the early morning sunshine. At 0830 hrs we reached the end of the line and after an excellent breakfast we boarded one of the great features of "Ooty", the narrow gauge rack railway which, in three hours, carried us up the first 6000 feet on an almost continuous slope of 1 in 12. Thus we passed from the humid jungle into the freshness of grassy downs and, in the town, eucualyptus trees. Due to the change of dates, the guest house into which we had booked was unable to take us, but we were directed to another that would. We knew that army officers could obtain a place in a tiger shoot, run by one of the white hunters in Ooty in exchange for a box of small-bore ammunition and had come prepared. Contact was made and clouds and mist making the first evening unsuitable, we were out on the second.

We and four others including the hunter, filled a large American car bristling with weapons, mine a mere 12-bore, which was to be used with discretion.

Proceeding slowly we dropped downhill from the short grass of the downs into thick vegetation, prepared for the tiger known to be in the area or perhaps a panther, but seeing only black monkeys. When we left the car we split up, I and a chap with a rifle moving cautiously along a path to a crest where we looked down to a water-hole. Seeing nothing we continued to a hill where we sat to observe the valley below and where, incidentally, there was a grand river with rising fish. We then spotted a barking-deer move out into a clearing about 400 yards away and, with my companion leading, we moved back and around the hill and into a valley, stalking our quarry without success. Hearing the grunt of a wild pig and realising that we were on ground that he had been disturbing, we pulled back, by then aware that the light was fading. In the gathering dusk we made our way back to the car, there to take refreshment before journeying home in moonlight, with empty bags. I for one was well content. It was the excitement of the chase and not the killing that attracted.

With time for the necessary preparation an organised 'shoot' could have been arranged, but I doubt that we would have wanted to bear the cost. The days soon passed in being out and about much as at home. We paid our respects to the famous club which dates back to 1830, which we thought looked its age and which, with its atmosphere of genteel decay, had little to offer us. In the months of November to March the day temperatures at Ooty are those of an English summer, with a strong sun, but the nights are sufficiently cool for a fire and for beds to need a couple of blankets. And there are no mosquitoes! Perfect conditions for a holiday and it was with reluctance that we departed on the final half of our 1,760 mile train journey.

A bumper mail was at The Fort to greet me, letters from as far back as early August. With demands on officers being what they were, I would not have been surprised to find myself duty officer on return, and scheduled to turn out the guard at midnight. Thus I sat down and made an immediate start on the acknowledgement of those letters. One of them is before me now.

Life continued to be full of change and it was no great surprise that, two days after our return, 'A' Company was relinquishing its special duties; our successors being one of the rifle companies the Cameron Highlanders. Thus it was that our return to Stud Farm was made behind their pipes and drums, a rare opportunity and with such a stimulus one could almost march forever!

When we embarked in April, Japanese naval forces were operating in the Indian Ocean and soon their planes were bombing the east coast of India, a situation made more critical by their broadcasts advising Indians that worse would follow and that they should make a separate peace, for by so doing, they would participate in the collapse of the British Empire. Such propaganda was made credible by the disasters we suffered at that time, in the Mediterranean and elsewhere – 1942 was a grim year, thankfully it improved towards its end.

By November, although the Japs had completed their occupation of Burma and were at India's eastern frontier, the immediate threat of their invasion of India had been reduced, for they had pulled back their naval fleet. The situation could also be considered as stabilized for both India and Ceylon had been reinforced with men and with aircraft. But the demands of the extremists in India for the immediate withdrawal of the British had increased, as had the 'Quit India' campaign. Living as we did in camps or cantonments within areas long accustomed to the armed forces, we were isolated from the peoples of India as a whole. It was a time when a visible presence was desirable.

At some high decision-making level, plans were made for British regiments to tour into the hinterland. So it was that on 30th November, we Dorsets, as one element of those troops, entrained at Ahmadnagar Station. From there we travelled north for a few hundred miles to the small town of Anand, reached in the morning of 2nd December. We were then at the same latitude as Calcutta, but had remained in the west, being tucked away at the head of the Gulf of Cambay, in the District of Ahmedabad.

This was an arrival best exploited by a formal parade. Accordingly we entered the town with bayonets fixed and our long column marching three abreast and in companies, headed by the Corps of Drums. At such a moment the finer points of musical skill are subordinate to the drama of the occasion and in that setting of narrow streets, so confined within their flanking buildings, the full volume of those beating drums reverberated most satisfactorily. We marched with pride, as had our ancestors in a thousand such places, progressing between silent crowds, intent on us. Perhaps some were so versed in local history as to know that the City of Ahmedabad, a place of great splendour under the Mogul Emperors, had been captured by the British in 1780.

Our immediate objective was a camp about one mile beyond Anand; there the battalion divided into two, with 'B' and 'C' Companies continuing to the larger town of Nadiad.

We had left behind the brown plateau for the green of the coastal lowlands, in that part 100 miles or more in width and fed by many rivers. By Indian standards this was good agricultural land of mixed farming and plantations, growing cotton, bananas, limes and oranges.

In order to cover the maximum territory companies set off on individual 100-mile marches, 'A' doing so three days after arrival. In the intervening period we visited the town and a temple. At all times we were in groups and any officer wishing to go shopping or sight seeing had an escort of two, for although we did not anticipate any hostility against us as individuals, we had to be ready for the unexpected.

We set off for our second camp on 5th December, a distance of 19 miles along a tarmac road which, as we neared our destination, had been freshly painted at intervals in large white letters – QUIT INDIA. This became commonplace and was accepted with an amused tolerance and a general reaction of 'wish we could'.

The following day we covered 12 miles to Mahuda where we occupied the Inspection and Travellers Bungalow and grounds. Such buildings were adjacent to the towns and larger villages to provide accommodation for the visiting magistrate and other officials, thus supplying an essential service in a country of great distances where, for the educated traveller, there was no other resting place or base suited to his needs.

Life settled into a pattern of afternoon arrivals and then calls on us by the local police inspector, with some senior and influential residents. Over tea we discussed our plans and enjoyed making social contacts with them.

We were fortunate to have as our company commander the good looking Tony, whose personality epitomised the English soldier sahib and who communicated, and when necessary commanded, with the assured self-confidence that our visitors expected of those in authority. And Tom Molloy, busy visiting his companies and meeting many locals likewise impressed.

The majority of our visitors were prosperous agriculturalists and business men, concerned to show themselves as friendly to us in what was said to be the first such visit in living memory. One, a Mr Bhatt, wearing European dress but for his rimless Indian cap, was very active on our behalf generally and it was he who was responsible for most of the photos taken at that time. He loaned me his shot-gun and a lake for a day, on and above which was a vast quantity of duck, keeping their distance, which suited me as I had no desire to shoot them.

On the 7th we were away north to Kapadvanj, a march of 18 miles, where we stayed for three days. En route we detoured into two villages and were greeted with tea and garlands. The latter were for Tony, Clive and me, and I remember at one of the villages Clive and I were given posies instead – we felt proper pansies! The following morning I marched the company to the bazaar for shopping. That evening a 'flag' march was organised through the streets with the aid of the police, which terminated at a sacred well where we were again given tea. A faded photograph shows the company sitting around a vast well below three and four story houses, the well sides being stepped down in the manner of the seating in a Roman amphitheatre. One section stands at ease at the rear with fixed bayonets – the Indian police are also present. Strangely, our chaps sitting drinking have not sheathed their bayonets as was customary before falling out from parade. It seems that we were taking no chances. During the march we had made our way through winding streets busy with people accepting us and showing friendly faces, as was the norm, the children enjoying themselves as children do when soldiers march.

While we were in India I was never aware of any overt hostility; we believed that the majority respected us and the British administrators more than they did their own leaders, and had no wish to see us depart.

Those few weeks had a great fascination, for we were in towns built in the middle ages which showed many similar characteristics to our own buildings of the same era, sometimes upper floors were jetted as ours had been, and as the internal combustion engine was still a rarity it seemed as if we had stepped back in time. Among the timber buildings were stone examples of Saracenic architecture, richly ornamented, some having elaborately fretted timber to oriel windows, designed so as to enable those within to observe the outer world unseen. In one place the stone buildings spanned the street on semi-circular arches and by so doing isolated the wealthy quarter, of which they were part, from the remainder. The strong shadows alternating with bright sunshine made the narrow streets seem like canyons alive with carts drawn by bullocks, donkeys or even camels. Darting about within this free for all were children of every size, and animals likewise. It was the India of Kipling.

Our next place was Savli Tank, a march of only six miles on the 10th. Tanks in India are artificial ponds or reservoirs for water storage but, as we were then in an area that was naturally wet and marshy, the name could have related to an ordinary pond or lake. We had not been there long when a native arrived asking if the sahibs could kill a mugger at his village four miles away, as it was eating babies. Mugger is the name by which the broad-nosed Indian crocodile is known. This was a challenge willingly accepted by Tony and he and I and one or two chaps with rifles departed in a truck with a native guiding. At best we were on rough tracks and when half way we got stuck in a muddy hollow, only resuming our journey after a tantalizing delay with the help of a team of bullocks. We found the village to be on the margin of a large pond and opposite an island, on the sandy shore of which were one or two muggers, no more than 40 feet or so away. A few moments of enthusiastic shooting ended in splashes as our targets dived into the depths. Having lost valuable time on the journey and the hot sunshine which brings the reptiles out of the water then fading, we gave up for the day, it being arranged that I would return on the following one with a Bren. That I and my two Bren gunners did, arriving at the village with visions of mass slaughter, but the day was overcast and no 'crocs' were out sunning themselves, so we had to depart frustrated and the babies to continue at risk.

That day we marched 16 miles to Dakor and completed the day with an evening parade through the town. We did another 20 miles the next day, having returned to one of our earlier camps for a week of 'flag' marching, on some days going out to villages by bus.

Tony was away for a month or so and Clive was in charge when the company went to a special reception at an area police station, an event of sufficient importance to warrant the addition of our Corps of Drums. There 50 residents were gathered to meet us and be presented after Clive and I had been duly garlanded. Tables were laid with sweetmeats and fruit for everyone, all these happenings being of great interest to the usual crowd of spectators, in this instance gathered outside the gates. At the conclusion Clive made a well received speech of thanks and there was much hand clapping and general goodwill. We decided that the Indian police officers we were meeting, all well educated and smart in their drill uniforms and Sam Brownes, were grand fellows. It may be naïve to think it could be otherwise in such places and communities, where there was no hint of discontent or hostility to us or the status quo. But that was how it was and for most it must have been inconceivable that the politicians would, so soon, bring it to an end.

This memorable tour came to a conclusion at the camp near Nadiad where we remained over Christmas, during which time I was confined to my tent with a fever. Thus I was unable to attend at the cinema for a special presentation of the film Ben Hur, in that wonderful 1925 version, but minus the two final reels and therefore no 'Great Chariot Race'. The language greeting this so unexpected an ending to a great drama was perhaps fortunately, not fully appreciated by the Indian management, unaccustomed to us English, and the same could be said of the comments and repartee during the preliminaries – the playing of gramophone records, amongst which was our National Anthem. It was claimed, possibly with slight exaggeration, that the audience rose to its feet five times!

At Christmas we had an exceptional gathering of local missionaries representing American Methodists, New Zealand Salvationists and Spanish Catholics, said to be the only 'whites' in that area. All were generous in their hospitality and to such an extent that everyone had an invitation to a meal. They complimented the work of our Padre 'Gus' Claxton, a doer of so much since early in France when he became our C of E Chaplain. We had the customary and memorable Christmas Day, by tradition a family occasion and observed no matter how difficult the circumstances, and good fare and cheer were essential ingredients. Carols were sung, there was a liberal ration of beer and seven camels arrived, goodness knows how.

Amongst photographs of the trek are the two that follow. One is of an 'A' Company guard under Corporal Chipp Smith, standing at ease preparatory to the arrival of Major-General Grover. They stand immaculate as was expected of our guards, but at a time when we were constantly on the move and clothes had to be in and out of kit-bags, that perfection is remarkable.

Another shows the equally smart figure of Private Burden, on guard at the sacred well.

During the evening of 27th December we entrained for Ahmadnagar and, travelling via Bombay, reached our destination during the morning of the 29th. We had done what had been asked of us and in so doing enjoyed a month away from formal routine, and perhaps we had dispelled a few myths about the British in one small corner of India.

And so we moved towards 1943, which could be described as the year in which we became familiar with landing-craft and the jungle. Months that were to be of preparation for a leading role in combined-operations and jungle warfare. How typical of service life that we were to carry out no assault landing and that we were to do very little jungle fighting when, at last, we faced the Japanese.

1943

Mail had become patchy – too many moves perhaps. That our letters home arrived with a constant irregularity is not surprising, but remarkably few were lost. Correspondence home had the choice of surface mail – mainly parcels and packages – or air-mail letters, which were not all that the name suggests, for they flew only for that part of the journey between South Africa and the UK. Best were the letter cards, ready gummed sheets not requiring envelopes and thus easy to carry and use and therefore popular, but rationed to one a week. They travelled the whole way by air.

Stud Farm was to be our home for less than three weeks and mine for only ten days, for on the 8th January I left by train for Bangalore OCTU, there to attend an Aircraft Recognition Course. Due to a timing error I arrived two days early, staying for that time within the splendours of the Staff Officers' Mess, where I shared a bearer who had been with 2 Dorset in 1921. To switch from the Dorset's rustic bashas, as the native type huts were called, to this establishment certainly added contrast to the daily routine, but polished tables with glistening cutlery, fine china, flowers and table decorations, and behind each chair a turbaned and brightly sashed bearer, was not something for which I lusted. But the course was an agreeable period of instruction and, although we did not fly we did examine planes on the ground. I learned (with partial success) to distinguish between Japanese and American aircraft and to talk of leading and trailing edges and even dihedral which, for those who have not been on such a course, is the angle of a wing with the horizontal. Such esoteric matters can be important when you are wondering whether the approaching plane is going to shoot you up. Ten days later I returned to reality and my friends who, on the previous day had arrived at our new address, Juhu Beach, to the north of Bombay.

That was the start of concentrated training for amphibious warfare, with swimming daily for everyone. We were well sited for not only were we camped on the beach, but adjacent to a creek, on the far side of which we were to do our training. At low tide we could wade across, but at all other times it was anything between two and three hundred yards in width and with a fair current. Thus when crossing we had rafts for our weapons and for the support of the non-swimmers. With every encouragement and from sheer necessity those who couldnot swim learned to do so, apart from a resolute five, who preferred to keep their feet on the ground.

To be under canvas within a grove of palm trees on the shore of the Arabian Sea, that ocean seen across a wide beach of golden sand, the water blue on which sailed the traditional craft of the local fishermen and the beach uncluttered by civilians – what a paradise! Certainly it was a very different world from that of Pashan Camp or Stud Farm but, when you are somewhere not of your own choosing and are preparing for a battle which is fast approaching, that beauty can dim and, anyway, living on sand is no joke!

Ours was a remote world, for the houses lining the shore behind us were empty and but for native fishermen, casting their nets on the surface of the creek, we had the place to ourselves.

Two days of lectures on combined operations were followed by a night exercise, when we swam the creek and crossed the mud flats beyond, into which we sank to our knees and then did battle, or whatever, within a tongue of semi-wilderness. Returning the way we had come and thankfully back on the home shore, 8 Platoon was found to be lacking Private Dudman, who did not reply to much bellowing of his name across the creek. With thoughts of bed fading, Lance-Corporate Bryant and I returned in what was to prove a fruitless search.

It seemed beyond belief that Dudman had vanished (although disappearing when wanted was commonplace in 8 Platoon) and in my imagination he had sunk in the mud, without trace, or had been trapped in the sea holly which was the very devil even in daylight. Back again at the creek, very weary and faced with what looked like half a mile of swirling water, I called back to Clive who had offered to remain ready to help. He set out with some more chaps towing a rope as Bryant and I swam out. We met in mid-stream and thankfully seizing the rope, were hauled in and able to stand again on firm ground. After all this – imagine our feelings when Dudman turned up, seemingly unconcerned, having taken some devious inland route of his own!

Next day we had a landing-craft and practised beach landings, noted by me as 'very wet'.

My earlier reference to char-wallahs omitted that equally familiar figure, the fruit-wallah. 'A' Company was favoured with one whose cheerful brightness and enthusiasm for us was such that at football matches, he not only cheered our efforts but, at least once, rushed onto the pitch to aid an injured player. A keen business sense brought him out on exercises (the fruit basket carried by a small boy), though how he tracked us down was an oriental mystery. And there he was at Juhu having followed us from Ahmadnagar. Bumping into him in the dark I was greeted by an unceremonious salute and a cheerful "Good evening sahib, remember me sahib? 'A' Company fruit-wallah".

Prior to our departure from Ahmednagar we, in common with other battalions, established a Guerilla Platoon: a carefully selected body of 'toughs', whose fighting skills in extra difficult situations were to prove their worth. For their training and leadership Lieutenant Harold 'Jonah' Jones was extracted from 'B' Company, to weld them into a cohesive unit with an identity and to do so as a matter of urgency in a few weeks.

Another change, but during those first weeks at Juhu, was the departure of Tom Molloy, to the regret of all, following his appointment as Second-in-Command of 5 Brigade and promotion to full colonel. Geoffry White then moved up in a logical progression to Acting Commanding Officer.

On 1st February we changed beaches for one ten miles away to the north at Marve, where we were to carry out two weeks of practice landings. We were told that following our landing in the operation for which we were preparing, we would immediately advance ten miles inland, there to capture and hold some high ground. This new beach, with open space of similar geography behind, provided us with the opportunity to rehearse that operation and day after day we did so. When a landing-craft was not available, we formed up on the shore in the positions that we assumed we might be on landing, then to do that critical ten miles dash as fast as we were able. Daily the temperature increased as we entered the dry pre-monsoon months and by the time we had attained that high ground against opposition, for in reality we expected to have to fight for it, we were just about scorched by the sun and whacked by the toughness of the going. I, to my dismay, found myself so exhausted as to be barely able to see.

My photograph of that beach, shows two landing-craft on a placid sea, which itself looks hot, and shows the wide and scruffy shore, which has no boundary, for sand extends inland among palms and under-growth so sunbaked that they too wilt.

One day, encouraged by the ever lively John O'Driscoll, we chartered a local fishing boat and had the thrill of sailing and handling it in a stiff breeze. It was a craft with an open flat-bottomed hull and a lateen type of rig, filling a role like that of the English coble of past days on the north east coast, both built to be run-in and beached at night. This one however, in the absence of any metal fastenings, was literally tied together by hand-made cords, thus for a few hours we had gone back in time and entered into so different a world.

We returned to Juhu for more training and on 19th February were told that the time and the place of our operation had been decided.

On the 26th, following a consultation with Joe Chamberlin, I was examined by a heart specialist in Bombay who recommended me for medical regrading to B. Permanent. Feeling both depressed and resigned, I wondered as to my future.

Landing craft off Marve.

At Juhu we concentrated on our long distance swimming, spurred on with thoughts of how necessary it might prove to be. By then, with the steadily increasing air temperature, the sea was too hot to refresh and the place had lost its charm – it was time for us to be on our way. That our days there were numbered was made obvious when, on 13th March, our Quartermaster Teddy Edwards and I left with an advance party to establish a camp inland at Bhiwandi, a place that was to be as ghastly for extremes of heat as Pashan had for rain. We found ourselves in a desolate land of rocks and scrub dried out and barren in the great heat, made worse by some misguided ass who thought to clear the scrub by burning and failed. It was a place that even Geoffry described as appalling. There we experienced the highest recorded temperatures of anywhere during the years we were abroad, a place where everything one touched was hot. The shade temperature on 30th March was 113 F and on 6th April it had increased to 116 and with a high humidity. Training had to continue and, as was customary in such a situation, we started early (0800 hrs) and finished late (1900 hrs). Of the daylight hours there was nothing other than an hour or so following dawn that was even tolerable, in the afternoons we lay naked and dormant. Dick Purser sat up a tree for two nights with a rifle and a wretched tethered goat below. On the first night a panther passed but too quickly for a shot. There were plenty of snakes about and one of the platoon killed a black scorpion, decidedly nasty.

From 1st to 4th April the battalion, less a rear party of whom I was one, refreshed itself on an assault ship as a further element of our amphibious training and one that was greatly enjoyed.

Life at Bhiwandi ceased for me on 10th April when I left by road, thankfully complete with batman, for Tobruk Lines, Poona. There I was to be acting Motor Transport Officer, while the newly appointed holder – Lieutenant 'Dixie' Deane, attended a course and Dick returned to the battalion. This resulted in another complete change of circumstances – a room of my own, furniture, carpet, electric lighting – wonderful! And no formalities or bugle calls. Actually I delight in the bugle but in those last weeks at Juhu, Geoffry's love of obscure calls of which "All officers at the double" was one, made life difficult for those, such as I, whose recognition of them was zero.

But for signing letters there was little to occupy my time but to mount one of our glorious Norton motor bikes and to learn to ride it over rough country, of which there was plenty. The only parade seems to have been the one for swimming, when at 0915 hrs we departed for an hour at an outdoor pool.

At the beginning of May the battalion turned up at a much improved Pashan Camp en route for Mahabaleshwar, a small hill station on the Western Ghats, there to do jungle training. I visited them in connection with their transport.

All good things come to an early end, as when on 8th May we moved back to Stud Farm. But there I was seen by a medical board and re-categorised as 'B' for three months.

Then on the 22nd we were off yet again, making a two day journey to a new place – Nira. On these moves I was able to ride the Norton and when on this particular one, we were hit by a pre-monsoon storm I and the vehicles had a battle to remain on the road. The rain struck us horizontally and at right angles, conditions I likened to Bournemouth promenade during a winter gale. Three days later the Norton and I with six trucks were off on a 70 mile journey to collect tents and tent pegs, our road a rutted track of loose sand.

Nira-Galunchi was, as far as our camp was concerned, no more than a plateau 100 feet above the surrounding country and 50 miles from the nearest town. But I was not to get to know it then for I was off again, on 30th May, bound for 'Staff Duties' at the Secunderabad leave camp.

The camp to which I had made that one visit was tented, but for a few bamboo framed and thatched buildings, of which our officers' mess was one. It was commanded by a Captain Ewins to whom I became second-in-command, being the senior of three subalterns. When full it held about a thousand, not always from 2 Div. At one time we had men from the RAF Regiment, which I remember from an after breakfast parade and inspection, held daily for no other reason than to ensure that everybody remained reasonably tidy. Work started (for us staff) at about 0700 hrs and finished by 1700 hrs. Messing was my main responsibility and I went daily to the Secunderabad open market, accompanied by an Indian cook for haggling, returning with a surprising amount of fruit and the like for the equivalent of, about, six pence a head. The camp kept a flock of ducks for fattening and we endeavoured to have duck on the menu once a week. Parties of 100 men or so would come and go and, on their departure, I and the mess staff would weigh and prepare travelling rations – perhaps for three days – then deliver them to the train. What different work it was to that of a platoon commander!

I renewed my membership of the Secunderabad Club being determined to get fit, made a point of having a daily swim and, whenever possible, a game or two of squash. Billiards in the evening too and perhaps a meal. This for a monthly membership fee of 12 rupees, the equivalent of just under £1. Of course one paid for meals and perhaps other things, but the charges were so reasonable that they were well within the modest pay of a subaltern. Of the many staff, I think of the white-bearded attendant of the changing room, to whom you gave your wallet for safe keeping while you played squash or tennis. He placed it in his wall cupboard and you never doubted the safety of what, to him, would be a great amount of money. Then, when you returned hot from your game, he filled your bath and brought a cooling drink for consumption in that bath and folded your clothes, just part of an unforgettable service with a mutual respect. Sad that such behaviour is not the norm! So impressed was I that when I did my post-war final for membership of the Royal Institute of British Architects, my thesis design was of a similar club on a fine site near where I then lived. I need hardly say that it was never built.

For the first time I was in contact with British residents who were providing hospitality to troops. Soon after arriving, in an outing organised by one of these hard-working ladies, I accompanied a group to an ancient fort about ten miles away. There we were given a conducted tour and tea in the shade of an elephant tree, said to be one of only three in the world and with a trunk diameter of 20 feet – well named. At some homes a regular fortnightly tea party was a part of our leave programme. One couple who were generous with their invitations were the Secretary to the Resident of Hyderabad and his wife, who opened their large garden and home to us. And what a magnificent garden and home!

That year the monsoon was late, with only isolated storms until September, by which time plans were made for the evacuation of the half million inhabitants of Hyderabad City, so desperate was their water supply. Then torrential rain put matters right, more falling during the first week of September than in the previous months. We in our thatched mess were busy dodging the leaks.

In that month I was able to arrange a flight with an RAF officer who, on a sunny morning at Begumpet airfield, took me up in a Tiger Moth. I had asked to loop-the-loop as aerial somersaults were known, a familiar stunt when there were still a number of the open cockpit slow flying biplanes in general use. We stuck at the top of the first and hanging in my harness I contemplated my feet; our speed as we reached the apex had been insufficient to carry us over the down, but we managed the ensuing ones and performed vertical spins and dives in a thrilling spell of unconventional flying. To end we flew low over the great city, seeing into the seldom seen and for the European, seldom entered, tangle of alleys and dwellings, unknown to those confined to the principal streets.

There had been a marked falling off in September of the numbers arriving on leave and then, from a Dorset party, there was talk of things 'hotting-up'. I had enjoyed a splendid break and was feeling fit (swam 20 lengths) and was only too aware that I would never forgive myself were I not with the battalion when they were doing the things for which we had trained so long and hard. I applied to return and did so on 4th October. That return was to a battalion commanded by 'The Link'. Lieutenant-Colonel Linklater had arrived from the UK soon after my departure and rumours had travelled about this so disliked a leader, a situation that was endangering the morale of the battalion at a most critical time and one that must have made his life hellish also. We smiled when the fitters, with whom it was almost impossible to argue, had his Humber Snipe car 'off the road' almost always when wanted. There was little else to smile about.

People seemed pleased to see me and cracks were made that 'I had been caught at last'. I rejoined 8 Platoon and a somewhat different 'A' Company with John Bowles commanding and Dick Castle as 2 I/C, sadly no Clive, who had become 2 I/C of the Carrier Platoon.

The operation for which we had prepared at Juhu and Marve had been abandoned as I was well aware, now everybody (and I should mention that we were still at Nira-Galunchi), was hard at work on another. When, on the 10th, we set out for a week of living under groundsheets, I was inclined to think that I had mismanaged the timing of my return. But the site that we reached was a good one, being within a broad valley running into the hills, the land green and bordering a river. There we were visited by the Divisional mobile cinema, the film that evening being seen against a background of lightning above distant hills. A 17 mile foot-blistering march took us back to base, from where we were off again for four days. Blistered feet were, and probably still are, one of the bugbears of infantry life. Given a combination of wet feet and a long march or a march where the going was unusually difficult, blisters up to an inch and a half in diameter were commonplace, as I well know, being one who suffered. We marched on them until they burst and that eased the pain and all the time we had a longing for the moment when we got our boots off. At the end of a testing march the platoon commander inspected feet, knowing full well that there would be some so blistered and bloody with abrasions as to need first aid, particularly when the next day, we marched again.

This activity was the culmination of weeks of preparation for exercise 'Swordfish', which was to be our final dress rehearsal for the long awaited 2nd Division assault landing. At 0030 hrs on 2nd November we departed in trucks for Poona Station, to entrain for Bombay Docks, reached the following day. There we embarked on the Bibby Line MV *Empire Pride*, a veteran of Madagascar, North Africa and the Sicily landings. For me, nothing compared with the delight and satisfaction of being within the well ordered world of a ship and seeing and smelling salt water. Those first few days while still off Bombay were memorable for me, providing as they did my introduction to the world of contract bridge. Dick Castle, 'Snagger' Highett and Graeme Gordon-Wright (Graeme joined us soon after our arrival in India) were experts. From then on the fascination of the game and their company and that of one or two others, was to give me hours of intense pleasure and a host of happy memories.

With the convoy assembled and ready, the 2nd Division set forth, sailing south within the protection of a Royal Navy escort and supporting force; our destination an area with a coastline similar to that on which we were to land – in Japanese held territory. The earlier landing, abandoned soon after my departure for Poona, had been for the recapture of the Nicobar Islands, north of Sumatra; unknown to us, our eventual objective was now the Port of Akyab on the coast of Burma about one hundred and fifty miles south of Chittagong. To avoid a direct assault on the port, we were to land on a beach due north of the creek south of which was Akyab. A complicated operation, in which surprise was essential, for once we were ashore we had to change direction in a right-wheel, then to re-launch ourselves into assault boats to cross the creek, almost certainly under fire from the enemy in Akyab, who, by then, would be well aware of our landing.

In the pitch blackness of 0400 hrs on 7th November, we clambered down the scrambling nets into the landing craft, a little tricky for they were rising and falling on a deep water swell, the convoy having halted far out to sea. Helping hands got 8 Platoon into our boat without mishap, together with our heavy burden of equipment and weapons. Then, in an orderly progression, the boats headed for the invisible shore. These boats or LCP's (landing-craft personnel) were of an obsolete pattern without a ramp, they could have been no more than commandeered ship's lifeboats. Thus to disembark from them one stood on the gunn'el behind the bows and jumped down into the water, On that first bump of keel on sand I, ready to lead my men through shot and shell, leapt into the sea which I expected to be of wading depth and not, as was the case, four feet. Our bottom had touched a sandbank and we were dropping into deeper water beyond. That unexpected difference caused me to half fall backwards and to lose my grip on my Sten-gun. A quick scrambling dive recovered it amongst a shower of other bodies. We then made for the shore onto which we staggered, weighed down as we were with water in every pouch and pocket. We had then to throw ourselves flat on the sand to pass below a line of barbed-wire entanglement, seen dimly in the pre-dawn at 0515 hrs. Any élan I may have had was long gone when I led my very wet and sandy platoon through dry loose sand to beyond the beach. There to shed such water as we could and count ourselves all present, as we did also in thankfulness that we were not faced by the Japs. The subsequent events of what was to be a very long day as we milled around and slowly dried out and became our usual selves, went unrecorded. It was at best a shambles. There would have been plenty of remarks to the effect that we "were well and truly up the ....creek". Some would have referred to it as just one more SNAFU – Situation Normal All Fouled Up. The same adjective can be substituted for Fouled as for the ... before creek, without recourse to much imagination. If ever there was a time for swearing that was it. Perhaps we Dorsets were particularly unlucky, I just don't know.

It was the following afternoon when we re-embarked and, with troubled thoughts of the shambles of the day and what it foretold, again in convoy retraced our route back to Bombay through blue seas. There to sleep on board and entrain on the 11th, arriving the next day at a new camp near Visapur, to the west of Ahmadnagar, for a brief halt before yet another move.

For us ordinary mortals, whose lot it was to obey, amphibious operations were an agreeable break from routine. Again fate was on our side and, thanks to the RAF, we were not to meet death and destruction at Akyab. A reconnaissance flight disclosed the arrival of Japanese forces of about one regiment, behind our intended landing beach. Surprise having been lost the operation was abandoned.

We Dorsets were now to learn the art of living within and, to some extent, off the jungle and for this we departed at 0700 hrs on 26th November; travelling south by road until 1800 hrs, repeating this on the second of two days through the all too familiar sun-baked landscape of rocks and scanty vegetation, until halting for the night near Belgaum City. On the third day a final 50 miles took us through jungle, our well known world replaced by one of lush vegetation and in this our journey ended. We were then a few miles inland from the Portuguese enclave of Goa, believed by some misguided service personnel to be a neutral 'Garden of Eden', in which if reached, they could complete the war on a tropical beach attended by dusky maidens, an error of the first magnitude, as some (not Dorsets) discovered.

We were travelling light, having the minimum of spare clothing and bedding and our first task was to erect shelters, not in anticipation of rain but of dew, sufficiently heavy by early morning to drop off the trees like rain. These shelters were to be made from materials gathered locally, the most useful being bamboo of a size which astonished us, for we were in a place where heights of 40 feet were commonplace. We would sleep on charpoys made of bamboo framing, interlaced with small branches and vines. Even string off one of my parcels played a part in the construction of our platoon HQ, which I was to share, as platoon commanders were to live with their men. Cutting was done with machetes, which were also ideal for clearing the dense undergrowth in which our shelters were sited for concealment – they were to be invisible at five yards.

This concealment did not prevent another visit from the mobile cinema.

8 Platoon was soon out on patrol in such a thickness of vegetation that we only covered one mile in two hours. But we reached a clear and fast flowing river, with small exotic fish and swooping over the water were birds similar to our kingfishers, and there were butterflies in abundance. We stripped off and were soon revelling in the water, indifferent to the pug marks, made our 'experts' said by a tiger.

At that time I was seen by a 5th Field Ambulance medical board and regraded 'A'.

It was not long before platoons were 'enjoying' the experience of moving through the jungle at night, a slow single file advance in complete darkness, made hazardous by fallen trees. Jungle and forest differ in that in the former the vegetation dies naturally so that decaying trees are everywhere. To progress at all one had to move on a compass course, thus fallen trees in all stages of decay had to be clambered over and through; our progress, such as it was, was marked by the sound of oaths and falling bodies amongst breaking branches, as a well and truly 'browned-off' platoon thinking longingly of tarmacadam, expressed its opinion of the proceedings.

On 10th December the battalion left camp for participation in a five day brigade exercise, our company being under the command of Dick in the absence, on leave, of John Bowles. Late that first afternoon Dick decided to cut bamboo for the cook-house dixies, so that there would be fuel available for the company cooks when they arrived. Using a kukri in an attempt to cut a large bamboo he had a ricochet and nearly lost his left hand. Having got him to Joe, thankfully not far away, I took over the company for the remainder of the exercise. An exercise that made very clear how much we had to learn about operating in the jungle. As usual when we were 'en masse' wild life kept away, our nearest contact being a herd of elephant some miles distant. We received notice of such herds, presumably it was reckoned better for both parties that we did not clash. Later we learned of the great excitement back at Rear Details, as our administration base was known, when a tiger entered our old camp site and shots were fired and one of our regimental police spent an hour up a tree.

The 23rd saw us marching to a brigade camp of hardscale tentage, seven miles from Belgaum City, where we were to rest and celebrate Christmas. To our delight we were reunited with our kit and thus able to change into clean clothes, after wearing a suit of overalls for the past weeks. Those were the dying days of the long epoch of shorts for the British in India, a garment which exposed legs to scratches or worse and to leeches – hence the overalls. And I and my friends had our camp beds and sheets again. So, in this organised camp, we had facilities for the proper enjoyment of Christmas, for there were chairs to sit on and plates to eat off, after a session of sitting on the ground and eating from mess tins. And the great influx of Christmas Mail was waiting for us, from airgraphs to parcels. We had our customary days of comradeship and on the 25th, officers maintained the tradition of serving the Christmas Dinner. Dry temperate weather did much for the success of those days of rest and recreation, which were aided by visits from the mobile cinema and our visits to a city with a reasonable bazaar.

This static camp made easier the due observance of Christmas Day by Padre Gus whose age, personality and temperament made him so fitting a person to be our Chaplain. His service was enriched by a mobile organ, generally known as the 'assault organ' which we envisaged as being rushed ashore from a landing-craft, in the manner of some secret weapon in the hands of armed acolytes. The latter being the honorary battalion organist, Private Stroud, an expert also on the 3-inch mortar, and by Gus's batman, the indispensable Private Hounsome.

As the year ended we set off on a two day road journey back to Visapur, which we reached at 1700 hrs on 31st December. Went to bed early.

1944

This new year started with what I noted as ... "Indications that operations are in the offing". Those indications were

Issue of tropical battledress
Equipment to be dyed green
All bills to be paid
The re-issue of greatcoats.

Despite all this, it would not have surprised us, any more than it would the readers of these pages, that our next instruction was a contradiction, one that confirmed what had been anticipated almost since we had disembarked at Bombay in November – our assault landing was off and we were to return to the jungle. In the jargon of today, we were back to 'square one'.

During the training at Bulford OCTU, so long ago, I and my fellow cadets were told that when we departed, we would be fit to lead 30 men into battle. Brave words!

Now, after a further three years of preparation, it was not to be my lot to lead 8 Platoon into action. Probably a good thing for the platoon, as it was in a very different way, for me. But how much I wish that I had, could I have done so in the manner that they deserved to be led against a fearsome enemy. Since Pashan Camp my ability to match the physical requirements of a rifle company had been suspect. In December, Colonel Linklater had proposed that I should be considered for a staff appointment at an Area HQ or within a Field Survey unit, on the grounds that I was too old a subaltern for an Assault Battalion. That recommendation had been returned by Corps HQ with an annotation that – 'Only medical regrading or an adverse report will enable an officer to leave the 2nd Division.'

On 11th January, John Bowles returned after an absence of five weeks and resumed command of 'A' Company and two days later, I was appointed Battalion Intelligence Officer, superseding Michael Morice. This was a very different assignment, being less physically demanding and also one in which I would be able to use some of the professional skills of an architect. I was to hold it for the remainder of my time with the battalion. There was much to learn and no immediate possibility of going on a course but, with Sergeant Marlow and nine veteran members of the 'I' Section, I had great support. With an office, a truck and a motor-bike, we were a small self-contained unit with all that could be desired.

Having the new jungle green battledress and the webbing of our equipment dyed to match (not to mention green pants and vests), we blended with the vegetation. As we also did when among rocks and scrub, for the shade was a neutral olive. What wrecked our camouflage was white flesh, of which there was an unexpected amount. This we set about eliminating as far as was reasonably possible, through a policy of everyone wearing no more than shorts until mid-day. We also discarded our sun-helmets for the wide brimmed, khaki bush-hats.

A visit in late January by our 'Supremo' – Lord Louis Mountbatten, Supreme Commander South-East Asia, gave us a great fillip at a time when our future seemed to be without purpose. Officers were presented and all were given an inspiring address by this so different and so charismatic a leader. Standing on a box and with his audience tight packed in a circle, he told us how, when the time came, we would defeat the Japs. But the 2nd Division, now that all landing-craft were concentrated in Europe, might have to wait for the defeat of Germany, something he believed to be possible by the end of the year.

We had a very different visit when the concert party administered by 2 Div., one drawing on a great wealth of talent, such as that of the actor Jack Hawkins, arrived and set up its stage. They were always excellent and topical. Officers attended with feelings of anticipation which could border on dread, knowing that the introduction into the script of their names was an expected feature. On this occasion both my bridge playing and my name of 'Tiger' were introduced to a mixture of groans and cheers. I squirmed and tried not to blush! That substituted name stuck so well (so much easier to remember and say than my difficult surname) that it continues in use and when asked if I mind, I am able to say that "it makes me feel almost young again". It is a product of Bulford and a wrestling match with a fellow cadet, a splendid Scot by the name of Moffat but who, I fear, did not survive the war. At the end of that barrack room encounter, someone said "Gosh you're Tigerish" – and so it started.

From time to time we had our own battalion entertainment, very much on the same lines and in its way almost better, for everybody knew everybody.

In the afternoon of 28th January, Colonel Linklater and I, being part of an advance party for our return to the jungle, set off to spend that night at a town 70 miles away. It could only have been Poona. Next morning the two vehicles carrying all but the C.O., who remained to come down later by train, pressed on as fast as the indifferent roads permitted. We shared the driving for the 220 miles, completed by 1730 hrs, a considerable distance on such roads in one day. Collecting the C.O. from the station next morning, we started a 100-mile recce of the jungle, 25 of which were over tracks. Some of the flanking vegetation was of bamboo in abundance and of great height, stems with a base diameter of six inches and all so dense as to be virtually impregnable, made more so by thorns.

On the following day we did a first recce of our allotted area, one of a more open character than where we were before and being hilly, there were hills of a few thousand feet in the distance, it was possible to find great panoramas over a landscape of jungle. This was a scenery with a richness and a scale unknown at home and one in contrast to that with which we had associated India. Our introduction to the fauna came when a couple of wild pig charged across the track.

Busy days were to follow as we prepared for the arrival of the battalion on 4th February.

Now as I.O., having been instructed to prepare a plan of our jungle base, I was able to use my ability to produce scale drawings.

We were simulating an infantry battalion with its supporting arms advancing along a jungle track and then dispersing left and right into the trees; there to establish a position with all-round protection – known as a 'box'. Thus 1,000 men had to be got below ground and so concealed that users of the track would be unaware of our presence. All spoil from trenches had to be dispersed and camouflaged and, also camouflaged, were the trenches, our vehicles and weapons. We occupied a most irregular rectangle – 450 yards in length on the axis of the track and roughly 200 yards in width. On my plan, which I fortunately retained, the general pattern of slit trenches can be seen, together with the arcs of fire from our Brens and the positions of our 3-inch mortars and various headquarters. We had 'B' Company of the 2nd Manchester Regiment (Machine-Gun Battalion) attached, their positions are shown, as are the eight 25-pounder guns of the 51st Battery, the 10th Field Regiment RA and two 3.7 howitzers of the 30th Battery. Vehicle parks are to the north of the track which snakes through from east to west. 211 slit and similar trench positions are drawn, in an historical record of a defended locality, in jungle, in 1944.

The exceptions to all this training for battle had to be the provision for those who were sick and who it would be unreasonable to treat in a dug-out, as would happen were the Japs around. Anyone using the track would have seen tents for Joe Chamberlin and company and for Captain Swallow, one of the RAMC doctors of the 5th Field Ambulance, who were in support, all of whom were sited within clearings along the line of the track. It was Norman Swallow who was involved in the one excitement of that camp when, in the pre-dawn of a quiet night, a couple of buffalos charged through his tent, taking him and his bed through the far wall. One can imagine this pair ambling along a familiar trail and then, suddenly, they were aware of the scent of humans on all sides. In terror they put their heads down and accelerated, thankfully without inflicting casualties.

Other but smaller residents were accepting us – a bird-eating spider (pretty revolting) and a friendly parrot of green and yellow plumage, who liked to perch on a tree and drop berries on us, were just two. Beyond our lines bears were being seen and patrols carried a few rounds of ammo for self protection, since they were known to be more likely to attack than the tigers, traces of whom had also been observed.

Like the earlier camp, we had the blessing of an attractive river. Being only three miles away, it was almost a 'life saver', for our environment was one where washing was, at best, difficult.

On the 31st January 61 British other ranks (BORs) were posted to us from Deolali, that base through which so many men in transit passed. They were a welcome influx to make good our wastage from sickness.

An appointment vital to the efficiency of the battalion was made in February when Graeme Gordon-Wright became Adjutant. He superseded Tom Hughes who had followed Tony Bridge and who now departed to use his skills in a higher formation. Graeme was a good administrator but no more than a shadowy, unknown figure, behind the façade he presented of the carefree, swizzle-stick-using socialite. For one so fastidious our rough living would have been abhorrent.

The even tenor of our life was broken on the 23rd when, during a field firing exercise, a 2-inch mortar bomb fell on a group of spectators, all of whom were battalion officers. Jock Wilson, Harold Jones, Lionel Halahan, Jimmy Hodder, Dick Purser and Joe Chamberlin were all injured, the first two seriously. Jock, commander of the Carrier Platoon, received a shattered femur and was never again fit for service. Thus we lost one whom we could ill afford to be without. Harold, with an injured knee and severe blood loss, returned months later. It could have been much worse, but a feeling of resentment has not faded at what was attributed to carelessness.

Clive succeeded Jock in command of the Carriers and received his captaincy.

As a break from jungle living everybody was having a 48 hours leave in Belgaum City, going in batches of 150. Dick Castle, just returned with a hand made good again, and I were the only officers in our lot, most being away umpiring a big exercise. It was good to have a bed and a chair and to eat at a table, but the return was grim – one and a half hours by train and then an hour in the back of a truck, reaching home at 0330 hrs.

On the 3rd of March, Lieutenant-Colonel Linklater departed unlamented and we awaited his successor. While welcoming the change we had feelings of dismay: our new C.O. was unknown and the first non-Dorset to command the battalion for 11 years.

Lieutenant-Colonel R.S. McNaught of the Royal Scots Fusiliers arrived, very fresh from the UK. He immediately moved around in the jungle, with not only the expected enthusiasm of one who was determined to impress, but with the added vitality and fierce energy of a tough Scot. He left me gasping and thinking that the promised break of a week on the coast for the whole battalion, due in seven days, would be doubly welcome. That night we were out on a battalion compass march.

For some time the 'I' Section had been planning a jungle trek, a feature of which was to be rafting down the river and, with our plans almost ready, it had to be postponed. Then, suddenly, we were told that we could go but only for three days, the rafting abandoned for lack of time. Making a pre-dawn start by the last light of the moon and using a dry nullah as the easiest route to the river, we covered that ground in just under two hours, pausing only to try to shoot a jungle cock which was too quick on the wing. We arrived at a pool where a dug-out canoe was launched but which capsized when boarded. Thinking back, it obviously needed ballast. We waded across, a fire was lit and our cook busied himself with porridge, bacon, fried potato and a pint of tea. In theory we were living off the country, hence the attempt to shoot the fowl. What we were then eating was a generous part of our emergency rations. That cooking and swimming (we could dive from rocks into deep water) occupied a couple of hours and it was mid-morning before we continued. Our map showed a village in a clearing beyond the jungle and at the end of a pack or cart-track; there we expected to purchase eggs and chicken. We had unexpected difficulty in finding the track, crossing it and then retracing our steps only to pass over it again without realising we had done so; it being so little used as to be barely discernible within the trees. Thus it was at the end of the afternoon when we arrived at a collection of huts, dust coloured like the sandy soil in which they stood and empty but for two ancient males squatting in the sun. At such a remote and isolated place I doubt that Urdu would have proved to be more effective than our English which, even when spoken loudly and slowly in the traditional manner of the English abroad, caused no reaction from these two, who seemed incapable of understanding anything, including what it was that we wished to buy. And the outlines of birds and eggs, scratched in the dust and arm flapping to denote wings, were deadpanned. During this pantomime a number of women, obviously returning from a day in the fields, could be seen making for home – until they spotted us, whereupon they turned about and were gone. We seemed unwelcome. With the hamlet so isolated, the only path eight miles to a road, it was probable that we were the first white faces seen for years and understandably armed soldiers were to be feared. Among the huts were a form of grapefruit of which we gathered eight or nine and, giving the old gents a generous handful of coins, we made for the river which we knew to be away in the trees beyond the sun-baked open ground we were then crossing. We struck it opposite an island, tree covered and looking most attractive and an ideal location for the night. It was an elongated outcrop of rock within a margin of sand and easily approached across shallow rapids above a series of pools, an unspoiled paradise if only we could catch fish. As usual we were near starving but with a fireplace constructed in a matter of minutes, our cook was soon busy producing an 'all-in' bully stew. Later we slept replete, on the sand, our bodies forming a ring around a camp fire of drift wood, kept burning all night.

We had what I can only describe as a generous supply of hand-grenades, that familiar product of World War 1 – the Mills Bomb. This was a no nonsense occasion, for the fishing had to produce fish and those grenades would surely do so. It was soon obvious that a grenade lobbed into even the largest pool was producing nothing. This we attributed to the splash of its entry causing the fish to dart for cover during the three seconds fuse delay. Using two or three in quick succession did however do the trick. Presumably the first detonation brought the fish out of hiding and they were then stunned by the subsequent ones. With the stunned fish rising to the surface we had a series of hectic and hilarious moments as we swam after them, some escaping just as we made our grab and we determined not to go hungry. It was 1130 before they were all cleaned and fried and we had finished a breakfast unlike any other.

There was no doubt in our minds that it would be folly to leave such a place, this Shangri-La, and the day continued much as it had begun. We swam and fished and ate and lazed in the sun, relishing the proximity of clear fast-flowing water and the solitude of that remote place. At 0700 hrs the following morning we departed from our haven and, following the river, made for our crossing and breakfast place of the first day, to find the pool occupied by an angler, from goodness knows where for we had seen no habitations. He, as yet unlucky, watched with amazement when we produced from our packs and proceeded to cook twenty fish. Those fish I should mention were accompanied by bread, prepared and baked on the island. Afterwards we carried on down river for four miles, there to laze in the enjoyment of our own company until 1630, having had our final swim and meal before an hour's march to the road, where we stopped a passing truck and so to camp. All agreed that it was the best three days that we had had for years.

My letter from which this 'holiday report' was taken, ends 'am now preparing for a big exercise, following which we return to base and go on leave'.

Awaiting me, to bring back memories of Poole Harbour, were a number of Yachting World magazines.

That anticipated week on the coast had been overtaken by events for, although leave was high on the agenda, we Dorsets had first to be the enemy in a 6 Brigade exercise known as 'Shawk'. In preparation we moved on 19th March to Dandeli, about thirty miles south of Belgaum City. We commenced to dig-in ready to defend our area against attack and more than content in having the static role.

Earlier in the month Major-General Grover had returned from GHQ India, having received confirmation of what Lord Louis had told us informally – that all landing-craft were required in Europe and consequently his Division would not be in action during the year. Our so familiar routine of training, of which the brigade exercise would be the first, was to continue – and what then? This was a situation that must have caused deep concern, for training can only achieve its aims if for a purpose. To remove that objective yet again and for so long, could be a recipe for disaster. And, as if that were not enough, he would have been subjected to disquiet, in the knowledge that the Indian Army would do its best to justify the dismemberment of so unwanted and costly a formation.

But in war, when your actions are so often determined by those of your enemy, circumstances can and do change with bewildering speed as, unsuspected by us, they were doing then. Far from continuing, our years of preparation for battle were at an end. How well the 'I' Section had timed that three day break!

March 1944 brought to a conclusion the three years and more during which, under six commanding officers, we endured the exacting routine of which this account has been an outline. That those C.O.s succeeded in preparing us for action against a formidable enemy was due, above all, to the 14 months under

George Wood, whose drive and determination and belief in us produced a close knit 'family' unit with that pride and self confidence that is essential for success in battle. And how fortunate we were that 'Jock' McNaught was tough enough to withstand the trauma of taking over an unknown battalion, which he was advised would not be in action that year, but which was to be in a few weeks and doing so with confidence.

Our pride in ourselves was enhanced by the support and affection of two individuals who were not transient as were commanding officers, but who steadfastly remained with us from the early days of the war until its end – staunch Dorsets indeed were Gus and Joe, of whom brief mention has been made. They were more correctly known, respectively, as Captain L.E.M. Claxton of the Army Chaplain's Department and Captain J.A. Chamberlin of the Royal Army Medical Corps. Both were to be awarded, to the satisfaction of all, much earned Military Crosses. It takes a better man that I to describe Gus, apocryphal stories of whom and his tussles with a 'higher authority', which caused his name to languish at the bottom of the leave roster, brightened many a dull day. And who could describe Joe, of whom there was no criticism, even when one staggered away from one of the perpetual inoculation parades, having seemingly been pierced by a square ended needle. They were wonderful, and a thousand of us say so.

The shortage of photographs of those years is lamentable; thus I value this one of 23 members of 8 Platoon. The senior NCO is Corporal Binding, for we seem to have discarded our sergeants.

Back row	*Ptes. Jones B, Male, Wright, Hole.*
Middle row	*Ptes. Millington, Blackmore, Cpl. Binding, Ptes. Dudman, Burden, Wealands, Buckley, Zeitmen, Jones D, Mullins, Gray, Blanch, L/Cpl. Bryant, Pte. Feldman.*
Front row	*Pte. Marsh, Self, Ptes. Carvell, Pierce, Whitton, L/Cpl. Grandfield.*

This narrative now changes to one that is more of a diary, where dates and times have an increased importance. The preparations for battle, the clashes with the enemy and the manner in which we lived, are detailed to the extent made possible by my records. Having complied with the order debarring diaries I am deprived of a great asset, but I have a collection of documents brought from India and gathered since, also the letters to my mother are accompanied by ones to Eileen, my future wife. In 1947 she and I drafted a record of what follows, an invaluable spine on which to build and one that has been augmented by reference to the Battalion's War Diary. In addition to those sources I have received many reminiscences from old comrades and others who were there.

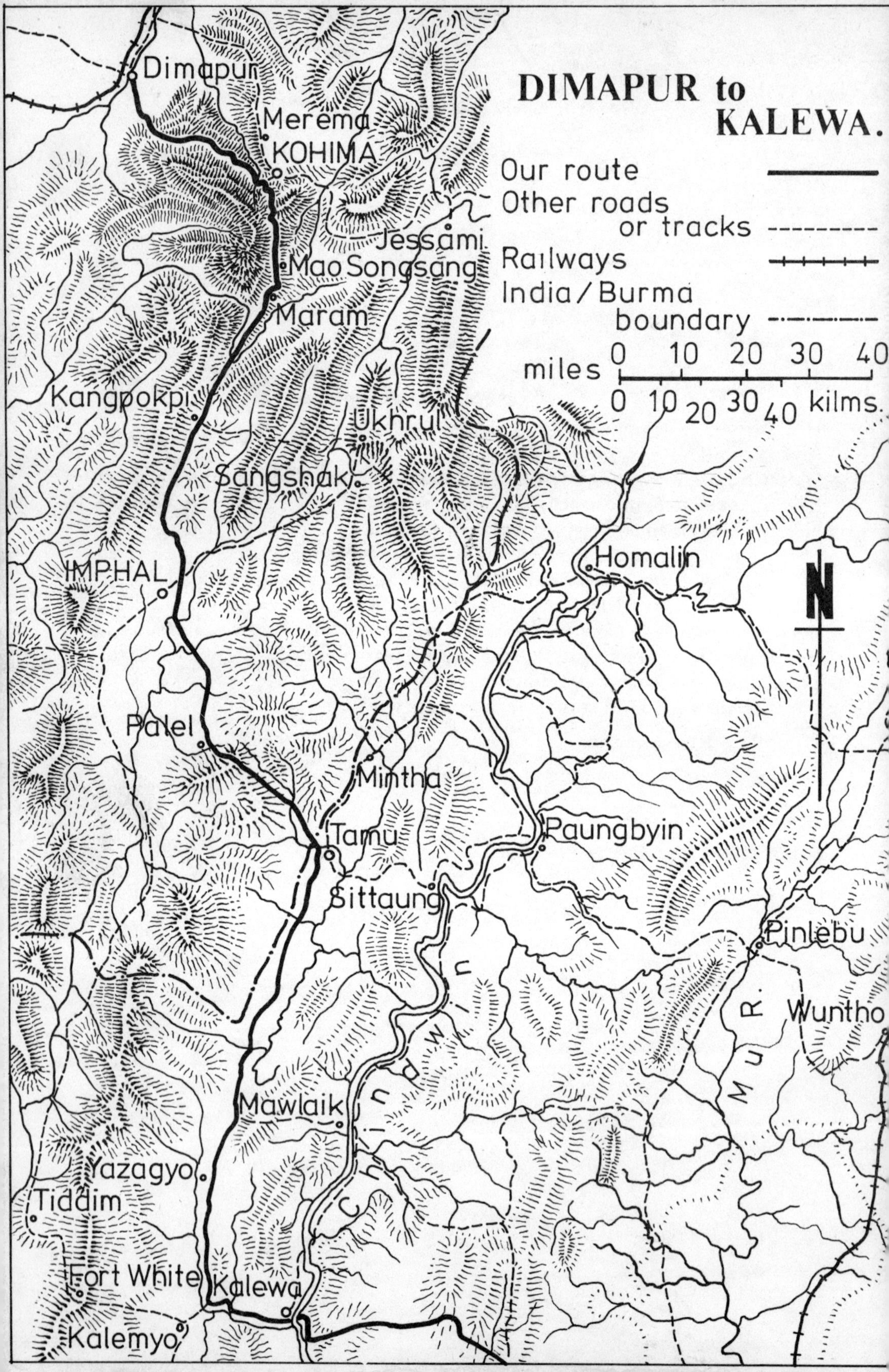

DIMAPUR to KALEWA.
Our route
Other roads or tracks
Railways
India/Burma boundary
miles 0 10 20 30 40
0 10 20 30 40 kilms.
Dimapur
Merema
KOHIMA
Jessami
Mao Songsang
Maram
Kangpokpi
Ukhrul
Sangshak
IMPHAL
Homalin
N
Palel
Mintha
Tamu
Paungbyin
Sittaung
Pinlebu
Wuntho
Mu R.
Chindwin
Mawlaik
Yazagyo
Tiddim
Fort White
Kalewa
Kalemyo

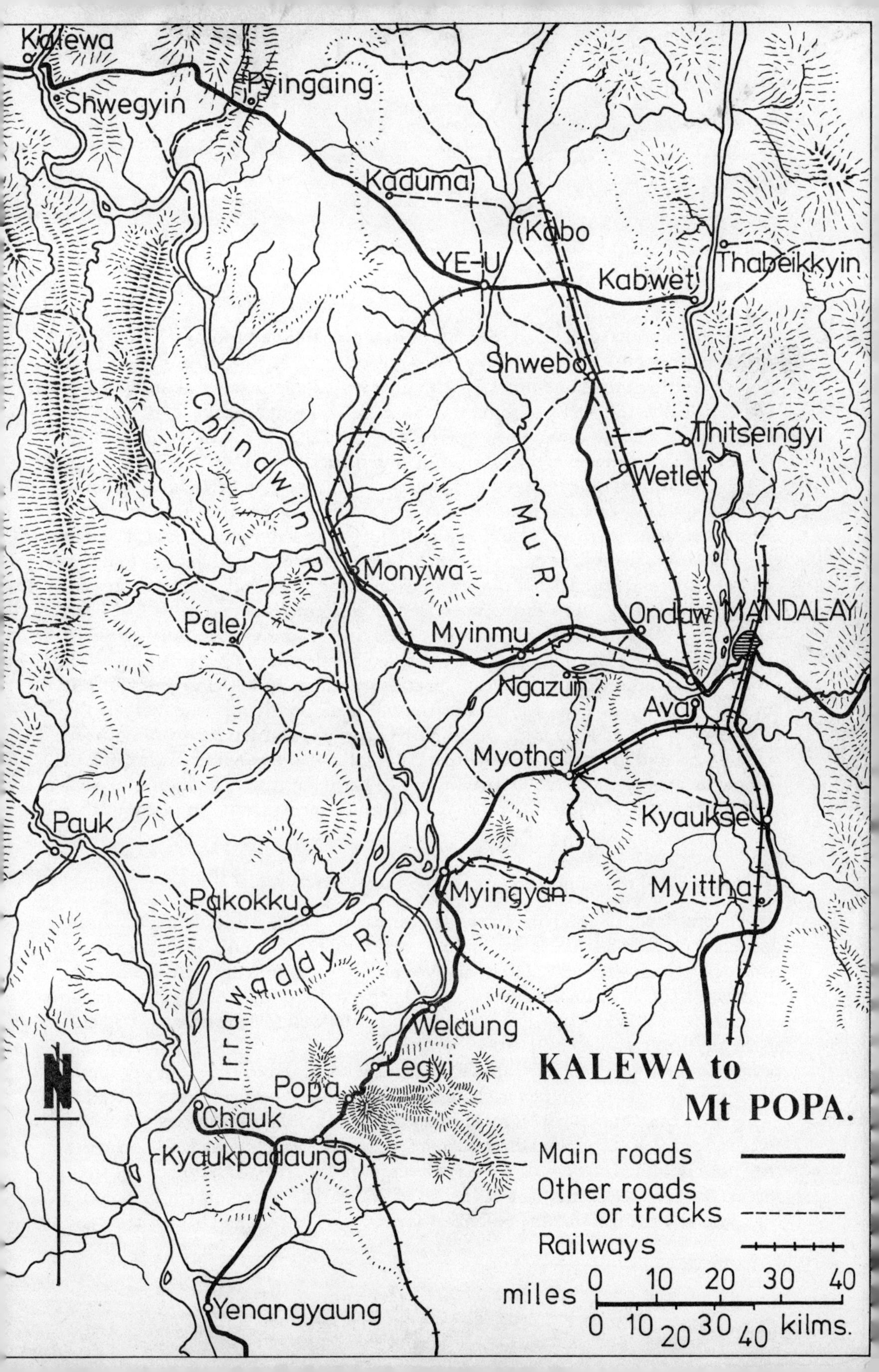
Kalewa
Pyingaing
Shwegyin
Kaduma
Kabo
YE-U
Thabeikkyin
Kabwet
Shwebo
Thitseingyi
Wetlet
Chindwin R.
Mu R.
Monywa
Ondaw
MANDALAY
Pale
Myinmu
Ngazun
Ava
Myotha
Kyaukse
Pauk
Myingyan
Myittha
Pakokku
Irrawaddy R.
Welaung
Legyi
Popa
Chauk
Kyaukpadaung
Yenangyaung
N
KALEWA to
Mt POPA.
Main roads
Other roads
or tracks
Railways
miles 0 10 20 30 40
0 10 20 30 40 kilms.

CHAPTER FOUR

Kohima

20th March

A day that started with us continuing our long established routine, I setting off for divisional HQ by motor-bike, carrying plans of our defences for exercise Shawk, at much the same time as the C.O. and Adjutant left for a conference at the same place. There I was told by Captain Bill Lough, one of the Intelligence Officers at HQ, that the exercise was off and that I should return without delay, there being big changes in the offing. On his return, Colonel McNaught reported that the division would be leaving the jungle, in a move that was to be considered as an operational one and that we would be starting our journey to our base, at Ahmadnagar, tomorrow. Also, I was to bring the Indian Army trucks allocated for our move, from their camp to ours. Hurried packing, the filling of trenches and site tidying ensued, all to the accompaniment of speculation as to the reason for this sudden flap. On the wireless and in the newspapers reports had been appearing of a Japanese invasion across the River Chindwin, in north western Burma and towards or into India. We had taken little interest in something so far away and remote from us and our specialist training; now the urgency of our move, exceptional even for us and our nomadic existence, encouraged the coupling of our activity with the enemy incursion. But having so often been falsely prepared for action, the fact that the medics had condemned our patch of jungle as one of the most malarial in all India made many, including myself, believe that this was just one more false alarm resulting from the threat of that disease.

21st March and succeeding days

In the pre-dawn of 0630 hrs, I departed as yesterday, but going for the transport which was about 30 miles away, a ride I well remember, seeing again the jungle through which the gravelled road wound its way, initially lit only by my headlamp. On rounding the many bends I half expected to meet a tiger or similar inhabitant of that lonely place, where nothing showed but the narrow road and flanking never ending vegetation which, at times, where the trees were tall, enclosed the road even from above; so that they seemed to crowd in upon me, their trunks and branches ever changing and distorted by shadows. I arrived at what was a busy unit, where it took time to sort and gather our vehicles, then they were all pointed in the right direction and we set off, reaching the battalion at the late hour of mid-day. Having been ready and waiting since partaking of a hurried breakfast their welcome, if it could be so called, had a certain coolness, only tempered by the fact that the convoy was intact and once it had been loaded the move north could start. That loading must have been time consuming, for it was after dark when we reached our staging camp at Belgaum. Next night we were at a similar camp at Satara, having covered 140 miles, and the following afternoon the final stage was completed when we drove into the familiar East Ridge (Stud Farm) barracks.

As many of the section as could do so, travelled in the 'I' Section truck and, as our driver was unwell, I took over. Being of the opinion that I drove rather well, particularly when changing to a lower gear on approaching corners at high speed, I failed to understand the less than enthusiastic attitude of the rightful driver to such a display of motoring skill.

Having been advised that we were, at last, going into action, our seven days at East Ridge were hectic ones. Although our objective had not been named, we were pretty sure that it would be somewhere around Imphal, a new place name and one of increasing importance in news bulletins, which were also confirming that the Japs were across the Indian frontier.

To our delight Kirkee Arsenal was literally thrown open to us and thus we were able to go to war with the best of weapons and, with other depots likewise made accessible, we had new boots, clothing and equipment as required. The issue and receipt of all this bounty kept us busy and as our kit was to be limited to a total of 60 lbs, our minds were much occupied with the matter of what to discard.

One who was happy at that moment of exceptional generosity to the regiment he had served so long, was that true Dorset, our lovable, roly-poly Quartermaster 'Teddy' Edwards, for whom there was a universal respect but who, to our dismay, was soon to leave us for the less physically demanding but similar appointment at Corps HQ.

Our War Establishment for officers, at that time, was:

Lieutenant-Colonels	1
Majors	5
Captains	7
Lieutenants	17 and 1 QM

On 25th March our nominal roll accorded with that establishment, being:-

Lieutenant-Colonel	McNaught	Commanding Officer
Majors	White	Second-in-Command
	Baynes	O.C. Rear Details
	Fretts	
	Watts	
	Molyneux	(posted away)
Captains	Bowles	
	Howard	
	Gordon-Wright	
	Harris	
	Castle	
	Davies	
	Purser	

Lieutenants	Edwards	Quartermaster
	Deane	
	Mayer	
	Chettle	
	Hodder	
	Murrills	
	Havers	
	O'Driscoll	
	Halahan	
	Highett	
	Morice	
	Clarke	(medically regraded B)
	Day	
	Prebble	
	Doran	
	Sick - Wilson, Jones and Turner	

During the voyage Captain Giles DCM, O.C. 'C' Company, had been disembarked as a result of an old injury, depriving us of one of our most liked and valued regulars. He was succeeded by Donald Baynes and then, for eight months in 1943, by Major Derek Gill Davies DSO RE, who had been attached to us and then, to our profound regret, was posted elsewhere.

26th March

Our unit motor transport left for an unknown destination.

29th March

Our last day at Ahmadnagar, for with preparations at an end and transport arranged, we could depart from this small Indian Army hutted camp, to which we had first come in October 1942 and which had so few attractions. Now we were to cross a continent and travel more miles in a single train journey than most would do again.

Late in the afternoon the battalion paraded and with a minimum of fuss took the dusty road to Ahmadnagar Station and entrained that evening; leaving behind a small Rear Details party under Donald Baynes and Lieutenants Prebble and Clarke, this in accordance with service procedure. An unenviable job and one I was thankful never to have to do. The 'I' Section did however remain to search the barracks, by then forsaken, for any breaches of security such as documents relating to our future, not destroyed by burning as ordered. Out of the whole camp we found only one lapse, that being a part of the Top Secret movement order. It was in the C.O.'s dustbin and had been issued to Geoffry White. This was not unlike finding hidden treasure and we departed well satisfied. On our way to the station by truck, we passed the battalion marching along the road in the good old and very familiar 2 Dorset way (a sort of fast and in a way a 'rolling' amble that covered the ground with the minimum of effort) and what a grand lot of chaps they looked.

The close friendship which had developed between Clive Chettle and myself had been diminishing as we went our separate ways within the battalion, and the coming train journey was to be almost the last time we were to be together for more than a few hours. Clive was to remain in the army after the war and to distinguish himself in Oman, but from where, despite that physical toughness which caused him to be known as 'The Bull', he was to return home to die of cancer. How inexplicable that I, the one who had been medically downgraded and given the less physically demanding job of I.O., was to survive into old age.

The five in our compartment were bridge players, this having become an accepted drill on our journeys by train, so often of three days or more, and what better way of passing the many hours! From the time we entrained on this journey to Assam until our arrival at the Brahmaputra River five days later, bridge was played almost continuously; one of us taking it in turn to rest while the others played on – the hours and the days seemed to melt away.

The train halted for meals, which were dispensed by our cooks on those station platforms which had been selected for this purpose. At such organised halts each carriage was guarded by two sentries with fixed bayonets, one being on each side and we detrained and entrained in response to bugle calls. Explicit orders were given that no fruit other than bananas and oranges was to be bought and the only drink that might be purchased was char from authorised vendors. All ranks were issued with anti-mosquito cream and mepacrine tablets were to be taken after the evening meal. But for these breaks we were travelling day and night, albeit often slowly and between halts in some remote spot for no apparent purpose, as is the custom of trains everywhere. Nevertheless, that we travelled so well, was surely to the great credit of the railways concerned, who had more than our 'special' with which to contend at a time when whole armies were on the move. We did occasionally watch the passing scenery, so often one of rocks and scrub, animated only by our passage through towns and therefore, in our eyes, much of a muchness and done as much as anything for the cooling breeze available to the viewer, sitting on the step of an open carriage door.

Our route commenced with a run of 100 miles north to the town of Manmad where we joined the Great Indian Peninsula Railway. From that line we turned east for Nagpur and the Bengal Nagpur Railway for Calcutta. It is of interest that the rail distance from Bombay to Calcutta is 1223 statute miles, with a pre-war train timing for the journey of 37 hrs 21 mins. Such speed was not for us, but Calcutta was reached and there we turned north on the Eastern Bengal Railway, for the rail junction of Parbatipur. There we changed trains onto the narrow gauge line of the same railway, this taking us north east to the Brahmaputra River opposite the east bank town of Gauhati. This was a place that became known to service men, not only because of the river crossing but because of its hospital, the 52nd Indian General Hospital (C). That 'C' is short for Combined, denoting that British troops were catered for as well as Indian. During that night we crossed the river on one of the monstrous ferry boats, with its barn-like superstructure dwarfing a surprisingly modest hull and into this the battalion disappeared.

Then the disembarkation on that east bank and into Assam, an operation that could be aptly described as a 'tactical exercise without lights'. Envisage 800 or more well and truly 'browned off' men after five long and weary days of train journeying, each festooned with his impedimenta of equipment and weapons, landing in an unknown Indian town and then moving on foot to a railway station outside that town; the whole operation being done in darkness; there to board a train devoid of lighting and, to make it really difficult, one having mini-sized carriages of a type with which we were unfamiliar. The wonder is that it was done at all. But on such occasions an inherent sense of good order, so strong in the Dorsets, quietly took over.

Under more normal conditions this would have been a moment of romantic adventure, for we were about to journey into one of the more remote places of India and of the world, doing so on the metre gauge Assam Bengal Railway. Primarily built to serve the tea and rubber planters it runs for 300 miles in an east-north-east direction, roughly following the line of the Brahmaputra until terminating just short of Sadiya in the Sadiya Frontier Tract, this bordering eastern Tibet which rises as a great barrier. North east of this remote place are the almost unknown headwaters of the mighty rivers the Salween, Mekong and Yangtze Kiang, while to the north the Brahmaputra descends from the Tibetan plateau.

Any romantically inclined motorist of today might thrill to the annotation on a road map of India, dated 1939, to the effect that at Sadiya – 'petrol may be obtained from cans'.

At that period of the war the railway was run by the American Army as an essential supply line for their new trans-Burma road. Known as the Ledo Road, from the place of that name 40 miles south of Sadiya and to which ran a branch line. There the road started on its long journey east, passing through the almost impenetrable jungle-covered valleys and mountains of north Burma, to the town of Myitkyina and then on to connect with the pre-war Burma-China road, made inaccessible by the Japanese occupation of central Burma. Leaving Burma it climbed into the high western plateau of Yunnan and the city of Kunming with its airfield, and finally China's wartime capital of Chungking. The Americans brought to this formidable task an essential ingredient, a willingness and an ability to do what others found impossible and to which they were able to add road making plant and machinery, the like of which had not been seen outside North America.

4th April

It was some hours before dawn when our train moved off from Gauhati Station, by which time I had settled down on the wooden seat of the Intermediate Class compartment in which I found myself and was trying for sleep that would not come, for my mind was too active in speculation on the coming day, of which we knew nothing. Although the darkness of Gauhati had only temporarily broken up the battalion, it had completely dismembered the bridge party. Not that that mattered, for with daylight the interests of us all were on the world outside and we were keenly scanning the passing scene. That we found to be a very green world with some jungle and pools of water, suggestive of pre-monsoon rains.

Our marathon journey ended that afternoon when, at 1230 hrs, we alighted onto the platform at Bokajan, a small place ten miles up the line beyond Manipur Road, the name given to the station at Dimapur. Some places have importance thrust upon them by seemingly unconnected and distant occurrences. One such was Dimapur, host to a military base and a staging post for us and many others. A name to be implanted in our memories and of which more anon.

We were met by our advance party who, under Captain Pryke Howard, had arrived two days earlier and, guided by him, the 'O' Group went to recce our allotted positions within 5 Brigade's Defended Locality.

The country in which we found ourselves was that which bordered the Brahmaputra and which, although so very far from the sea, had an altitude of only a few hundred feet. Thick jungle covered all but the cultivated areas and of those we saw little. To the south and quite close were the Naga Hills, which we were to come to know so well. To the north, at a much greater distance and isolated from us by the Brahmaputra, were the hills of the Balipara Frontier Tract, above which lay Tibet.

The 'O' Group returned and companies dispersed to their positions as did Battalion HQ to its portion of jungle, none of us I imagine having anything but what we carried on our backs. My home for that first night or two was under a bush; a desirable place, for the ground was dryer there and one was less likely to be walked on in the dark. The pools of water we had seen en route were the product of an habitual shower at about 1600 hrs, a timing that seemed designed to make us damp when least able to dry out, for it was dark within an hour or so from the rain ceasing. During the war the media, then no more than the wireless and press, designated the jungle a 'green hell' or 'stinking' and we doubtless obtained much credit at home for our fortitude and courage, when forced to endure it. While the monsoon was on, the very thick jungley bits could indeed be grim and the jungle of the Kabaw valley, just inside Burma, was then a place to be avoided, if only to lessen the likelihood of getting malaria or some equally horrible disease. Otherwise I was all for it. One was out of the interminable and exhausting sun and away from the almost perennial dust of the open ground, from which there was only relief during the monsoon and then that dust became mud which was even worse. In this jungle there was a peace and quiet (the Japs were still some distance away) and relief from the external glare and enjoyment in the green of grass and foliage; much as in one of the thicker deciduous woods in Dorset. Admittedly the near-by slow flowing river was not another Dorset Stour, for this really did stink and had what an angler would describe as a pronounced colour and, at home, in its dark depths would lurk large pike.

The 'I' Section had been reduced in number by two and now consisted of –

Sergeant Marlow; Lance-Corporals Churchman, Green and Smart; Privates Hoffman, Miller, Randell and Voller. At opportune moments they would engage Gus Claxton in spirited debate, which was no small achievement. There could be no better summing up of them and their excellence than that given by Joe Chamberlin, who wrote describing them as 'a Brains Trust, whose word it never occurred to me to doubt'.

5th – 9th April

During this time Division decided that interpreters would be necessary while we were among the tribesmen of the Naga Hills and these, in the form of two sepoys of the Assam Rifles, duly arrived. It was a little unfortunate (to put it mildly) that neither could understand English or even Urdu, but such matters are of only minor consequence to the British Tommy and we welcomed them into our midst, to be immediately impressed by the speed with which they built themselves a lean-to roof over their square of living space. A few minutes of cutting with their kukris and the job was done. Quite obviously our jungle training had concentrated on the wrong things! They were to remain with us until we reached Imphal in June and, although they served no useful purpose other than providing the section with the best 'sheltered accommodation' in the battalion, we missed them after their departure, for we got on well together and especially they and Private Voller – countrymen with a natural affinity.

Life in the 'I' Section was being made memorable by a positive flood of Brigade and Divisional Intelligence Reports. Almost hourly, news of 500 or 1000 Japs, in some obscure village or on a ridge fringing our portion of the plain, would be notified and these were often said to have with them one or more elephants. This information originated from our good friends the Nagas who, at this early stage, presumably assumed that a generous estimate of numbers would give greater credence to their reports.

We were at a time of understandable confusion at our end. Reinforcements were arriving daily by train, road and air, to counter the presence of a Japanese division at Kohima, just under 50 miles away by road. When the enemy was reported to be making for Kohima it was assumed that a regiment (the equivalent of one of our brigades) would be the largest unit that could traverse the 80 miles between their starting point on the Chindwin River and Kohima. Thus, with the Japanese 31st Division surrounding the small force at Kohima and their patrols only 30 miles away and assumed to be probing towards us in an area having no geographical barriers to their further advance (in fact it was all down hill), it was logical to believe that Dimapur, with its vast wealth of munitions, clothing, food and the like, plus the railway, was their prime target. To counter this threat we and the brigade were split up to protect as large an area as possible. During this initial period when the 4th and the 6th Brigades had yet to arrive and, with our transport and artillery also en route, it was fortunate for us that our first contact with the enemy was to be at a time and place of our choosing.

By one of those strange quirks of fate we had prepared for everything, in all our years of training, except the mountain warfare now facing us. Strange too that our mechanisation was to be no asset but actually a hindrance, when we operated on the axis of one overburdened road.

Soon after our arrival the battalion established an advance force on a secondary road known as the Merema Track, consisting of our 'C' Comany under Dick Castle, 3 and 4 platoons (mortars and carriers) and our Guerilla Platoon. They were strongly reinforced by 'B' Company, the 2nd Manchester Regiment, the Divisional Machine-Gun Battalion. More directly to the north we had 'A' Company under John Bowles and 'D' Company under Paget Fretts, they being split up into platoons and holding stations on the line north of Bokajan, with 'A' Company at one time 30 miles away at the larger place of Jamuguri. This track was an unmetalled road taking its name from the village of Merema, north west of Kohima, through which it passed. Although rumoured impassable in places it remained a likely route for enemy patrols, being a secondary road linking Bokajan with Kohima. Between the 7th and the 9th members of The Shere Regiment (part of the Nepalese Army) and the Bombay Sappers and Miners came down this track and were given biscuits and water and, when possible, tea. On one occasion when I was there we watched a steady trickle of Gurkha-type soldiers making their way down from the hills and Kohima. We viewed one another in silence, they perhaps looking upon us as British troops avoiding battle while they suffered; while we thought that here, yet again, were men for whom the Japs had proved to be too good.

Once, in a spare moment at the end of a day as dusk was falling, I and a companion walked across to where there was a stationary train, and chatted to and shared cigarettes with its American sergeant driver. His conversation and standard of education was impressive and far above what we had anticipated, being so at variance with the brash American depicted in films. With the Japs so close and apparently still advancing, he had good reason to fear for himself and the railway, but was too polite to show it.

During this period I had remained with Geoffry, who as 2 I/C was in charge of the residue of HQ Company and the platoon detached to provide defence. To give us a reasonably secure base against marauding Japs we were situated within a loop of the river to which I have referred and, with the addition of a barbed wire fence across the neck, we had a form of all round protection. One evening after dark, Geoffry and I were sitting in the unlighted HQ tent, having a peg of whisky before turning in, when a single shot rang out loud and clear, the sound coming from the apex of the loop. I was directed to find the idiot who had discharged his rifle at a time when there was a strict ruling that no weapon was to be fired other than at a Jap. There having been no follow up shots, it was unlikely that we were being attacked and I made my way along a narrow pitch-black footpath, flanked by vegetation, more concerned with staying on the path than anything else. About half way I bumped into my friend 'Snagger' Highett coming in haste towards me and we returned together to Geoffrey. There he told how one of his men, seeing a tiger swimming across the river towards him, had fired in an act of self preservation. Just then we heard the roaring of what was, very obviously, an extremely angry tiger down at the wire and getting lacerated as he did his best to force a way through. After a crescendo of feline oaths, there was a sudden and blessed peace and quiet and we breathed sighs of relief. Those who had devised our defended position would not have anticipated our sharing its confined space with such an animal, although we had, of course, met them in Belgaum. It had been there that we had laughed about an incident involving Clive Chettle's batman, the redoubtable and very lucky Private Russell, whose aggressive temperament was so well matched to Clive's. During a jungle exercise he had heard movement in adjacent undergrowth which he had parted to peer through, only to find himself in what would be described today as 'an eyeball to eyeball' confrontation with a tiger. As an 'A' Company man and prepared for almost anything, he raised his Lee Enfield and fired two rounds of blank at the unfortunate animal and then fixed his bayonet. What must have been a bemused tiger left Russell to survive unscathed.

Snagger, or to be correct, Lieutenant Lintorn Highett, was considered a true Dorset despite a home in Hampshire, by reason of his father the original 'Snacker' and a Dorset of the previous war. Lintorn was soon to distinguish himself at Kohima and in subsequent battles. Of his skills the game of bridge was not the least, and after the war he was able to enjoy playing in more suitable surroundings, of which Crockfords was one.

My references to individuals as 'Dorsets' suggests that, as with those who play cricket for Yorkshire, we too when designated so, were born and bred there. On the contrary, the majority were from London and Birmingham. We were what we were because we wore the Dorset badge and a bond, fostered by adversity, tied us to each other. An infantry battalion is sufficiently insular, by reason of its numbers, as to delight in isolating itself from others, be they even the battalions in the same brigade. Thus individuals become dependent upon one another and if, as in our case, they have a pride in their abilities, morale is high and time knits the whole together as a family, quietly self confident and formidable. With the approach of battle those emotions were intensifying.

10th April

Things started happening in a big way, for the battalion was ordered to pack up, wherever it was, and move to Dimapur using any trucks that could be obtained. By night we were concentrated there and in camp.

While the C.O. attended a conference at Brigade HQ, we officers gathered together, and keenly awaited him, though as the evening hours passed we began to believe that there could be no move next day. However, soon after his return at 2200 hrs we learned that we were indeed to start and would do so by moving up the first stage of the road for the relief of Kohima at 0900 hrs tomorrow.

So at long last, the years of training and preparation for war were about to be put to the test, and in the all too familiar circumstances of a British force in dire straits and near defeat, and should that defeat become a reality, a brutal slaughter by the Japanese would follow. Since our arrival in India 6 Brigade had, for a short time, been in action in the Arakan but, from the little we had learned from their experiences, not with much success. But now that the two other brigades had caught up with ours, we were to operate as the British 2nd Division. That was what we wanted and furthermore, we were to do so within 33 Corps under our respected Corps Commander, Lieutenant-General Montagu Stopford who, on 2nd April, had taken overall command of troops in this and the Kohima areas. Morale in 2 Div. was high. We really did believe we were the best.

The story of Kohima has been told by Arthur Swinson, in his book – KOHIMA. Lord Louis Mountbatten described the battle as 'probably one of the greatest in history' and Field-Marshall Wavell as 'one of the turning points of the war'. Certainly, following their defeat at Kohima, which accelerated and made complete their subsequent defeat at Imphal, the Japanese began a retreat of utter disaster, so heavy had been both their casualties and material losses.

During the weeks when we in the 2nd Division had been travelling to and then gathering ourselves at Dimapur, the Japanese had almost surrounded the Imphal Plain, held by 4 Corps, and great battles were in progress. At Kohima a small force, consisting of the 4th Royal West Kents and bodies of men from units in that area, the 1st Assam Regiment and the 3rd Assam Rifles, plus detachments such as those of the Shere Regiment (a Nepalese contingent), seen on the Merema Track, had been desperately and with great valour holding a shrinking perimeter, the vital part of which had become 'Garrison Hill'. That hill was the conical end of a major spur, extending towards the town of Kohima from mountains to the south. Around it ran the Imphal Road, thus it dominated that portion of the road as it did the approach to the town. These physical features made its possession one of strategic importance and were it to fall, our task would have become infinitely harder and the morale of the enemy would have been enhanced.

Prior to the war an unmetalled road traversed the 130 miles between Dimapur and Imphal. From there a series of tracks and footpaths formed a tenuous link with the small Burmese town of Tamu. Following the Japanese invasion, our loss of Rangoon and withdrawal northwards, there was the desperate need for a road into India, through the mountain barrier separating the two countries which their governments had chosen to maintain, at a time when communication by sea was preferable. Such a road would not only provide salvation for those refugees who could reach it but a route for our return. These factors gave the necessary impetus and in 1942 the tea-planters of Assam, using their own and local labour, plus the expertise of British and Indian sappers, commenced the construction of an all-weather road from Dimapur to Tamu and sufficiently completed it to help in the final stages of the evacuation. Excepting ten miles near Dimapur, its 200 miles through the Naga and the Chin Hills had an average altitude of 4,000 feet, at which height it was seldom without a cliff rising on one side and an almost sheer drop on the other. There you could look down onto the tops of trees amongst which were wrecked vehicles, most of which were Indian Army trucks whose

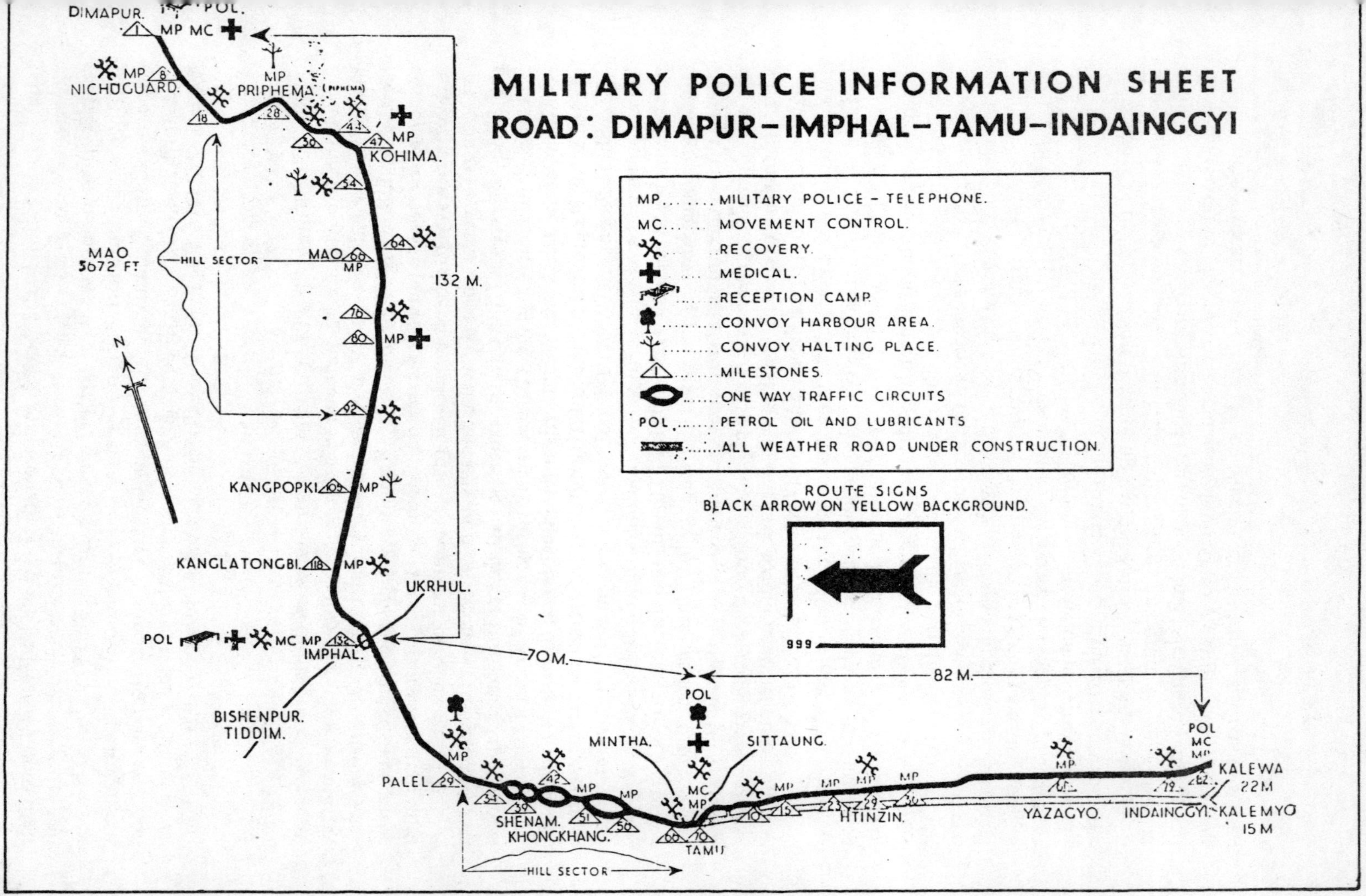
MILITARY POLICE INFORMATION SHEET
ROAD: DIMAPUR–IMPHAL–TAMU–INDAINGGYI
MP....... MILITARY POLICE – TELEPHONE.
MC....... MOVEMENT CONTROL.
RECOVERY.
MEDICAL.
RECEPTION CAMP.
CONVOY HARBOUR AREA.
CONVOY HALTING PLACE.
MILESTONES.
ONE WAY TRAFFIC CIRCUITS
POL........PETROL OIL AND LUBRICANTS
ALL WEATHER ROAD UNDER CONSTRUCTION.
ROUTE SIGNS
BLACK ARROW ON YELLOW BACKGROUND.
999
DIMAPUR.
POL.
MP MC
NICHUGUARD.
MP
PRIPHEMA.
KOHIMA.
MAO
5672 FT
HILL SECTOR
MAO
132 M.
N
KANGPOPKI
KANGLATONGBI.
UKRHUL.
POL
MC MP
IMPHAL.
70M.
82 M.
BISHENPUR.
TIDDIM.
PALEL
SHENAM.
KHONGKHANG.
MINTHA.
TAMU
SITTAUNG.
HTINZIN.
YAZAGYO.
INDAINGGYI.
KALEWA
22M
KALEMYO
15 M
HILL SECTOR

drivers had been forced by the demands of war to drive on a hazardous road for which they had not been trained. Road maintenance was continuous and gangs of men, women and children cleared up after land-slides or made good after subsidences. This was to be our axis of advance, and it would have been hard to have found one more dangerous or constricting.

Imphal was the tiny capital of the minute state of Manipur, the greater part of which was the Imphal Plain, some 30 by 20 miles of precious level ground; then a place of air strips and military stores, comparable with Dimapur and as vital to us as its capture was to the Japanese, who as a preliminary struck at Kohima, thus breaking Imphal's main supply route.

After the defeats of 1941-42 Burma had remained within the British sphere of responsibility and the only area where we could and did engage the enemy, and of interest to the Americans only for its land link to China. A British advance into Burma from Imphal had been planned for mid-1944. Because of the geography of this remote and mountainous country and the newly constructed road, any British concentration for such an offensive had to be at Imphal and the only approach from India, other than the inadequate and isolated Silchar track, was the one which we were on.

To some extent we had been forestalled when Lieutenant-General Mutaguchi, the commander of the Japanese 15th Army (the equal of a British Corps) had crossed the Chindwin with 80,000 troops in the first week of March, his 31st Division in the north making for Kohima, while his 15th and 33rd Divisions and the regimental sized, renegade, 1st Indian National Army Division enveloped Imphal, preparatory to the annihilation by them of the Indian 4 Corps, a task for which they were allocated three weeks.

This followed a Japanese attack early in February in the Arakan, planned as a preliminary to the capture of Imphal and both were the early phases of the occupation of India, under the title 'The March on Delhi'.

11th April

At the designated time of 0900 hrs we were dressed for action and paraded, by companies and platoons, on the road prior to packing ourselves into a convoy of 3-ton trucks; just as we had done many times in training and, as always, men had been counted and checked as 'all present and correct – Sir'.

Was there ever a moment more fitting for ceremony and the showing of a flag or two, at this final opportunity for our colonel to review those he was about to lead into battle? But we had no banners in our drab, camouflaged lives, and Jock McNaught was not given to vanity. Thus to have passed down our lines would have seemed to him to be a display of personal aggrandisement, rather than a salute and tribute to those who, under his leadership, were about to face the enemy. As with all commanders at every level on the eve of battle his inner feelings would have conflicted with his external display of confidence, something made possible by years of training and many more years of British tradition.

The sun was out, the distant hills looked magnificent against the blue sky and we were in good heart at the prospect of sharing in a great experience.

One hour after parading we moved off behind our advance guard – Clive Chettle in the one armoured car assigned to us, and so began our travels on this road we came to know so well and which was to be our life-line.

As we advanced towards the hills and looked up at them, marvelling at their extent and grandeur, we wondered how it would be to fight in such country. What we could see were the lesser western peaks and foot-hills of the Barail Range, jungle-covered, as are those some 30 miles to the east, where they are at their most majestic and extend up to 9,890 ft. at Mount Japvo. Below that crest at 5,000 ft. is Kohima, partly on the mountain's northern slopes but also spreading over a saddle, to the west of which is the deep valley of the Zubza or Dzuza River, flanked on its south side by our road and on the other by the Merema Track. To the north and east a medley of green-clad hills extend for many tens of miles until, after crossing into Burma, well to the north, they merge with the most remote mountains of that country.

My information comes from my much treasured Kohima map, printed in June 1943, which has on it at the point where we were to fight our greatest battle, smudges of the brownish-red Kohima soil, left by muddy fingers. Like the map cover for all this area, it is to a scale of 1 inch to 2 miles, what we called the 'half inch map', and is based on the surveys of 1922/23 and '24, by the Survey of India. It is almost impossible to imagine the immensity of a task undertaken by unsung heroes, whose dedication produced maps showing contours at 100 foot intervals and every stream, village and patch of open ground, in country where there is very little open ground and hardly any that is flat. Remarkable also are the lines of communication, from footpaths to pack-tracks linking the villages one with another.

Then, following another ground survey in January 1943 the road appears, and the best tracks are annotated as either 'motorable in dry season' or, on the editions printed by 14th Army as late as April 1944, 'jeepable in dry season'.

During the time that we were in those hills and beyond, it was a standing battalion joke that I did not know where we were. Actually that was often so, for when surrounded by trees and hills that all appear the same and having no convenient church spire (as at home) on which to get a bearing, it could be the very devil of a job. But we managed, thanks to those surveyors of blessed memory.

Leaving the plain, the road climbed almost continuously between milestones 10 and 25 and we noted the changing atmosphere, realising that whatever might be the shortcomings of the hills, they had the immeasurable asset of a moderate temperature, a reduced insect life and, as we soon found, an absence of rain. We passed the first locals – refugee Nagas moving in family groups from the battle areas – and were impressed by what we saw. Later, as we came to know them better, that admiration increased.

Our convoy had progressed without incident or hindrance and, on reaching milestone 31, we scrambled out and adopting the familiar order of dispersed companies, platoons and sections all under their respective leaders, we advanced up the road with our weapons ready for use. It was good to be on our feet and

OUR FRIEND THE NAGA

Three Nagas return from a patrol. As allies and observers they played a vital role in the defeat of the Japanese.

on our own; like members of some exclusive club we regarded all strangers with suspicion. Our vehicles had yet to arrive but the all important artillery must have been coming up, for it was in action a day or two later. We felt conspicuous on an open road, so different to the jungle at Belgaum and then the one near Dimapur and no doubt our pulses had quickened, but nothing untoward happened and we reached milestone 32 and then, when half a mile beyond, we turned left onto a gravel track. We were in an area where Japanese patrols had been seen; however we were not alone for somewhere ahead were the Camerons and Worcesters. Our track was just to the east side of a ridge running north and south at right angles to the road and led to the village of Khabvuma (height 3649 ft.), two and a quarter miles away.

During the next few hours the battalion split up, 'D' Company setting off for the village and 'A' Company following behind to the apex of our ridge, three quarters of a mile short of the village. 'C' Company remained with Battalion HQ, just to the north of the road and astride the track. Back at Dimapur were our Rear Details under Geoffry White and with them parts of HQ Company, such as the personnel of our Carrier Platoon. On the orders of brigade we had departed prepared to function on foot and away from the road. We were not to know that we would be one of the battalions who, until after Kohima, would remain quite close to our precious road.

In the early evening our one uncommitted rifle company – 'B', guided by two Sikhs, set off for the village of Kiruphema on the other side of the road and some two miles to our south. They found the going hard, for once off the tarmac they were faced with a steep climb of 1,200 ft. on a narrow footpath and in failing light. This was only the first of many such climbs in the ensuing months and the first is never easy, also on this occasion, all the factors were against them. Probably the severe physical characteristics of the route had not been fully appreciated from the map and consequently they started too late. There is nothing so tiring, frustrating and slow as a steep ascent in single file, with the leaders pausing for the tail to catch up and that tail so often desperate in its efforts to maintain contact. In 2 Div. one was, in theory, never exhausted, but 'B' Company was at the end of a day of nervous tension and out of condition, as we all were after so much travel. The outcome was that they took longer than anticipated and arrived after dark. There, pinned to the narrow track on a steep hill face, they were fired on from the village and the column leader, Lance-Corporal Nursaw, was killed. Kiruphema was occupied without resistance and interrogation of the villagers disclosed that a Japanese recce patrol, consisting of an officer and two men, had arrived just before we had and after firing had retired the way they had come.

Thus we suffered the first of many fatalities, all tragic, but this somehow particularly so.

Kiruphema may have been exceptionally difficult to approach, but all Naga villages were sited on hill tops or mountain spurs for self defence. This was a relic of inter-village hostility and head-hunting, customs that British administration had eliminated, except possibly in the more remote areas and the villagers were grateful; now they had time for more fruitful pursuits. However, this had not stopped the men from carrying a spear or a bow and arrows in those days and, with their splendid physique, they looked the virile warriors that they were.

One final event on that first day, was a night patrol from 'C' Company, which went out under Lieutenant Mayer, a very recent arrival in the battalion. They had gone up the road to make friendly contact with the Worcesters, whom they duly found, only to be greeted by a shower of grenades. It was said that our chaps returned rather browned off.

At Ahmadnagar our kit had been reduced and before leaving Dimapur more had been discarded, in anticipation of a final assault across country, when we were not to have more than would go into our small packs, which was precious little. Extra clothing at night was to be a pullover and gas-cape, the latter being carried as a waterproof.

That first night on an open hillside was bitterly cold, after being within the enclosing and protective jungle. Any digging-in at Battalion HQ must have excluded me, for I spent that night lying on, of all places, the gravel track. With my knees drawn up I lay cocooned in my cape and longing for the dawn, when with the light one could move about. Fortunately, such had been the drop in temperature, that Brigadier Hawkins ruled that everyone must have a blanket.

Unknown to us on that day of first contact with the enemy, our Catholic Chaplain, the Reverend Father J. O'Callagan, had been killed, while with the Worcesters, by enemy gun fire. In the ensuing days as the news filtered down there were feelings of disbelief; for such a person to be killed and so soon, shocked us in a way that other deaths would not. The harsh reality of our situation was made clear by the loss of a man of peace and one for whom there was an exceptional degree of respect and affection.

12th April

'D' Company left their overnight position just short of Khabvuma and moved forward to the village, establishing a defensive position there on a small plateau on its east side. There they had uninterrupted observation across the Zubza River valley, on the edge of which they then were and towards Kohima at the head of the valley, a distance of six miles. Some idea of the generous size and scale of the country is obtained by examining the footpath from this village to the Merema Track on the far side of the valley, a horizontal distance of four miles. The path drops 1,800 ft. to the river and rises 2,400 ft. to the track, a journey made almost entirely within jungle, which was to the advantage of the Japs when they used this route to attack us, for looking into the valley all that could be seen was trees.

That villagers had to make routine journeys such as the one across this valley, or up and down such slopes to attend to their paddy-fields, explains their exceptional physique.

That morning the battalion, less 'B' and 'D' Companies who remained in their respective villages, moved forward up the road passing the village of Zubza and, after milestone 36, turned right into a wide re-entrant within rising ground. There we joined 5 Brigade's defended position, known as the Zubza Box.

'Boxes', such as our earlier practice one, in the Belgaum jungle, had enjoyed a vogue within the Indian Army, particularly in the Arakan where those within them had stood and fought the advancing Japs and not, as in the past, retreated.

Now they were in less favour following new thinking that such places encouraged a defensive and not the more prized offensive mentality. But this was a rare and thus precious open space, which was partly level and by the afternoon most of 5 Brigade was in position. Infantry provided an outer fringe to what was a rough oval, about 400 yards wide and rather more in depth. We Dorsets faced east and towards Kohima, the Worcesters west, and the Camerons linked us together and closed the far end. Thus we protected the artillery, the vehicles and Brigade HQ, dispersed near the road. Much of this clearing had been paddy and tracks led to Kiruphema and also to the south, where the Camerons had a two company outpost in the village of Sachema.

Earlier, the Worcesters had gone forward about a mile to capture an enemy position which dominated the road and thus blocked our advance. After two separate company attacks had been driven back, badly mauled, it was appreciated that this was a formidable bunker. They then discovered they had returned without a new weapon, the PIAT*, which they had had to test. They were ordered to recover it and great must have been their relief when they succeeded in doing so – they had our sympathy.

In late afternoon we experienced enemy artillery fire for the first time, when about 25 rounds from a 75mm gun or guns fell amongst us. While our gunners returned the fire, the rest of us disappeared below ground. Afterwards I busied myself enlarging my trench which had seemed all too shallow, and completed the job with an earth roof of doubtful security. In the early hours we were to be at the receiving end of more shelling and some Indian supply troops, firing their rifles in panic, killed a staff captain sent by our brigadier to stop them.

13th April

Between 0940 and 1015 hrs at Khabvuma, a Japanese patrol of twenty men advanced from the Zubza Valley and attacked that part of 'D' Company's sector, manned by Sergeant 'Yorky' Seale's 17 Platoon. These attacks were driven off.

Lance-Corporal Alan Critchley relates how, during a lull, he and CQMS Hayward investigated the report of a wounded Jap whom they found severely wounded and calling for what they assumed to be water. Critchley, who was a stretcher-bearer, injected him with morphia, only for him to die as they dragged him back; action which brought down on them a positive fusilade of fire.

The ruthless butchery of the Japanese Army was starkly demonstrated when four of our stretcher-bearers ran out to bring in a wounded man. As they started back they were machine-gunned and the casualty, Private Calcott, and Privates Atkins, Bash and Taylor were killed. Critchley, the fourth of the stretcher-bearers, was wounded. This horror intensified our loathing of a race whose

Projector Infantry Anti-Tank. Fired from the shoulder and launched a high-explosive armour-piercing missile. ~~A flat trajectory mortar bomb.~~ RUBBISH

bayonetting of helpless prisoners, nurses, doctors and the like, was well known and recorded. We who were brought up in the 1930's have been described as 'damned innocent, so simple so pleasant'. And we were, for we believed that we British and other peoples like us did not hit a person when he was down and that the Red Cross and similar organisations were sacrosanct.

Intelligence would have been delighted to have had that early prisoner, especially as all prisoners were rare. The Japs did not have stretcher-bearers but after a battle they would go to great lengths to collect their dead and wounded. The removal of the dead would be attempted no matter how difficult, so that a portion of each body could be returned to its homeland, through cremation. We became accustomed to finding envelopes containing ashes in enemy packs, and some packs that were full of such envelopes.

At Zubza we were quietly settling in, offensive action being confined to the gunners who were 'softening-up' the Japanese strong-point. They also fired in support of the troops at Kohima, where the situation continued to deteriorate and fierce attacks necessitated a steady contraction of the defended area. The 'I' Section set about the construction of an observation post, close to the perimeter, from which to keep watch on the bunker. We could see it clearly, yet not the slightest movement or sign of life was perceived and I, for one, thought that the Japs had gone. Fortunately others knew better and the shelling went on and increased in intensity as the days passed. This was our introduction to the thoroughness with which the Jap would go to ground. Not only was he prepared to remain motionless for days on end and deceive us as to his presence, but he was brilliant in camouflage, to the extent that one could fail to see defences, even at a few paces. And brilliant too in the construction of bunkers that could withstand just about all that we could throw at them. In a world of trees, to make multi-layer roofs, secured with steel bolts and sometimes concrete, plus some tons of earth on top required only time, and when they had that time, we had problems.

14th April

The day started with a dawn attack by a strong party of Japs against the Worcesters' perimeter, which was only driven off after some hours. During the afternoon Welch Fusiliers passed through us on their way to the hills behind Sachema (1,000 feet above us) and to relieve the two companies of Camerons at that village. As they moved into our open ground they were spotted and Jap guns opened fire, causing a number of casualties. Seeing that there was a shortage of chaps to carry the stretchers and get them to our Regimental Aid Post, I went across to help and had my first close contact with injured men. Looking down on them and in particular the one I was helping to carry, I felt a wave of pity and sympathy for these unknown soldiers who had injuries we all dreaded. I remember saying, "Don't worry, you'll soon be in good hands and away from this frightful place."

And what a strange place it was, with jungle on three sides, from time to time at the top end where it was most dense, carrier pigeons would be released by the

Japs we knew to be there and who were watching us. The birds would circle just above the trees and we would try to shoot them down before they flew off with their messages.

One night after dark some of us went down to the road in order to look at the fiercely burning northern part of Kohima, following aerial bombing of Jap positions. The flames showed as a continuous belt which lit up the horizon and in which it looked as though nothing could live. But when examined through binoculars, Japanese signalling lamps could be seen flashing messages so that they appeared to be using the flames to conceal what they were doing.

One event which has stayed fresh and treasured in my memory was the arrival at the 'I' Section of a delegation of Nagas under their chief, a splendid figure who marked the importance of the occasion by wearing his cloak of office – a red hospital blanket issued by the government to village headmen. It was then that language become a problem. We could do no more than make them welcome through smiles and gestures to sit down with us; our intention being to look after them until they could be taken to an interpreter. Having settled themselves, they brought out a cylindrical wooden vessel containing their rice beer, of ill repute, known as zu, made under conditions that would have ceased in Britain at about the time of coming of Christianity! Perspiring only slightly we drank, knowing that under Joe we had a remarkable medical service. None of us died as a direct result of this conviviality. Being unable to reciprocate with liquid refreshment we offered them army biscuits and were delighted at their very obvious enjoyment of them. We were keen to discover the reason for their visit and a week later we heard that we had shelled their village injuring some of its inhabitants, something that they accepted during a time of battle. However, should we do so again, would we please warn them so that they could temporarily move out.

We hoped that it was not *our* guns that had shelled our Naga friends, but such mistakes do happen at a time of great and urgent activity, with gunners fully into their stride, as they gave support both to us and the besieged survivors at Kohima. Often positioned between the guns and their targets and with one troop only 50 yards away, we literally got the full blast, which happened when we had our visitors, who chuckled with delight. Then and later, the sound of the guns and the shouted commands signalling their firing, thrilled in a way that has to be experienced to be understood.

It was about this day that 'B' and 'D' Companies came forward from their villages where they had remained to protect our rear, in anticipation that Jap patrols might cut or harass our line of communication with Dimapur. That link, now a mass of traffic bringing up supplies for thousands of men and their weapons, had to be left to its own devices. Getting forward and relieving those at Kohima was the task, the urgency of which increased with every passing day.

At mid-day the Camerons attacked the bunker which had so effectively performed its task of blocking the road to our advance. Having learned from the attack by the Worcesters, this time the assault was preceded by a final artillery concentration of 1,500, together with 750 rounds from the infantry 3-inch mortars, all in 20 minutes. When the Camerons reached and surmounted their

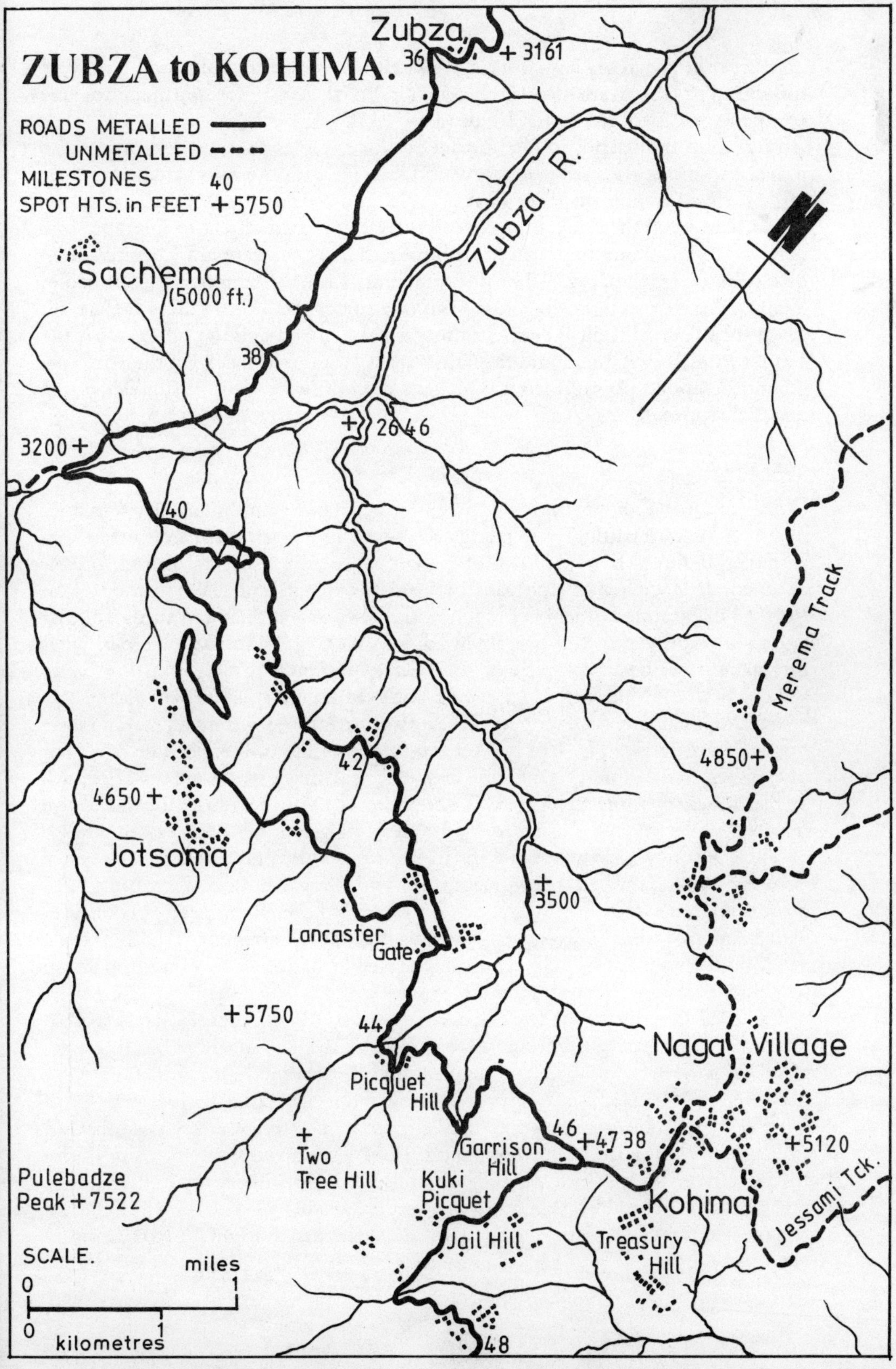
ZUBZA to KOHIMA.
ROADS METALLED
UNMETALLED
MILESTONES 40
SPOT HTS. in FEET +5750
Zubza
36
+ 3161
Zubza R.
Sachema
(5000 ft.)
38
3200 +
+ 2646
40
42
4650 +
Jotsoma
+ 3500
Lancaster Gate
4850 +
Merema Track
+5750
44
Picquet Hill
Naga Village
Garrison Hill
46
+4738
+5120
+ Two Tree Hill
Kuki Picquet
Kohima
Jessami Tck.
Pulebadze Peak +7522
Jail Hill
Treasury Hill
SCALE.
miles
0
1
0
1
kilometres
48

objective the surviving Japs, but for a few who were able to stand and fight, were too dazed to offer resistance. Only a handful of the defenders, estimated as one company, escaped; the rest were dead.

Now that the barrier to our further advance was gone, we were ordered to prepare to move forward tomorrow and join up with the two battalions of the 161st Indian Infantry Brigade. That brigade, under Brigadier Warren, had flown into Assam from the Arakan in the early days, when the threat to Dimapur was believed to be greater than that to Kohima and had been caught by events, more or less between the two. When the attack on Kohima commenced, Brigadier Warren decided to fight the battle with one of his battalions – the 4th Queen's Own Royal West Kent Regiment, forward at Kohima and the other two – the 1st/1st Punjab Regiment and the 7th Rajput Regiment, back on the road in a second defended position from which he could use his guns in support of the forward troops.

15th April

We were up and about soon after first light in preparation for an early start and, in anticipation of battle, I stripped my Sten-gun and magazine and cleaned them as never before. 'B' and 'D' Companies were remaining at Zubza and in compensation we had 'A' company of the Camerons attached. We formed up on the road in extended order of companies and platoons, all facing towards Kohima and then stood waiting, as one always did on such occasions. We were in what might be described as a spirit of subdued expectancy; anticipating the battle which, with each passing day, became both closer and more inevitable.

Advancing up the road we passed the position captured yesterday, making slow but steady progress. The Japs had set fire to one of the timber road bridges, but our advance guard put it out before any serious damage was done. Just beyond, a road block of three vehicles was encountered, but it was not held and the 'Honey' tanks leading our column pushed and blasted them out of the way.

Those 'Honey', or Stuart tanks (from an America now producing much better 'armour') which looked so antiquated and with thin armour plating, must have been vulnerable in this hilly, wooded country where their speed was of little value. And how those crews must have sweated in the knowledge that their Pratt and Whitney radial aero engines, although reliable, had, because of using aviation petrol, a tendency to 'flare up easily'.

It seemed that the Japs had fallen back to the country more immediately around Kohima and by early afternoon we reached 161 Brigade, noting with interest a number of well-ordered ridge tents near and just above the road. If they were occupied there was no sign for no one appeared to note our passing, or even to say, hello. Brigadier Warren, generally known as 'Daddy' Warren, was admired and liked by those under his command. But in common with so many of the British officers in the Indian Army he disliked the British Army and was very ready to say so. Thus he disliked and was very critical of 2 Div., whom he believed to have been far too slow in getting forward. We in turn thought him to be bloody idle and living soft – which squared things.

We dug-in for the night, in very scattered positions, with 'D' Company, now commanded by David Harris, in occupation of a village on a ridge south of the road and about 500 feet above it. During the evening, after the attack on his company on the 13th, Paget Fretts had been shot through the chest while guiding a friendly patrol and we were to be deprived of him for months. Thus we lost another of our small band of regular officers when most needed.

16th April

Contrary to our expectations, we had not been attacked during the night and in the morning we looked forward to further progress, only to receive the staggering news that we were to return to Zubza. We were to be replaced by our old friends the 2nd Battalion of the Royal Norfolk Regiment in 4 Brigade. So close had been the association between the Norfolks and ourselves during the First World War that, at one time, we were known as 'Norsets'. As would be expected, the return to Zubza, from where we had advanced with such high expectations, produced a flood of uncomplimentary opinions about those responsible for our operations – and their parents.

Unknown to us, the plan for the deployment of our division in the battle for Kohima was being formulated. What we knew as Garrison Hill, but which was sometimes known as Summerhouse Hill from a summerhouse that had been on its apex, or Hospital Hill from the hospital at its base, was to be the hub and the responsibility of 6 Brigade. 4 Brigade would do a wide hook to the right, starting from the village of Khonoma and would battle their way through the jungle-clad lower slopes of Mount Japvo, their objective being the Imphal Road, south of Kohima, which they would cut. 5 Brigade would go in the reverse direction and cross the Zubza valley to Merema and from there they would fight the Japs in Naga Village and clear Kohima from the north.

But there was some shuffling to be done, for we were to be with 6 Brigade on Garrison Hill and Lancashire Fusiliers were to temporarily replace us in 5 Brigade. It is fascinating to speculate as to why that switch was made. Were we – the 'Swede Bashers' – considered better temperamentally suited to life on the beleaguered hill and the Fusiliers to the hard going of crossing that deep valley and the movement of the left hook? Were we fortunate or very unfortunate, who can say?

17th April

That night at Zubza, which was indeed to be our last, has passed from memory. I do know that we set off again up the road as yesterday, this time going ahead of 161 Brigade to the high ground above 'Lancaster Gate', the name given to a road junction where a secondary road led to the large village of Jotsoma, south of and 1,000 ft. above the Dimapur to Kohima road. Jotsoma was within the defended area of 161 Brigade and was the place from which the gunners had given, and were to continue to give, supporting fire to Garrison Hill and the battle areas. We were there during the critical days when 6 Brigade relieved the gallant survivors on the hill who, contrary to expectations, had managed to hold on.

18th – 25th April

It was on the 18th that Clive and his Carrier Platoon, in borrowed carriers (ours arrived two days later), assisted in the escort of a convoy of ambulances that reached Garrison Hill and evacuated the wounded.

From our forward positions Kohima and, more closely, Garrison Hill could be clearly seen standing above the low ground of the head-waters of the Zubza River, the hill being at a distance, as the crow flies, of a mile or so. I spent much of my time watching all that could be seen from our vantage point and although movement on the ground on Garrison Hill was not visible, the effects of our shelling, much of which was in close support, was very obvious. We watched the dive-bombing of enemy positions in and around Kohima and along the line of Naga Village on the town's northern extremity. In the afternoons the Dakotas flew over and dropped supplies, the parachute canopies of coloured silk – reds, blues, greens and yellows (colours that indicated the article being dropped) but, in the main, the familiar white – provided a brilliant picture against the blue sky, so that it was difficult to realise that a grim battle was in progress below.

All was not peace and quietness, for 'A' Company on a hill to our right had a sticky time. Japs were very active on a ridge above them and patrols sent to remove them had no success. A patrol at 1930 hrs on the 20th did manage to grenade a bunch of five Japs and inflict casualties, but the terrain was so difficult and the potential for losses so great that the patrols were withdrawn. From then we restricted our action to mortar harassing fire.

My batman, Bert Jones, and I visited 'D' Company in their village behind our HQ. Our first to a Naga village and of interest in itself, but specially so in that we were among Nagas, of all ages, at close quarters. What, I wonder, did they think of us with our guns and our planes, the like of which they had never seen and the cause of the mass destruction all around them?

Our chaps were feeling sorry for themselves for they suffered from flea bites, having been sleeping in the huts. Thus we learned that the villages were for the villagers and not for us. We were told of where there was a dead Jap so, thinking that I might get some useful documents, we went to look for him. We walked into a delightfully wooded hillside where the sunlight dappled the ground and below which was a stream. A lovely place but for the smell which guided us the last hundred yards: he had been dead for some time and we left well alone.

I was fortunate in my batmen, of whom Bert Jones was the last, and we developed a close rapport that continued after the war, when he achieved his desire and returned to his old job of postman in the Forest of Dean. He was a great chap, but sadly the last time I saw him was the day before his death.

When in action or involved in the Indian riots, no one went alone, so batmen became gunmen and we were dependent on one another. Harold Jones has reminded me of the emphasis given to this by George Wood and that, when in contact with the enemy, nobody was ever to be alone. To make his message clear he ended by saying, "If on an exercise I find anyone alone, officer, non-commissioned officer or man, they go straight to the guardroom."

Kohima was the place of residence of the Deputy-Commissioner, Charles Pawsey, who had been there for 20 years. One of those remarkable men from our islands who, in the days of Empire, worked in far-off places and whose dedication to those within their charge and amongst whom they lived, bound them with ties of affection, much as with a parent and children. Needed as never before, he was helping us with his unique knowledge of the country and its people and providing a link between us. And he was caring for his Nagas; hundreds had lost their homes or had left them ahead of the advancing Japs.

One of the educated Nagas with whom he had close links was Dr Sevilie, the administrator of the medical station and the district of what, on our maps was shown as Phakekedzumi, but which was more correctly Phikrokedzemi. With such names it will be no surprise that we called it 'Phek'. A place within high, remote mountains, towards the far end of the Jessami track; one of those 'motorable in dry weather' roads winding its way to the east from Kohima to Jessami, close to the Burma frontier. It was along this route that the bulk of the Japanese division advanced on Kohima, after overcoming a brave stand by the 1st Assam Regiment at Jessami at the end of March. Also on this track was a detachment of the 2nd West Yorkshire Regiment, a battalion whose future was to be at Imphal and the battle there. Dr Sevilie had been instructed by Pawsey to stay at his post and assist the army and help and receive refugees. He was to do so until the arrival of the Japanese when he was to depart.

My informant is his son Niketu Iralu, born at Phek in 1935, who records –

> "I was nine years old then. Refugees began to flood back. Soldiers patrolling forward would stop at my father's medical station. Often they would ask 'Doc ... got any tea?' He referred them to my mother who always had a cauldron on the boil. We remember one corporal, so young .. perhaps 20 .. his mug hanging on his belt. He spoke of his loneliness far from home. The returning patrol reported he had been killed. We mourned a friend and thought of his family. My father had to slip away. The Japanese arrived. I am wearing my tribal shawl not against the cold but because as a Naga on such an occasion as this among soldiers .. without it I would be improperly dressed. A Japanese soldier entered our house. He began to take things and picked up a shawl belonging to my sister. He was about to tie it around his waist when my sister who was 20 years old took a hold on it and said, 'No. That is mine', pointing to herself. My mother was terrified .. we had heard what the Japanese could do. My mother was praying. The Japanese soldier drew himself up. Then .. with a touch of formality he handed the shawl back. Something had happened to him. Some good responded to my sister's courage."

Mention has been and will continue to be made of our Bren-gun carriers, open-topped vehicles peculiar to the British and Commonwealth forces. They were the 4-ton Carrier Universal, evolved pre-war by Vickers-Armstrong to transport the new .303 Bren and a crew of three, within 12mm armour and at a maximum speed of 30mph. They were indeed universal, carrying anything from men to rations that could be fitted in either side of the centrally placed 65 hp engine. They were unique amongst tracked vehicles and had their own steering system. A steering wheel moved the front suspension unit laterally, bowing the tracks and further turning of the wheel operated brakes causing a skid turn. We had a profound affection for ours, so often our only armoured support, and we had admiration for their drivers.

In the very early hours of one of the last mornings before we reached Garrison Hill, having been awakened by the noise of battle, I walked across the rounded spur on which we were to where the ground fell away to the east, providing an uninterrupted view of that much larger spur at the tip of which was Garrison Hill. There I and others watched in silence the ghastly scene, where the flashes of exploding shells and mortar bombs showed within a mass of flame and billowing black smoke from burning trees and goodness knows what. From the inferno came the continuing sound of small arms fire and the thump of explosions. This was one of the last of the major attacks against those on 'the hill', as the Japs became more and more desperate. At the receiving end were the Durham Light Infantry who suffered grievously from a battalion instructed by their general that 'the position must be captured'. Men fought in close combat with the bayonet and grenades, in the light of burning trees and exploding ammunition. Out of sight from us, on the northern perimeter where we were soon to be, the Royal Berks were attacked by three companies but held their ground as, but for a few yards lost, did the Durhams.

It had been on the 20th that the two leading battalions of 6 Brigade had taken over the defences on this, so vital, so-called hill. The 1st Battalion Royal Berkshire Regiment and the 2nd Durham Light Infantry now had the 1st Royal Welch Fusiliers and ourselves, waiting in support. The issue of rum with our evening meal on the 25th had a considerable significance to those who had read of such issues, in the Great War, prior to 'going over the top'.

26th April

After so much expectation and so many false starts, from the day of our arrival at Bokajan until this day, we were at last at our objective. Four days earlier, 'B' and 'D' Companies under Geoffry White had taken over from a similar force of Durhams the occupation of Picquet Hill, a hillock around which the road to Kohima passed. Thus on this morning at 0830 hrs it was 'A' and 'C' of the rifle companies with battalion HQ and Headquarters Company, less the carriers and mortars, that started off along the road.

I had to see everybody into Garrison Hill and, in order to do so, positioned myself at the tail of our column. As we rounded Picquet Hill I climbed above the road to where I could squat and, through binoculars, observe the road ahead. It turned south along the near side of a re-entrant in which was a tributary of the Zubza River and, after crossing the stream, reversed direction north on the far side along rising ground which became the flank of Garrison Hill. Moving up that distant length of road was a carrier in which were the C.O. and the Adjutant and

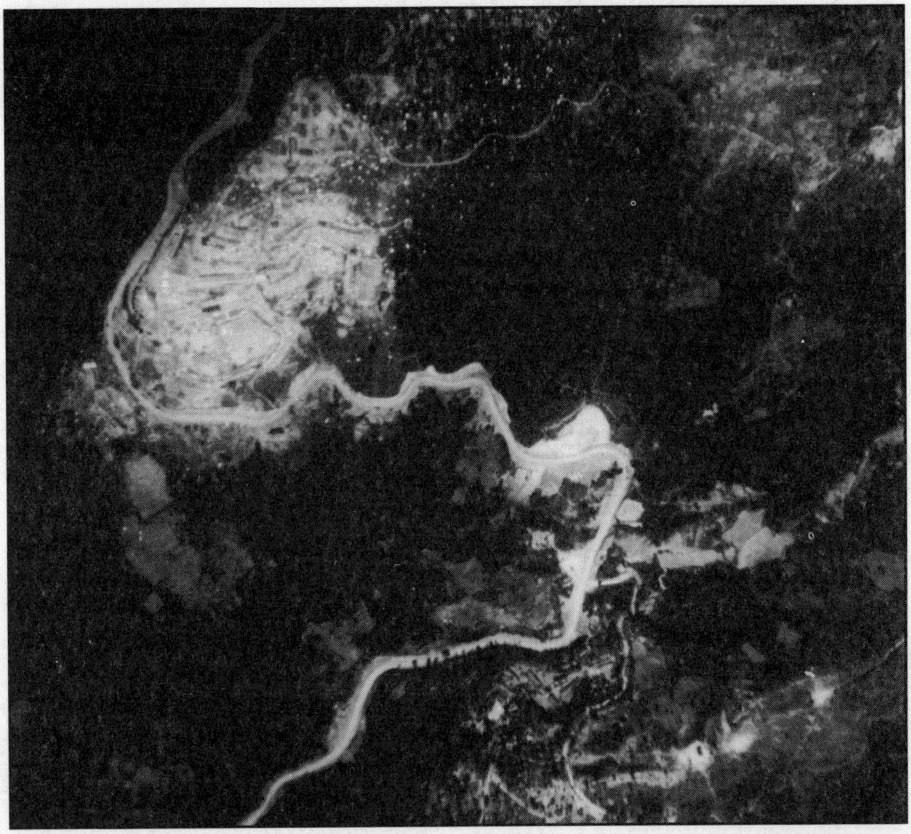

The approach to Garrison Hill with Mortuary Corner and shattered hospital. The white spots are parachute canopies entangled in the trees.

as Bert Jones and I watched they halted; simultaneously, a mortar bomb exploded a few feet away, an encouragement for them to leap out and waste no time in getting off the road. Very deliberately we were well dispersed and I was soon watching the head of our column advancing along that same section of road and coming under fire from a machine-gun to their rear. They ran in small groups through this long-range fire which there, at least, seemed to be inaccurate. Two stretches of the road were being fired on, these were separated by a short bend where the road was shielded by the cliff which flanked its right-hand side. That cliff, and the much deeper drop on the other side, confined us to the road, where one felt conspicuous and vulnerable. The road had an uphill incline and when my turn came, my load of pack and equipment, plus so many things from map-case to grenades and my Sten and pistol, made the road both long and steep. Once around the corner at half-way we flung ourselves down, secure but for the occasional mortar bomb.

During their advance the Japs had captured numerous 3-inch mortars and bombs to go with them, a galling situation that was aggravated by our awareness that their ample supply also resulted from inaccurate air drops. In those early days we were receiving only one third of the supplies dropped from the Dakotas, the remainder were missing our tight perimeters and were feeding and arming the enemy.

So that they could pass through the small-arms fire, invariably directed at them, ambulances were protected by armoured plate and one was to our left in the small re-entrant. Joe Chamberlin, helped by Lieutenant John O'Driscoll, was busy attending to casualties who were further up the road and both carried a number of stretcher cases down the road to the ambulance. The Guerilla Platoon was protecting that length of the road to where it turned east, hence the presence of John, for he had taken command after the injury to Harold Jones back in Belgaum. He was an ideal choice for a difficult and dangerous job and was universally liked, in part due to a willingness to become involved in all things, but also for having that modesty so often associated with courage.

We lay on the tarmac as close to the rising ground on our right as we could get, a bit winded and very aware that there was a certain amount of blood about, as was to be expected in this prelude to the occupation of Garrison Hill. Suddenly, those in front picked themselves up and we followed, doubling up that last stretch where vehicles littered the road, blown up and burnt out in earlier fighting. The bodies of a Jap and an Indian at the side of the road, swollen to many times their normal size and quite black, were part of a sombre scene. Such bodies and their associated stench were to become an all too familiar and nauseous background to our lives.

We were then at what was appropriately named Mortuary Corner, from the abandoned hospital mortuary, standing in isolation on the left of the road. There our column had its worst losses, a mortar bomb having landed amongst a group, killing or wounding most.

Thinking back to our advance up that road with the odd bullet or two whizzing past as we doubled up the incline, we were not then as well dispersed as we had been when we started, for we had bunched, contrary to all training. Presumably, those who ran the fastest would not pass the slower ones, for to do so would give the appearance of running away.

We had some way to go to be within the actual perimeter, the nearest part of which was about 200 feet above where we left the road, to commence this final lap up a steep and open hillside. We then had another wait of what seemed to be an age, while we were alongside the shattered and burnt-out remains of the 53rd Indian General Hospital. Then those in front were moving and, after helping to push a couple of chaps up a vertical bank, I in turn was heaved up and made the climb partly by crawling and partly by short rushes, from cover to cover, some of which was in trenches. And I remember so clearly the alarming swoosh of our artillery covering fire, the shells being from the guns at Jotsoma away at our backs and apparently passing within a few feet of my head. So, what with that and the belief that we were being sniped from our left front, I kept my head down.

All, other than the Guerillas who rejoined us at 1745 hrs, were within the security of the perimeter by 1300 hrs; there we busied ourselves in this strange

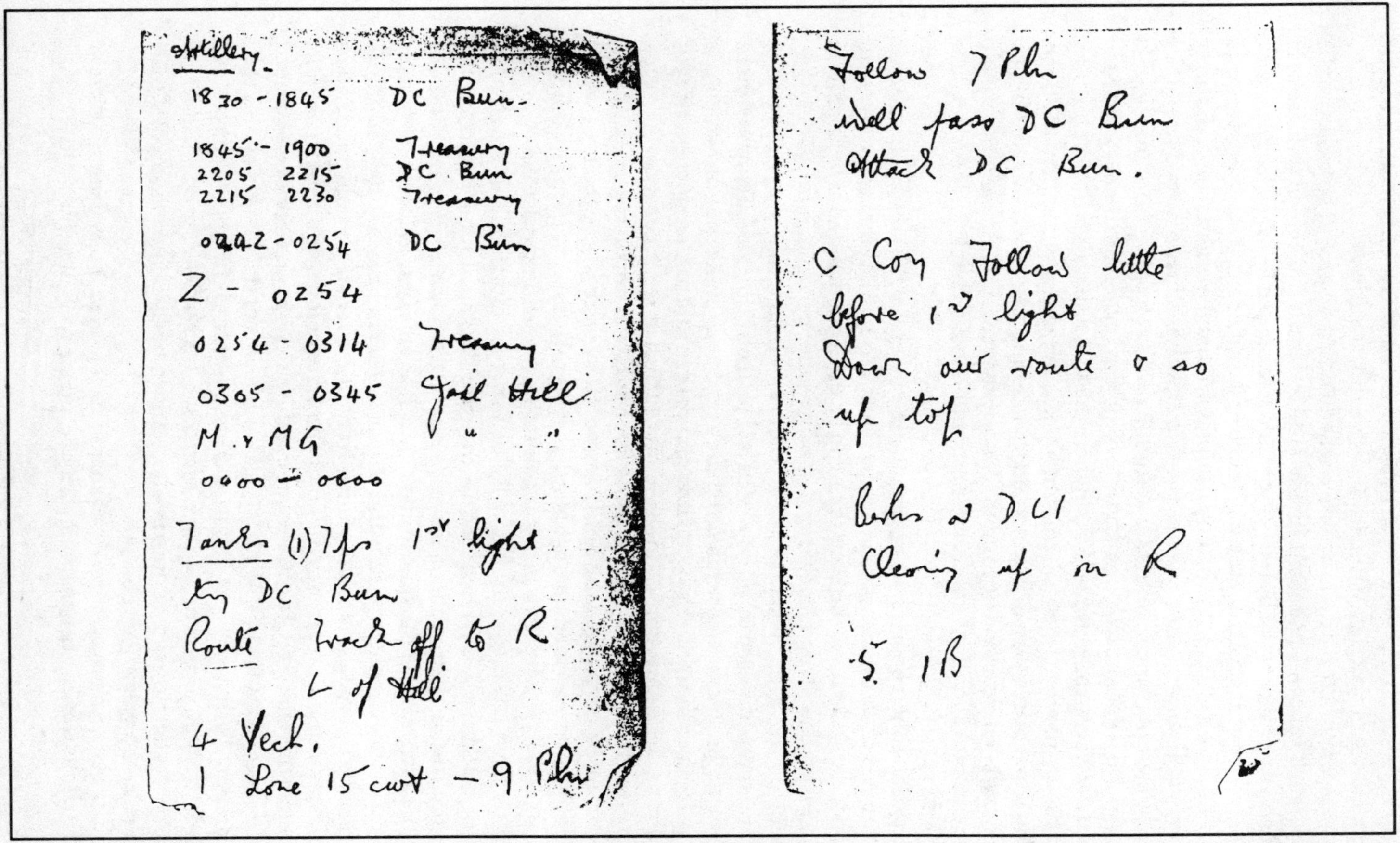

Artillery

1830 - 1845 DC Bun.

1845 - 1900 Treasury
2205 2215 DC Bun
2215 2230 Treasury

0242 - 0254 DC Bun

Z - 0254

0254 - 0314 Treasury

0305 - 0345 Jail Hill
M + MG " "
0400 - 0600

Tanks (1) 7 Pls 1st light
by DC Bun
Route Track off to R
L of Hill

4 Vech.
1 Lone 15 cwt - 9 Pln

Follow 7 Pln
will pass DC Bun
Attack DC Bun.

C Coy Follow little
before 1st light
Down our route & so
up top

Berks & DLI
Clearing up on R

5 1B

Notes made by Lieutenant Murrills at John Bowles 'O' Group 26th April. They show the phases of the artillery supporting fire. Also that 8 Platoon was to follow 7 and pass the District Commissioner's bungalow which they were to attack. The Royal Berks and the Durhams are mentioned and the covering fire from 0305 - 0345 on Jail Hill, of artillery 'M' (mortars) and MG (machine-guns) would have been for them, Jail Hill being on their front and not ours.

patch of polluted earth, that had to be denied to the Japs. Battalion HQ took over the old HQ of the Berks, who were depleted after six days of defending the hill and able to fit in on our right flank, from where they were to attack in conjunction with the operation for which we were scheduled.

Our signals officer, Lieutenant Jimmy Hodder, and I had agreed to share a slit trench and were allocated a hole in the ground some seven feet long by three wide and just over five feet high to the underside of a timber and earth roof. It was to be my home until 15th May, Jimmy having soon moved elsewhere, and during those weeks I came to know it so well that I can visualise it now. It could be described as utilitarian and functional, for the roof's soffit was about nine inches above ground level, thus making possible firing slits on the north side, where the ground fell away to the perimeter. Elsewhere the roof sloped down to the ground, but for the south west corner where rough steps gave entry. Other than the floor, the only storage area was a nine inch margin around the trench, formed by the roof having been extended beyond the hole by that amount. At night rats would scamper around and to my fury scatter grit onto my face while I lay on the floor trying for precious sleep.

To describe the geography of our hill and of our neighbours from personal observation is not possible; of necessity we kept our heads down and only went where necessary. Maps make clear the main features but disagree as to the minor ones and battalion areas, trenches and the like suffer accordingly.

Before the arrival of the Japanese this had been a delightfully wooded place of numerous footpaths used by hospital staff and patients, club members and others. Somewhere for an evening stroll. Extending north east is the spur on which was the Deputy-Commissioner's bungalow and garden and at the junction of spur and hill was the tennis court, one side of which had been cut into the rising ground. This spur, with a length of about 250 yards, was not unlike a swan's beak and if the hill be considered the head, our positions were where the eyes would be. What was strange then and has puzzled everyone since, was our inability to see the spur. There were two prime reasons, the trees and the fall in the ground.

To our great advantage the majority of the trees remained, although after weeks of battle most were reduced to their trunks and stouter branches, the enemy not having the weight of artillery required to blast them away. With our positions so high above the spur, some as much as 100 feet, to look downwards was to do so through the tree tops and in places one could see virtually nothing. But this in turn saved us, for without the trees all movement would have had to be along communication trenches. To obtain areas of level ground on the spur, and of these the tennis court was the largest, the rising ground had been terraced into two or three giant steps. With Japs in the remains of the bungalow and club house and the corrugated iron ancillary buildings east of the court, no one was able to look over or down onto the terraces. To say the least one had to be circumspect when moving about and then only in well-defined places of which few were in the vicinity of the spur.

We had become seriously short of majors and missed Tony Bridge, then at Quetta training prior to becoming brigade major to 5 Brigade; and Donald

Baynes, who had been with us since France, was a sick man. We were also short of junior officers, but the stalwart 'Preb' had come up from Rear Details and had joined 'A' Company. While in India and before Assam, a mixed bag of officers had circulated and, at varying intervals, had departed unlamented and soon forgotten.

But forming the battalion's backbone were our seasoned warrant officers, on whom with our sergeants and corporals the success of almost any task depended. Their tolerance of us, the junior officers, and their steadfastness and good humour at all times, was wonderful. 2 Dorset had good ones in abundance.

On this day during which we had moved into Garrison Hill, 5 Brigade had reached Merema, having cross the Zubza River valley in an all-night trek under horrifying conditions, the natural hazards of that gorge made so much worse when overburdened men, moving in single file, traversed precipitous and slippery tracks in total darkness. They were preparing to advance on Kohima and faced a series of battles where all the advantages were to an entrenched enemy and for which, to obtain some balance, they needed the support of armour. Accordingly a troop of tanks was to join them at their tomorrow's objective but, because of that Zubza Valley, they would have to move by road and pass unescorted through Kohima and its Japanese occupants.

For this venture the American Lee/Grant tank, generally known as the 'Grant' and described as being as big as a house, was chosen. With a 75mm gun in a sponson on the right of the hull it looked almost of World War 1 vintage and it was virtually obsolete in other theatres of war. But at 28.5 tons it was big and tough and served us well until gradually replaced by the improved version, the Sherman.

In order that the route of these tanks might be protected by us as far as the road junction opposite the D.C.'s bungalow, our 'A' and 'C' Companies were to attack and capture that area by dawn on the 27th, hence our arrival on the hill. Our plans were based on the belief that there was one Japanese platoon on the spur but, as we found to our great cost, their actual strength was one company.

Acting as a guide to 5 Brigade during their crossing of the Zubza Valley was the brother-in-law of Niketu Iralu, Savino, then a young man who in later life was to become a Baptist minister. As the column inched its way up the steep slope below the Japanese positions, Savino was wounded in the thigh and was evacuated to Dimapur. He deeply cherished the memory of those he led, many of whom were to die, and claimed that that wound saved his life, as very probably it did.

At night that deep valley was used for the evacuation of the wounded from our three brigades, the stretchers being carried by Nagas, sometimes under mortar fire, but always on narrow tracks and in difficulty and danger. That there was the chance of meeting an enemy patrol made no difference to the care and understanding shown by our friends, who fulfilled a role no others could have done.

My account of the traumatic battle of our companies is helped by a written report, made by John Bowles and which I managed to retain.

At 1300 hrs, when some of us had just entered the perimeter, John Bowles and Dick Castle were receiving their orders from the C.O. Those orders were that 'A' Company was to capture and hold the end of the spur and by so doing, cover the road below the spur and at the important road junction, where the road into Kohima branched off eastward and north. 'C' Company was to take possession of that part of the spur abutting the hill, in which was the tennis court, and they were to continue to the corrugated iron buildings known as the 'tin huts'. Coinciding with all this the Royal Berks would attack from their position, towards the same huts. Had all these objectives been attained, the spur would have been cleared of the enemy.

John and Dick had the near-impossible task of formulating a plan for a night attack over ground that could not be seen and to attack and capture unknown enemy positions. Thus they had the nightmare of dealing with an unseen enemy in prepared positions. They were supplied with a plan, of sorts, on the basis of which they allocated platoon objectives.

As was customary in the British Army, our four rifle companies consisted of a headquarters and three platoons. They were commanded by a major or a captain and, when up to establishment, had a second captain as the second-in-command and a lieutenant commanding each platoon. It was considered desirable for the 2 I/C to be left out of battle, thus he would be ready to take command if needed. Sickness, together with wastage from our years in India and the casualties suffered on the road, can be assumed to have reduced 'A' and 'C' Companies to strengths of about 90. Their platoons would therefore have had not the 40 men we paraded in England but less that 30. Japanese rifle companies were comparable.

We took care that officers were not easily recognizable as such. Thus badges of rank were pieces of uniform, cut to the appropriate shape and stitched on flush, making them identifiable only at short range. For further disguise, weapons were carried that were similar to those of the men. A fortunate few, however, preferred to take a chance and carried the deadly American Thompson submachine-gun, much favoured by the Chicago City gangsters in the '30s. As a secondary weapon, a pistol was carried in a webbing holster on the belt. Its use for shooting oneself, in the event of the Japs overrunning us on the hill, was seriously discussed; for we had no illusions as to the horrors that were meted out to captured officers.

More than the brief references made so far of John and Dick are due. John Bowles was small in stature and a doer of things without fuss. He had been a Platoon Sergeant-Major in France, where his accomplishments had warranted a Mention in Despatches and a direct commission. He was universally liked and respected and, having the bonus of 12 years of service with the Dorsets, had a knowledge of soldiering denied to most of his fellow officers. Dick Castle, like so many of us, was a 'temporary job' and was already planning his return to farming in Essex. Thick-set and rock-like and with all the qualities necessary for being labelled a Dorset, he too was universally liked. His natural unflappability was soon to be sorely tested.

'A' and 'C' had about 13 hours in which to settle in and reorganise after their casualties, hours in which they must prepare for action as well as feed and rest.

That they were crowded into too small an area and were generally bloody uncomfortable and that it would soon be dark, did not help. That the place stank from decomposing bodies, makeshift latrines and the garbage of a battlefield, would not have troubled them unduly. Most would have been contemplating getting some kip, or 'shut eye', not only from an instinctive desire to 'recharge batteries' but so that they might withdraw into an inner self and think of loved ones and places that were far away. But such an indulgence would not be possible for the platoon and section commanders, busy with 'O' Groups and doing their best to digest a mass of information and orders. These would define how they and those for whom they were responsible would capture their objectives, irrespective of anything that the enemy might do. Admin in the form of quartermasters would be doing wonders, producing boxes of grenades and ammo generally. Grenades had to be available in generous quantities and had to be primed by those who were to use them. Weapons would be cleaned yet again, to minimise the risk of stoppages, the Bren-gun magazines checked as fully loaded and spares distributed.

And someone had to set out the white tracing tapes, so that the companies would move off in the right direction.

27th April

'A' Company had to traverse the north west side of the spur and, taking the lead, moved off at 0254 hrs. Moving slowly and with difficulty along a steep and wooded slope that fell to the road on their left, they had covered only 50 yards when a light machine-gun opened fire from above. They halted while Corporal Hill and two men attempted to silence it but failed, a similar gun having commenced firing, 15 yards away to a flank. The company pressed on, crossing one line of fire and then two more by moving in short rushes and using the folds in the ground. 'C' Company to the rear of 'A' had their Company Commander and two Platoon Commanders, with runners, in the lead. Both companies halted while John and Dick liaised and Dick Castle, having decided on his line of attack, turned to the right and up the slope, the companies thus diverging. At that time 'A' came under further fire from a bunker which they silenced but which they were unable to occupy. On reaching the top, Dick and his men were immediately subjected to machine-gun fire from three or four directions, despite which they eliminated a bunker at the near end of the tennis court. In brave attempts to silence the bunkers from which the fire was coming, Lieutenant Mayer was killed leading 13 Platoon; also killed was his Platoon Sergeant, Sergeant Perrett, and two others of this platoon. At the same time the commander of 14 platoon was wounded, as was Dick Castle. Dick was attacking a bunker and had a grenade in his right hand preparatory to throwing it through one of the bunker's firing slits, when he was shot through his right elbow. Almost simultaneously he was hit in his chin, probably by a fragment from his exploding grenade, which it is assumed he dropped.

Captain Michael Morice, Dick's 2 I/C, had been left out of battle and command was taken by Company Sergeant-Major Keegan. With Lieutenant Day having been one of the wounded on the road the previous morning, there were then no other officers in this company. On the spur, but in particular around the tennis court, the Japs had developed the 'classic' defence of strong points mutually protected by fire from automatic weapons, probably firing on fixed lines, so fully effective in the dark or through smoke. Little wonder that further attempts by Sergeant-Major Keegan to clear this opposition failed.

Harry Newcombe of 13 Platoon gives a vivid account of those horrific moments, when the air was full of small arms fire and bursting grenades, light from the latter giving glimpses of figures crouching or darting and of some standing and firing, one being a chap with a Bren. Someone stumbles over something. During a lapse in the firing quiet words of command are heard and groans are mixed with swearing, and the call for stretcher-bearers is repeated and repeated and someone shouts "the Company Commander's hit".

During this fighting 'A', with 7 Platoon in the lead, had pushed on along the left flank and reached the spur's tip above the road junction. Behind was 8 Platoon, temporarily under Lieutenant 'Jock' Murrills, moving out to the right flank of 7 Platoon, enabling 9 Platoon and Company HQ to close in behind, and doing so without opposition other than sniping from the vicinity of the bungalow.

Maps show the D.C.'s bungalow well back from the road and at an angle, so that it looks to the west of north and down the Zubza Valley. This is as would be expected, for the extensive view is not spoiled by the town or road. A peacetime photo shows the garden terraced down from the bungalow, a fall of about eight feet to a fairly level area before the drop to the road, of, at a guess, 20 feet.

It would have been this fairly level part of the garden which 7 Platoon had selected for the control of the road junction and, being exposed, they had to get below ground quickly. 8 Platoon away to their right were preparing to attack the bungalow and, under the cover of their right-hand section, the other two and their HQ crawled to within 15 yards of it and waited, while two of their men with pole-charges rushed the battered bungalow and exploded them inside. Under the cover of the explosions the two sections charged into the ruin, but meeting no opposition they withdrew and the whole platoon reformed to the west of the bungalow. At that time Sergeant Varley was carrying out a recce in preparation for the arrival, at first light, of the tanks. It was then fast becoming daylight and very heavy fire was directed at 8 Platoon from the 'tin huts' area, pinning them to the ground. Their platoon commander signalled his rear section to pull back down the slope above the road and there he joined them. Meanwhile 9 Platoon had moved above the road until they contacted 7 and they too dug in due north of the bungalow, in what was their agreed position. At about 0530 hrs, Jock Murrills set off with a section with the intention of silencing the Japs whose fire had caught 8 Platoon's two sections in the open, and of doing so by attacking the Japs from their rear. Starting west of the road junction, Jock and his party moved along the road towards it and came under fire from a bunker within the tip of the spur. With Jock was Corporal Softly and together they rushed the bunker and eliminated it, killing seven Japs and capturing a Bren-gun. That was a remarkable achievement by any standard, even on a day when there were so many brave deeds, of which many went unrecorded. To their amazement and that of the remainder of 7 Platoon, they realised that a two-man trench was being dug, by them, into the bunker's roof. They had also been amazed when a group of about five Japs had run from the spur side of the road into a bunker on the opposite side, and doing so without helping the one that was under attack.

Jock's patrol continued along the road and entered the one leading to Imphal. As with the one with which we were familiar, this one was below a steep drop, where the falling ground contained the drive to Charles Pawsey's home. It was a steep one, best approached from the direction of Imphal, roughly parallel to the road, but as it climbed so it diverged and ended in an acute bend. Jock continued to what was probably the start of the drive and deep into enemy territory. They reached their objective but, while trying to locate the machine-guns at the top of the slope, Corporal Softly was killed; thus we lost another irreplaceable Dorset. They then withdrew under fire, realising that their task was beyond them.

Company HQ had been digging in at their agreed position, north of the bungalow, but as the light strengthened John realised, with dismay, that the trench which he, his wireless operator and batman were occupying was dominated by a bunker on the north edge of the tennis court. At about 0900 hrs John Bowles got a wireless message through, that he commanded the road junction and that the tanks could proceed. That they did and safely reached 5 Brigade. An hour later John received a note, thrown to him inside a cartridge-case, that 8 Platoon had lost two sections, but that all three platoons were dug in.

During his adventures, Jock Murrills had one particularly remarkable escape from death, for three bullets were found to have grooved his forehead and nose.

Another remarkable escape was that of Privates Hoddnit and 'Snowy' Horlock of 8 Platoon who, when caught in the open, had managed to crawl into an enemy slit trench. There they hid until the afternoon when a Japanese officer walked to it and, mistaking them for Japs, started a conversation. While Snowy tried to slip a round into the breech of his .303, Hoddnit shot the officer, and scrambling out they dashed back the way that they had come and got away with it.

Before dawn, 'C' Company, knowing how impossible was their task following heavy casualties, had pulled back to the hill. There Jock McNaught, having called up Michael Morice, put him in command. His instruction was that they had to occupy and hold what was known as the club square, a rectangle of level ground immediately above the tennis court, and there they dug in, having reorganised on a two-platoon basis. They reported losses of four killed, three missing, 34 wounded.

Private Harry Newcombe, a recent reinforcement and only 20 years old has described that weary return through the trees, during part of which he carried a small fellow who had been hit in the shoulder, until two pairs of hands reached out and a voice said, "OK, chum, we've got him." Finding himself back in the slit trench from which he started and of which he was now the sole occupant, he wondered whether the wetness on his thigh was his blood, or the casualty's. Great was his relief to find that his water bottle had been pierced by a bullet. Checking his weapons he found that he had used three of his Sten magazines and had one grenade left out of four. He couldn't remember using any! Lighting a cigarette under his gas cape, he heard, "Are you all right, lad?" and saw a craggy unshaven face peering down, was offered and took a double swig of water. Harry could think of nothing to say but "A complete f— up." The face grinned and said, "You're so right, lad." The big chap tapped him on the helmet, and disappeared.

Months later, Harry discovered that his visitor was Sergeant Major 'Tanky' Williams.

During that night the Royal Berks had no more than a limited success in their attack, which was tragic for John Bowles and his men. Behind us, the Durhams held off another attack on their part of the perimeter.

Those pole-charges need explaining. They were ideal for bunkers that resisted shot and shell, and were sufficiently simple for production by those who were to use them. To one end of a five or six foot bamboo was taped a block or two of an explosive, such as ammonol; the weapon was then completed with a fuse which could be set for timings of between four and twenty seconds. When slung through firing slits by brave chaps, they were deadly.

One wonders how the Japs allowed 'A' Company to survive that first day, when disorganised and vulnerable. Probably they were complacent and saw no reason to leave the security of their impregnable bunkers, within which they were prepared to live for as long as might be necessary. Certainly they were very different in temperament to us, as was apparent from the way that they allowed us to do certain things that were to our advantage, without responding, and then some invisible line would be crossed and their reaction would be violent.

What did make our survival possible, and it applied to all of us, was close artillery support; without it Kohima would have fallen.

The 2nd Division had the 10th, 16th and 99th Field Regiments, Royal Artillery, armed with the 25-pounder and the 3.7 howitzer – to a total of 72 guns. Thus a brigade could assume the permanent support of one regiment of 24 guns, and a battalion one of the three 8-gun batteries. In addition there was the 100th Light Anti-Aircraft/Anti-Tank Regiment, Royal Artillery, with the Bofors gun and the 6-pounder anti-tank gun.

Nevertheless, we remained at a disadvantage until later, for none of these guns were of the size required to destroy the well-constructed bunker, such as the one that had dominated the road at Zubza.

When we were in close contact with the enemy the gunners would provide a Forward Observation Officer who, given the time and opportunity, would range his guns on carefully chosen targets and areas. Thus, when needed, he could bring down immediate fire on them and many were the occasions when it brought success to us and disaster to the Japs. The pity was that John did not have one from the start; when he and his successors had a F.O.O. later, he could be said to have saved the position from being overwhelmed.

We developed a profound respect for the Japanese artillery; its deadly accuracy was such that an appeal went out for gun sights, to be returned for expert examination. It is unlikely that the Japs reached Kohima with anything larger than their 75mm gun and how lucky for us. When we were on the Tamu road and in Burma we were to be familiar with ones of twice that calibre. Their antiquated look belied their efficiency. They also had a modern high velocity anti-tank gun, which we were to suffer from in Burma when fired not only at tanks but also at us.

With all our thoughts concentrated on 'A' and 'C' Companies, nothing that we on the hill did that day has registered. Obviously we were doing our best to settle into that battle ground and learn its geography. Paper work had to continue, hence adjutants and their staffs. The 'I' Section had to make Sitreps (Situation Reports) to brigade at dawn and dusk and maintain the War Diary on Army Form C-2118; also information was coming in from a variety of sources and it had to be digested and circulated. Maps were scarce but not a great problem. Later when we were on the move their receipt and issue was almost a daily occurrence. Also in the future, we were to have air photographs, enabling us to see 'the other side of the hill' and when in overlapping pairs as was customary and viewed through a stereoscope, one had that wonderful third dimension.

Looking back on those days, the unremembered and unrecorded part is the daily routine. Generally I have no recollection of the actual business of eating, although I can visualise the stomach-filling bully-beef stews which, with hot and very sweet tea, were what kept us going.

My last mention of Joe Chamberlin was of him dealing with the casualties on the road. Now he and his splendid band of orderlies had established the Regimental Aid Post, and what a place it was – a cave burrowed out of the hillside, where what seemed like bright lighting (to us who had no lights) was screened from the exterior by a wall of blankets. Parting those blankets one was dazzled by a space where walls and roof were lined with multi-coloured parachutes – once seen never to be forgotten. There great things were done and fear and pain were mitigated.

Joe has advised me that:

> There were four stretcher-bearers with each company. At HQ we had Sergeant Osmond, Corporal Plantard, Lance-Corporal Davies (in civvy life a London bus conductor and a dedicated amateur chiropodist), Fred Fowles (drummer and batman) and Kingston, jeep driver.
>
> It was clear from the way the Japs behaved in the Arakan that the Geneva Convention was not on. We had rifles and grenades and Gus and I took turns at standing-to in the Garrison Hill R.A.P., which overlooked the ravine at the side of the club terrace: fortunately our skills were never tested. I remember Gus complaining of insomnia, the cause of which was found to be a pile of grenades – under him. When General Slim visited us, I told him that M.O.s should be issued with revolvers and this was later done.

Also with us throughout the battle was Norman Swallow and his section from the 5th Field Ambulance.

Very much with us were our signallers under Lieutenant Jimmy Hodder, often no doubt weary of so demanding a job and one that was so seldom rewarded with praise. They would be busy repairing and laying telephone lines and maintaining wireless contact with 'A' Company. Isolated companies had a pair of signallers allocated to them, complete with the infantry two-man No 18 R/T Set. By today's standards a monstrous lump of valve-fed machinery and not highly thought of then, particularly by those who had to carry it. At Battalion HQ a pair of signallers would be maintaining a listening watch.

In all our battles the familiar sounds were those of shots from rifles or light machine-guns and exploding grenades or mortar bombs – the basic infantry weapons.

Our main weapon was the famous Lee Enfield .303 Rifle, excellent on the rifle range but cumbersome and heavy at 8.8 lbs (we did not have the lighter jungle-warfare version). We envied the Jap with his small carbine and were tempted to swap, hesitating only because of its ammunition supply. Some unfortunates of whom I was one, had the Sten 9mm submachine-gun, weighing 7.8 lbs and having a range of only 200 yards. We viewed that piece of 'rough plumbing', which generated no respect or affection, as something of more danger to us than the enemy.

We were fortunate in the Bren .303 light machine-gun, also respected by the enemy who used those he captured. Weighing 22 lbs it was a brute to carry, but had an effective range of 800 yards and fired 500 rounds per minute. Rifle companies had nine, each platoon section having one, where it was in the care of two men trained to fire it in a well rehearsed drill. The Japanese had a similar weapon of smaller calibre and lower rate of fire. Their similarity results from a common ancestry, that of the Czech Arms Company who had supplied them to the Chinese Army, from whom the Japs captured some and copied them. Ours were made under licence at a later date; by then they had been improved.

Our rifle platoons had a 2-inch mortar, operated by two men. It fired a 2 lb bomb 470 yards. These were high explosive or smoke or had a parachute flare for illuminating night targets. In Yorkshire, 8 Platoon was issued with one flare bomb for a trial firing. With due ceremony we set up the mortar and fired the bomb which, hanging on its parachute and issuing fiery smoke, was very impressive. What I overlooked in the excitement of the moment was the strong breeze which, to my horror, was taking our firework towards a thatched farmhouse. We just missed it.

In effective opposition was the Japanese 50mm Grenade Discharger with a range of 65 to 175 yards, and deadly it was to those in close contact.

Our most formidable battalion weapon was the 3-inch mortar, of which we had six. They were the responsibility of Captain 'Dave' Davies and his mortar platoon. It was a heavy load at 124 lbs but it divided into three for carrying – mortar 42 lbs, mounting 45 lbs and base plate 37 lbs. It discharged a 10 lb bomb 1600 yards at five rounds per minute.

The Jap mortar was similar but interestingly different. It weighed slightly more at 145 lbs and at 81mm its bore was greater. Much greater was the long range of its smaller 6.93 lbs bomb – 3100 yards and that bomb could be fitted with a delayed action fuse.

Our main grenades were the old familiar 'Mills Bomb' which clipped onto one's belt and most officers carried a couple. The Japs had a less effective plastic-cased version with a spigot which, when struck, activated the fused detonator.

When we temporary officers obtained our commissions it was clearly stated that 'a sword is *not* required', which was just as well – for everyone. The Japs of course thought differently and had an even greater attachment to their swords than we British had to our pistols. Mine was a Mk.1 .38 Smith & Wesson, the handling of which gave me a boyish thrill, but I never fired it in anger.

28th April

It was in the early hours that the Japs made their last big attempt to overrun Garrison Hill; in preparation for which they brought up additional troops in trucks with their headlamps on and which were watched as they approached up the Imphal road. Those vehicles would have been some of the 30 they captured in and around Kohima, following their arrival.

The attack started with a mortar bombardment which awoke Jimmy and me, we then hearing an exchange of small arms fire along the perimeter. To cover themselves in what was bright moonlight, they laid down a heavy smoke screen and visibility was soon down to a few feet. Bombs, explosive and smoke were bursting around us, some within a few feet and close enough to spray phosphorus onto our blankets. The smoke became so thick in our trench that we started coughing and I wondered if gas was being used in a final assault after the failure of so many by more conventional means. As some protection we tied damp handkerchiefs over our faces.

With our weapons to hand and our grenades ready we peered through the smoke, wondering what was happening on the perimeter. after what seemed to have been an age the battle ceased and a blessed quietness descended; we then took turns to keep watch for the remainder of the night. Never have I been so glad to see the dawn. My watch having stopped, I had no idea of the time and peering out through those firing slits I hardly dared to believe that the sky, behind the trees, really was beginning to get lighter. The strange isolation of the trench (it had no neighbours) and our half expecting a hoard of Japs to swarm over us at any moment, had made it a nerve-racking experience. With the arrival of daylight it was quite wonderful to get out and learn what had happened.

The main attack had come from what was known as Kuki Picquet, a small hill on the ridge immediately to our south, which had been captured by the enemy about ten days previously in a night assault, that so very nearly overwhelmed the original defenders of Garrison Hill. On this occasion the Durhams had taken the brunt of the fighting and had suffered the loss of two of their positions. John O'Driscoll, with that casual generosity we knew so well, offered himself and his platoon to help drive them out again, a job that took most of the morning. He was later to describe this offer as utter folly.

In the hours before dawn, 'A' Company had been subjected to spasmodic attacks, during which many grenades were thrown by both sides. Throughout the day they set about improving their positions into a trench system, to the extent that was possible under conditions described as 'quiet but punctuated by sniping'. However, great efforts were made that morning to support them and a bulldozer, driven by a very brave sapper, travelled along the road and round the spur, preceded and followed by Grant tanks, their intention being to get one of the tanks up to the bungalow. Desperately they tried to use the drive and when that failed, to improve it. When that too failed they set about making a new and direct slope up from the road. Then one tank tried to haul the other up by means of a heavy block and tackle fixed to a tree at the top, again without success. The bulldozer then tried its utmost to haul a tank up and that was a failure. And all this time sappers and our men worked with picks and shovels to no avail and the project was abandoned for the time.

The Lee/Grant tank, such as this, provided our armour from Kohima onwards.

Supplies were getting through to 'A' and their casualties were being evacuated by means of a developing service of carriers, medium and light tanks and ambulances. That supply line provided just about all that 'A' Company and those who were to succeed them required. Also it provided us with those items that were not suitable for air drops.

Snagger had taken upon himself the task of getting food and ammunition to those on the spur. Arriving each day and often alone, in a lightly armoured scout car, he passed out dixies of hot tea with their rations. 'A' Company was unable to light fires for fear of the smoke attracting attention and, but for the tea, had cold meals. Also delivered to them and to us was the mail, only just beginning to catch up with us since our departure from Ahmadnagar. Later some mail was to be lost, but luckily not Snagger, when his car received a direct hit from a 75mm gun.

Each day was enhanced by the afternoon air drop when Dakotas arrived with supplies, mainly food and ammunition. As they flew over so we went to ground, for not all the parachutes opened and items such as barbed wire arrived by 'free fall'; one did not get in the way of those items arriving by parachute, for their speed was sufficient to break limbs, as we found on our first afternoon when a sergeant of 8 Platoon had his thigh smashed. Our admiration for those who flew was tempered by what seemed to be their excessive height, which contributed to the percentage that was lost or which supplied the enemy. Many that were on target became lodged in the trees and there, for fear of snipers, they sometimes remained.

Those that did arrive were unpacked and their contents taken to a central dump, their handlers and anyone on the spot being allowed to make use of the canopy, lines and the container, as they wished. Canopies were valued as sheets, for our one blanket was insufficient for warmth. Containers became glorified sandbags which, when filled with earth, made a substantial addition to the strength of defences and the shock-absorbing pads in their bases were removed for seats. Strips of coloured material became scarves and gave a spot of colour in a drab scene.

When I had first approached my trench I could see a book on the floor and picking it up found it to be Daphne DuMaurier's Jamaica Inn, a book that was new to me and which I was delighted to have to read, which I did a number of times. Since then, some to whom I have mentioned it have scoffed at my enthusiasm, showing an inability to visualise those grim days and how such reading transports the reader. When we departed I left it for another to enjoy. A letter home tells of how my carrying capacity had been so reduced that specially saved campaigning literature with plenty of 'meat' in a small space had been left behind, my pack having room for just one Penguin. But by early May, so efficient was our supply line that a steady flow of letters was arriving and even two parcels of magazines.

Following our arrival in India, an Airgraph home had told of our safe arrival. They were reissued when we were at Zubza and one survives. It makes the plain statement: "We are in action on the Eastern India front and in contact with the Japs." They were not liked, for much of the personal contact, so important in a letter, was lost. One wrote on one side of a prepared sheet of paper, which was photographically reduced to 4 x 5 inches (100 x 125mm) including the recipient's name and address, which when folded was visible within an aperture in the envelope. It was a brilliant idea for the postal services, being so small and light, and the wonder is that we only had to use them occasionally.

This Airgraph, dated 18th April, has a British postmark of 6th May. No postage was charged on them, but the Air Mail Letter Card, our normal means of communication with home, had postage of 4 annas (4 1/2p) until February 1945, when letters became free until our leaving India.

29th April

Not unexpectedly, 'C' Company were finding that any attempt to get near the forward edge of their plateau, so that they might fire down onto the Japs, was met by a shower of grenades or those larger ones, projected from the grenade discharger; a pattern of life that was to continue. Of necessity, they and 'A' established head cover to their positions.

On this day there was a profound change for the worse at 'A' Company. An enemy 75mm-gun on what was known as Treasury Hill, the first hill away to the north east, commenced ranging on them from about 600 yards. Also, during the night, they were subjected to a number of probing attacks which they repelled with grenades.

Major Geoffry White came onto our hill, having been instructed to hand over Picquet Hill to Captain Pryke Howard.

30th April

'B' and 'D' Companies, under Pryke Howard, together with 45 of our M.T. personnel, also joined us on the hill and, by so doing, relieved two companies of the Royal Berks. After a certain amount of juggling of positions, 'D' settled into the area to the right of 'C' Company. There they were more or less behind the battered remains of the corrugated iron buildings and a large steel water tank, long since too punctured to hold water, but now suspected of housing at least one sniper. Our mortars remained on Picquet Hill, being well sited for providing covering fire.

There was a worrying increase in the sniping of 'A' Company and the 75mm gun fired during the morning and the evening. It was on this day that they had a most welcome addition, a gunner F.O.O., one who I believe was a Sikh and thus, presumably, directing the guns of 161 Brigade. Tragically, his guns were short of ammunition and unable to blast the '75' out of existence. I have a note that the 3.7 howitzers of our division were so short of shells that they were silent for days on end.

Fortunately 'A' Company had a quiet night.

1st May

This May Day was not one for celebration although the Durhams might have thought so, for it was when the Welch Fusiliers took over from them. Their exhausted survivors would have been more than thankful to be departing after a series of battles, as terrible as any endured throughout the earlier siege. Bloody affairs in which they and the Japs had fought hand-to hand.

Further attempts to get a tank to the assistance of 'A' Company, then enduring their fourth day in isolation, had failed. Partial alleviation did however arrive when 11 Platoon of 'B' Company made their way up the road, under the protective fire and smoke laid down by our artillery and mortars, and reinforced their dwindling numbers. They were just in time. During the day Japanese guns had inflicted more casualties. Then at 1800 hrs a gun opened up, presumably the one on Treasury Hill, and devastated ten positions on their north flank. It also hit Company HQ, killing and wounding a number who were there, Company Sergeant-Major Downton being one of those killed. That shelling also destroyed the wireless set. By 1900 hrs there had been a reorganisation of the defences, enabling that north flank to be held by Bren-guns sited at each end and, in its centre, Lieutenant Prebble and three men.

At 2300 hrs, there appeared out of the darkness beyond our Command Post, Corporal Mansfield of the Signals Platoon and two companions; somehow they had got through to us from 'A' Company. They carried a communication from John Bowles to the C.O. It reported their heavy casualties and requested permission to withdraw as, in John's opinion, no useful purpose would be achieved by remaining. Jock McNaught 'phoned the brigadier but was told, after Brigadier Shapland had consulted with General Grover, that the position had to be held. Accordingly, the decision was made that 'B' Company would relieve 'A' during the day that was then commencing. Corporal Mansfield volunteered to return with the message and later set off, accompanied by two signallers and a replacement wireless set.

These were moments of great emotion, ones in which we had had confirmation of what we had feared; the virtual destruction of 'A' Company. And the agony and the suffering was to continue.

For John and his men it was one more never-ending night of harassment, by an active enemy sensing how fragile were the undermanned defences that, against the odds, held him at bay.

2nd May

Our gunners, as if to compensate for past shortages, were generous with their covering fire and the changeover of the companies took place with shells falling as close as 25 yards from our positions. Thus Alan Watts and the remaining two platoons of his company joined the advance one of yesterday. A task completed by 1030 hrs and, as on the preceding day, our enemy chose not to interfere. Later we paused to watch and stand in silence as John led two officers and 29 'A' Company men still capable of walking, so slowly, up the hill. Our eyes searched for familiar faces amongst men so battle weary as to be scarcely recognizable.

Such had been their bravery that John was able to prepare a list of 15 names, worthy of recognition. They had to remain with us for a couple of days, then they were away to Dimapur and a rest.

'B' Company were grenaded during the day and then, at 1845 hrs, the '75' put three rounds into their position, the final one being a direct hit on their HQ. Seven were killed and eight wounded, one of the dead was Company Sergeant-Major Draper.

It is said that this gun, which had been and was to continue firing over 'open sights', was concealed in a pit from which it was hauled up a ramp and, having fired, was lowered down again. Hence our inability to eliminate it.

3rd May

On this day it was falsely reported that the dive-bombing of Treasury Hill, by Vultee Vengeance planes, had driven the Japanese from it. At best they made no more than a temporary evacuation. 5 Brigade were in action to the north of Kohima and with them was 33 Brigade of the 7th Indian Division, newly arrived from the Arakan. They were to advance south on our left flank. At that time 4 Brigade was some 2,000 feet above us, on their right hook. They were having an appalling time in jungle so dense that the sun never penetrated and which really did stink. It was where dampness was perpetual and the vegetation was coated in a fungus. In this they had to exist and fight. And to do so always upwards, on slopes as severe as those in the Zubza Valley (at times they had to provide handrails), and do battle with an expectant and waiting enemy.

Our crazy situation on the hill was such that few knew where other units were or even who they were, unless in close contact. Not only was it unwise to move about, but there were outspoken objections to being visited, as movement invariably drew fire from the Japs.

4th May

Our friends of the 149th Regiment, Royal Armoured Corps, decided on another attempt at getting a tank up to the bungalow; at last all went well and a Grant, with Jock Murrills inside as a volunteer guide to the enemy positions and those of ours which he had left only two days before, reached the D.C.'s garden. Shielded by and under the covering fire of the tank, 10 Platoon with the Company 2 I/C, Captain Dick Purser leading, leapt from their trenches. Charging forward and up the slope of the terraced garden, Dick and the platoon entered the bungalow and killed five Japs. However, after firing the remains of the building, they were forced to withdraw with the heavy loss of six killed and four wounded. Even with the protection of the tank the ground outside our position was a deadly place, swept as it was by fire from the bunkers in the bank below the tennis court. If you had to cross it your only shelter was in shell holes, little more than places in which to get your wind, before another dash for cover.

Dick Purser, who was alone amongst the officers at Bhiwandi in building a tree-top machan, in the hope of shooting a 'big cat' and in which he failed, was getting bigger game. Before first light he would take up a suitable position and shoot at least one Jap before standing-down. And as killing Japs was what we had to do if we were to survive, that was an excellent thing. Dick, who became much admired for his bravery and disregard for personal safety, had been with us from Selby, as had Stanley Prebble and both were true (and self-effacing) Dorsets. The rather ancient (in the eyes of his fellow subalterns) 'Preb' who seemed to come and go more than most, but unlike some was around when needed – as then, was universally liked. His thoughts during those long night hours with 'A' Company were perhaps on his very different soldiering in 1942, when he was ADC to the Governor of Bombay Presidency.

That lone tank which we had imagined as so effective in slaughtering Japs had to get out for, like 'B' Company, it was vulnerable to fire from bunkers at a higher level and could only operate with its hatches closed.

At 1600 hrs 'B' came under renewed fire from the Jap gun and amongst the wounded was Alan Watts, Dick Purser then taking over command. Alan was evacuated and was not to be seen again.

Looking at a letter to my mother, written on that fourth day of May, I read that I was 'perfectly fit and well, if a trifle untidy in appearance, for we are in our ninth day without a wash or shave and have not undressed for nearly a month.' Untidy hardly describes our appearance – unwashed and unshaven faces above filthy clothing, made worse by the smell. It would have been about then that Joe arranged for everyone to make one visit to his R.A.P., so that feet might be immersed in a bowl of disinfectant, probably potassium permanganate. A moment of blessed relief!

We were beginning to experience the mixed blessing of rain, for the monsoon was approaching and preliminary showers were falling. Then we had a few hours of rain and, with the aid of a tarpaulin, some of us collected enough with which to wash and, later, to shave. Subsequent showers provided further opportunities for a wash and shave every two days or so. Throughout the siege water had been a problem and, until the rains, was strictly rationed to one pint, or so, each day for all purposes. Much came from a source near the road, access to which was a chancy business and, such was our need, some arrived by air.

5th May

As on the previous day a tank climbed up to 'B' Company, then to be joined by Dick and 11 Platoon. All that is known is that they claimed to have inflicted 11 casualties at a cost, to them, of two killed and one wounded.

6th May

For the third day a tank operated in the area of the bungalow and was able to claim the destruction of some bunkers. Up on the hill routine was enlivened by artillery concentrations on the enemy and dive-bombing was directed at the small adjacent hill, Kuki Picquet. The latter was so close that we were ordered to take to our trenches. Good advice, for one of the Hurribombers deposited two bombs on Brigade HQ; thankfully no one was hit.

During this period the Welch Fusiliers, who were behind us and thus facing south, were having an equally rotten time. Their outlook was not over falling ground as was ours but along the spine, a wasteland from earlier fighting back to early April, when the Royal West Kents and others were forced back by overwhelming numbers. To their front was that small hill, Kuki Picquet, against which they directed two attacks, first descending into a deep gulley and then climbing the far side. There they received heavy casualties from a concealed machine-gun and achieved nothing.

Such attacks and those in which we were involved counted for little by those in distant offices, and General Grover was being harassed with more accusations that his division was falling badly behind schedule. To these he countered that he was fast running out of troops. A problem that was about to be indirectly lessened by the reinforcement, at Kohima, of the 7th Indian Division, under Major-General Frank Messervy, whose 33 Brigade had arrived earlier. More directly, Indian units were taking up positions within our perimeter.

The pre-monsoon rains, in this area of a high rainfall, were becoming frequent and this night a particularly severe storm caused the collapse of a number of our trenches. These included that of the 'I' Section, who escaped as the roof fell and buried their kit. 'C' Company had a number fall in, including one in which two men were buried. Michael called out his company and they commenced an urgent rescue dig, only to be fired on by an Indian unit behind them. By the time these Indians could be made to stop, the men were dead. Skilled helpers in that rescue attempt were a couple of volunteer ex-miners from the Welch Fusilers.

Our contacts with the Indians seemed fated, we experiencing then as at Zubza wild uncontrolled night firing by men who should not have been in a forward position.

That afternoon about 20 fighter aircraft had appeared and began circling above us. Not suspecting that they were other than ours, I was idly watching their manoeuvres through the tree tops when I spotted their red roundels. After that aircraft recognition course, I should have instantly realised that Oscars, which these planes were, while not all that unlike the Hurricane which I took them to be, had radial engines. Someone gave the alarm and we disappeared below ground, only too aware of what our planes could do in similar circumstances.

Luckily for us they decided to bomb Kohima's line of communication and chose to do so in the vicinity of Zubza, doing remarkably little damage. By then we were above ground and, those who could, watched the proceedings. We were impressed by the effective anti-aircraft fire put up by 2 Div's Bofors guns, sited in that open ground where we had been, now an all-important advance admin base. There 'B' Echelon, the home of quartermasters and their staffs, worked to supply us, and it was the base for our M.T.

It was said that the 2nd Division's transport, at the regulation spacing between vehicles, would extend over 150 miles of road. It is, therefore, not difficult to imagine the congestion on the forty-odd miles back to Dimapur for, though there were only essential vehicles in use, there was more than our division at the end of the supply line. But for the shortage of howitzer ammunition, and that was not a local fault, we were provided with the essentials for living and for doing battle. After Kohima and later, when we were deep into Burma, the excellence of our administration, as much as anything, made victory possible.

7th May

After five long days on the spur, 'B' Company's casualties matched those of 'A' and they too had to be brought out; although such was our diminished strength that another company could not be spared. Accordingly 16 Platoon of 'D' Company, under Lieutenant Lionel Halahan, was brought up to full strength and carried out the relief. Inexplicably, the Japs, apparently tiring of their attacks and failing to appreciate how deadly they had been, left them alone throughout their occupation of this so vulnerable a position. There they remained until the final battle.

Lionel, generally known as 'Hal', must have marvelled at his luck. He was another adopted Dorset from our days in England, but a tendency to be 'bolshie' did not endear him to commanding officers, which was a pity for he served the battalion well. Hal was an English volunteer from the Argentine who could boast of having served in their army. To our regret, but for a glimpse in London just after the war, no one has seen him since, so he probably returned to South America.

8th – 10th May

When the surviving few of 'B' Company came back onto the hill they took up a position on our right flank, where they overlooked the road to Imphal, and they also swung round to the south so that they were, in part, to our rear. Our losses made a shuffling of appointments necessary, one being the transfer of Graeme Gordon-Wright from adjutant to the command of 'B' Company, his job going to Lieutenant Colin Doran. Colin had joined us as recently as February, when his request that he should desert his staff appointment at division in favour of some real soldiering had been granted, and he had been a platoon commander in 'D' Company. To the surprise of nobody, John O'Driscoll had been wounded and the command of the Guerillas was passed to Dick Purser, and Pryke Howard took over the command of 'C' Company.

As might be expected we were being increasingly plagued by flies, mostly bluebottles. They swarmed over everything. Blankets, when spread on the ground to air, became covered, and the knowledge that they had hatched from maggots infesting our own and the enemy dead made them so much more revolting. Rats too were multiplying in this place where there was so much to feed on. Most of the dead lay out in the open, where they had fallen, and there they had to remain until the battle ended.

'A' and 'B' Companies had been so confined within their defensive positions that some of their dead had to be buried within them; the stark horror of that, with shells continuing to blow those trenches apart, can be imagined. And everywhere we were within the shattered remains of trees, standing like skeletons over our rounded and, in parts, steeply sloping spur. The stony ground had become devoid of living vegetation and was a brown wasteland, featureless but for the trenches, sheltering under their crude, earth-covered roofs. No wonder that senior officers with experience of the First World War said that Kohima was like that ghastly field of battle – The Somme in 1916. It was being said that it was unwise to go downwind of Garrison Hill and, with so many unburied bodies, that is understandable. And we, who had the good fortune to be still on our feet, also stank in our unwashed state; made worse by sweat-soaked, mud-encrusted and, for some, blood-caked clothing. We had become so accustomed to our condition that personal odour was of little consequence, but how we did long for a bath!

For the many who suffered the debilitating and sheer bloody awfulness of perpetual diarrhoea, it was all so very much worse. One carried on and drew some comfort from our static situation.

For what was to be our final week on the hill, the 'I' Section had an observation post from which we were able to take offensive action. Following the felling of a tree or trees by the Indian unit behind 'C' Company, a portion of the spur appeared in view and, initially, one of the Guerilla Platoon was sited there with a sniper's rifle. At about then a Bren-gun was found under the body of a Japanese officer who had been carrying it, when leading an attack up a gulley on our east flank. That gun was given to us for use in this position, which we then took over. Being able to borrow a telescope from the gunners and tying it onto the gun so that it was aligned with the sights, I converted it into an effective weapon for sniping. Being more than keen to get it into immediate use we gave the Bren a quick clean and set it up. The gun fired down the slope into enemy territory beyond 'C' and in clear view was a section of trench with open ground beyond. The first shot was at a Jap who obliged by climbing out of the trench, but the gun jammed. Cursing our luck, we did what we should have done before and stripped a very filthy weapon, right down. Taking it in turn on a daily rota, we had the satisfaction of shooting at many of the enemy, particularly in the open ground. We claimed seven killed out of some 20 shot at; at last we were making a positive contribution.

Away behind us and further up the hill, in that broken ground of Kuki Picquet and Jail Hill, names that meant nothing to us, but which had been fought over from the earliest days, Jap bunkers continued to withstand repeated attacks and shelling. There, the wearing down of the enemy continued, with even more vigour. That we remained absorbed in our own tasks and took so little notice of our friends, was a sure reflection of our confidence in them; at no time did we fear for what might happen on the long southern flank.

Following monumental efforts by the sappers a self-propelled flame-thrower, known as a 'Wasp', had been got up to us and was sitting on the plateau above the tennis court. Having got it there, those whose responsibility it was decided that it would be suicidal to drive it forward to where it could be used. Once there it would be above the 'C' Company trenches which, if things went wrong as they might well do, in so hazardous a place, would be as much at risk as the Japs below.

11th May

To our amazement a pair of B.B.C. War Correspondents arrived and, as with the Nagas at Zubza, they were passed to the 'I' Section. We did our best to describe our confused and confusing situation and each had a look at the Jap trench through our telescope. They probably departed disappointed, for the Japs were keeping their heads down and there was no cause for the Bren to be fired.

Having civilians on our besieged hill did make us wonder a bit. We looked upon ourselves as marooned in a dangerous and hostile world, one that was the exclusive province of soldiers and although we obviously had a 'back door', with things coming in and casualties and the like going out, it was not for us and was ignored. That was sound psychology, for resolve could have been weakened had we contemplated an emergency exit. Visits from senior officers were to be expected, but they were rare. But for General Grover, who looked in at our R.A.P. at least twice and who did his best to see something of the spur, we only remember the welcome figure of George Wood, now Brigadier General Staff, at 33 Corps. Thoughts must have flooded his mind as to how things might have been had he remained O.C. 2 Dorset.

Another new face was that of P.J. (Peter) Feeney, posted to us from Divisional HQ, where he had been a Staff Captain, now to become 2 I/C of 'B' Company. Peter was a stockbroker whose keen brain had been sharpened (or otherwise) at the Staff College, Quetta. He would have liked to have succeeded Colin as adjutant, a job for which he was well fitted, though I doubt that he would have suited Geoffry, when he became C.O. It was Graeme that he was to succeed, taking command of the company and leading it through highly dangerous times.

12th May

In the very early hours Snagger Highett, together with Sergeant Spiller and 12 men, accompanied by four sappers under a sapper officer, set forth to lay anti-personnel mines in the area to the east of the road behind the D.C.'s bungalow. Venturing into enemy territory at night was always a suicidal and nerve-racking undertaking and this patrol was more than usually chancy, the territory into which they were going being the Jap's only remaining approach to their positions on the spur. Snagger would have found that it was not possible to negotiate the steep slopes, in the silence needed to maintain surprise. On halting near their objective, they found that their presence had been discovered by some Japanese who were following them – a dicey moment. Most leaders would have decided that they had had enough; however their extra numbers disappeared, and Snagger took his patrol down into the low ground, a place where the road was 30 feet above them. Then, what has been described as 'a strong force of Japs' appeared, and ran down onto them. With surprise lost and any hope of laying the mines gone, they scrambled out and by some miracle were all in our lines by 0200 hrs.

On this day we lost David 'Dixie' Deane, killed by a sniper. Dixie was one of our diminishing band of old Dorsets and was valued for that, but more so because we liked him. As Motor Transport Officer he had just led our vehicles across India and through to Dimapur, only to be shot almost on arrival. We were later to find brilliantly camouflaged sniper positions, high in the trees from where a marksman could fire down into what were believed to be safe areas.

A few days earlier Clive Chettle had been ordered to leave his Carrier Platoon and assume command of 'D' Company, an appointment which he was to hold throughout our time in Burma. His company position is the only one of which I have any memory; that no more than an impression of trenches (into which you quickly leapt) in an open and battered patch of bare earth. To the front and left falling ground held our enemies and to the right the battered iron huts remained a hunting ground for them. Those snipers thought to be in the water tank were believed to have out-smarted us, by concealing themselves below it.

Experience had convinced us that the spur could only be taken by an attack on it from where we were and, were we not to be decimated, we must have tank support. To that end, sappers had been making a route up through and beyond the hospital ruins.

During this day a Grant tank climbed up to us and by evening was safely parked, and camouflaged. Its commander, Sergeant Waterhouse, attended the conference that night, during which it was made clear that our capture of the spur depended on his ability to get his tank down the terrace and onto the tennis court. Brigadier Shapland emphasized that the drop was about ten feet and that, although the face had originally sloped, it might now, due to the bunkers formed at its base, be vertical. If, when he reached the top, he found that it was so, he need not proceed. He replied that a sheer drop would not deter him and that, if necessary, he would go over and chance landing the right way up. With him would be Snagger, as his guide and for wireless liaison with us.

Away to the north, Brigadier Hawkins had been seriously injured and command of 5 Brigade was to pass to a new brigadier – Michael West (Brigadier Michael Alston-Roberts-West). Also, at about this time, Tony Bridge took over as Brigade Major, his predecessor Ian Thorburn having been killed during the fighting at Naga Village.

13th May

At 1000 hrs the tank advanced to the edge, found that the terrace face was not vertical and safely reached the tennis court. With us in our O.P. and soon at a better vantage point, were Colonel McNaught and Geoffry, plus the two B.B.C. men, one of whom was Richard Sharpe, a well known personality. Four days later, it was his report on the day's work that was broadcast after the 9 o'clock news, on the B.B.C. Home Service. Soon we could see the tank on the court, within drifting smoke, so that we saw it and occasional figures only indistinctly; those figures moving with an unexpected lack of haste denoting that the enemy there, at least, had been overwhelmed.

When it was all over, Snagger told of how he had watched through a periscope as the tank's 75mm gun blasted away at the bunkers; ones that until then had been impregnable. From inside, those capable of doing so fled to the open air, only to be shot down by the tank's machine-guns, or blasted by exploding shells.

The two platoons of 'D' Company that remained after Halahan's relief of 'B' waited under Clive in readiness to follow the tank and, within minutes, they were doing so. Those indistinct figures were those of the leading platoon under Sergeant Given and, as the smoke lessened, we watched him use the telephone, carried at the rear of the tank, to speak to its commander within. Then the news came through that the whole company was there and meeting with very little opposition.

That the tide had dramatically turned, became evident when there were shouts – 'The Japs are getting out'! We moved to where we could look out to the east and over the Imphal Road, and there they were – running from battle. Not in any controlled groups but in ones and twos, frightened men wanting to save their skins. Quite incredible! The seemingly fearless enemy had had enough. Close by was Sergeant Marlow. He had been watching the road in the area of yesterday's patrol and, as the flight over what until now had been safe ground increased, he used his rifle until it became too hot to hold.

During this critical and momentous phase, in which so much had happened, I had become increasingly frustrated at being, yet again, a spectator. Eventually I persuaded Jock McNaught to release me and, together with two of the section, I went down to the plateau. There Clive was giving out orders for the destruction of a number of bunkers, on which pole-charges were to be used. Those charges being ten pounds of ammonal on a fuse reduced to three seconds. To my dismay he would not let me help and it was he and Russell who did the majority; they heaving the explosive through the firing slits and well into the interior, before activating them. When it was all over Clive told me that he had primed himself with rum and that he had been doing a lot of mad things: as a result of which the long-suffering Russell had said, "You bloody drunken idiot, you'll get us both killed if you're not careful." That Russell had some justification was proven when Corporal Siggins was killed while pole-charging one of those bunkers.

By 1115 hrs we had obtained the occupation of all the enemy territory on the spur, but the blasting of bunkers continued. 'B' Company had been standing by in reserve and it was one of their sections that at midday, under Sergeant Fox, helped in clearing a particularly difficult bunker, one on which a massive 25 lbs of annomal was used for the pole-charges.

Thanks to Sergeant Waterhouse and his crew, our casualties had been one dead and four wounded, a fraction of what had been dreaded.

There was a delay and then all who could went to see the place for which so many had suffered, or had given their lives. Everywhere there was the debris of war, bodies of friend and foe, shattered and unrecognizable buildings, bunkers and trenches, discarded weapons and equipment, and crumpled corrugated iron. The ground, where not dug up for defences, was broken by shell bursts, so that few natural or original features remained unchanged. We found one or two steps where there had been a flight to a terrace. As everywhere, trees were reduced to little more than torn and broken stumps. There was no life, it was a place of desolation and very horrible. By the pile of wreckage that was the bungalow, out of which rose a stone chimney stack and a piece or two of walling, there were bodies, some much as they fell in that first attack, a long 17 days ago. Now Gus was to have the grim task of identification and the removal of one of the two identity discs worn by all of us, on a cord around the neck. And the Pioneer Platoon began the burials.

Garden and bungalow after the battle.

The 'I' Section set about collecting documents, for which a start was made within the bunkers at the east end of the tennis court, some that had remained intact were of interest in themselves. Being at the base of the high bank they went in horizontally and did so for such a distance as to leave daylight behind. We progressed on hands and knees, through a warren of narrow and, for us, all too shallow passages. We were thankful to return to the open air.

We were soon the possessors of a mass of literature, a fair proportion of which were military training manuals. Then and later, we were amazed to find that the Japs seemed to be as keen on having army bumf with them as we were at leaving it behind.

During the afternoon 'C' and 'D' Companies moved forward to the periphery of the spur and dug in, ready to defend the area against a counter-attack. Later the 75mm gun that had caused so much devastation opened fire, and all who were not needed to man positions were ordered away.

At dusk faint sounds were heard from one of the bunkers and it was partly opened, disclosing an officer and four men. As they gave no indication that they wished to come out and surrender, there was no alternative but to kill them where they were.

A particularly nauseous sight on a day when there were many, was the body of what could have been the officer commanding our enemies. He had squatted in an open space and, holding a grenade against his stomach, committed hari-kari.

Unknown to us the Japanese 31st Division had, by early May, all but exhausted its food and ammunition. Denied further supplies by reason of their isolation and the onset of the monsoon, their situation was by now so desperate that their commander, Lieutenant-General Sato, was preparing to do the unthinkable – withdraw. It would commence at the end of the month, behind a rearguard. One with which we were to do battle.

14th May

After a quiet night there was a general gravitation to the spur, where an abnormal silence prevailed, much as is experienced after a great storm and for the first time people stood upright and greeted one another.

We began to appreciate that a significant victory had been achieved, but fighting continued to the north of Kohima where 5 Brigade, under their new brigadier, had some distance to go before their task was done. And 4 Brigade, after a terrible time within those jungle clad slopes of Mount Japvo, were finding determined resistance from bunkers to our south and by the Imphal road. There, operating with Indian units displaying that bravery and discipline which few could match, the brigade had lost their commander – Brigadier 'Willie' Goschen of the Grenadier Guards who, in an endeavour to save his injured orderly, was himself killed.

The 'I' Section decided to excavate a bunker at the back of the tennis court and set to with pick and shovel in an explosion of energy seldom seen; but which we soon found was no match for Japanese construction and the project had to be abandoned. However, we collected further documents and it could have been then that we made a significant find – maps produced by the Survey of India, overprinted in Japanese, one being of Calcutta. One can imagine these and others like them, being purchased by Japanese or their agents in India, prior to the war. These were not just part of the customary Japanese bumf. Were these front line troops expecting to reach so far into India? To my considerable regret, I passed all these maps over to brigade; I should have retained at least one.

15th May

The security of Garrison Hill was materially improved when the 4th/1st Gurkhas of 7 Div. took occupation of Treasury Hill, in an operation that had commenced the day before and to which there had been only token opposition. While this was in progress Halahan decided to look at some abandoned enemy positions near Treasury Hill, and there he shot a Jap he found hiding in a fox-hole. Pulling him out, he sent him off en-route to a P.O.W. cage. This was our first prisoner.

This was an important day for us, the fortunate survivors, for it was when we packed up. For most, a simple task when all you had was always within arms reach. It was also the day of reunion with our Mortar Platoon, whose invaluable covering fire had come from outside our lines.

We had no idea how many Japanese had been killed and injured, or that from this time on it was to be they who would be in retreat, for this was the turning point in our war. We now loathed the Japanese as did all who fought them. As expected they were a formidable and skilled enemy, with differences in temperament that had to be learned. Their use of bunkers in contrast to our preference for being in the open, was one. And so much in contrast to our thinking, was their belief that death on the battlefield was a sure entry to paradise.

Before leaving Garrison Hill I pause to think of Corporal Softly and the many like him. Of Lieutenant Mayer, leading his platoon, of the sapper who drove the bulldozer and of Sergeant Waterhouse, whose bravery in driving his tank over the ten foot drop made that final day possible. I think of the decimated 'A' Company and of the incomparable 8 Platoon. Of Jock Murrills (one of the few who survives) John Bowles and 'Preb'. I remember Lance-Corporal Smart of the 'I' Section, who on the 27th had picked up a Bren-gun and fired it without regard to his own safety, until shot down and killed. Also buried there among his pals is Private Dudman who, a little over a year before, got lost on the night exercise at Juhu.

The move back in trucks, driven by Indians as before, occupied all the latter part of the day. A move that was marred by the injury of 16 men, whose truck went off the road soon after leaving Kohima. However the rest of us moved into a tented camp at Dimapur and there removed our clothing for the first time in five weeks. I remember the sensual delight of sitting in my canvas mini-bath and allowing warm water to dissolve the accumulation of sweat and grime. Then to put on clean clothes was to be rejuvenated and what a tonic it was to have a hat that was not a steel one. Those delights to be followed by an undisturbed sleep, stretched out and relaxed.

16th – 20th May

The pleasure of our first day was blighted when we found that the kit we had left behind and which contained items that were irreplaceable had been rifled, some losing all that they valued. I was lucky, for although someone had been through my things, the only item taken that I valued was my fountain-pen.

The opportunity to relax was all-important and being again in an area of high humidity, there was no incentive to be energetic.

The rest period of four days was extended to seven, which was no more than adequate if we were to unwind and recover after so appalling an experience.

Recovery was helped by an Elsie and Doris Walters concert on the first night. Letter writing flourished and, for some, bridge continued far into the night. We were having a hot bath every day, and those unfamiliar with the ways of an army in the field might wonder how thousands of men are bathed, even though that number is reduced to batches of a hundred or so. At times such as this a bath company would arrive, complete with machines for heating water and a generous supply of baths. These, for us, were oil drums halved longitudinally, no taps or plug-holes of course, but they did their job and men could even be heard singing in them.

On the 19th we paraded for an open air Memorial Service, there to pay tribute to lost comrades as we stood, with the minimum of formality, within our companies. The name of each of the 80 killed was read in what seemed to be a never-ending succession of names, our emotions intensified when, amongst those whose names meant little, there were those whose loss meant a great deal.

Also on this day, thankfully unknown to us, the continuing threat to our division took the form of a notification to our corps commander from General Sir George Giffard that so great was the shortage of manpower, that the 2nd Division might have to be disbanded to provide drafts for other British units in 14th Army. General Stopford counter-attacked with a memo setting out how we could receive reinforcements.

To our many battle casualties had to be added those who had succumbed to sickness, in all a sufficiently large total to cause 'A' Company, with the smallest number on parade, to be temporarily disbanded and the other companies to have their strengths slightly improved as a result. The similarly diminished Guerilla Platoon had its numbers made good with reinforcements from HQ Company and Dick Purser was confirmed as their commander. Pryke Howard was again shifted, returning to HQ Company and taking command. And our Motor Transport was reorganised on the much reduced basis of 8 jeeps, 8 15-cwt trucks and 7 carriers.

It was after four days in this camp that Joe decided to pack me off to hospital, something of a shock and accepted with mixed feelings, particularly as I had not been a hospital patient and wondered what kind of a place it would be in this remote corner of India.

21st – 26th May

Arriving at the Casualty Clearing Station a mile away, I joined a crowded dysentery ward which, in common with the other buildings, was of native construction – jungle timbers clad; with woven matting and thatch. My recollection is of a dim interior, lighted by pressure lamps at night and having the customary rows of beds, actually they were charpoys, along each long side. This was my home for two uneventful days while we waited for the hospital train, which we learned had been involved in an accident. This seemed to be a regular occurrence, the Americans hustling the trains along at speeds well in excess of those for which the line had been designed, the many bends being their downfall. However it did arrive and though memory grows dim after more than 40 years, my recollection is of entering that immaculate train; going from the pre-dawn darkness into brilliant electric lighting in almost a state of shock, so great was the contrast. I can still see the white ceiling, the whiter than white sheets and the walls in that so familiar pale green of the period – eau-de-nil. Whether that colour resembled the water of the River Nile, or not, was immaterial, what made it so important was that this was something from home – a bit of England, and the train was wonderful. Such were its standards that I had barely settled myself between the sheets when a nurse arrived with a whisky. The journey to Gauhati was completed without accident in just over 24 hours. Detraining after breakfast, we were taken in ambulances to the Indian General Hospital, where we promptly sat down to another breakfast. There I remained for another 24 hours, saw a film in the evening and next morning set off, again in an ambulance, but now for Shillong the capital of Assam. A fine hill station at an altitude of 5-6,000 feet.

This 70-mile journey concluded with a 40-mile gradient on a road so restricted for width that one-way traffic was enforced by gates, movement between them being either up or down during set periods of the day. The military hospital was full and I was passed on to the Welsh Mission Hospital; a permanent civilian hospital which was accommodating up to 70 army officers. Single bed wards now contained four, which was a crush but no matter, we were so very fortunate to be there. We had a real bed (what luxury) and a room with a view – and what a view! One of distant mountains seen across a wide valley toward which the lawn outside our verandah fell away.

Matron, sisters and doctors were British and they controlled a staff recruited from the local Khasi tribe. This was a Methodist Mission, providing an essential service to the community and which trained Christian girls as nurses – and excellent they all were.

Back at the battalion things had been happening, for on the 23rd, at the end of their seven day break, they had departed from Dimapur and had reached what was known as Two Tree Hill, west of the Imphal road. This was beyond Garrison Hill and they now faced south with 5 Brigade, which they had rejoined.

27th May – 22nd June at Shillong

Life settled into the more than reasonable routine of a chota hazari of tea and a slice of bread and butter at 0600 hrs, preceding the doctor's visit and breakfast. Then there was a morning cup of tea, and lunch at about 1300 hrs. Tea proper was at 1600 hrs and dinner at 1900 hrs. The day ended with yet another cup of tea and lights out at 2130 hrs. All this did not deter the mobile ones from a mid-morning visit to a café, run by voluntary workers for local charities. This was so much like home, of which we had further reminders in the pine woods, the occasional showers of rain and the crisp air.

In between the good times there was treatment and how well I remember the stomach pump. To swallow the metal nozzle and follow up with yards of red rubber tubing was quite an accomplishment. And, typically, I was perplexing my doctor with renewed gippy tummy and nights with a high temperature. To get fit, those who could were out and about on foot in our small world, set so high in the hills. There was much of interest in the place itself and from certain viewpoints, that we soon discovered, one could look down for hundreds of feet over ravines. They opened the view and were visually exciting with their waterfalls dropping almost sheer through the coniferous woods which isolated us from the familiar jungle and paddy, so many more hundreds of feet lower still.

During all this time I had received no news of the battalion and then a letter arrived from Colin Doran, writing as Adjutant and telling of the deaths of the three captains – Morice, Davies and Purser. He continued by asking when I might be returning. It could truly be said that anyone voluntarily leaving a life of such care and comfort as provided at that 'hospice', for the squalor and horrors of battle, needed to have his head examined and I would be the first to agree. That letter, however, changed everything. No longer could I enjoy these indulgences and I arranged with matron my discharge and return journey.

Horrendous tales circulated in the mess about such returns, which not only took an age due to their difficult nature, but which included the hazard of being grabbed en route by undesirable units desperate for new blood. There was also the lesser but more likely fate of languishing in a transit camp, from which no transport seemed to be going your way.

Having said goodbye to those always jolly nurses I joined a group to travel, by taxi, to Gauhati. A journey at headlong speed down that 40-mile incline and in the same manner to the transit camp, where we were to spend the night and which we were relieved to reach in one piece.

23rd – 25th June

I travelled by train to Dimapur, reaching that transit camp in the late evening, after the time for obtaining a place on the daily officers' truck up the Imphal road the next morning. Many people had a rotten war and I find it difficult to imagine one much worse than staffing a transit camp, of which there were so many and thousands needed for their staffing. An unrewarding and obnoxious job anywhere, but so much more so when in a place such as Dimapur, with a bad climate and few redeeming features.

How great was my relief when, on the second morning, I travelled up the now familiar road into the clean mountain air – it was like returning home, as indeed I was. There at last were the Dorsets, to the right of the road near milestone 100 and thus a long way beyond Kohima. On such occasions one does not expect much of a welcome; they had endured hardship and danger while I had been in safety. My aim was to slot back into routine quickly and unobtrusively. Good old Preb had been acting for me and it was the easiest of things to take over from him.

CHAPTER FIVE

The Advance to Imphal

Before continuing to report on the battalion, last recorded as at Two Tree Hill, some mention has to be made of the fighting at Imphal which we, occupied as we were with our own situation, tended to forget.

Early in March the southernmost of the three Japanese divisions, their 33rd, had crossed the River Chindwin at Kalewa. They then advanced against the 17th Indian Division, doing so through Tiddim and along the Tiddim Road, on which a series of fierce battles ensued as 17 Div. carried out a planned withdrawal to defend the Imphal base. To their north the Japanese 15th Division attacked the 20th Indian Division who were on the Tamu – Palel – Imphal road, along which a similar fighting withdrawal occurred. That enemy division had a second line of advance, which enabled them to infill between their main thrust and their force at Kohima; their objectives being the large village of Ukhrul and the subsequent cutting of the Kohima – Imphal road. They were to engage elements of the 23rd Indian Division. By early April the 5th Indian Division, less its 161st Brigade at Kohima, had arrived by air and had reinforced a very much over-stretched garrison.

These bare facts suggest a preponderance of Indian Army over the Japanese, but the strengths of their divisions differed. A British or Indian division would have been under 15,000 officers and men, the Japanese could be as much as 22,000. Also with the enemy was the, so-called, 1st Indian National Army Division, a force that never met the expectations of the Japanese, for it was in the liberation of India from British rule that they were to be fully exploited.

For weeks, bitter fighting had raged around the vast base of Imphal; with a wealth of stores and two all-weather air-strips, it had a value that was even greater to the Japs than Kohima and Dimapur. At this time of late May, despite all non-essential personnel and 30,000 casualties having been flown out, the supply of the day-to-day essentials had become desperate; the planes although numbered in hundreds, were insufficient. Our advance and that of the 7th Division, had to relieve beleaguered Imphal as a matter of extreme urgency.

23rd – 28th May

At Two Tree Hill the Dorsets were something over 1,000 yards west of the Imphal road, deep into the jungle clad slopes of the Pulebadze ridge, to the north of Mount Japvo. From this position Garrison Hill was about 1,500 feet below and a mile away to the north east. 'B' Company was away on detachment up the mountain slope, further into the trees and must have wondered whether they would find their way out again. The battalion was fortunate in not having bumped into the Japs, known to be in the vicinity, but heavy rain made life a misery.

On the 28th they moved east and slightly south to take up positions on the road with the Worcesters, near milestone 48. Snagger was soon patrolling forward through the ground east of the road, 'C' and 'D' Companies then moving into the same area, leaving 'B' back in reserve. An advance to coincide with a parallel one by 4 Brigade, to our right. It was at that time that all our brigades (6 Brigade was to the right of 4) came up against well concealed and cunningly prepared trench positions, prepared by the enemy on the tops of the multitude of hills and spurs.

During the latter part of this day Michael Morice had gone forward with Company Sergeant-Major Keegan. They were together on a reverse slope studying enemy positions ahead, when Michael was killed by a shot in the back: one believed to have been fired by someone outside our battalion who, coming over a rise in the ground, mistook them for Japs.

This was a major tragedy and the killing of a young man for whom all had a great affection – one more for whom there could be no substitute. That night the battalion pulled back in a state of profound depression and a day or two later it returned to a rest area at Kohima.

The physical discomfort of a perpetual wetness made worse the dawning realisation that, from now on, we had to overcome determined Japs in prepared positions. A daunting task when we were a mere shadow of our normal selves, and three very under-strength companies could see themselves being asked to do those things for which four strong ones had been needed in the past.

3rd June

During the coming weeks there were a number of clashes with the enemy, the first of which, Dyer Hill, started on this day. This was no great geographical feature in a land of mountains, but it was a fine defensive position and the Japs were always good at exploiting such places. Little more than a bump, it sat on the extremity of a major spur from the Pulebadze ridge and was 1,500 yards to the east of the road. It shared that spur with the slightly larger Big Tree Hill, 600 yards to the west and thus further up the spur. Between these two features was a well named hillock – The Pimple. Counting contours from the stream on our approach side, Dyer Hill rises 1,000 feet and the Pimple and Big Tree Hill rise another 100. Thus they look down on to and over Dyer Hill. To the north, the east and the south the ground, after falling, rises in great jungle covered mountains, across which all progress had to be on foot and which at best was slow. But then that world was one of a seemingly perpetual and never-ending wetness, where to stand upright was difficult and any advance was a slithering and wearisome progression, which made a nonsense of any customary reckoning of miles that might be covered in the hour.

On this morning 5 Brigade set off again, moving south to clear the country east of the road, while 4 Brigade tackled the road and the known and anticipated road-blocks. To their right was 6 Brigade, flushing the enemy from the high ground west of the road, at heights in excess of 5,000 feet.

As the leading battalion in our brigade, we had been allocated the occupation of Dyer Hill, approached over two miles or more of difficult going, which initially crossed ground flanking the west side of Treasury Hill. Our objective was said to be clear of the enemy but was suspected by us as very probably anything but unoccupied. At 1030 hrs Snagger and half a dozen men from 'C' Company went forward to find out. Five and a quarter hours later, by which time the battalion was in the low ground to the north of the hill, the patrol rejoined them, Snagger reporting that the hill was clear but was under fire from Big Tree Hill. Later however, our leading company which was 'D', came under fire from Dyer Hill. Jock McNaught decided that, as it was not long before last light, he would close the three companies into a defensive position and there they were to remain – cold, wet and unfed. That night was later said to have been the most awful, weather-wise, of all the rotten nights during that period; one that was so wet that the trenches filled with water.

4th June

In the early hours Clive and his company climbed the hill again and at 0700 hrs they occupied vacated enemy positions. Our target was now Big Tree Hill, which had to be occupied if we were to remain on Dyer Hill.

At 0905 hrs, following ten minutes of shelling by our artillery, 'C' Company and the Guerilla Platoon under their two captains, Dave Davies (newly appointed as the company commander) and Dick Purser, commenced a combined assault on The Pimple, which had to be eliminated as an outpost to Big Tree Hill. On nearing the top 'C' was halted by fire from light machine-guns and by grenading coming from positions on a reverse slope, towards which Dick led his platoon in a left-flanking movement until they too were checked by the same fire, and took cover. Dave then tried to get around the opposite flank with one of his two platoons but, after a scrap in which they killed four Japs, they had to pull back, having been met by a hail of fire as they breasted the crest. Then and while withdrawing from that untenable position, a number of casualties occurred, one of whom was Private Collis, a stretcher-bearer, who had been shot in the stomach. After two attempts to rescue him failed, Dave went out, only to be killed as he knelt beside the dying Collis.

Away on the left, Dick was giving out orders when a Jap came out into the open and fired two shots, the first fatally wounding him in the head, his assailant then in turn shot by Sergeant Maule.

At 1155 hrs the C.O. ordered a general withdrawal under the protection of further shelling.

The loss of two of our best leaders in so short a time after the death of Michael, left us woefully short and in a state of shock. Dave and his great friend Michael had been around for so long that they were known to all and were universally liked and admired. Dick, the loner, was so reserved and so uncommunicative as to be barely known to anyone outside those he was commanding, but his outstanding qualities as a fighting soldier had gained him respect and admiration. All three had made a great contribution to the battalion and we were to be much the poorer without them and remained so.

The Camerons had come up and, taking the lead, they climbed that formidable hill, initially having better fortune than ourselves, for by then the enemy had vacated The Pimple. Turning their attention to Big Tree Hill they were met by heavy fire and found, just as we had, that it was more than ever difficult to endure when on steep and slippery grass slopes in torrential rain.

During this period Joe Chamberlin was lower down the hill and he recounts the following:

> We shared the hill for a while with the Camerons – never a dull experience. I found myself alongside Peter Barkley, their M.O., a gentle and dreamy Edinburgh man. With rain cascading off his tin hat and Jap guns getting the range, he looked across and said "It's a verrry beautiful view from here." A while later there were shouts of 'get out of the bloody way' as four Jock stretcher-bearers charged urgently down the slope with Angus Douglas dying from a bullet wound in the neck. Their medical sergeant Jock McEvoy said to Angus, "I'm afraid I've only whisky in ma water-bottle." Angus looked pleased and closed an eye in a wink and took a glorious last dram.

Major Douglas was their Second-in-Command and during this engagement had been commanding their leading company. He was described as a small dapper man, with Highland courtesy, one who was immensely popular and whose death brought a tremendous melancholy.

But no Highland warrior could have wanted a better way in which to die – shot while leading his men under appalling conditions and, a few last moments, among friends.

Another warrior to die that day was Private Lawrence Hobby, one of the three Hobby brothers who served so splendidly in our 'C' Company and who, to spread their risk, had been distributed within its three platoons. We had been lucky in having these true men of Dorset. Born on a farm at Lytchett Minster, midway between Poole and Dorchester, they had 'pulled strings' to be in the same battalion.

Snagger Highett brought 'C' Company out of action and assumed command, their fourth commander in a few weeks. Snagger, who understandably prefers his proper name of Lintorn, must have been the leader of more patrols than any other, and favoured in that he was to suffer nothing worse than wounding. His reputation for involvement in hazardous enterprises was such that it was said amongst the men – "go out with Snagger and you'll get your bloody head blown off"; or "he's sure to get in a fight" and "mad as a March hare". Doubtless there were others.

Our losses on that hill of five dead and 14 injured further sapped our strength and we were well aware that there were more to come. But our efforts had not been in vain for we had made the Camerons' lot easier, and they were able to clear Big Tree Hill in 24 hours. Those skirmishes had shown that, even where so much favoured defence, the Japs were not always ready to fight to the last man.

5th June

On that morning a 'B' Company platoon under the recently promoted Sergeant Mansfield, was dispatched to have a look at the village of Pfuchama, a mile away in a straight line. There are no straight lines in the Naga Hills and for them the path dropped steeply and wound its way along, before a final climb of 1,300 feet to the top-most point of the ridge, on which is the village. Pfuchama sits at the north end of a spine running away south west to the road and the village of Phesama, a distance in excess of a mile. On a clear day the views would be stupendous, over ground falling on three sides to streams and then rising in a succession of mountains where, at that time, the only man-made intrusions (excepting ourselves and the Japs) were timber huts.

The village was reported clear and the platoon dug in. At noon a heavily burdened battalion, there could be no trucks on those narrow footpaths, set off behind a Naga guide and, but for some hesitation when the path forked and 'D' Company went away right in error, they had no problems. Until, that is, when nearing the summit where Snagger's leading platoon came under close fire from a light machine-gun. With sides to the path too steep for dispersal, the battalion less 'D', scrambled back down to the fork and then followed 'D's route, their progress hampered by the need to carry one dead and three wounded. They were at the village at 1830 hrs and as Clive and company had been through it and confirmed the absence of Japs, they dug in. Earlier, Mansfield's platoon had seen laden Japs moving east from the village and had engaged them, killing three. It was assumed that the gun that had shot up 'C' had been there to cover that withdrawal.

There the battalion remained for a couple of days. Time in which to patrol the ridge, with little contact with our enemies, but for the unfortunate wounding of Sergeant Mansfield, not to be seen again. Graeme Gordon-Wright was also wounded – shot through an arm. He was not to return to us until early December.

During this 'away from the road' period, the battalion excluded the mortar and carrier platoons, also those things and personnel for which there was no use in what was, in effect, a strong fighting patrol.

7th June

After two days at Pfuchama, days so wet that the battalion sheltered in the village and suffered from flea bites which made wet clothing even more of a torment, they set off along the ridge for Phesama and the road. Turning left onto unfamiliar tarmac, they passed through the Worcesters and reached the next village – Kigwema, eight miles down the Imphal road and there, after overcoming a token opposition, they settled in for a couple of nights. Ahead were the battalions of 4 Brigade – the Royal Scots, Royal Norfolks and the Lancashire Fusiliers. Somewhere to the rear was 6 Brigade under a new brigadier. Shapland had been wounded and an Indian Army officer, Brigadier Smith, had taken over. Later he was to write: 'I was amazed at the fortitude of these soldiers and their officers and their powers of recovery.'

The battle for Kohima, that furthest point into India reached by the Japanese, was considered as ended. So important was its defence and so heavy the fighting that it is rated as one of the great battles of the Second World War.

I quote from one of our past enemies:

> I have fought three times in my life: in the battle of the Shanghai line, in north China, and in Burma. Each time there was heavy fighting, but the heaviest was at Kohima. It will go down as one of the greatest battles in history.
>
> Major Tokuji Morimoto.

8th June

Early that morning Geoffry White was called forward from the battalion's 'tail' to Kigwema, there to be met by General Grover and appointed our Commanding Officer, on the promotion to brigadier of Jock McNaught to the command of 4 Brigade. For our C.O. to have been promoted after only three months with us was, of itself, an indication of his qualities and there were many who regretted his going. As for Geoffry he achieved the command that he, as a regimental officer had sought before all others; one that he had begun to think might pass him by.

When mustered so that Brigadier McNaught might say farewell, the six weak platoons which constituted the battalion made all too clear the extent of our casualties.

On compiling his order of battle, our new colonel was able to give Clive Chettle his majority and Lintorn Highett his captaincy.

9th – 16th June

The news of the Normandy landings had 'lightened loads', for victory there brought blighty nearer and the rain-sodden world became slightly less daunting. Our advance south had to press on and, situated as we Dorsets were, it made sense for us to be under command of 4 Brigade for a time, thus indirectly under our old C.O. Ahead of our leading troops, on the near side of the village of Viswema six miles away, the Japs had blocked and mined the road and were discouraging our attempts to clear it. A tricky situation on a road carved into a very rugged mountain and where even tracked vehicles were confined to that same road. Due west of Kigwema is Mount Japvo, the highest of the peaks, but Phepu at 9,852 ft. two miles to the south is almost as high, as is another, just to the south again. Thus we had a 5,000 feet high right flank and on our left a frightening drop into jumbled valleys out of sight below.

The battalion moved up to a small spur short of Viswema, from where late in the day, 'B' Company and the Guerilla Platoon were dispatched to assist the Norfolks, on what we knew as Shaving Brush Spur. This was a thickly wooded and steeply rising central feature on our right flank, where the road curved eastwards around a large peak on the lower slopes of Phepu. It dominated the road and Viswema, making its possession essential to the Japs if they were to maintain the road-block. Peter Feeney, who had taken command of 'B' Company following the departure of Graeme, had to get his men up a steep and slippery slope in the dark and on an almost non-existent track, said to have been 'cut' by Japs. Led by a Norfolk and with each man grasping the water bottle of the man in front and at times progressing on the remaining hand and knees, they eventually made it at 0300 hrs the next morning. The Japs thankfully had gone.

Onto the scene now comes the unflappable Andrew Mac, the first of a number of post-Kohima reinforcement officers, that were to join us during the remaining months of that year. Captain Andrew MacKenzie had come out from England, where he had worked as a journalist after leaving his native country of New Zealand. Mac was a considerable gain at this most difficult time, he fitted in so well, becoming and remaining a true Dorset. Fortunately for him he had the toughness of body and spirit required for the situation in which he found himself. What happened is best told by him in the following extract from a letter to me in 1988. It commences on the previous day, at the time that Jock McNaught was handing over to Geoffry White.

> When I arrived I was sent up a hill on which I was soon meeting walking wounded making their way to the rear. At the top was Colonel McNaught who looked me in the eye and said that I would be taking on the Guerilla Platoon from Captain Purser, who had been killed. My first night was a tame affair as we did not know if the Japs would be back and we did not see them. On the next day we marched down the hill to join up with the battalion preparing to attack Viswema. The road was blocked by a strong Japanese presence on the hill overlooking the road. The Norfolks were in position higher up on the ridge and more Japs were beyond that. Geoffry White, then presumably in command, sent me up with the platoon to report to the C.O. of the Norfolks, who I remember as Colonel Carroll. He ordered me to establish whether or not the Japs were above him in strength – they were. We fired at them to draw their fire, during which one of the platoon was hit. I crawled out with my batman to pull him back and we did so while shielded by artillery fire. Somehow this wounded man was evacuated and, to the surprise of Joe, after such a journey, he recovered. The following day a combined patrol (Norfolks and the Guerillas) under a Norfolk major drove down the ridge to dislodge the Japs, but there were several ridges – all wired. We found that we were on the wrong one with the result that we then had to attack the correct one from below. We did not know where the Japs were until they fired at us from directly above. Luckily I was shielded by a dip in the ground but was as near damned killed. Oddly enough I was conscious of great calm and of being outside my physical body, I have never been closer to death. We rolled down the hill to safety shielded by the undergrowth. One of my men had been hit and a stretcher party sent to bring him down was able to do so. This was the only time the Japs were to show this sort of chivalry. That night they withdrew from the ridge and the attack on Viswema was able to go ahead.

The account condenses a great deal into a few lines, but they suffice to portray something of the horrors of fighting under grim conditions, where the defender can hear your laboured approach and shoot you from a few yards. The hardened veterans of Kohima respected a newcomer who could go into battle in such a place and not succumb.

Mac's task on the 10th, when he and his platoon set out to locate the Japs, was partly achieved by his encouragement of them to fire at him and by so doing disclose their positions. They established the location of seven automatic weapons, presumably light machine-guns, an achievement which produced a letter of thanks from Colonel Carroll. During those days when Norfolk companies were harassing Japs, 'B' Company was stiffening the Norfolks' base, from where a gunner F.O.O. was directing artillery fire.

Joe Chamberlin has let me have some recollections of this hideous portion of jungle clad hillside:

> It was the most unpleasant, dense jungle we had been in and we were not reassured by some Norfolks at the bottom of the track, who said the way up was cut by a flame-thrower. Happily, we found no evidence of this. The only people who managed to do anything other than dig holes to escape the very heavy mortaring, were the Guerilla Platoon. Mac made an impressive first appearance, locating the Japs by drawing their fire with calm deliberation. The mortaring was such that even Sergeant-Major 'Gary' Cooper found it necessary to throw himself into someone's trench, regardless of who was underneath him. And such was the warm respect that

The Imphal road at Viswema, part of which is seen.

everyone had for him that he was credited with having deliberately protected the occupants. He said that nothing was further from his thoughts. He was hit by a fragment and consented to have a dressing on it. I have a very distressing memory of something that happened during this mortaring. Someone who had been hit – invisible in the dense scrub and trees – was crying for help. The cries went on for so very long and we couldn't even begin to try and find him. By the time someone got to him he was dead. He was one of the draft of recently joined and very young soldiers, who looked as if they should all be at school.

The attack on and capture of Viswema and the road block had become a joint effort by 4 and 5 Brigades, as might be expected when they were so hugger-mugger on that strip of road, cluttered also with guns, tanks, trucks and jeeps galore. There too were brass hats wishing to see, so easily, a front line.

We were considered to have played our role in these manoeuvres and, on the 14th, it was the Royal Scots in the centre, the Camerons on the mountain side (how well chosen) and the Worcesters in the valley, that cleared the road and village.

Early next morning 6 Brigade passed through and with the support of an armoured column, made for Mao Songsang but, being beset by demolitions and pockets of enemy, stopped short.

17th – 18th June

The battalion moved forward to Khuzama village, two miles short of that major village, Mao Songsang, which was the hub of a group of hamlets and the anticipated centre of enemy resistance. As we were the most depleted of the three battalions, it was the Camerons and the Worcesters who were chosen to clear the place in a night attack. But our shelling sufficed and, to the delight of all, the Japs were found to have gone.

Ever since Kohima our road had been slowly climbing throughout the 20 long and difficult miles, now it was to be downhill. We had attained a watershed. With the country opening up, for Mount Japvo and the Barail Range were almost gone behind our right shoulders, we had a much needed psychological boost to jaded spirits.

The second day was one of torrential rain so that the road was awash, but that road was clear of the enemy and we passed Mao Songsang and, supported by a couple of troops of tanks, covered a dozen miles right through to Maram. Then Maram was just a place with geographical features to be exploited by the enemy. Later it was to be where we would live and prepare for battles within Burma. Again Camerons and Worcesters did the fighting and it was not until the evening that Dorsets were scrapping with Jap patrols.

19th – 26th June

A change to brighter weather helped the other 5 Brigade battalions clear Japs from this very rugged area of steep mountain slopes and gullies which, although of less height than those to our rear, remained formidable at close quarters. By evening much had been achieved and we were past Maram and companies were having to be dispersed. 'C' came under machine-gun fire while still on the road and Snagger was shot in the hand. During active night patrolling we were to suffer the death of one of our leaders, Corporal Robinson.

That the nature of our surroundings was altering is indicated by the need, on the 20th, to deal with a high point on the left of the road – Point 4,643. As before it was our artillery, this time from the calibre of the Bofors gun (used most effectively in a ground role) that broke the spirit of our opponents who, not having had the opportunity to prepare bunkers, had to fight from open trench positions. It was the Royal Scots who dealt with Pt. 4,643 and then continued with 4 Brigade in a dash down the road, leaving our 'D' Company to mop-up at their rear. No longer were we to be confined to a road carved out of rising ground, for we were slowly entering an ever widening valley, at the end of which was the Imphal Plain. Our armour and our mobility could be used almost to their full effect and, when we Dorsets went forward, we were to do so over the unprecedented distance of 18 miles.

In the early morning of 22nd June the Durham Light Infantry, the leading battalion of 6 Brigade, with a vanguard of tanks, met an advancing column of tanks from Imphal. Imphal had been relieved at milestone 109, 63 miles beyond Kohima.

Hands were shaken and photographs were taken. Men sat at the roadside and smoked while generals congratulated themselves and arranged divisional bound aries. The sun shone; it was a lovely day.

For a few days our advance towards Imphal was to be checked and we received orders to establish a base at ms. 100 and a two-company position at the village of Mayangkhang, a mile or more to the east and about 2,000 feet up. An important location, being on a route parallel to the road and one that led into the interior where there were many villages, of which Ukhrul was one and Sangshak another. By then Japanese resistance had collapsed, so completely that we had no expectation of meeting anything other than stragglers, whose only concern would be to avoid us and get away to the east. This was a moment of success, one that could be enjoyed in an atmosphere of cautious relaxation.

A period of contemplation that was well timed for the 23rd was our own, very special, Plassey Day. Signals appropriate to the occasion were dispatched and complimentary ones were received. And a glass of beer and an extra ration of rum helped to make it quite a day.

After Kohima there were expectations that a goodly number of those who fought on the spur would receive decorations. To my knowledge there was just the MM to Corporal Mansfield. Well earned, as was the same award to Sergeant Given of 'D' Company and the MC to Clive Chettle. An award to John Bowles would have delighted the battalion as due recognition of his leadership and his years of service to the Dorsets, and what happened to those 15 listed by him as worthy of recognition!

Is it not strange that the two weeks of action in France earned the battalion more medals for bravery than did the months in Assam and Burma! Was this one more manifestation of those at 'Delhi' denigrating our division? Arthur Swinson in his excellent book 'Kohima', goes into the political considerations and confirms the belief that our achievements were concealed. I remember how the publication of that book changed the attitude of an Indian Army Officer who had fought at Kohima. What had bordered on contempt, changed to respect and admiration, so that he spoke of the British infantry as 'the bravest of the brave'.

To our relief the total number of casualties on the journey south from Kohima had been less than anticipated after the many at that place; nevertheless grim is a fair description of those days. To be repeatedly cold, wet and without hot food, under conditions of utmost danger and to be only too aware that one is part of a dwindling force, and still to respond when called upon to attack or advance, as they did, showed an outstanding fortitude. We admire those who were so very brave in the defence of Britain; to be brave in that remote place, and the many others in Burma, all so far from home, required a very special quality of bravery.

When we reached milestone 100 we had lost 92 killed in action, three had died of disease and 235 had been wounded. Roughly two men in every five had been killed or wounded.

Not being in contact with the enemy at ms. 100 we were encamped in 'bivvy' tents – two men per tent. With a floor area of about six feet by four and a ridge height of three feet, they took a bit of getting used to. Also, of getting into when, as then, the adjacent ground was a sea of mud. But once inside we were, at least not rained on. Having wriggled into mine, there to lie uncomfortably in fitful sleep, my thoughts were of those white hospital sheets of but a few days before. How I did kick myself for not delaying my departure.

27th June – 18th July

Trucks arrived from somewhere and on 27th June we set off towards Imphal, 35 miles distant. Our destination was a rest camp of bashas and tents, mainly the latter, set in isolation away from the town. There we could, at least, stand upright and had time to dry out and rest, to get clean and to reorganise. The latter was a continuing problem when casualties and sickness exceeded our very few reinforcements and the numbers returning from hospital. Mepacrine tablets held malaria at bay to a remarkable degree, but the bugs of dysentery and dysentery-type sickness were the despair of all.

It was not long before our Corps Commander, General Stopford, came to see how we were, as did Lord Louis Mountbatten. Stopford, later to be knighted on the battlefield, was so English in his looks and quiet personality, that just to see him occasionally was reassuring. He personified those qualities we most admired – a calm authority, courage, honesty and a keen brain brought to a peak after many years of soldiering. Lord Louis was, of course, another with great qualities of leadership, to which were added the presence, the looks and the flair of royalty. Thus he was different and in personality superior to all others. He was generous in his praise of our achievements and he gave the sort of address that everybody wanted to hear and for which they felt much better.

In contrast, one week after reaching Imphal and probably due to a clash of personalities between himself and his Corps Commander, General Grover was relieved of his command. There was shock and anger at what seemed shabby treatment of the one to whom we owed so much, in fact we were indebted to him for our very survival. It was to his credit and that of those he commanded, that all ranks saw the real and very private man who had dedicated himself to leading 15,000 men in battle, from behind the austere facade of one seeking neither publicity nor popularity.

However, we were to be fortunate in his successor, Major-General Nicholson CBE, DSO, MC. He was to command the 2nd Division for the remainder of our war and was to prove himself to be a much less fearsome character.

Our expectation was that we would be in camp for some weeks and it was only logical that the division should restart the leave that we had been about to enjoy when we were in the Belgaum Jungle. Peter Feeney, newly promoted major, shot off to make preparations for a leave camp at Calcutta, shortly to be followed by a leave party, with whom was Colin Doran. Like the others he was off for 28 days and the job of Adjutant was passed to me, I then temporarily doing two jobs.

On the 28th we were glad to see Donald Baynes again, sufficiently recovered to take command of 'C' Company. At about that time we also welcomed a new face – that of Major Tommy Tucker, not a Dorset but nearly so for he was of the Hampshire Regiment. Geoffry was greatly cheered that at last we had with him a regular whose service dated back to pre-war days. Thus he was able to slot him into the job of Second-in-Command and lessen his burden of administration resulting from an 'office' that had been closed for weeks. Tommy's cheerful equanimity was to be needed in the often difficult and testing times ahead, when he was to command 'C' Company.

A number of promotions were given at this time and I was one of the subalterns to be made a captain.

We were then in the native state of Manipur, whose Rajah was said to have a weakness for jewellery and scent. Certainly the Manipurians were very different to their neighbours the Nagas and the Chins, who must have considered them effete in their preference for a life that did not necessitate living on top of a mountain.

As so often, my memory fails and I remember nothing of the town of Imphal, which very probably was 'out of bounds', neither can I recollect our camp. The scenery in the Naga Hills, when one was able to enjoy it, was always splendid but there, if anything, it was even better. We were in a green plain surrounded by hills and mountain peaks, brilliant in their clothing of trees and grass. And in the plain, and terraced into the lower slopes, was the richer and uniquely vivid green of paddy fields, glistening with water, through which the rice was growing. Emphasising the fields were the bunds, the narrow earth banks confining the water within each minute field; of necessity they were horizontal and showed like contour lines, as they profiled the ridges and valleys of the rising ground.

Impinging on this beauty were areas of brown earth where war had blasted away the vegetation and shattered the trees. Darker rectangles of slit trenches and loop-holes testified to the recent fighting. Along the roads were lines of vehicles and guns, over which camouflage nets were strung. Bivouac tents and tarpaulins, beneath which mud-stained figures sheltered from the rain, added to the contrast of our world with that which had preceded us.

With the breaking of the siege of Imphal we entered a brief period of calm and of an awareness of the enemy in retreat to the Chindwin. As the weeks passed, so became apparent the extent of that flight to Burma by starving remnants of a defeated army. In March, 1944 the Japanese had some 200,000 men in Burma, of which the best 80,000 were in their 15th Army. That strength is understood to have reached 85,000 of whom, following the Kohima and Imphal battles and their retreat to the Chindwin, 53,000 became casualties – 30,000 of which were fatalities or missing.

Since Kohima, our vulnerable left flank had had the protection of the 7th Indian Division, whose similar flank had been covered by the 23rd L.R.P. Brigade, one of Wingate's long-range penetration columns detached from the remainder.

Ahead of 7 Div. was the village of Ukhrul, a focal point in an area of many villages and one with a hospital and post office. It sits astride a long north to south ridge, 45 miles to the north of Imphal, to which ran one of those 'jeepable in dry season' roads. From it tracks radiate to villages at altitudes of 6-7,000 feet, from which the ground drops for 1,500 feet and more. Thus Ukhrul and the village of Sangshak, the latter eight miles to the south and on a jeepable track to the east, had been natural objectives for the Japs in March. It had been at Sangshak, that a battle had raged from 19th to 26th March, one as bloody and terrible in its hand-to-hand fighting as any subsequently at Kohima.

Early in July, two brigades from 7 Div. together with the 23rd Division, started operations for the taking of Ukhrul from the north, while the 20th Division did likewise from the south. By the 14th the area was clear of the many Japs for whom it had been a rallying point, as they retraced their earlier line of advance. Mopping-up continued to the 20th, on which day 20 Div. was withdrawn and replaced by our 4 Brigade who 'hustled' the retreating Japs through the hills to the Kabaw Valley.

We should have known that plans for leave invariably come to naught, as was happening then. Orders were that 5 Brigade was to provide a reserve to the 23rd Indian Division, about to advance across the Chin Hills on the axis of the Palel to Tamu road, their objective Tamu, in the Kabaw Valley.

Thus the placid life of a battalion in camp was ending almost as soon as it had begun. For the first time I found myself juggling with the production of a Movement Order, so that we might transfer ourselves and our vehicles, within a strict time-table, along the congested roads to Palel.

To use to the best our small numbers, we reorganised as a unit of four rifle companies. And chaps from the specialist platoons had to forget, for a time, that they were mortar experts or whatever, and shoulder a rifle.

But first, on a fine Sunday evening, 5 Brigade held an open-air service, at which the conducting Padre spoke of how we welcomed the dawn of a new day. We did indeed, for it represented one small step towards home, that 'Blighty' so far away but dominant in our thoughts. Hymns were always important and on this occasion the last of four was 'For all the Saints who from their labours rest.' Its sentiments -

> O may Thy soldiers, faithful, true and bold,
> Fight as the Saints who nobly fought of old,
> And win, with them, the victor's crown of gold.

could have been ridiculed elsewhere. There, a congregation of hundreds, for on such occasions almost all who could attend would do so, sang with a great and vigorous enthusiasm and, by so doing, relieved pent-up emotions. Ones resulting from lost comrades, and an awareness of unknown dangers in an uncertain future.

Those weeks following Kohima had enabled us to get to know and admire our new Brigadier. Again, in Brigadier Michael West, we had a leader with the qualities expected in a high-ranking, front line, infantry soldier; one who would neither flap nor wilt. We liked the look of him for he was physically tough and, being approachable, one soon sensed a disposition that was equally robust. Others were impressed for, in the next war, the one in Korea, he was to command the Commonwealth Division and be knighted.

A letter of mine dated 13th July, was written under the address of SEAC (South East Asia Command) and not, as before, India Command. We had moved into the sphere of the 14th Army and were no longer within India Command. And with the passage of time, censorship had been relaxed, making it possible to 'tell something of our campaign.'

CHAPTER SIX

To the Kabaw Valley

19th – 28th July
Our convoy delivered us to Palel, without mishap, and we settled into a basha camp that was terraced into a hillside. Palel, no longer a minor village, now had a dual importance, being not only at the end of that road to Tamu, but adjacent to one of the Imphal air-strips. That strip had been under recent attack from Japs moving unseen through the jungle north of the road, then having to be fought off at close quarters. Attacks that ended only nine days earlier, when a small but determined patrol destroyed eight planes.

In 1943 a General Reserve Engineer Force had been established to carry out the many major engineering works necessary in Assam. It was provided with engineering and transport companies and a labour force of tea plantation labourers, Army Pioneers and civilian ones, to a total of 26,000 men. Initially it improved the Imphal Road, but its great achievement was the making of the road to Tamu, one that had to traverse an almost impenetrable barrier of jungle clad mountains. There a road was constructed where, but for a hastily made track which enabled refugees from Burma in 1942 to reach Imphal, there had not been one before. This was the road along which we were to advance and see the full magnitude of its undertaking. Unlike the Imphal road which was generally within the lower slopes, this climbed to the upper hill faces, some so steep that narrow, dual one-way sections were all that could be formed.

Back in June, when we had been at milestone 100, we had not been far from the village of Kangpokpi, an objective of the Japanese 15th Division and designated by them as 'Mission'. Ben Bazeley, an officer at the Headquarters of G.R.E.F., the builders of the Tamu road, tells an intriguing story.

The HQ was housed in a compound carved out of the hillside for the personnel of the American Baptist Mission's leper colony, all of whose medical staff had gone, leaving a sole missionary, the Rev. W. Brock, in charge of the Mission. The lepers remained in the isolation of their colony at the top of the hill, within the garden on which they were dependent for food. During the final weeks, before their move into the Imphal Plain ahead of the Japs, Ben had seen huts under construction above them, the size of which and the unfriendly, villainous and surly looks of those building them, made him suspicious.

Feelings that were not decreased by the Political Agent to the Maharajah in Imphal who, when questioned as to what was going on, replied that the Kangpokpi villagers had been given permission to build a new village. An answer that did not lessen Ben's doubts, who checked again as the houses grew in size and number. Still the same answer. He continues:

'The growing village above the mission station was forgotten in the turmoil of the evacuation. HQ G.R.E.F. was ordered out of Kangpokpi because it was very isolated and we had no combat troops to defend the position. On the day before we left, while standing-to in the late afternoon, a column including elephants was spotted working its way up a ridge on the hillside above us. A patrol was sent out but failed to make contact. We left for Manipur the next morning and later that day the Imphal road was cut by the Japanese at Kangpokpi.

Months afterwards, I learned that our mission had been used by the Japanese as a Div. HQ, and the new village above it as an Army Depot. Had the column of elephants been the first hook across the Imphal – Dimapur road cutting off 4 Corps from its base and was it the Japanese who were the builders of that supposed village on the way to the leper colony?'

On the map the distance from Palel to Tamu is about 40 miles but, as the road rises 2,300 feet from Palel and then drops 4,200 feet to Tamu and throughout its length it undulates over ridges and hollows, the road distance must be nearer 50. For much of its length there was a road in use and a parallel one under repair, such works being often the reconstruction of a length that had disappeared, the original having slid wholesale into the valley. These duplications were just wide enough for one large vehicle, to reduce the amount of cut, and so steep were these slopes that one route could be 600 feet above the other.

For me Palel had but one redeeming feature. A view seen between showers, of distant paddy fields showing brilliant in the clear sunlit atmosphere, and so much in contrast to the shaded timbered slopes, between which they could be glimpsed.

After a few days at Palel the time came for us to start up the road and we covered the ten miles to Recce Hill, on the apex of Shenam Ridge the highest point on the road. There, when not enveloped in cloud, as it was for us other than one evening and the following morning, the view extended in every direction over jungle clad mountains to distant horizons. We had actually been there some days seeing nothing, when suddenly the mist had gone and we found ourselves on top of the world and chaps who had never bothered with a view before, stood agape at the immensity of a land of mountains that seemed to have no end. Someone said of those same hills that one saw the world as God made it. A rare privilege even then.

This 5,250 ft. feature had, by reason of its height and location, been the dominant position on this the most direct route from Burma to Manipur and indeed into India. Its defences had been constructed by the 20th Indian Division and it was there that the Japanese advance on Imphal had been halted. Repeated assaults by them on it and the line of which it had been the focal point, ended only on 13th July.* Now we found ourselves in this 'earthworks', one that would have been all too familiar to a soldier of the 1914-18 war.

* Grevious losses had been suffered by the 1st Devons of 80 Brigade who, in April, had endured these assaults and the desperate fighting of attack and counter-attack, as formidable as any at Kohima.

Shenam Ridge. Enemy Weapons and equipment litter the ground. The winding road can be seen in the left background

A place of firing positions, communication trenches and dug-outs, the whole deep in mud after weeks of rain which, during the monsoon at that altitude, was nearly perpetual.

I was to live in the Command Post throughout our five days of occupation, the appearance of which is depicted in a sketch I made at the time and is described in a letter. The drawing looks out through the entrance, beyond which a short length of trench links the dug-out to a communication trench, running to left and to right. Clearly shown is the flight of steps, by which one dropped the four or five feet from trench to dug-out. The steps were made from short lengths of timber and these irregular branches from trees also formed a floor of sorts. Clearly shown is the bottom step, twice the depth of the remainder and which was such a curse to the inhabitants as it was to those who came to visit. They, unable to see in the dim light, would drop the unexpected 18 inches into a pool of liquid mud, constantly replenished by rainwater down the steps. This 'office' was about ten feet square by six in height to tree trunks which, with three or four feet of earth, formed the roof, made moderately watertight by a tarpaulin on top. After dark, the entrance part way up the steps and about four feet high and two and a half feet wide, was blacked out by a loose end of the tarpaulin.

Packing cases formed a central table and two smaller ones and a 'bunk' were against the earth walls. Wall recesses provided shelves, the one by the bunk having the field telephone, which together with all other 'phones was only to be used at night in the event of an enemy attack. An oil lamp provided the lighting. It was a cold, smelly and thoroughly disagreeable abode, made more so at night when out came the rats. I described them as being as big as cats and, having fed off a battlefield for three months, they probably were. After being over-run by them during the first night, I spent the remainder on the central table within the protection of my mosquito net which I strung up from the roof.

Telephones were not encouraged after dark as they gave away positions and all movement was banned, so that any moving body could be assumed as hostile and something to be shot.

Even there, behind the forward troops, the suicidal Jap or Japs had to be guarded against and nerves were taut after sunset. One night I awoke to the sound of someone scrambling over the roof and sat up in a sweat of terror, my Sten cocked and pointing at the tarpaulin (the lantern was always lit) expecting it to be swept aside by Japs.

Although a loner, those long nights at the end of that hated telephone were dreaded. Being on my own at night was the norm, although not out of sight and sound of others, as there. Life at Battalion HQ lacked the camaraderie that was so special at 'A' Company but it was, of course, a damned sight safer. We knew little of what was happening up the road but, throughout the 24 hours, there would be unexpected bursts of artillery fire from the guns supporting 23 Div. Those shells passed low over our elevated position and were a welcome and exciting sound.

On the 23rd, Mac and the Guerilla Platoon set off on a three-day fighting patrol, having in support – two stretcher bearers, three signallers, an 'I' Section corporal, a porterage party of one sergeant and seven other ranks carrying reserve ammunition and digging tools and a Captain Cohen (of the Foresters) attached. To help them find their way they had a couple of Gurkha guides and also a Gurkha interpreter for when they reached the village of Phalbung, their main objective.

Phalbung, centrally positioned on a ridge to the north of the road, 500 feet below us and, as the crow flies, no more than five miles away to the north east, would seem to be so close as to be reached in a gentle stroll. But those miles were to be in thick all-enveloping jungle including the most difficult of all, the tangled mass proliferating in the perpetual dampness of the lower slopes. Going that would not only be sodden but steep-sided by reason of the many watercourses, tributaries of the river in the main valley, running at right angles to their route.

They had an early and easy start of a couple of miles along a ridge-top track going north to Saibom, a place about which nothing is recorded. At 0630 hrs they turned almost east for the river and Phalbung. Leaving the ridge they dropped 2,000 feet to the river and then set about the climb of 1,700 feet to their objective. It was in the anticipation of these hazards that they had the carrying party but, so difficult was the going and made more so by having to force a passage through elephant grass, that those doing the carrying became exhausted. And their progress on approaching the village was hampered by fog, very probably the same cloud which enveloped us. Once at the top they were on a track running along the ridge and roughly parallel to the road. The village, supposedly still occupied, was a burnt-out shell and they reported it as containing nothing but a mule and a sword scabbard. That night Mac and Captain Cohen took out patrols. The following day they combed the whole area, finding numerous abandoned Japanese positions, together with both Japanese and British equipment which included weapons and ammunition.

When terrain and distance permitted, contact with such patrols was by wireless. Reports from them were expected at 0800 hrs, then at around noon and at the end of the day. On the second evening Mac reported that he had a Jap position under observation at 500 yards and that he had hopes of a prisoner. The latter suspected by us as an unwarranted extra by Mac to enliven his dull reports.

They were back with us at 1300 hrs on the 26th, weary and extra wet, having crossed the river where it was waist deep and requiring the use of ropes.

That patrol, and others like it, were a guard to our vulnerable left flank from what a week or two before would have been Jap territory, as deadly as had been those hills to the south of Kohima. For all we knew it held spirited Japs, wanting nothing better than death in the glory of a suicidal attack. One such could well have been the possessor of that missing sword.

On that patrol the new jungle rations were used for the first time and considered to be excellent.

On the 24th Tommy Tucker, whom Geoffry had made his Second-in-Command at Imphal, but who, in the absence of Peter at Calcutta, had temporarily taken command of 'B' Company, was spared a return to battalion HQ by another new arrival. The new face was that of Major Mervyn Jones MBE, a Territorial Army officer of the Monmouthshire Regiment (his home county), posted to us from a staff appointment in the Arakan. To be decanted into a close-knit unit induces stress as each side assesses the other and, for the newcomer, is a severe test of character, particularly when the appointment is that of a second-in-command. Fortunately Mervyn's abilities and amiable disposition enabled him to slot in and hold, for the remainder of our active war, what many would consider to be the least desirable of battalion jobs; one with a heavy burden of administrative responsibility and precious little real authority.

29th July – 3rd August

Ahead of us, following a series of skirmishes, the 23rd Division had broken through the last of the enemy positions and road blocks and we moved forward nine miles, on an even wetter morning than usual, to a wooded spur above the road at milestone 46, its distance from Imphal. En route we passed large quantities of abandoned Japanese weaponry – shells of all calibres predominating. It had been on this, the most direct route from Burma to Imphal, that the Japs had lavished their heaviest artillery and much of it had been halted there by the combination of the natural barrier, from which we had just descended, and the monsoon.

While we were there Mac and his Guerillas were off again into the wilds north of the road, on a two- or three-day patrol. For some inexplicable reason, I remember briefing him and can visualise that open woodland south of the road, to which the ground fell, and that the sun was shining and that I had wished that I could have accompanied him. That suggests that I had not studied the map as closely as I have today, for they had to drop 1,000 feet to the Khulei Lok. That river would have been running in spate and had they crossed it and continued up the far side they would have entered a world of tangled slopes rising 2,000 feet, so steep and broken that I find it difficult to imagine any human progressing at all. Mac says that he is unable to remember any of his patrols, which is a pity. Probably he prefers not to do so, for even Mac, when faced with such a climb, might have proceeded with less than his customary diligence. Anyway, I did manage to get away from the 'office' with the 'I' Section on a number of sorties to abandoned trenches, where our findings ranged from quantities of documents, which we collected, to three 150mm guns, which we examined with interest.

Our next move, one of about ten miles, took us across the Lokchao River, of which the Khulei Lok is a tributary, on a temporary bridge just completed by the sappers to replace the one blown by the retreating enemy. That steep sided valley and the all-important bridge across the only major river between Palel and Tamu, were as vital a geographical feature as Shenam. A determined enemy on the commanding heights could have trapped and ambushed us there for weeks. But starving Japs could do no more than delay our advance and there, as elsewhere, they were content to do the obvious and wreck that part of the bridge spanning the river. Had they stopped to destroy the abutments, the check to our progress would have been considerable. As it was it had taken from 24th to 27th July to achieve that crossing.

Being provided with only half the number of trucks required to move the battalion, I arranged that one half (the lucky ones) would march down to the bridge and then be carried, the others doing the reverse. Being past the apex of the Chin Hills, with high points 3,000 feet lower than those behind us, the 1,000 foot drop to the bridge and the ensuing climb were done under conditions of high humidity and temperature, not experienced since leaving Dimapur. I had been able to jeep the whole way, but in the afternoon Geoffry asked me to return to the bridge where Jock Murrills was checking everyone through. My return was for the dual purpose of ascertaining that they had passed through and what were our numbers, but also and I imagine more essentially, to look for his carbine. Sitting in the truck I was comforted by the knowledge that even C.O.s lose weapons. However all was well, numbers had been counted and I had the carbine. On the way back torrential rain and storm winds started and the 15cwt truck had difficulty in making the steep gradient, for the road was mud-covered and awash and we were packed solid with chaps in need of a lift.

When, after something of a struggle, we neared the top, a fallen tree blocked our way and the driver and I sat contemplating the dismal scene through a steamed-up windscreen. A deathly hush prevailed as those in the back pretended that they were miles away. Only too conscious that I was without my groundsheet-cape, but also aware that this was when one set an example, I got out and into the deluge; with help the truck's tow rope was secured to the tree and it was pulled clear. That night was not a good one, for besides having wet clothes, I spent it lying on a sheet of corrugated iron, the alternative to lying in a sea of mud, the only remaining area not 'bagged' by my comrades-in-arms. Something must have gone badly wrong in my absence for, while I had soon discovered that I.O.s lived hard, it was not customary for adjutants. And may I add that this is no figment of my imagination, for that night I learned that such a 'bed' is only tolerable when lain upon bottom up with one's head resting on forearms. That night's ghastly stench from a dead Jap, which one of our drivers thought to cremate with a can of petrol, is another memory.

On this day 5 Brigade took over from the 23rd Division, which began its return to Imphal and to rest in India.

Jap guns and gun tractors lined the road by the bridge, more stark evidence of their desperate straits. Today it seems unbelievable that they lacked the four wheel drive of our vehicles which enabled us to keep going.

The pounding of the road by a multitude of vehicles, often during periods of torrential rain, was so breaking it up that in places it was described as 'having to be seen to be believed'. Also where sections of the road had collapsed and had slid away into the depths, and where there had been no time for more than a quick repair job, it could be very dicey. The wonder was that it still functioned and, in places, was quite good. If ever there was a road for four-wheel drive, that indeed was it!

On the Tamu Road

As was customary when we had pushed on ahead of base there had been a break in our mail, but by mid-July it was coming through and magazines were being enjoyed and shared. I was engrossed in Evelyn Waugh's Decline and Fall, lent to me by Geoffry.

4th – 11th August

We were fortunate to remain just one night in that muddy camp above the Lokchao river before advancing, on 4th August to the edge of the hills overlooking the Kabaw Valley. We were then about five miles from Tamu and had moved into a site on the left of the road, which I remember as quite thickly wooded.

This, with the exception of patrolling in the vicinity of Tamu, was to be the limit of our advance at that time, for during the monsoon the Kabaw Valley (then generally known as 'the valley of death') is one of the most malarial districts in all Burma.

Marching up the road to our rear was the 11th East African Division, brought in to relieve the 23rd Division and to whom had been given the task of recapturing the valley down to Kalewa. That place, 110 miles south of Tamu, was where a bridgehead across the Chindwin was to be established. That done, a revitalised 2nd Division would cross the river and drive deep into Burma and to that end we were to spend the remaining months of the year.

Throughout the advance we had been the reserve battalion in our brigade and, although the Camerons and the Worcesters had had no active opposition, they had collected prisoners. To the Camerons fell the distinction of taking by far the largest number that our division was to take at any one time. Entering Tamu they found dead and dying Japs in hundreds, within every building be it hut or temple, under trees and wherever there was protection from the rain. It is said that 198 were taken. Exhausted remnants of the 15th Army, some of whom had made their way from as far north as Kohima. Lack of food, wounds, disease, the elements and the shock of defeat for an army that had never suffered defeat, reduced them to such a state that they were not even capable of committing hari-kari.

Tamu was declared to be a closed area and thus we were not to see the place that had so often appeared on our plans and maps.

From one of the spurs jutting out towards the valley, we could see across the low ground to the hills beyond and east of which was the Chindwin River. A great moment, for we were looking over Burma, a new land with new interests where we were destined to be and to fight. Below lay dark green masses of jungle broken only occasionally by the lighter patches of grass where clearings had been made. I longed to be down there!

Here there was no noise of battle, and the only sound that disturbed the silence of this remote, unspoiled world was that made by our own vehicles.

Our move that day had been in trucks provided by a battalion of Jats. The 3/9th Royal Jats were in the 5th Indian Division and I assume the vehicles were theirs. That night their Adjutant phoned complaining that their trucks had not returned, and that they were needed for moving more troops the following day. As Adjutant, I should have organised their return, a task I had overlooked. I had also overlooked the simple fact that some drivers failed to appreciate that it was necessary to turn round in order to return the way they had come... Working on the assumption that they must have gone forward I prepared to carry out Geoffry's orders, which were "Find them." Bumping into John Bowles who, in his customary generous manner offered to help (saying that he couldn't sleep anyway!) we set to to organise a truck and driver. A quick look at my maps revealed that the Jats could either have run out of road near Tamu or, having swung south, they could be making a very premature approach to the river town of Kalewa. My imagination pictured the headlines, 'Motorised night column meets disaster in the Valley of Death. Japanese success due to poor Intelligence. Anger in Delhi'. But for the annoyance of the lost trucks, we would have enjoyed the excitement of travelling down that unknown road with its virtually undamaged surface and flanking jungle, just like the roads in Belgaum. We reached the Worcesters without incident and to my joy – there were the Indians. We stirred them up, pointed them west and off they went and so did we.

In retrospect I wonder how far they had to drive that night, with all the dangers and difficulties of that 'broken' road. A folly of their own making if, as would appear, they had no competent person in charge. For us there was an almost complete language barrier.

Next day was spent settling in and but for a trip down the road by Geoffry, into Burma, so that he might claim to have been 'Primus in Burma and Primus ex India', a distinction that was probably due to John and to me, nothing happened.

Being first, for or with the Battalion, meant a great deal to Geoffry and many were the occasions when we were reminded of the year 1757, when we were adjudged the first in courage as well as the first of the King's regiments in India.

On 6th August a patrol was instructed to go north of Tamu and establish an ambush at a ford, where the unmetalled road to Mintha and beyond crossed a stream, a task given to Mac and his Guerillas. My request to Geoffry that I might accompany them for the day was granted, on the understanding that he received the first flag that we found. Trucks dropped us close to Moreh, north of Tamu. That was no more than a cluster of huts and not the great army dump sharing the name and sited just to the south, a store that had been built ready for our planned advance into Burma, but which had been overrun by the Japs, only after its contents had been largely destroyed.

We moved up the road in patrol formation and, after crossing the ford, halted at the junction of a track just beyond. There and all around was stark proof that our world had indeed turned full circle. It was as if we had walked into some great dumping ground, for everywhere there were vehicles and equipment, abandoned by the Japanese. While Mac deployed his men, Bert Jones and I walked across to some bashas, dispersed among the trees. The first contained three dead Japs lying side by side on charpoys; the stench was appalling. Close by we discovered two 150mm guns and a gun tractor, then other vehicles and masses of documents. When Mac was free and together with those of his platoon who were not wanted on the ground, we strolled up the so-called road for a quarter of a mile, counting 20 trucks and staff cars. And with them were two more gun tractors; all had been sufficiently immobilised as to put them beyond salvage.

Just before we departed I spotted a Japanese flag, neatly folded and placed on the ground with a land-mine on top. They looked most suspicious. Playing safe and sending the others back a bit, I got behind a tree and with the aid of a long stick, pushed the mine off. There was no explosion and Geoffry was able to post this forsaken emblem of a blood red sun to the Mayor of Dorchester who, it is said, displayed it in the town.

Our days in this camp were ones of relaxation in a reasonable climate; at 2,000 feet we were adequately elevated above the heat and humidity of the Kabaw Valley and my recollection is that sunshine exceeded the rain. Six days in which to enjoy the knowledge that, at home and there, the tide had turned. And it was great to know that most of the Naga and the Chin Hills and their people had been freed from the invader.

Firmly fixed in my mind is the belief that the battalion was 292 strong, including our 'B' Echelon at Imphal. Sickness was depleting our numbers, at about the same rate as those returning from sick leave were augmenting them.

While at this camp we were made aware of tick typhus, a particularly virulent addition to our tropical diseases. The tick was prevalent in elephant grass, a belt of which was near us, and Mac and his patrol from Recce Hill had passed through some of this man-high vegetation and had been at risk of infection by the mite, through contact. Our depleted strength was about average within the division, thus the rebuilding of 2 Div. was essential before it became so reduced as to have virtually nothing on which to build. Thankfully, that rebuilding was to commence once we had handed over to the East Africans and had reached our base camp. 4 Brigade, away to the north, were to do likewise.

In notes made at the time I recorded that the road to the south, in the Kabaw Valley, which had been partially metalled, was a sea of mud varying in depth up to axle levels. Advancing in time, to the third week in October during the last of the monsoon, I noted that the mud was such that convoy timing for the 37 miles from Moreh to Khampat was five days!

Reference to the Kabaw Valley suggests a 'V' shaped depression within the hills but, as with the country as a whole, it was on a generous scale, having a width which varied between six and eight miles. That land was a network of rivers and streams, flowing east and draining it and the Chin Hills into the Yu River; along the east side and parallel to the Chindwin River, 15 miles further east, the two were separated by a strip of hills. With jungle and forest covering 90 per cent of the land, the combination of water, vegetation and a high temperature produced conditions that were ideal for mosquitos and similar pests.

Joe Chamberlin gives his recollections of Tamu, which he entered in his medical capacity:

My memory of Tamu is of a Buddhist shrine, totally dark inside apart from a shaft of light falling on the Buddha, with a very dead Jap lying at his feet. The Kabaw Valley was hideous with blue-bottles bred from corpses, but yielding for me an excellent ear-syringe by Allen & Hanbury, no doubt looted from a British Medical Hospital, but no longer required by the nearby decaying Jap medical orderly.

There was little on our maps but contour lines, rivers, villages linked by tracks, our road and the one in the valley and infrequent yellow blobs denoting clearings, annotated as impermanent, for they tended to be cultivated and then abandoned. The indication of an air-strip a little way up the valley above Tamu, attracted my attention and from our spur I could see a clearing within jungle, more or less in the right position. From the daily intelligence reports, I knew that none of our troops had been or were going into that area; and I became intrigued by it and the thought of going there myself; picturing more abandoned vehicles and weapons – perhaps even planes. I put my idea to John Bowles who became equally keen and who said that he would come. Geoffry took a lot of persuading but did at last agree, providing I was away for no more than hours and could obtain a stand-in, and that I did. This made possible one of the best-remembered days of my life, one that is often relived in my imagination.

Thus it was that on 8th August, at 0800 hrs, John and I set off in his jeep driven by Private Wareham of 'A' Company, whom I knew so well. Also of the party was John's batman and a sergeant, enough to fill a jeep. And I can visualise as clearly as if it had been yesterday, sitting behind John, with a rifle across my knees (I had swopped my Sten for Jones' rifle), the sun was out and fresh green jungle flanked the road as we sped downhill into the valley. And I thought to myself how lucky I was to be there and not one of the unfortunates, about to start a day's work in an office.

After travelling a mile or so beyond the ford we branched onto a jeepable track running east and then, when roughly south of the strip, we turned left onto a similar one going north. Only to be abruptly halted by a ditch, straight sided as if dug for a drain. It crossed the track and continued into the trees on each side and was, as those who dug it intended, a barrier to vehicular traffic. For some time we had been in a teak forest, one where the trunks were substantial and the trees perhaps 30 or 40 feet in height. This was the first such forest of Burmese teak that we had encountered and although free from undergrowth, those who dug the trench chose its position well, for it could not be by-passed. Being unable to continue in the jeep, we decided that it should remain there in the care of the sergeant and John's batman. It was therefore Wareham, John and I who continued on foot and to discover what was almost certainly the reason for the ditch. Some 30 or 40 Japs had preceded us and quite recently, for their footprints were clear in the muddy track. There was no mistaking them, for their boots had rubber soles with a separate section for the big toe, as for the thumb in a mitten. There were also the wheel-marks of two heavy guns which, we assumed, they had been man-handling in an effort to save them, their tractors doubtless immobile. Theirs must have been a slow and agonisingly laborious progress.

We had to cover a distance of about a mile, perhaps a little more. When at about half-way, the forest was succeeded by a marsh with shallow water every-where, including the track; so that we stepped as best we could from tuft to tuft of the tussocky grass, just as one would at home in similar circumstances and wanting to keep one's feet dry. Our route passed over two or three hillocks and there on firmer ground trees grew – so that they appeared as islands in a lake. Among these trees were Japs, dead from exhaustion, disease and starvation. It was as if they had thought that these were agreeable places in which to die.

The marsh ended in a strip of jungle through which we passed to enter what would have been the south west corner of our air-strip. Continuing slowly forward, for 100 yards or so, we could see that we were looking at the early stages of a runway, for ahead and down the centre of the clearing were heaps of hardcore, work that had been halted by the Japanese advance. My vivid imagination had let us down, little wonder that other troops had not been here. We stood together in contemplation of this unexciting open space, discussing how best we might use this day so free of the constraints of battalion life. The obvious alternative was to continue along the track, which at a distance of about two miles crossed a river and where it seemed probable that the guns might have had to be abandoned. There in that remote place were perhaps the gun sights we had yet to find. Our thoughts were broken by Wareham saying "What's that?"and pointing to a dark object showing within the jungle edge, 200 yards or so to the right of where we had entered the clearing. It seemed to be a concrete mixer or some other item of contractor's plant and not worth the trouble of inspection. In that confined place of great heat and high humidity, made worse by an abundance of flies and mosquitos, we were drenched in sweat. Every gland exuded moisture which started from the crown of one's head and trickled into eyes and dripped off noses. Clothing that one longed to shed but could not, was black with sweat and, as always, flied buzzed and irritated. Having almost committed ourselves to another four miles, to go off at a tangent even for a short distance, was a waste of precious energy. However, the decision was made that we would see what it was, and we started diagonally across the rough grass. When about half-way, we could see that we were looking at the rear half of an enclosed bullock cart but, of far greater significance, was a Japanese flag flying from an adjoining tree. We were moving at a shambling run and laughing, someone having said 'First there gets the flag,' to be brought to an abrupt halt when a face, clearly that of a Jap, appeared through the back of the wagon and shouted at us. Throwing ourselves on the ground and bringing our weapons into firing positions we, for the first time on that holiday, behaved like soldiers, though hardly efficient ones. I had a stoppage and had to hammer with my fist on the rifle's bolt handle to free it and get a round into the breech. Luckily, we were not at the receiving end of any hostility and scrambling to our feet and duly chastened, we proceeded but now in line and moving slowly, the face having disappeared. As we closed on the cart we stepped over three dead Japs lying by the ashes of a camp fire. While John and Wareham went on into the trees beyond the wagon for a quick look around to check that there were no others, I went round to the open front and there he was, sitting on the floor, behind the shafts, with his hands up. Reaching down, he picked up a grenade and handed it to me. It had had its safety pin removed, so taking it quickly, I threw it into the trees, clear of the others, who were soon back having found no one. The grenade did not explode.

We three stood in line in front of our Jap (as we came to think of him), who indicated that he was hungry, but having no food we offered water, which he then showed us he had. We compromised with a cigarette, which was eagerly accepted and the four of us lit up. But for a couple of revoltingly filthy Jap prisoners, this was the first live one that I had been near, and for Wareham it was probably a new experience; unlike John who had been in close contact with dozens. We studied our enemy with considerable interest, becoming aware that he and his cart were quite clean and tidy. Except for the grenade there were no weapons, that grenade presumably retained so that he could commit hari-kari. Our Jap, whose badges of rank denoted a Private 2nd Class, seemed to have all his kit including, to our surprise, his respirator.

We entered into a dialogue in which something of what we said was understood. We gathered that he had been in the fighting at Ukhrul, very probably he was therefore a member of their 15th Division. Ukhrul was something like 100 miles away, a journey over mountain tracks and he and his companions had done well to have got so far. Hunger may have defeated them; indications were made that he had not eaten for five days and one can imagine that they had precious little before and during their trek.

Unknown to us, their 15th Division was establishing a base and headquarters, on the east bank of the Chindwin at Paungbyin, a little over 30 miles to the east and north of Tamu. These Japs who were so inexplicably moving north would have been en route.

This unexpected meeting with one of the hated enemy astonished us for the manner in which we were becoming emotionally involved, with feelings of compassion for this young man, so much in need of help if he was to survive. Help that had to come from us. What, I wonder, would those of other nations have done – in so remote a place. Some would have shot him then, or earlier, at that critical moment when he made his presence known. It would have been so easy to have riddled his flimsy shelter, as we closed upon it, using the probable presence of further Japs as justification. And why trouble ourselves and others with an unimportant Second Class Private, when we had so many prisoners? To walk away would leave him no worse off than before, and with ample time to regain his grenade.

Any doubts that we might have had were however eliminated for us. Being the first to have reached him I was standing directly to his front and it was of me that he asked the question – "English Master?" I nodded and said, yes. Whereupon he brought his hands to his forehead, palms together in salutation, and then laid back quite flat, relaxed and smiling – so clearly showing that he no longer worried as to his future.

Considering the attitude of the Japanese to those whose tragedy it was to become their prisoners, this surely was a remarkable tribute to us British. How was it that this young soldier, I was later to assume as Kesahichi Takahashi – the name on the flag – one of an army taught to look upon us with contempt and hatred, did not do so?

But irrespective of this demonstration of trust, we and the majority of our comrades would not have thought to do other than what we did.

It must have been soon afterwards that he had made signs that the flag should be lowered and torn up. Wareham, John and I tossed for it and, to my great delight, I won. That flag was to be far the best in quality and interest that came my way and, some years later, a friend of Eileen's was able to translate the writing on it. A sample is:

> Do your best Mr Takahashi, from Gojo. Be loyal. Banzai! from Imano. Bomb them from Matsoda. Make a good show from Fuku. Fight to the end, from Sato. Be patriotic. Beat the Americans & English & Siamese. Please win the war! Be gallant! Be strong! from Tanaka.

Sentiments that we might have received, in similar circumstances.

We now had a prisoner for whom the walk back would not be possible and were in need of a stretcher party. Wareham offered to return to the jeep and drive it to our ambush where there was a wireless set, through which an ambulance could be summoned. Thus he would eventually return with a stretcher and bearers. I need hardly mention that Wareham was one of our old and treasured Dorsets.

Knowing that all this would take some time, John and I, following the departure of Wareham, decided that we would continue and resume the escape route as earlier intended. Our Jap took a poor view of our preparations. I sketched an ambulance on a scrap of paper, thereby partially, but only partially, reassuring him that he was not being abandoned.

Instead of retracing our angled approach we wandered straight out into the dazzling sunshine of the clearing and, when about half-way across, seeing a Japanese helmet lying on the ground, we decided that here was an opportunity to test its penetration by our weapons. We duly shot at it from varying distances until, having holed it to our satisfaction, we proceeded to the far side.

There we halted at a cleft stick some three feet in length and stuck upright in the ground, within the cleft a sheet of white paper, cluttered with Japanese characters. Behind it a narrow footpath wound its way into the jungle and, like the other bigger one, its surface showed the familiar footprints, both clear indications of an escape route, with the notice providing information to those about to use it. The paper was fresh and it and the ground were clear indications of the path's recent use. To my lasting regret I did not pocket that piece of paper; how fascinating it would be to know its message.

We decided to follow the path and with John leading we disappeared into vegetation so dense that the only view was ahead, and that precious little. As we moved deeper into a silent and frightening world, where the trees enclosed us on all sides and above, it was as if we were entering a trap. How far we had progressed when we moved to the right, clear of the track to halt for a smoke, has faded from memory. There we sat, back-to-back, so that we had an 'all-round view' – one that did not extend much beyond our boots. On finishing our smoke we mutually agreed that what we were doing was a frightful sweat and not worth the effort, and so we retraced our steps. And what a blessed and wonderful relief it was to be again in the open.

Earlier I described this day as one that was 'free of the restraints of battalion life'. In effect a holiday, and holidays are when foolish things are done, but our irresponsible behaviour, especially after the departure of Wareham, was utter folly and we were unbelievably lucky to have got away with it. To have fallen foul of a few Japs would have been to disappear without trace. Looking back through so many years I almost laugh at the thought of what the reaction of George Wood would have been – we broke so many of his rules.

Our Japanese friend was delighted to see us and we three spent the ensuing hour or so smoking, John and I reclining on the ground. Then Wareham and the stretcher-bearers arrived and we all set off, reaching the ambulance without incident, it and Private Takahashi going to brigade and we back to the battalion.

One hopes that the recipient of all that effort was able to return to a welcoming family and to Gojo, Imano and his other friends. Perhaps he, from time to time, thinks of us?

It was probably on this day that the East Africans arrived and moved down to near Tamu, in preparation for their advance south on the 9th. Also on this day the C.O. of the 5th Field Ambulance visited Geoffry, to ask if he might have an escort for a dash down the Kabaw Valley, before the Africans got going. He wanted to be first at a Japanese hospital which, it was believed, they had established at a village some 12 miles south of Tamu. It was arranged that he would have Mac and as many of the Guerilla Platoon as could be squeezed into a jeep and two 15cwt trucks. This looked promising and I was delighted when Geoffry agreed that I might accompany them.

So on that following day, at 0600hrs, we set off down the now familiar road and then to turn south down the unfamiliar valley road. There we soon passed between long lines of giant Askaris maintaining an impressive march discipline, their sections properly and accurately spaced out and alternating on each side of the road. We progressed slowly, partly due to the rotten state of the road but more so that we might, we hoped, have an appearance of respectability. As we got forward, so our advance slowed and we could see ourselves being scrutinized, just as if we were suspected of being gate-crashers at a party.

On reaching the HQ of the leading brigade we were halted and our doctor C.O. disappeared, leaving us aware that we had probably reached the end of our road, and so it was. It was agreed that he could accompany the brigade; we were to return. Mac and I decided that as we could not go south we might as well go north and explore one of the supply routes to Ukhrul. As we progressed beyond where I had been, on that unmetalled road, so the going got worse, bogged vehicles were everywhere. After some miles we, very reluctantly, decided on discretion and turned about.

Seeing and being amongst those abandoned vehicles, some Austin and Morris cars which had been collected by the Japs in their progress through Malaya and Burma, made us aware of how great an ally the monsoon had been. The 'I' Section found nothing of importance but there were beneficiaries, for our fitters amassed a collection of tools the like of which they had never seen. And when lower down the valley in December, two three-ton Japanese trucks were mobilised and, under the names of 'Tojo' and 'Tokyo', did great service in augmenting our transport.

Harold Jones has a story to tell of what was our final day:

> I was ordered to escort a colonel in the Royal Army Medical Corps from 2nd Division Headquarters, into the Kabaw Valley.
>
> He arrived in a jeep towing a trailer. With him was his driver, a gunman and a very smart orderly in starched jungle green. I had not until then realised how good the laundry arrangements were at Div. HQ.
>
> I accompaned the colonel with one section of my platoon, in two jeeps.
>
> The forest through which our road ran, (the jeeps in four-wheel drive, so bad was the going on a surface reduced to a morass), was humid, gloomy, depressing and unhealthy, the trees and undergrowth dripping water. After about three miles we stopped near a roadside basha of bamboo and plantain, some 150 feet in length, 40 feet wide and 20 to the ridge. It had been used as a shelter for the sick and injured and inside were 60 charpoys, 30 a side and three feet apart. On every one was the bloated corpse of a Japanese solder in an advanced state of decomposition. Other corpses were on the floor.
>
> The colonel picked up the sword of a Japanese officer as a momento.
>
> Our medical services had told us that the valley was an unhealthy place, the scene in the basha confirmed that dreadful diseases lurked everywhere.
>
> We then moved away from the road to a more open area within the trees. The sun shone brilliantly, the ground steamed and all manner of insects buzzed. It was intensely hot and humid. There we made some tea and discussed what we had seen. Presently I thought I heard a moan and went with my batman to investigate an adjacent track. There, in the mud, was a Japanese soldier in an advanced state of malnutrition. He was in a pitiful state. We summoned the colonel and then bore the soldier in a blanket, gently, to our vehicles. The colonel prescribed – not hot sweet tea – but crushed biscuit, sugar and warmed tinned milk and water, and that was fed in small teaspoonfuls. After about half an hour our captive, who was in no condition to talk and thus unable to indicate what had happened to him, was placed on a blanket in the trailer. We moved off but almost immediately he cried out in pain and we stopped. It was then that the young, immaculately turned-out orderly did what I shall always remember. He said to his colonel 'Drive very slowly and I will jump into the trailer and nurse him.' Then, without a thought for the consequences he cradled the pitiful figure in his arms. I have often thought of that soldier's conduct and his complete disregard for the risks he took in nursing the lice-infected and, perhaps, scrub-typhus ridden body.

We commenced our return on the 10th, August at 0600hrs, marching for three hours and again for four hours from 1800hrs. Timing that avoided the heat of the day. But it was a rotten march, in rain, the road often deep in mud of which some was very liquid. It ended with that 1,000-foot climb from the Lokchao River to our old camp site within the trees. But we cheered up on arrival, two pints of hot sweet tea and a cup of rum put a different complexion on life. On the next day trucks whisked us to Palel, 23 days after our first arrival there. Days remembered for the rain and the almost universal mud. To the best of my knowledge we saw none of the native population, either in the Chin hills or the Kabaw valley. They would have dispersed into remote villages, ready to return after a nightmare that had started early in March.

CHAPTER SEVEN

Maram: Recovery and Renewal

12th August – 4th September.

On the 12th we arrived at a new camp, one in which we were to be refreshed in spirit, in training and in numbers; then to depart to do battle within the heart of Burma. Our home was astride a spur to the east of the Imphal road at ms 82 and one mile south of Maram, at a height of 4,500 feet. It was an extension of the mountain, west of the road, on the apex of which at 6,167ft, was the village of Maramei. Steep slopes continue to the river, the Sangu Lok, 1,200 feet away in the depths. There we viewed spectacular scenery from our tents for, being on the tip of the spur, our outlook was over mountains and valleys for as far as the eye could see.

6 Brigade had not been involved in the recent operations and, in consequence, was well established. Close to the road were the Welch Fusiliers, our allocation was the open ground beyond them. Thus we had not only to develp a camp but access, in the form of a vehicular track, which would encircle the Welch on their south flank. There we were to be for some 15 weeks, during which the division as a whole recovered and was reinforced. And we changed from a wholly motorised transport to a mixed one – trucks, jeeps, carriers and such, and mules.

Tentage was sufficient for all but the largest buildings, two of which were our church and mess. The former, as was our custom, was dedicated to St. Aldhelm. For these, forest timbers were clad with tarpaulins, some probably 'borrowed' from those vehicles that went into other hands. Wherever they originated their products were remarkably satisfactory. Officers had a 40lb. tent with a floor area of six feet by five, ample for a camp bed and kit. So we were very comfortable and I have most happy memories of mine. Even the 'I' Section had an office tent, one that developed into an information room, where were displayed maps and charts of our front and the others, particularly Europe, the area of greatest interest as we and the Americans fanned out into France. Later we were to add a section of drawings and photos describing the Jap, his equipment and organisation.

To my delight I was to depart for an 'I' Course at, of all places, Shillong. Thus I was to see again that most agreeable of places, one to which there had been no expectation of returning. With Colin back from leave and in the adjutant's chair, I was very happy to relinquish that demanding position and make arrangements to do as much of the journey as possible by air. Bert Jones, who was to be with me, was to go by train; thus on the day, he set off for Dimapur and I for Imphal, there to board a Dakota.

Leaving the Imphal Plain in brilliant sunshine, the atmosphere clear and bright between the monsoon showers, we turned west over the high ground and the widening valley of the Silchar track and so on to the town of Sylhet and its air-strip, a flying distance of 150 miles. A journey with the thrill of crossing that mountain barrier, which had prevented the Japs from taking this direct route into India. Then there was the contrast of the plain, much of which was under flood water which shimmered with the reflected sun. At 0600hrs the next morning I was away on the third stage, travelling in a small convoy of trucks bound for Shillong, a distance of 70 miles. A letter describes this as the most beautiful of all my road journeys; first the low ground and then up into the Khasi Hills, climbing 6,000 feet. Finally the spectacular conclusion of a road on a 'knife edge' ridge, flanked by sheer drops of thousands of feet – seen at its best in the bright sunshine.

My destination proved to be one of a number of hutted camps, four miles from the town. There students had their own rooms complete with that rarity – a proper bed. What with clean clothes, a cool mosquito-free climate and floors to walk on, life was to be very pleasant. The mess was agreeable and the food excellent, with teas that included lettuce, radishes and tomatoes grown locally and the quantity such that we could eat as much as we liked.

I was glad to have Bert Jones, so that he too could relax away from the never-ending battalion routine. Very often, in those days of individual batmen, as will have been apparent, a relationship of trust and understanding developed. And we junior officers were pampered in a way that few would experience again.

The course kept us busy during the day and sometimes into the night, and study occupied most evenings. But across the road was a cinema, no plush seats and a place that lacked the finer points of showmanship: nevertheless somewhere to enjoy that rare treat of English or American films, on one's doorstep. One evening, having decided that the crowd of hopeful patrons was so large that there was no chance of admission, and also aware of an increasing internal uproar, I was turning away when the Indian manager hurriedly emerged and in passing said, "Booking clerk he sell seats twice, sahibs very, very angry, I go away." And so did I.

One half-day holiday enabled us to shop in Shillong. There local craftsmen had on sale items such as fur-lined leather gloves and slippers which, being easily packed and unbreakable, we snapped up as ideal presents for the folks at home.

When forced to be part of a communal life, one that lasted for seven days in every week, time to oneself was precious. Perhaps it is for that reason I remember a Sunday walk, in morning sunshine after rain, strolling alone along gravel-margined asphalted road through pine woods. So reminiscent of such places in Dorset. The roads and the trees were true to scale and not only looked right but, in a warm and damp atmosphere, smelt right. It is easy to understand the affection that such places generated and that they were homes from home for their British expatriates.

Of the three weeks, a third was devoted to the study and interpretation of aerial photographs. Training that was to prove essential subsequently, when we received them in large numbers and which it was my job to interpret and build into 'mosaics', in which each could be seen in its relationship to others.

We studied the fall of Singapore and, in the role of Japanese commanders expecting an Allied attack, did 'appreciations of the situation'.

Having learned much and so agreeably, it all ended too soon for my liking. To my surprise I had done sufficiently well to have a recommendation to do such work at a 'high level' headquarters. An attractive possibility had I a desire to leave the battalion.

5th September – 12th October.

It was good to be back among the familiar faces and to see the established camp; much had been done and it was a happy and generally healthy place. There we prepared for the demands of Burma, in anticipation of which our lives were totally directed. One of those faces was that of Paget Fretts, superficially as fit as ever, despite the bullet received at Khabvuma, still lodged in a lung. Joe describes him as one with 'more lives that a cat', for his wounds had started prior to Dunkerque.

Of particular interest, then and later, were the new arrivals. With spare infantry in very short supply and the Japanese air force only an occasional threat, it was from the anti-aircraft gunners that battalions received most of their reinforcements. When they had recovered from the shock of their changed role, they probably welcomed the chance of a more active life. Certainly they became one with us and they excelled in training and when we were in action.

In the period September/October we received, from seven Light Anti-Aircraft Regiments of the Royal Artillery, 339 new faces, of which four were officers. A further 26 were to join us from the 8th Heavy Anti-Aircraft Regiment.

In October we had a much valued influx of 66 foot sloggers, 25 coming from the Somerset Light Infantry (Mac's old regiment) and we also had 41 from the South Lancashire Regiment.

In all, 472. Enough to be classified as a massive blood transfusion into a battalion with a total strength of approximately 800, all ranks.

Newly arrived subalterns included John Main, John O'Donnell and 'Fish' Mullet. They were followed by Colin Beale, Robin Cuthbertson and Gerry Overman, of whom Colin and Gerry were Dorsets. Later, Roger Johnson and John Joslin arrived.

After we had been in camp for about a month, cases of the dreaded typhus were found amongst ourselves and adjacent units and a number died, one being a newly arrived Captain Smith. To travel half around the world and then to die in such a way, epitomizes the waste of war. A number of us went to Kohima for his burial service in the war cemetery, then being established on the spur we had known so well, and where work was in progress on a memorial to the dead of our division. Above the spur, most trenches had been filled and a prolific growth of vegetaion made the recognition of our old positions almost impossible.

Joe wrote to me about the typhus:

> At ms 82 we had 25 cases, five of whom died. One got a sense of foreboding when a man reported sick with fever and examination revealed a small inflamed black spot (the site of a mite-bite) and enlarged glands in the groin or armpit. This fit looking man would for certain be desperately ill in ten days time. One of the 2 Div. Field

Ambulances set up a treatment centre which did a very good job – the mortality would have been even higher if cases had made the long journey to a base hospital. Paget Fretts got it when just back from a remarkable recovery from his chest wound and again managed not to perish.

Gus must have been busy with the aftermath of battle and widespread sickness, people in and out of hospital and others concerned with the blitz and home problems. Church services were part of a well ordered routine. There was no mistaking St Aldhelm's-in-the-Jungle, with its cross at the roof apex and, in the traditional manner of battlefield churches, a suspended brass shell-case sounded in substitution for a bell.

With thousands of men in a confined area and precious little level ground it was not easy to make provision for spare time. However, our sappers excelled when faced with a challenge, and constructed a theatre able to accommodate 1,000. The framing was Bailey bridging, with which they spanned the 100-foot width, without internal supports. Amazingly it was roofed and walled with tarpaulins. Earth-filled sandbags constituted the seating, the front rows of which were allocated to those other than officers, who sat at about the half-way line. There our mobile cinema units put on film shows and the concert party delighted us with its professional skills. One hardly needed ENSA.*

The sappers also managed a football pitch, of sorts, and no games were watched or played with greater enjoyment.

Many of the memories of those days are of the views to the south, seen at their finest and most spectacular in the early morning. At that hour we looked down, as often as not, on a sea of mist blotting out the lower ground and, standing out of that whiteness, would be the distant hills and peaks. With the rising of the sun, so the mist dispersed and the lower ground would return to view throughout the seven miles of the valley of the Sangu Lok, over which we looked. The hills within our vision, flanking the far western side of that valley, have their topmost peak seven miles to the east – Paduhu, 7,508ft. The highest ground then runs to the south and towards the west through a chain of villages just under 6,000ft., with names such as Prayatemei Thingba Khuien and Prayatemei Thingba Khunou, and terminates due south at the village of Khabung. West of that place the ground falls some 2,000 feet into a tributary of the Sangu Lok.

A wonderful place in which to have lived, for that short time, and how favoured we were to have been there, though I doubt that all my comrades would agree.

Because of the fear of the typhus bug in the low ground, patrols to the Sangu Lok and beyond were few and far between. My visits to habitations were restricted to Maramei, where Geoffry claimed he had found a Japanese position, so well concealed that he could walk me through it without my knowing. Accordingly, to put it to the test, we set off and climbed the 1,600 feet to Maramei and, skirting the village, we walked across a wooded spur and halted. Turning

* The British war-time Entertainments National Service Association, which travelled the world, taking entertainment to the Services.

about I was advised that I was looking at the concealed defences, having strolled right through them. They took some finding even then. Of the many I remember only a one-man standing position, in a hollow tree. We were astonished that so much effort had been expended on something of so little value, with the road out of sight and so far below.

As these so carefully sited and constructed slit trenches and so on were in what might be described as 'mint condition', they were considered worthy of careful examination and recording. Consequently, the 'I' Section spent a couple of days in carrying out a survey, from which I was able to plot a detailed plan.

During those days we were able to see just a little of the life of Maramei, a rarity for us in that it was a village so little affected by the war. It included a meeting on a promontory of the village elders, under their Headman, he proudly wearing his red blanket of office. They might well have been discussing us and what we were up to, but made no attempt to interfere. A woman was working a loom, producing the coarse woven material, attractively patterned in the reds and browns of their outer garments. We admired the exteriors of their long low huts, a feature of which were the gabled ends, decorated with animal skulls, trophies of the chase and evidence of the prowess of their inhabitants.

The Nagas were our trusted friends and allies. It is said that there is no known instance of them betraying our trust, or doing other than assisting us to their utmost. We in turn respected them, and we admired them for their virility and their ordered way of life; one in which the wheel played no part. Loads were conveyed in conical baskets, supported by a head-strap. The women being the carriers, so that the men might be unencumbered, and thus free to use their spear or bow.

When on that formidable climb to the village, we were resting where a gap in the jungle enabled travellers to enjoy the view, over and beyond our camps. We were joined by an elderly Naga. He, to our horror, had a five-inch gash in a shin in which the leg bone could be seen. We did our best to indicate that the soldiers below would attend to it for him. For his part, of greater interest were our binoculars, we had been studing the view, and he was soon also peering through them and grunting fiercely – whether in amazement or frustration wasn't clear.

We had one night up there, spent around a camp fire on which we cooked our supper, and in the morning we were spectators of a superb dawn made more so by the view from this the highest of any near-by peak. Nights at that height, above 6,000 feet, were definitely chilly and even in our camp we were glad of pullovers after dark.

On 13th September, one week after my return from Shillong, I was flying again. In the knowledge that in our future operations air transport would be our main and possibly, at times, only source of supply, the planners decided that as many officers of the ground forces as possible should learn about the flying side. By knowing something of their difficulties in reaching and finding us and then delivering, we would be better able to co-operate. To this end, each front line unit was given four places on planes dropping supplies to fighting troops, for us the 5th Indian Division advancing on Tiddim, a small but strategically placed town, about 100 miles to the south of Imphal.

It did not take long to contact Colin Doran and make clear my interest, and it was he and I who formed one half of our allocation. Leaving camp at 0600 hrs, we were at the Imphal strip at 0800 hrs and taking off 15 minutes later. Flying south we were soon over mountains, one moment just clearing a peak and the next looking down thousands of feet onto jungle, with virtually no clearings, tracks or signs of human habitation. However we found our objective, a group of native huts on a spur among the lower slopes; as we lost height so they became visible to Colin and me and then we spotted the dropping zone, a microscopic patch of lighter green adjoining the huts and marked by the regulation linen strips, laid on the ground to form a cross. We had been preceded by two planes which we now followed more closely as they commenced to circle for the drop, during which Colin and I looked up the mountain slopes, which by then were rising 1,000 feet or move above us, a most peculiar and thrilling sensation.

We were, of course, in a Douglas DC-3 Dakota and, with the fuselage full to the roof with our load, Colin and I were looking out through the rectangular windows provided in alternate bays of the fuselage's transverse framing. Those planes carried a maximum load of 7,500lbs and had a dropping speed of 120 mph which, although seeming relatively slow, did necessitate split-second timing, for the plane was travelling 100 yards in one and a half seconds. In the port side near the tail was the opening, about four feet six inches wide by five feet six inches high, through which the load was discharged. This was to be a 'free' drop and thus from a height of about 100 feet, as against 6-700 feet for parachuted loads. We had been sitting on and amongst the cargo of sacks and set to, helping the two aircraftsmen dispatchers or, as they are also known, 'kickers', by dragging sacks to the opening where they were built into a pile. The indicating light over the opening would light up and on this signal out went the sacks, the dispatchers holding on with one hand and using the other and their feet in a mighty heave. We passengers having dashed to a window to watch the fall, returned to the cargo to repeat the proceedings while the plane climbed and recommenced circling. We soon had our jackets off, for the sacks took some shifting and, as more were dropped, so the dragging distance increased; but as with most such jobs, we thoroughly enjoyed ourselves. In all on that flight we made 45 runs (as reckoned by me) over the zone, in each of which six or seven sacks were jettisoned.

The flight had been so marvellous that on our return, we went straight to the office of the squadron-leader in charge of the drop, to see if we could 'sign on' for a repeat performance. There was no difficulty, they were always happy to take officers from the 2nd Division because of their willingness to help with the work.

Forty-five minutes later we were on our way in the same plane to the same place. This time we were carrying a half load of sacks to be dropped as before, the remainder of the load was fitted with parachutes and was to be dropped in threes. As before when we ran in for the low drop, so we swept down on to and over the huts, seemingly at roof height; this was followed by a steep bank to avoid the mountain and an 'even keel' circling in the valley, while the load was stacked and the plane positioned for a repeat.

What a terrifying intrusion this must have been in a way of life devoid of extraneous noise. No motor vehicle could have reached them and prior to the war 'motors' would have been rare anywhere in those mountains. No inhabitants could be seen, presumably they moved out complete with their animals, to as remote a corner as they could find. There were not even many troops visible; my memory is of little more than a cluster of men and mules, most of our sacks being fodder for the latter.

The 5th Indian Division were engaged in fighting the 33rd Japanese Division which continued to live up to its reputation of being the most formidable of the divisions in their 15th Army. As our road building and maintaining resources were insufficient to maintain the Tiddim road and to upgrade the one in the Kabaw Valley, the one to Tiddim was being allowed to disintegrate behind our advancing troops. Thus, for 5 Div., air supply by dropping (in that country no plane could land) was the only source of supply. Their resulting isolation made them unique in having nurses with them, there being no way by which their casualties could be got to hospital.

On our return flight Colin and I lay on the floor with our heads behind the door opening, enjoying the wonderful panorama until, as we approached the Imphal Plain, we were invited into the cockpit. Standing behind the pilots we were told that they were diverting from the direct route, as they wished to see a Dakota that had crashed when returning from a similar mission, but we failed to find it. That ended, we completed the flight at a height of about 20 feet, to the alarm and consternation of the many locals returning to their homes from Imphal market.

Luck had been very much on our side in the allocation to us of those flights, for only a day or two later the Japs shot down all the planes that were flying, killing amongst the crews two gunner officers, who were experiencing what we had so much enjoyed. On each side of the fuselage of those Dakotas, a window had been removed and an antiquated Vickers machine-gun with a drum magazine inserted, so that the dispatchers might provide a token defence against attack. We could visualise them desperately trying to sight those inadequate guns on to fast-flying fighters, probably their restricted arcs of fire prevented them aligning their sights on their attackers, who would have approached astern and unseen. As a result of this disaster 'Division' decided that such losses could not be afforded and the liaison ceased.

Returning to the routine of daily life: that could be said to be nothing other than the training of ourselves and our newcomers for the tasks ahead within Burma. It was the departure of our many vehicles and the arrival of the mules that affected all; as did the realisation that we were returning to the life of the foot-soldier of earlier years, advancing in columns accompanied by baggage-carrying animals. In that way we would move into and operate within Burma, doing so in the small formations of battalions and brigades, fighting in engagements often at company level, much as we had done after Kohima. Not for us the massed battles of Europe, with all their particular horrors and in that we were to be very fortunate.

Our new scale of vehicles was:

8 Jeeps, four of which had trailers.
1 Jeep, towing the Battalion HQ office trailer.
6 Dodge 15cwt trucks, five for company cooks and one for the QM.
4 Bren-gun carriers.
1 Water truck.
2 Motor-cycles.
These to be augmented by the two Japanese trucks.

One jeep was allocated to the R.A.P. and its trailer was fitted with a frame to hold double-banked stretchers. (A very uncomfortable ride says Joe Chamberlin.)

Those drivers of trucks and carriers, dispossessed by the departure of their vehicles, were drawn upon to provide the required muleteers for the 54 mules and two ponies which constituted the greater part of the Transport Platoon. This was the successor of our Carrier Platoon, no longer justified as such. To these was to be added a Japanese pony, a 'grey' named Judy, one that it was often my pleasure to ride.

Attached was an Indian Army Mule Company with 59 mules, six of which were riding mules for the evacuation of casualties. I think it unlikely that those six were used as designated, but they were ridden. Finally there were chargers for the Indian officers and splendid animals they were.

John Main, now a captain, became our Mechnical and Animal Transport Officer. It is with the mules that we associate him and his number two – Sergeant Park, an ex-cavalryman, also newly arrived. In close support was Private Churchill, another expert with horses and together they did a great job, one that was made possible by the exceptional efforts of the ex-drivers. They were to develop an affection for their charges which far exceeded their earlier regard for their vehicles and they who, before, marched the least now did the most.

During the weeks following the arrival of our animals, the camp enjoyed many diversions from routine as mules careered through our lines and across country, shedding their loads en route and out-pacing their muleteers. And we discovered that it is not only the cowboy's pony that can buck.

A unit of the Women's Auxiliary Service (Burma) arrived, and were alongside our lines from time to time with their mobile canteen, which was attached to 2 Div. Their cups of tea and cakes and the so different non-regimental and feminine atmosphere, in a totally male world, was almost a touch of Blighty not only then, but later when we were into Burma.

The 'I' Section was happily running the 'Information Tent', where the display was expanding with an ever growing collection of photographs and our own drawings. These dealt with the war generally, but we concentrated on our particular enemy, his organisation, weapons and equipment. We had a number of Japanese weapons, mainly carbines and machine-guns, which we not only displayed but demonstrated. Thus their characteristics could be understood, and the variations in the rates of fire of their and our automatic weapons could be heard and recognised.

In that September our establishment was changed by the formation of an Administrative Company, thus dividing the cumbersome Headquarters Company into two, as follows.

Headquarters Company.	
Officer Commanding	Captain MacKenzie.
Company Sergeant-Major	CSM Osmond.
Signals Platoon	Lieutenant Eagle, platoon strength 34
Mortar Platoon	Captain Murrills, platoon strength 36
Defence Platoon	Captain Highett, platoon strength 41
Pioneer Platoon	platoon strength 23

Administrative Company.	
Officer Commanding	Captain Harris.*
Company Sergeant-Major	CSM Vaughan.
Quartermaster	Lieutenant Smith.
Regimental Quartermaster-Sergeant.....	RQMS Hayward.
Regimental Sergeant-Major	RSM Goldson.
Transport Platoon	Captain Main, platoon strength 62
Medical Section	Captain Chamberlin, Medical Officer.
....	Sergeant Critchley, Medical Sergeant.

The Transport Platoon's personnel included 10 drivers and 42 mule leaders for the 54 mules.

In the Medical Section there were 20 stretcher bearers and 4 sanitary orderlies of whom 2 were in charge of water.

13th October – 28th November.

On the 13th Geoffry sent me off to Kohima to contact the C.O. of the Norfolks, and also an old 2 Dorset of Yorkshire days – Sam Symes, then in command of the 2nd Worcestershire Regiment, in the 19th Indian Division who were moving into Assam, en route to Burma. But Sam had not arrived.

That journey preceded our 'Sarah Sands Day', for which I was carrying invitations. In 1857 the transport *Sarah Sands* was conveying our predecessors, the 54th Regiment, to India and when in the Indian Ocean the ship caught fire. Exploding gunpowder blew off the stern, but the courage and discipline of the troops not only saved all on board but the ship as well; which, although reduced to a water-filled dismasted hulk, they sailed to Mauritius, a distance of 800 miles.

Successive C.O.s have believed that such deeds can be best recognised by formal parades. But at Maram, in the absence of level ground, even Geoffry had to admit defeat, and celebrations suited to our situation were substituted.

One merit of that camp was that it so suited the bugle calls, beloved by Geoffry,

* David Harris had a personality having much in common with that of Joe Chamberlin and everybody liked him. The multitude of admin jobs that became his responsibility were executed with a cheerful excellence.

and so well sounded by Corporal Cripps. In such a place and time, there was an uplifting of spirits on hearing the daily calls, so clearly, within the vastness of that remote world.

The training of our reinforcements in the ways of the infantry, as practised by us, was in the hands of Andrew MacKenzie, an instructor at battle schools before coming to India. Such schooling aimed to break down the tendency of recruits to move and do things according to the text book, as had those Askaris in the Kabaw Valley. Our world had to be that of the crouching, darting run to cover and its constant use, we becoming part of the landscape, outdoing the Jap in what he did so well.

In October, as many as could made the journey to Kohima for the dedication of our Dorset memorial to those who had died there and in the fighting towards Imphal. Built in the local rugged stone, it stood four-square on a plinth of two steps and, in that solidity it epitomized the battalion. A bronze plaque has the inscription – "In Memory of all ranks The 2nd Battalion The Dorsetshire Regt, who Fell in Action in these Hills between April and June 1944. Who's Afear'd?" A short service, which included the singing of that great and favourite hymn, 'O God our help in ages past', was followed by the reading of the names for whom the memorial had been erected, and the firing of a salute. General Nicholson performed the unveiling, and our bugler sounded the Last Post and Reveille.

A month later we returned for the unveiling of the memorial to the dead of the 2nd Division, the central feature of which is a monolith carrying the words, so often repeated on occasions of remembrance:

> When you go home
> Tell them of us and say,
> For your tomorrow
> We gave our today.

That stone, of 17 tons and 16 feet in height, was a Naga obelisk and was donated by them. It had stood near Maram, from where it was conveyed by a tank transporter to its final manhandling by a team of Nagas. It stands supported on a stone base, forward of a curved retaining wall built by craftsmen in the division, to a design by an architect in the division, Lieutenant Ferrie RE.

At that time, we did not look many years ahead and none would have contemplated the Service of Commemoration in York Minster, on Sunday 13th, May 1984. It marked the 40th Anniversary of the battle. An apt date, for on that day we Dorsets had taken the tennis court.

In that magnificent building, filled to overflowing by a congregation of whom many were old or young soldiers, we had a service that the Church of England, when it has the mind to do so, does extremely well. With the Reverend L. E. M. Claxton MC in the pulpit, we had an address which awakened memories, touched hearts and brought tears to old eyes and possibly, also to young ones. Then making our exit through the west door into the bright sunshine of early summer, a day when it was so good to be alive, the morning concluded in a march

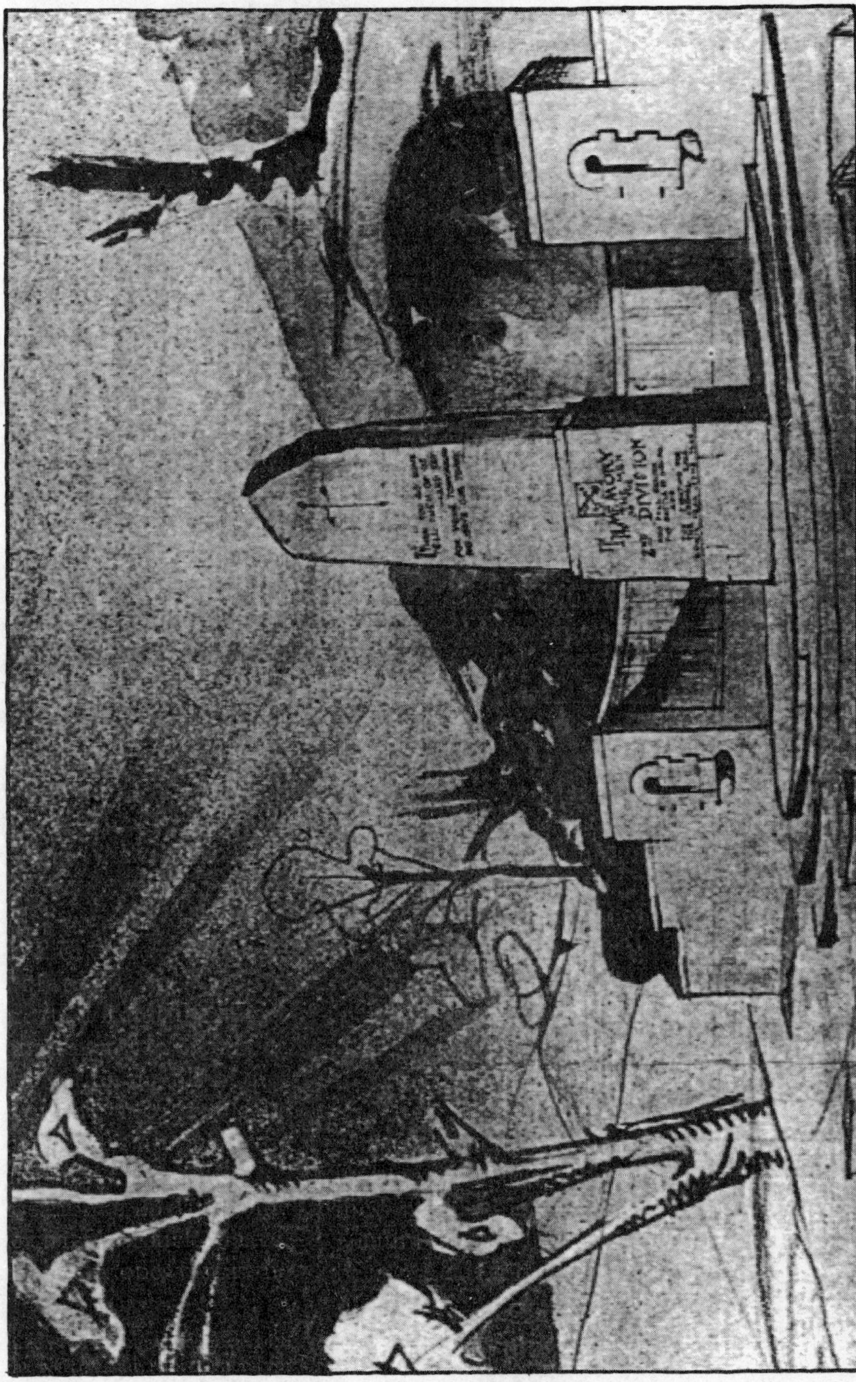

Sketch design for the 2nd Division's War Memorial.

past. Led by the band of the Royal Corps of Signals, which had accompanied the service, a contingent of Burma Veterans marched off, to the cheers of the crowds filling the street.

At Kohima, the Catholic Community of Nagaland (as it is now known), were preparing to build a Cathedral Church close to Garrison Hill, to the everlasting memory of the fallen. The brochure of this ambitious project has photographs of that hill and the famous spur. Both are changed beyond recognition, for they are one of the many worldwide cemeteries maintained by the War Graves Commission. There the rows of graves are set within mown grass and flowers. And within that mown grass, as a permanent reminder, are the lines of the tennis court. A picture of the town shows many white walled buildings, set in a generous abandon, within a green world. It is not only in Britain that, in these post-war years, towns have spread beyond recognition, for Kohima extends as far as Zubza. Within that town there is a new hospital and a school, both financed by the British Government.

During that month of October, 1944 I had occasion to visit Bill Lough, last seen just prior to our departure from the Belgaum jungle. He invited me to attend a conference he was about to hold; one for the briefing of Brigade I.O.s on our forthcoming campaign. I was provided with a pass to the tented Division Planning Room, surrounded by wire and guarded by military police. There I learned that the Dorsets' first objective would be the town of Ye-U, in the Burmese central plain to the north of Shwebo. We were shown maps and an aerial photographic mosaic of the proposed route. This was immensely intriguing for it was a first leg that would take us well into Burma.

As the date of our departure approached the details of our role were made available to the whole battalion, so that everyone had as clear a picture as was possible of the tasks ahead and the nature of the country.

The move forward of our division was dependent on the clearing of the Kabaw Valley and the occupation of Kalewa on the near bank of the Chindwin. When that had been achieved and a bridgehead has been established on the far bank, 2nd Div. would cross and take over the advance, moving east and then south east along the road to Ye-U, a distance from the river of about 95 miles. Little was known of this road, despite every effort being made to obtain information from those who had used it in the 1942 retreat. Aerial photographs were of little help, much of its length being concealed by the jungle through which it ran. It proved to be little more than a sand and gravel track, sufficient however for our restricted scale of vehicles. Although a poor road, it had the redeeming feature of being within wide valleys in hills rather than mountains.

During our three and a half months at 'ms 82', steady progress had been made by the East Africans and the 5th Indian Division, as they continued the good work of driving the Japs back to and beyond the Chindwin. The Africans, in addition to their main task of advancing down the Kabaw Valley, had also moved a column east of Tamu to the town of Sittaung on the west bank of the Chindwin, reached on 4th September and found to be another 'Tamu'. From there they were able to form a small bridgehead on the far bank. That crossing was followed by a second on the 10th of November at Mawlaik, 50 miles to the south. A few days later they achieved their principal objective – occupation of Kalewa.

By then 5 Div. had passed Tiddim and had also taken the mountain-top village of Fort White (named after Sir George White, commanding the Burma Field Force in the late 19th Century) and in mid-November linked up with the East Africans at Kalemyo, a village to the west of Kalewa.

I remember discussing with Paget Fretts, who was weary and bored from so much inaction, the reports that we were receiving on the fighting by 5 Div. in their long and gruelling advance to and beyond Tiddim. We decided that we could learn far more about fighting the Japs, could we accompany such a division as observers.

In the Kabaw Valley, the main enemy had been the sheer wetness of the monsoon. There five inches of rain in a day was commonplace and we appreciated how very lucky we were to be out of it. The enemy who, in March, had advanced north up that valley so confident of success, by then must have been as desperate to get out.

Much as we had enjoyed our camp we knew that we could not remain there for ever; a job had to be done and the sooner we did it the sooner we would be going home. With the monsoon ending, conditions would be as ideal as they could be for our advance and it was right and proper that we should be off.

Mac and David had settled into their commands of the divided HQ Company and Jimmy Hodder, so long a signaller, was with John Bowles as his 2 I/C. Jock Murrills had become familiar with his mortars and Snagger Highett was amongst known faces in the Defence Platoon, the name by which the Guerillas were to be known. Throughout the battalion, the new faces had become familiar ones.

Geoffry decided that we should have a battalion trek before our departure, so that we might see how well we functioned after so long in camp and, with much new blood and our mules, we could be said to be almost reborn. The chosen day was 20th November, we moving off at 0215 hrs and, crossing the road, attacking the Maramei mountain in a slow but steady climb of about 1,200 feet, the last third of which was through jungle so thick that we were in complete darkness. There we continued a climb in which we were guided only by the upward slope, until at about 0430 hrs we halted to await the dawn and then progressed another half mile to a crest, a place where we could sort ourselves into a reasonable order, brew-up and eat two of our four bully sandwiches and admire the view. If, as I believe, we were south of Maramei, we would have been towards the top of the 2,500-foot drop down to the Barak River. And seeing mountain range after mountain range for as far as the eye could see to the north and west. From there the going was easy, on a native track running west and inclining down towards the river, into country which changed from jungle to forest. This was a place without villages and thus no clearings, but we progressed without difficulty, in sunshine, along a path within low ground and which could have been an animal track as easily as a human one. At times I must have been in the lead and enjoying the 'magic' of that remote and unknown world, on a track going nowhere and I perhaps the first European to have trodden that ground. Certainly I would have been map reading for all I was worth and only too aware of the wrath that would descend upon me were we to become lost in what would have so soon become 'damned hills'.

At mid-day we were at the entrance to a ravine with sheer cliffs enclosing the fast-flowing river in which were massive rounded boulders. Geoffry thought it a sound idea to accept its challenge and return that way, for should it be passable we could avoid retracing our outward route over that early climb. While the battalion sat down to a brew-up and the remainder of their haversack ration, I and two of the section set off to find a way through what we found to be a half mile long chasm. With the easing of the monsoon the water level had dropped, leaving some dicey but passable going, for us and the mules, so we were able to return with a favourable report. Whereupon Geoffry said, "Fine – off we go." And off we went. After that, to the relief of all, the path was reasonable and on the general line of the river and at one time over paddy fields. We hit the road about three miles south of our spur and were home at 1830 hrs, there to enjoy not only a hot supper but an issue of rum. When we were lucky that hot supper would be steak and kidney pudding and plum duff, real stomach fillers.

At Kohima, 33 Corps had expanded from a top-heavy formation responsible for the 2nd Division and those miscellaneous infantry battalions in the Assam Area, to include the 7th Division and the 161st and the 268th Brigades. Then, for the advance on Imphal it had the 23rd Long-Range Penetration Brigade, out on our left flank. Later, for the advances on Ukhrul and Tamu, the 20th and 23rd Division were temporarily transferred from 4 Corps.

Just how serious was disease, during the post-Kohima months, is shown in the following figures. Average weekly strength of 33 Corps – 88,578.

Casualties and Sickness – Period 22.6.44 to 16.12.44.

Malaria and N.Y.D. fever	20,430
Dysentery and Diarrhoea	6,849
Typhus	2,245
Battle Casualties	2,868
	32,392

CHAPTER EIGHT

To The Chindwin and Beyond

29th November

0400 hrs had been decreed for our start, an early hour but justified, for we were to be 5 Brigade's leading battalion. Despite the darkness and our distance from the road, where our convoy of vehicles was waiting, the business of moving some hundreds of men from camp to trucks, together with all their bits and pieces and how many of these there were, went almost perfectly. There was one slight hiccup with the Welch. John Main, wishing to avoid the outer road with all its hazards for frisky animals, thought to take the direct route through their lines but was refused passage. However, they survived the perils of the flanking track and all was well.

We were soon away and traversing the familiar Imphal road and then the one to Tamu, last seen when it was deep in mud. That night we were at a staging camp below Tamu; there a nearby stream helped to remove the thick coating of yellow dust with which we were plastered, and which also covered our possessions and vehicles. One memory of that stop is of reclining on the ground, within a lighted jungle clearing and laughing at a monologue by Colin Doran. He was entertaining us with one of his impersonations of an Indian Baboo. Happy days!

30th November

We resumed our journey at dawn, our destination Yazagyo, 60 miles due south down the Kabaw Valley and the last lap of this preliminary move. As on the previous day, I was leading the convoy and able to avoid some of the dust. In India dusty roads were the norm but none was like the one over which we moved that day. It was where hundreds of vehicles ploughed through inches of dust having the consistency of pepper, their wheels throwing out bow waves and from which there rose a dust cloud to above the jungle canopy and potentially visible to the enemy. A matter considered sufficiently serious for the imposition of a 5 mph speed limit, the breaking of which was a court martial offence. To pass an oncoming vehicle was to enter an all-enveloping curtain of suspended grit, which reduced visibility to about the length of your truck's bonnet, you inching forward and trusting that the road was where you hoped it to be. The issued dust masks, if worn at all, were used reluctantly, being more of a hindrance than an aid to breathing. Grim as it was, it was a mere trifle compared to the conditions of only a few weeks earlier – during the monsoon.

I have no recollection of passing through Khampat, that place which was a five-days journey from Moreh in October, or of any villages. We progressed through nothing but dust-caked jungle. But, as elsewhere, that dreary route was of interest for the many abandoned vehicles, of which two were enemy tanks, which I was able to stop and examine. As was to be expected, our convoy had become nothing more than a number of individual vehicles, each moving as best it could.

We passed an elephant dragging baulks of timber for use in the rebuilding of a road bridge. This would have been one of 'Elephant Bill's'. J. H. Williams or 'Elephant Bill', as he was best known, had lived with his animals in Upper Burma since 1920, and had become a recognised authority on that part of the country we were then entering. As such he had visited us and Service units generally, talking of the jungle and how best to live in it and, when necessary, off it. At the beginning of March he had evacuated his elephants, their attendants and their families ahead of the advancing Japs, passing up this valley en route for Imphal. During the battle they had lived away to the west of Imphal, now they were returning to play their part in the defeat of the invaders and in the restoration of their country. Pre-war, the Bombay Burma Trading Corporation maintained some 2,000 elephants in the forests. There they hauled teak logs to the rivers, where they were assembled and rafted down to Mandalay or Rangoon.

I overshot our destination which turned out to be well away from Yazagyo, but on returning I found a side track and was delighted to arrive in a forest clearing.

1st – 19th December

This was to be another happy camp and made uniquely so by the celebration of an early Christmas. A place so different to the last with its hills and views; in this we were in a wide valley and enclosed by trees. With the leaf canopies high above our heads, we moved with ease over a carpet of leaves on level ground, among well spaced tree trunks and enjoyed the filtered sunshine. Conditions that could not have been more different from the heat and humidity of August. Now we had dry sunny days that were temperate and cool nights. Nights that were noted for their prolific dew, much as we had experienced in the Belgaum jungle, and which by 2200hrs was steadily dripping off the leaves and refreshing the vegetation.

The track continued beyond our camp, taking a course in the general direction of the important village of Kalemyo, where the Tiddim road joined ours. It was obvious that it had been much used by the Japs; they would have been thankful for the concealment provided by the trees. On our first day the 'I' Section set off along it in a journey of exploration, but so hard was the going that only a couple of miles were covered. We crawled along a deeply rutted surface or bumped over 'corrugated' sections – tree trunks laid crosswise over what had been deep mud, all dried hard and, in the absence of traffic, not turned to dust. We continued to find abandoned vehicles.

There was little danger of an enemy attack. However, to guard against stray Japs appearing out of the vegetation, we had a trench system in which we slept and from which we could have defended ourselves. My slit trench followed the general pattern in having a longitudinal step in the floor, thus one stood in the deeper part and slept on the higher. Sleeping on the ground had long ceased to be a hardship, though it helped if it was dry and from then on it usually was. What I did detest was the enforced use, in the absence of anything better, of the large pack as a pillow which, with boots and the like inside and straps and buckles outside, was a most indifferent one. About then I obtained a Jap greatcoat, seldom worn as I was reckoned to be in danger of being shot, but it made a wonderful addition to the light-weight jungle blanket during that period of chilly nights.

Offices were above ground and the 'I' Section produced a thatched hut; doubtless some of the skills of our old friends, the Naga interpreters, long departed, had been assimilated.

Newly with us were two English speaking Burmese from the Burma Intelligence Force, the members of which had been selected from Burma Army escapees in '42. We got on well together for we liked them and they reciprocated. They were to be indispensable in making effective contact with the locals, giving and obtaining information, and they were able to advise and reassure civilians about what was happening – locally and generally.

We were soon visiting a village and making a formal call on the Headman, who invited us to join him on his verandah, there to relax in chat and the drinking of tea from attractive china – English exports perhaps? We learned how these inoffensive people had suffered at the hands of the Japs, who had pillaged them, stealing their live-stock and more. Consequently they were able to do little in the way of ploughing and were short of food. Their houses were typical of those we were to see in Burma, being of one elevated storey, supported on seemingly inadequate timber uprights. Access was by way of a flight of steps to a verandah, often the length of one side, as that on which we were entertained. The covered space below was a protected place for those things not wanted in the house. Construction was naturally of local timber, the walls rough boarded or of interwoven panels. Our years in India had made us familiar with the way of life in remote places; thus we were immediately aware that, in Burma, even in so isolated a place as this, there was a superior standard of living. Not before would we have imbibed tea without fear of the consequences. And there was a standard of behaviour that we found admirable, as we did the absence of begging.

Our lives entered into an easy routine, in which we did those things that were necessary or which were chosen for their interest or enjoyment. Having found that among our own mules there were a few that could be ridden, I spent many an afternoon on a splendid animal known as Goggles. Sometimes alone, but more often accompanied by someone such as Randell, we would travel along forest tracks, where elephant and even tiger spoor, plus the occasional Jap telephone cable, added variety, as did places used by the enemy. When someone discovered a well concealed open-sided building, containing artillery shells, there was an infinite satisfaction in seeing thousands that had been conveyed so far and then so precisely stacked – to no purpose. More generally I would be with the section, sometimes on all-day treks, delighted to roam so freely where, but a short time before, our enemies had been. On one such excursion we met an elephant trailing a length of chain and obviously glad to see some 'white' faces, for all our efforts to shoo him away were rebuffed. Appreciating how unpopular we would be were we to return with so large and so unexpected a visitor, we detoured through the cook-house area of the Brigade HQ lines. It worked perfectly and we made ourselves scarce as cooks and elephant contemplated one another.

Informal and unofficial safaris were commonplace, one resulted in the discovery of a long deserted Jap sawmill, complete with bunkers. It had been well stripped of anything worth finding, but at least one bivvy tent went up in flames that night, for what had been assumed to be a store of paraffin, but which was petrol, was used in some individual solid fuel stoves. When a scrounged 'banger' or whatever, was available, these 'Tommy Cookers' were providers of cherished meals of meat and veg., cooked in a couple of mess tins, juggled with skill and determination over the single flame.

These light-hearted outings were intermingled with a programme of patrolling, some of which lasted a couple of days. Both reflected and confirmed our confidence in the defeat of the enemy west of the Chindwin. A party of Japs was caught on the road, about a mile from our lines and, even back at ms 82, a couple had turned up some time earlier. But these were strays, so long separated from their fellows as to have no idea of where they were, or what was happening.

Our southward advance, within 33 Corps, was in preparation for the decisive battle envisaged by General Slim,* in which his 14th Army would meet a similar force within the Shwebo plain. That plain, some 60 miles in width and the same from north to south, lies within the Irrawaddy on its east flank, the Chindwin on its west, and to the south it is contained by that length of the Irrawaddy which flows west from Mandalay, to where the two rivers meet. There, in so suitable a terrain – generally flat and open – our tanks and artillery would overwhelm the Japs and force them back to and beyond the Irrawaddy River. That our foe was likely to stand and fight there, or could be persuaded to do so forward of that great river, with all the problems it presented as a barrier to the movement of men and supplies, was in the expectation that they would see our situation as similar. Had we not, behind us, obstacles in the Chindwin, admittedly a lesser river but one that was reinforced by the Kabaw Valley and the Chin Hills! And the Japanese Command would be well aware of their shorter lines of supply and our ever lengthening ones. East of the Irrawaddy and Mandalay are the formidable hills of the Northern Shan States, the equal of the Chins but infinitely more extensive. All north/south movement of any consequence had to be within the plain, thus our enemy could prepare his defences, confident that our advance would be channelled to them. This was sound reasoning. That the Japs did not make the stand as contemplated was to prove to be to our advantage.

At about this time, our Command decided that an allocation of 28 days home leave, would be a morale booster for British troops. The chance of such a leave, be it almost as minimal as winning a football pool, would raise hopes just as the

* It had been in August 1943 that Lieutenant-General Slim had taken command of the newly formed 14th Army. Following the victories at Kohima and Imphal, and his receipt of the KCB, Lieutenant-General Sir William Slim was to lead his army through to victory and, by so doing, establish himself as one of the great leaders of the Second World War.

latter does of winning a fortune. We received an allowance and a meeting of officers considered how best to fill the vacancies. It concluded that they should go to those who, in the men's opinion, were most deserving or needy. But they would have nothing of it, saying that such a choice would not be possible and that selection must be by a ballot open to all. They were undoubtedly right and that was how it was done.

It became my turn for 28 days local leave, which I had planned to enjoy at Darjeeling, from where one went on trek with ponies and relaxed each night in the comfort of a traveller's bungalow. It now seems quite crazy to want to go so far to do what we were, virtually, then doing. It must have been those bungalows, the snow and that great mountain, Kanchenjunga, that attracted so much. But this conflicted with the advance from the Chindwin and the capture of that intriguing town of Ye-U and its railway station. There was only a little hesitation – it had to be Ye-U, and so it was.

Mail was being delivered in remarkable quantities; it included Christmas Cards and thus we had our snow scenes and such potent reminders of home. One of my letters included a cutting from the Dorset Daily Echo, reporting the arrival in Dorchester of our Jap flag.

Cigarettes and pipe tobacco, dispatched by generous relatives and friends, were greatly valued in an existence having many hours when there was little to do but smoke. That precious moment – the opening of a new packet of English cigarettes, with that perfection of packaging, the silver paper and that first sharp scent of the Virginia tobacco – aroused the senses of touch, sight and smell, in a unique way; being so much in contrast with our somewhat seedy world.

We had been told that we could expect to be on the road during Christmas. Accordingly we, not being designated to be within the leading units in the crossing of the Chindwin, were allocated 18th December, as our day of celebration. There was a universal determination that the day should be one that was truly memorable. That it was, and so much so that memories remain of the little things and, as I lean over my typewriter, I see again that timbered camp site where the brown of tree trunks and leaf-covered ground predominated. Trucks had been dispatched to Dimapur and returned well laden. Then, on that day, at mid-day, we fulfilled the time-honoured tradition of waiting on the men and, having ample to eat and to drink, we achieved our traditional Christmas in that so different and so distant place. There feelings of comradeship surfaced freely and uniquely and they remain treasured. All were aware that for some, and if we were to have another 'Kohima' – for many, this was our last Christmas. Probably it was one's own?

I think of us as members of an exclusive club.

With us on that day were 49 men of the 1st Battalion The Gloucestershire Regiment, under Major James Heath, they having been attached to us as an exceptional stiffening of our numbers, ten days earlier. How glad we were to have them, at a time when every man was precious. Some had been in the 1942 retreat from Burma and, in our eyes, were in a very special category.

Also returned was Graeme Gordon-Wright who, with the departure of Colin

Doran, resumed his role as Adjutant.

Until that time our lives and the manner of our fighting had been determined by the mountains and, to a lesser extent, the jungle. That was soon to change and it was to be our lengthening supply line, along those difficult and hazardous roads which were behind us, and those rough tracks which lay ahead, that governed our lives. But as those tenuous tracks lengthened, it was our supply by the ubiquitous Dakotas that kept us going.

Though we always thought of ourselves as, first and foremost, members of 2 Div., we were also proud of being within 33 Corps. We were soon to admire the dash and brilliance of 19 Div., and to become aware of the support we were having from 20 Div. advancing with us on our right. Those divisions and 268 Brigade on our left and infilling the often wide gap between us and 19 Div., away to the north east, were to constitute the principal formations in our corps.

The all-important task of bridging the Chindwin had been given to Indian sappers, and on 10th December they had completed a floating Bailey bridge at Kalewa – 1,154 feet in length and the longest of all such bridges at that time. Contemplate for a moment – all the bridging material and the hefty pontoons had been conveyed along our tortuous roads, that were but the conclusion of a longer journey. We were at the receiving end of a brilliant administration.

The great move east started when 19 Div., under Major-General 'Pete' Rees, crossed into the Sittaung bridgehead and 20 Div., commanded by Major-General Douglas Gracey, (they whom we in 5 Brigade had supported in the advance on Tamu) crossed at Mawlaik.

19 Div. were to march across the hills of the Upper Chindwin, as we would also but on an easier course. After their crossing, 20 Div. swung sharp right to advance south along the east bank of the Chindwin, with the first objective the town of Monywa. Thus, just as the Japanese had struck across the river in March, with three divisions and a regiment, so we were similarly striking east in December.

20th December

As invariably happens, a long period of waiting was terminating in a rush departure. During the morning we received orders that one company and our HQ would move that night. Then throughout the day, at almost hourly intervals, the numbers were changed until nobody knew where he was going to be that night, and it was in the late afternoon that we heard that we would all move after dark. Much of this flap resulted from the unexpectedly rapid progress of 6 Brigade who, on the 17th, had crossed the Chindwin and had advanced against almost no opposition. Those who had opposed the crossing and the initial advance, were only a fraction of the numbers of Japs reported by the East Africans. All the efforts by our division were being directed towards getting a second brigade across, as soon as the limited transport would allow. It was the difficulty in gathering a convoy that had caused the variations in our instructions.

A day or two before, General Nicholson had told us about the tasks and the objectives of our division and it was with high hopes and great excitement that I, for one, packed up that day.

Again, I was to lead the convoy and a jeep in which to do so. By then it had been decided that I was one to whom a jeep was essential and, although I marched with the others, its possession made life a lot rosier. It was a change of mind mainly brought about as a result of the many hundreds of maps that were coming into my keeping.

Not only had I some 60 or 70 copies of every One Inch Ground Survey sheet covering our route between the Chindwin and Ye-U and, in fact, as far as Shwebo, but also a lesser known number covering the country for some 50 miles to either side of the road. The latter were to guard against a change of route or the need for us to carry out a flanking movement. Over and above all these were a generous number of large scale sheets and a lesser number of small scale ones. All had to remain 'en masse', as security regulations would not allow an issue beyond those covering our immediate route. The indexing of this multitude had kept us pleasantly employed, but a far more complex task had been the listing of aerial photographs. Up to that time the issue of these had been on a meagre scale, covering particular objectives. With the receipt of the complete cover of our intended line of advance, we had established a system whereby we could produce a photo of any place or feature on request. For this we developed a series of marked maps, on which were plotted the numbered outlines of every aerial photograph.

In a tightening of security, I.O.s had been formally designated as Battalion Security Officers and had been given the responsibility, when necessary, for the destruction of documents.

It was at about 2100 hrs that our column of vehicles commenced assembling with, at the rear, our salvaged 'Tojo' and 'Tokyo'. After weeks of work by our fitters they were ready for the road and were, in spite of anxious moments, to keep going all the way to Mandalay, but there to be taken from us.

At 2200 hrs I started up and commenced the drive to Kalewa, 40 miles away.

21st December

Kalewa was to be reached at about 0600 hrs, but even when on a road such as that, it is the very dickens of a job keeping down to 5 mph and I was not surprised when we arrived an hour or so ahead of schedule. Interested as I was in the journey, it was anything but easy to remain awake as hour after hour passed with us crawling through – oh so very dusty jungle. We rested along a side track, just short of a village, waiting for daylight. There we parted company with the vehicles provided for this part of the move, as only our own were to cross the river.

Shortly before 0600 hrs I led the way through Kalewa, of which I saw no more than one battered pagoda and, on the hour, we moved down and on to the Bailey bridge. A memorable moment and one to treasure after so many trials and tribulations; for we were not only crossing a great barrier to our advance but doing so just as planned – without opposition.

Now we were to penetrate into Burma proper, territory that had been lost to the enemy since our ignominious defeat, two and a half years before. In the bright sunshine of that early morning, in a move that was as significant as when we departed from Dimapur, we were soon ashore and on to what we thought of as the Ye-U road. It started north before curving to the right and running south for about five miles in close proximity to the river, although taking a somewhat devious course along the fringe of impressive escarpments (thankfully free of the enemy) to our left. Occasionally there were glimpses of the Chindwin, its blue water framed by trees and now and then broken by rocks which, together with patches of yellow sand, formed tropical scenes of 'picture post-card' brilliance. At the end of the length of road was Shwegyin, where we turned away from the river, which we were not to see again, and passing through a break in the escarpment, found ourselves in an area of almost flat country.

Littered over open ground were some of the remains of the civilian and military vehicles, abandoned in 1942. Shwegyin in early May of that year had been the scene of desperate fighting, as the survivors of the Burma Army and hundreds of refugees strove to attain the relative sanctuary of the west bank. For their part, the Japs were throwing in all their resources, of which some were coming up river on naval craft, in a final effort to eliminate them. Many had died here from exhaustion and disease as the battle raged around them, but there were fortunate ones who made the crossing on the ferry boats, until their crews refused to sail them. Other survivors moved further north to where we crossed, and there they made use of such in the way of boats as could be found.

A mile or two up the road we passed the survivors of a regiment of Stuart tanks, which at the end of a long withdrawal had been parked, well back from the road, in perfect formation. One can imagine the heartbreak of those who had driven and fought with them, the length of Burma, then to be defeated by a lack of time to embark 12-ton tanks on to suitable craft. Efficient immobilisation prevented their use by the Japs, who would have been further deterred by the need of high-octane spirit for their aero engines.

Burma, in parts at least, would seem to have become a paradise for post-war scrap merchants.

As we progressed so we crossed a number of dry river beds, sandy stretches having a consistency like those of our coast beaches. In normal times these were crossed by rickety timber bridges, but the weight of traffic from 1942 had resulted in their destruction. Now that there was no flow of water, timber planks laid on the sand became an adequate alternative. After 13 miles, within sparse jungle, we had reached the camp site that was to be our home until Christmas Eve.

While we had been making this vehicular move the majority of the battalion had been ferried down the Chindwin to Shwegyin, from where they completed the journey on foot. Much further back was our Animal Transport Platoon under John Main and our Indian Army Mule Company, marching from Yazagyo.

22nd – 24th December

As with the last camp, this was another chosen by the Japs as a good place in which to live. Some of their huts remained, but needing concealment from the air, they were 300 yards back from the road and therefore much further than we, with air superiority, wished to be. It was while scouting around those buildings, that I found a number of tail units for the Japanese 400 lb mortar bomb. Monstrous weapons designed for use against the tight defensive position, which we favoured, in the jungle. A crude base plate and barrel would be dug into the ground and the bomb lobbed in to its target, from a range of about 500 yards. How fortunate for us that these tail units were all that we were to see of this freak weapon. Geoffry decided that one of these tails would be a suitable object for the Regimental Museum at Dorchester. A place that was understandably constantly in his thoughts, as it was equally seldom in ours; but even he was defeated by the problems of getting it there.

The dry watercourses were symptomatic of the 50 mile wide range of hills we were then entering. Country in which the rivers ceased to flow with the ending of the monsoon, and the jungle which clad them was of trees that were suited to dry and sandy soils. That villages were few and far between was a sure pointer to a lack of water.

To combat this shortage our sappers were provided with boring equipment, with which to sink wells in the river beds and similar likely places. I remember us digging at a bend below a river bank, where the bed had been eroded, and finding increasingly wet sand and finally a slow trickle of water. Provision had been also made for aircraft to drop supplies, in the event of a chronic shortage.

One night Japanese planes flew over our bridge, presumably intending its destruction, but were driven off by our divisional anti-aircraft guns. We could hear the exploding bombs and the distinctive sound of the Bofors, but it soon ended and I doubt that we felt concern that the bridge was at great risk.

During those days I was able to visit our companies and pass on the good news coming back from 6 Brigade. Contrary to expectations, the Japs were not attempting a determined stand on our, so called, road. One that at home would have been described as a cart track and which, with its almost continuous enveloping jungle, was ideal for blocking, for ambushes and for the development of strongly defended localities. They were covering their retreat by no more than a continuous felling of trees across the road, within which were scattered mines. Thus the rate at which we progressed was determined by the time taken to clear these obstacles, and not by engagements with an enemy taking advantage of every defensive position, as had been the case when we advanced south from Kohima. But had we not had a bulldozer with which to sweep aside these trees, they would have been a time-consuming obstacle, as the enemy would have anticipated. His thinking was probably that his first essential was to obtain time, for time was necessary to recover from a debacle greater than our defeat of 1942. He would also reason that he could the better win battles and inflict casualties in the central plain of Burma, where he had shortening lines of supply and where ours were not only lengthening, but doing so over roads that were increasingly tenuous.

So that we might be saved the strain of marching in the heat of the day, and then shivering under our single blankets through what were quite cold nights, our routine was to be reversed. And so it was that on Christmas Eve we fell in at 2000 hrs, ready to march the first of a number of night marches. This was a short one of about seven miles, our objective being the village of Thetkegyin. This village had been abandoned, as had the others on this route through to the Ye-U plain. One can imagine their inhabitants deciding that there was no point in remaining and being pillaged, when they could exist in the interior.

Our blankets, which were being carried on the Jap trucks, had failed to arrive and, after erecting my mosquito net and wrapping myself in my gas-cape, I lay down to spend a miserably cold night. We were aware that we were in a jungle clearing with long grass, very wet from the dew and in the blackness of a dark night we could just sense the enclosing trees. My net was propped up on sticks and had a value beyond that for which it had been made. Having carefully tucked the net under one's ground-sheet the air within seemed a little warmer, and loose possessions were contained and not lost in the grass.

25th December

The big snag about cold nights, such as those, was that it was not possible to move about and thus generate a little warmth. Movement after dark was forbidden and when in the close confines of the jungle, in particular, one's defence was to fire first and ask questions afterwards. But all was well that Christmas morning and when the sun came up we found that we were in a small irregular clearing, just off the road.

We had rightly anticipated the trees, but not a sadly battered monastery building at the east end of our open space. This elaborate timber structure, of a magnificence superior to any other such building I was to see in Burma, its aged hardwood showing black against a green background, had all the complexity associated with such buildings – multi-storied roofs over carved walling, boldly embellished by native craftsmen. We were unable to do more than view it from a distance, as it was assumed to have been booby-trapped. It was also assumed to have been used as a Japanese HQ, for scattered around and visible on the floor within were what seemed to us to be an incredible number of army manuals and booklets. Added to this military litter, there was evidence of our fighter-bombers having 'shot-up' the building in an attack on its occupants.

There would have been few of us whose thoughts were not of home and loved ones, or whose awareness of the significance of Christmas was not intensified, as we rested in the sunshine of that peaceful place. We and that day were not forgotten by the RAF, for they flew over us trailing a streamer, on which was written – 'A Merry Christmas from the RAF'. An offering that was received with some amazement but also with wit, ribaldry and laughter. What I wonder were the feelings of the Japs at such a manifestation of our superiority?

At 1900 hrs we were off again on another short march, this time eight miles.

One that finished in thick jungle which seemed to be miles from anywhere, although our destination was the village of Okhan.

26th – 31st December

A Boxing Day with a difference. But it was a holiday of sorts, and few people outside of 2 Dorset can claim to have spent that day at Okhan. Very probably we were then as far distant from a pub or place of refreshment or entertainment as we would ever be. Despite those drawbacks the jungle was pleasant enough and the sun shone warmly, which was probably not the case in Dorset.

That ensuing night was to be different from its predecessors, for we were to march 17 miles. Not a lot under ordinary conditions, but on the rough and dusty road, within an enveloping jungle and thus in almost total darkness – a different matter. We were then as hardened 'foot sloggers' as we would ever be. We had so easily completed our weekly 25-mile route marches in England, doing so as platoons complete with packs and weapons. Marches that to me seem to be particularly associated with Selby in 1941. There we 'fanned out' into the flat countryside and our progress was enlivened by song and witticisms flowing back and forth within our ranks. And the days were enriched by repartee with village locals and, of course, 'cat calls' – our irrepressible 'Eastenders', at the forefront. Proud days for a not long commissioned subaltern.

Now of necessity we marched in silence and the miles passed less easily.

With the arrival of our mules three days before, we were at full strength and, as darkness fell, were preparing for an early start to our march – an orderly bustling in the gloom as mules and vehicles were being loaded. Being still in reserve to 6 Brigade, we could send ahead our B Echelon trucks with their quartermaster stores, blankets and such essentials. There were a few odd spaces for passengers and I found one for my ever willing Bert Jones and they departed. This advance column was in the charge of Mervyn and Graeme who had to locate our camp which, we had been advised, would be allocated to us within two miles of 'Pink Gin', that being the accepted pronunciation of the village of Pyingaing. Also on board were our cooks, who were to have a meal ready for us on arrival. Whenever possible cooks were sent ahead to prepare a meal for those on foot, and that the number of our cooks seemed to multiply on such occasions, will not surprise any student of human nature, or that some waxed indignant when challenged as to their right to be so classified.

This was the first battalion march with mules of sufficient length as to need their being rested; which entailed their unloading and reloading, in all a break of 45 minutes. Doubtless fine for the mules but rotten for us humans; our march rhythm was broken and the stiffening of weary muscles made restarting more than a bit agonizing.

It was near the end of that break that Geoffry suggested he and I, (we had marched with the head of the column and then during the stop had joined the mules), should go ahead of the battalion so that we might see them pass. We found a place to the right of the road, where a break in the trees would enable us to stand back a few yards and see the column silhouetted against the sky, as they marched towards a battle then but a few days distant. Seeing those hundreds of men as a moving frieze, many so familiar as to be recognisable in that brief moment of vision, the silent night broken only by the small sounds of studded boots and hooves on gravel, and the clink of weapons and mule harness, produced feelings of such emotion that they do not fade with the passing years. Today I see it all again and treasure the memory.

Once beyond the half-way mark, speculation began as to which side of 'Pink Gin' our camp might be; the difference of four miles being no light matter for weary men, with anything up to 60 lbs on their backs. We were about five miles from the village when one of our D.R.s, as our motor-cycle dispatch riders were known, arrived with a message from Graeme, to the effect that the camp was indeed two miles from 'Pink Gin'. This useless piece of information was not at all well received and the D.R., who had no idea of the distance he had travelled or if he had passed through a village, was promptly told to return to the adjutant and come back with something more explicit. As we feared, the camp was the wrong side of Pyingaing, making those final miles a trial, the more so because of the loose sand of dry river beds we were then crossing. The largest, 200 yards or so in width, was the river Maukkadaw, a major tributary of the Chindwin.

Entering camp at 0215 hrs on the 27th, we found the all-prevailing darkness broken by the harsh brightness of pressure-lamps. There our cooks were putting the finishing touches to that most welcome of all meals, bully stew. And I was met by Jones with my green enamel mug, filled to the brim with hot sweet army tea, of a consistency found nowhere else, and drank deeply – nectar indeed! And that blessed moment of relief when, after unbuttoning the battle-dress shoulder straps and unbuckling the equipment belt, a weary heave of the shoulders allowed the large pack and equipment, together with the appendages of revolver and fighting knife, ammunition pouch, water bottle, mess tin and grenades, to drop to the ground.

Those marches are remembered by Andrew MacKenzie as involving complete physical exhaustion.

6 Brigade were having trouble up the road and we were to remain in what proved to be a quite reasonable camp – for two days. For me, one was to be partly occupied by a treasure hunt which, as is customary in such hunts, produced no treasure.

When the 1st Glosters, who had been one of the two English peacetime garrison battalions in Burma, had been a part of the retreat in 1942, they had come up the road that we were then using. With them was the whole of their officers' mess silver which they were then ordered to bury, as it was too much of an encumbrance. Unfortunately, there was no member of our Glosters, who had been present at the burial. When Jimmy Heath had learned of our route, he had obtained a map of the burial site from his battalion and it was with that map that he and I set out that morning. When making our plans we soon discovered that the map lacked a north point; there was therefore no means of telling whether the site was to the east or west of 'Pink Gin'. We decided to go east first and after travelling the stipulated five miles from that place, tried to find a stretch of road similar to that on the map, but without success. We then set off for a similar location west of the village, only to fail again. We concluded that the present road probably bore little resemblance to the one of 1942. Some months later, the officer who did the burying was able to return and did locate the site, after considerable difficulty. Only to find that everything worth having had gone.

When we had started our march from Shwegyin we had headed east, continuing so until near Pyingaing. We then inclined to the south east and passed over the apex of the hills at about 1200 feet, from where it would be gently downhill to Kaduma in the plain, to the east of which was Ye-U.

Our next march was of about 12 miles to another decent camp, adjacent to one of the many dried-up rivers that were so much a feature of that country. There we were among the head-waters of rivers running south west to the Chindwin, soon we would be amongst those dropping east to the Mu, a tributary of the Irrawaddy.

News was coming through of 6 Brigade's first encounter, since the crossing of the Chindwin, with determined enemy opposition and it was that that was the 'trouble up the road', a few days earlier. The enemy's stand was in a position of great natural strength, where our road crossed the eastern apex of the hills. There high escarpments dominated the road. Our attack had been reinforced by the 4/10 Gurkha rifles of 20 Div. who, after their crossing of the Chindwin at Mawlaik, 40 miles to the north of ours, were driving south through the hills and had synchronised their arrival, at this point, with that of 6 Brigade. The Gurkhas got on to the high ground among the Japs and, as was said at the time, 'slaughtered a very satisfactory number'. 6 Brigade then continued and the Gurkhas pushed on south to rejoin the remainder of their division.

Our next move was an early morning one and after marching eight or ten miles, we were picked up by vehicles and ferried through to what we then came to know as the Shwebo Plain, eventually halting for the night, just beyond the village of Kaduma.

At last and after so many months, we were entering a world without jungle, not to be seen again, or the mountains that had so dominated our lives. The single road, to which we had been confined, would continue as our axis, but it would be within relatively flat and, for the greater part, cultivated country. There our mobility could be used to full advantage; for our trucks and jeeps, with their four-wheel drive, were not dependent on roads and they and our tracked vehicles could deploy on our flanks. Our way of life and the manner of our fighting was to be that for which we had been equipped.

At Kaduma 6 Brigade had taken a left fork in the road and, moving due east and as fast as they were able, had reached the Kabo Weir before it could be blown up by the Japs. A destruction that would have been a major calamity, for it made possible and controlled the irrigation of that part of Burma.

During the day the C.O. and I had been at Brigade HQ for an 'O' Group, There, Mike West told us of how our brigade was to take the lead and allow 6 Brigade, but for their excursion to the weir, to rest in reserve. We Dorsets were to advance on the town of Ye-U tomorrow, in the expectation that we would capture it single-handed. Simultaneously the Camerons and the Worcesters would make a wide hook to the south and cross the Mu River ten miles below the town and then, striking north, catch the remnants of the Ye-U garrison from their rear. Only if we got into difficulties, would they be diverted to our more immediate assistance.

What a reversal of the situation on 1st May 1942. Then General Slim and his retreating Burma Corps had reached the far side of Ye-U, there to confer with General Alexander, C-in-C Burma. Also present was the American, General Stilwell, responsible for the Chinese forces. His detestation of anything British and our C-in-C in particular, was only matched by his stated contempt for the Chinese. It was a time of increasing disaster, of a magnitude that such antagonism was lost amongst the general exhaustion, near-starvation and despair. In the town, a mix of troops and refugees prepared to take the long road to Shwegyin, Tamu and Imphal. Few would have had any appreciation of its horrors, or of their need to cross the Chindwin ahead of the enemy. Already, some Japs were taking the short route by moving up the Chindwin in naval craft, having been ordered to see that none of our troops reached India.

We caught up with the battalion just before dark, finding our camp within a plantation of palms, amidst open country. For the next couple of hours, trucks were arriving and disgorging some 20 or so men on the road a quarter of a mile away, for security. Guided to their company localities, they set about with picks and shovels, to dig themselves in. We were up front and taking no chances. This continued long into darkness, with the minimum of noise, no easy task. To an outsider this would have been a scene of utter confusion – hundreds of milling men, the majority digging slit trenches. At such times we often found ourselves in something of a state of chaos and probably did so that night.

A word or two here about the organisation of Battalion Headquarters, when anticipating battle. It divided into two parts – Attack HQ and Main or Rear HQ. Attack fought the battle and Main organised the supplies and maintained the administration. Main also formed a reserve headquarters. Attack had to be small and mobile and was no more than the C.O., his gunman, myself and signallers, plus a defence group or section. To these could be added my gunman, an interpreter and a gunner F.O.O. and party.

The signallers operated the control wireless set, by means of which the C.O., or myself as his mouthpiece, directed the battalion. Messages were sent to and received from the sets that were distributed among the companies, any body of sufficient size or importance as to warrant one and, of course, Main HQ. At the latter there was a more powerful set, supplied by Brigade and operated by a couple of their signallers. This was our link with our Brigadier, messages that were channelled through the Second-in-Command, the Adjutant or the Signals Officer. All operational messages, other than those relating to the enemy which were sent in 'clear', had to be encoded, its form being determined by the importance of the message. For those to Brigade, the excellent system known as Slidex was employed. Scrambling was used within the Battalion to conceal place names, road junctions, map references and so on. Code names identified units and formations. On settling into a locality for the night or longer, telephone cables were run out so that we could dispense with the sets and, providing no line was where it might be tapped, speech could be in clear.

At night the Adjutant, the Signals Officer, and I took turns at sleeping by the control 'phone. Either in our own trenches or, when in a semi-permanent position, in the Command Post.

Few worked harder than the signallers – they who carried the heaviest loads and who, on reaching our destination, laid cable and serviced their sets. Probably also digging a hole for the 'phone exchange, in addition to a slit trench. In compensation they had job satisfaction and kudos from their technical skills.

At the conclusion of a momentous year and on the threshold of a second, we were ready to renew contact with the enemy; doing so with a battalion strength of 32 officers and 764 other ranks.

Donald Baynes, smitten with illness, had departed for an attachment at the Staff College, Quetta. And that other veteran, Pryke Howard, had been posted to 33 Corps Transit Section.

Our newly arrived Lieutenant Eagle, who had been appointed Signals Officer, was at the Army Signals School.

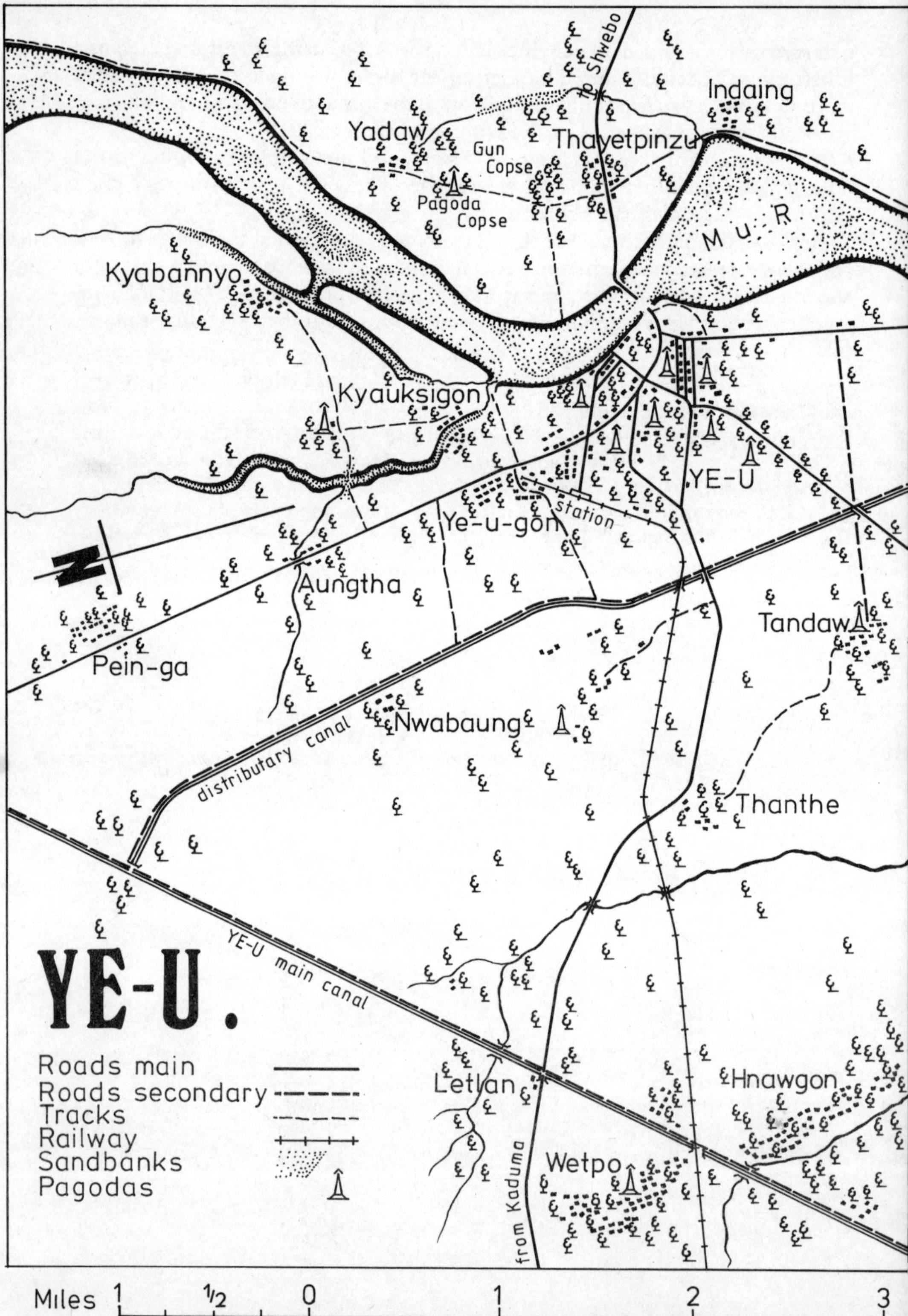

YE-U.
to Shwebo
Indaing
Yadaw
Gun Copse
Thayetpinzu
Pagoda Copse
Mu R
Kyabannyo
Kyauksigon
YE-U
Ye-u-gon
station
Aungtha
Tandaw
Pein-ga
Nwabaung
distributary canal
Thanthe
YE-U main canal
Letlan
Hnawgon
Wetpo
from Kaduma
Roads main
Roads secondary
Tracks
Railway
Sandbanks
Pagodas
Miles 1 1/2 0 1 2 3
Kilometres 1 0·5 0 1 2 3 4

CHAPTER NINE

The Battle of Ye-U

1945

1st January

At first light, looking east over a flat landscape into a shadowy distance, one could not help but believe that this was an exceptionally auspicious day. Our advance into open country, for which we had trained and been equipped, seemed so significantly to coincide with the first day of a new year and the optimism thus engendered.

Studying the small print on the One Inch Ye-U Map, one reads that it had a First Edition in 1909 and that it was only in October 1944, that it had a second, which was compiled from air photos taken in January and May 1944. Significant dates!

In that January, preparations were being made for a British and Indian advance into Burma from Imphal; plans that were overtaken by the counter-advance of the Japanese. In May, the battles at Imphal and Kohima were at their peak and anything but won. Yet Forward Planning was in hand. This demonstrates a remarkable air superiority extending to central Burma, and one of the standard required to achieve the meticulous flying of an aerial survey.

On that map of the country over which on that day we were very nearly to cross, being just off its left margin and our objectives very close to the right, a land is shown devoid of contours. Except for its western edge, the map is tinted yellow – the symbol for land under cultivation. Within that yellow a multitude of villages is shown, enmeshed and linked in a network of footpaths and tracks. Towards the top of the map is the west to east road to the Kabo Weir. That weir, spanning a narrow section of the Mu River, which elsewhere has widths of between 400 and 900 yards, feeds water into a pair of main canals running south on either side of the river to and beyond Ye-U, near the bottom of the map. Those principal canals feed distributary canals which irrigate the land adjacent to the river. In all that area, the only natural or man-made features able to check our advance, would be the Mu and its flanking main canals, all running north and south.

The nearer of these main canals, three miles west of Ye-U, formed so obvious a defensive line that it had been the subject of much discussion at the 'O' Group the previous evening. In particular we had studied aerial photos, on which our road could be seen crossing it on an iron bridge. It was expected that we would find the bridge blown and possibly covered by fire.

Thus, when at 0815 hrs, on the sunny morning, we commenced our approach march of 18 miles with objective Ye-U, it was the canal and its bridge that were considered as the likely climax to our day.

I was one of the few with a justification for not doing the miles on foot but in the comfort of my jeep, together with Jones and the two signallers and their set, crowded into the back. We were on listening watch so that Geoffry would have immediate advice on any enemy contact. My memory of that day seems crystal clear, a result perhaps of my grandstand seat. This was the battle for which we had been prepared for so long and which was to be quite unlike any other. There we were, after so many weeks, doing what we had so often studied and carrying out what we had so often practised – An Advance to Contact, in open country and all in accordance with the drill book.

With the battalion in an extended single file and sections taking alternate sides of that straight and level road, individuals and groups were so separated as to provide no easy target from a ground or air attack. And our column length of about one mile would, of itself, present a daunting sight. On our right flank and passing through many of the villages that so dotted the landscape, was Snagger and his men. Ahead were sappers, checking the six road bridges we would cross and looking for mines (none was found); it was they and our scouts that determined our rate of advance – some two miles in the hour. Our vehicles remained closetted within the column, by moving in bounds which took them slowly to the tail of the leading company, there to halt until repeating the operation, when the rear of the battalion approached.

Generally visibility was good, for this was agricultural land that did not support dense vegetation but, as would be expected, it was less open once we were within the area of irrigation. The road passed through only one village, although many were but a short distance away. Now, for the first time since Yazagyo, we were meeting Burmese. Naturally hesitant at first, more and more were coming down to the road in small groups, seemingly pleased to see us and some, with shy smiles, handed out bunches of bananas. All of which gave much pleasure, unaccustomed as we were to displays of welcome. That this was a very restrained triumphal progress, compared with those enjoyed in Europe and of which we had a natural envy, did nothing to lessen our enjoyment.

Through one of our interpreters I learned that no organised bodies of Japanese had been seen for some time but that, during the past weeks, small groups had moved towards Ye-U.

As we neared the canal we were keenly awaiting the first report from those up front – 'A' Company. It came from John Bowles at 1600hrs and was to the effect that the bridge had indeed been blown, but no Japs had been seen and there appeared to be none on the far side of the canal. The column halted while Geoffry and I jeeped up to our old company where, sure enough, most of the bridge was below the water.

We were then at Letlan, the name of crossroads comprising our road, the canal and the road flanking the east bank, in the manner of a towpath. To our left and adjoining the canal, were one or two ramshackle timber buildings which had seen better days. One I seem to remember as a distinctly seedy café. It was probably the proprietor and his patrons who reclined on chairs, so placed that they might best watch the passing show. And when, as then, there are strangers dealing with a manifestly insurmountable problem, the entertainment value is considerable. It was no surprise to us to find that these layabouts could not, or would not, advise us about the Japs.

Geoffry asked John to get his company dug in where they were and we then returned to 'B' Company, half a mile to the rear. Providentially, an educated Burman turned up and volunteered to guide us to an intact bridge spanning the canal, a short distance away to the south. Peter got his company moving and we set off, Geoffry and I tagging along in our jeeps. We were soon traversing a large village with the arresting name of Wetpo and the added interest of some remarkable pagodas. The need to attend to more important matters, prevented us from seeing more than their fantastically carved brick Chinthes, 15 to 20 feet in height – those mythical beasts that guard the entrances to major pagodas.

We had entered a land where pagodas were features of the landscape, the equal of the English village church. In their vicinity there would be a Buddhist monastery, known as a phongyi kyaung.

Just beyond the village we were at the canal again and where, for want of a better description, was what I can only call a bridge. It was in the region of 100 feet in width between parapets and but for the latter, it would have been easy to have thought that the canal was running underground. This was where the railway (the lines of which had been removed) angled across the canal, hence the width and the continuity of the ground levels, over and at the canal sides. A great stroke of luck this, for not only would it take all our vehicles, but its size and strength ensured its safety against attempts that might be made at its destruction.

'A' Company were then confirmed in their location, while the remainder of the battalion closed on us and 'B' Company, to form a bridgehead east of the crossing. There was another large village to our front and Geoffry and I and some others walked to it, hoping to be able to buy some eggs and, with luck, fowls. Not surprisingly we met with little success; the inhabitants were, however, able to confirm our own understanding about the Japs in Ye-U. Air observation during the day reported the preparation of defensive positions by small parties of Japs, in and around the town and that the roads were being mined.

At dusk Geoffry sent for Snagger Highett and instructed him as to how he was to take our four carriers into Ye-U, to see and report on the general situation and, if possible, to reach and report on the road running down to the Mu River bridge, which we knew to have been destroyed. Snagger had only recently returned from a course at Shillong and, not having had time to harden up again was, after his 25-mile flanking patrol, quite exhausted. As he received his orders Snagger, who was grey with fatigue, swayed so much that I expected him to fall. I now believe that, to some extent at least, his haggard greyness resulted from his conviction that he and his companions were going to their deaths. A belief shared by me.

Geoffry completed his orders and the carriers departed just after dark. Almost immediately a message came through from the Brigadier that Snagger was to be told that one of the bridges over the distributary canal, on our side of the town, was reported to have been mined. Wondering what good this information would be to Snagger, who would be unable to do anything about it or avoid that bridge,

I passed the message. Snagger, being the excellent man that he was, decided that his only chance of pulling off this seemingly suicidal patrol was to use bold measures, in the hope that the Japs would think his force stronger than it was. Accordingly he instructed his drivers to switch on their lights and, taking the lead, charged straight into the town and through to the Mu where, as directed, they viewed the remains of the bridge. Then north up the road from the centre and back again and out the way they had entered, only stopping at the bridge reported as mined. They found no mines, but on either side of the bridge there were newly dug trenches. To the relief of all and I include Geoffry, who acted on the instructions of Brigade, they had returned safely. That they had seen no signs of life raised hopes for tomorrow.

In the meantime Geoffry had been called to a conference at Brigade HQ, four miles back up the road in the village of Chaungzon. He and I set off in our jeeps with an escort of a 15cwt truckload of men, and on returning at 2330hrs Geoffry called his 'O' Group. Soon everybody was crowding into the Battalion HQ Office, which at that time consisted of the outer fly of a 160lb tent, the actual tent having been discarded to reduce weight and bulk. There, squatting on the floor, we learned the plan to attack for what was, by then, later that day.

This was that we were to clear Ye-U and its environs of the enemy and occupy the town – our primary task. This to be in preparation for our secondary task – the crossing of the Mu River.

For that secondary task, which entailed the clearing of the east bank of the Japanese, the battalion would split into two formations, to be known as 'Minor' and 'Minor', names that bore no relationship to numerical strengths, which were similar, their composition being:

Major.	'A' & 'D' Companies.
	Attack HQ.
	Pioneer Platoon.
	Detachment of mortars.
	R.A.P.
Minor.	'B' & 'C' Companies.
	Main HQ.
	The remainder of HQ Company.
	Admin. Company.

Our rifle companies, on whom our very existence depended, were struggling to maintain three platoons; this was inevitably a continuing and increasing problem. 'C' Company was uniquely at full strength, as they had our attached platoon of the 1st Glosters.

We were to have generous support from the Division in the form of:

10th Field regiment RA – 25-pounders.
99th Field regiment RA – 3.7 howitzers.
18th Field regiment RA – self-propelled Priest guns (one battery).

Attached throughout – one platoon of the 2nd Manchester Regiment, medium machine-guns.

Attached for the secondary task – a troop of the Carabiniers, in the form of three Grant tanks.

Ye-U is one of those places through which we passed in that long pilgrimage of ours, to which I would love to return and be able to stroll around and meet people, and to see what it was really like.

Very obviously it had developed as a result of a river crossing, as did so many similarly positioned English towns, of which the one in which I live is an example. The river at Ye-U had a ford before the bridge enabled the east to west road to cross. In addition, a north to south road passed through the town making it, in an area of few long-distance highways, an important junction. And it had that railway station which, since October, had been such an attraction. The station formed the terminus of the branch line running south to Monywa, a sizeable town on the Chindwin, before swinging east to a junction with the main line just north of the Ava Bridge near Mandalay. So it was a place of local importance, in spite of its smallness. One hopes that it has since prospered.

2nd January

Everybody was up early after a quiet and uneventful night, and we were soon sorting ourselves into the order of march and forming up along the east side of the canal. We moved off at 0800 hrs, going first along the road bordering the canal until we arrived at the blown bridge and there we turned right, so that we were ready to advance east on Ye-U, three miles distant.

With 'A' Company, our Order of March became:

'C' Company.
One platoon of 'B' Company.
Attack HQ.
'B' Company less one platoon.
Main HQ.
HQ and Admin. Companies.
'A' Company.
'D' Company.

Advancing at the gentle pace set by our scouts at the column's head, there was time to look around and about and at the tiny fields, with their tangled hedges, flanking our route. But for the prevailing brown colour, which was probably due to neglect during the past couple of years, we might have been in England, on a hot summer morning and engaged in routine exercise. The ever optimistic battalion had hopes that we were entering a 'civilised' town with a market and in which, through the delights of barter, they might supplement their 'meagre' rations.

We had travelled a couple of miles since leaving the main canal, and those who were not daydreaming were anticipating trouble as we arrived within sight of the small canal bridge, inspected by Snagger. Sure enough 'C' Company was met with rifle fire which came from either side, this followed by some shells from a 70mm gun across the river. Immediately, men and vehicles dispersed into cover on both sides of the road, we in Attack HQ going to the left among large clumps of brambles which were a positive menace, as we could see precious little and odd shots were buzzing past without hindrance. Harry Newcombe, one of the leading platoon of 'C' Company, had a better view and reports as follows:

> I had seen in the distance a small low-parapet road bridge and observed a figure sitting on the side and another crossing the road, both dressed in longyis. One of our leading scouts raised a hand and everyone went down on one knee and, at the same time, two shots cracked the air above our heads. It had been my turn to carry the Section's Bren and my 'Mucker' Tommy Thomas had the spare barrel and extra magazines. There was no way of getting it back to our regular Bren-gunner 'Tiny' Lewis. We were well hidden in tall grass and I said to Tommy 'How far would you say that bridge is?' 'About 4/500 yards,' he said, 'Here!' and handed me a magazine. I flipped open the dust cover, inserted a magazine and turned the drum sight to 500 yards. I had a clear picture of the bridge above the level of the road, down which shots were ricocheting towards us. Catching a glimpse of a figure behind the stone parapet, I sent a long burst and had the satisfaction of seeing chips and dust fly off the stone. I emptied the magazine by spraying the bridge. There were no more shots and all was silent. After a while I could hear Major Tucker calling to continue the advance, which we did with more caution than before.

Tommy reported on the set to us, saying that the opposition appeared to be an outlying screen and that he was pushing on. After about 15 minutes Geoffry decided that things were not progressing quickly enough and that he would go forward to spur on 'C'. He and I, together with his gunman and our signaller, crossed the road and advanced across fields and open ground to the right of the road. In the excitement of the moment I forgot our Defence Section, who were in firing positions and did not notice our departure. Geoffry passed a few pithy comments but would not wait for them to be fetched, so we four pushed on until the road forked, 600 yards beyond the bridge and on the edge of the town. There we made ourselves reasonably small behind a thick hedge. Odd bullets were passing close enough to make me think that we were being sniped and I regretted the absence of our Section, presumably defending nothing. We could hear 'C' Company as they pushed down the left fork into the town. The shelling had ceased and the opposition was obviously no more than a delaying force of snipers, within the excellent cover afforded by the buildings, trees and, in places, thick undergrowth.

While we had been advancing down the axis of the road, 'A' Company had been doing likewise along the railway line, away to our left. After running parallel to our road and crossing the distributary canal, the line curved to the north east to the station and its terminus some little way beyond. That was a route suited to their tasks of protecting our left flank, clearing the station, the north of the town and the nearby village of Ye-u-gon and then holding them against any incursion of Japs from the north.

'C' Company had asked for an ambulance to pick up a wounded man, and when it arrived at our road junction I directed it to them. After picking up the casualty the driver lost his way, going on into the town instead of out; he realised his error when he ran into what he described as a crowd of 20 Japs. Luckily, he was not alone in being surprised and, doing a quick U-turn, he returned undamaged.

It was about then that Geoffry decided to reinforce 'B' and 'C' with 'D' Company. This change, together with the fact that Tommy had taken the left fork and not the right, (it having been 'B' Company who were to go left in the original orders), had to be wirelessed to Main HQ. During our retraining at Maram, emphasis had been laid on the need for security, in the matter of which it was said the British Army was notoriously bad. Unwisely I decided that this was the moment for using 'Slidex' – a simple method of garbling messages between holders of the relevant data. But what with my slow encoding and requests from Main HQ for repetitions, that simplicity did not prevent a protected message. Understandably, Geoffry became increasingly impatient and had harsh things to say about Slidex and the like and those who operated it. Poor Geoffry, he was at times most grievously tried! But weren't we all?

Anyway, when 'D' Company was reported to be behind us, Geoffry asked Clive to spare a lance-corporal and two men to act as an Attack HQ Defence Group. They proved so successful that they became a permanent part of Battalion HQ, remaining throughout the campaign.

We moved forward, walking up the road taken by 'C' Company who, with 'B' Company on their right, they having a more direct route, were well into the town and advancing towards the river. The dwellings were the disappointingly familiar match-boarded, single-storied ones on stilts, their general dilapidation and neglected gardens suggesting that most of the population had abandoned the town. Eventually we halted at a road junction and dispersed into the shelter afforded by the 'open ground floors' of some houses, there to brew-up and eat our haversack rations.

When 'C' Company reported that two of those opposing us at the bridge had been killed in the fighting, we sent back to see if they were Burmese or, as seemed more likely, Japs in Burmese clothing. They were found to have been removed and the matter was not settled, although that removal of bodies was to be expected of the Japanese.

The left-hand road taken by Tommy and his company turned right after 500 yards, becoming parallel with the other fork until after a slightly greater distance, the right-hand road having turned left, they converged. From there a road ran down to the bridge, and other roads ran north and south.

Thus 'B' and 'C' Companies linked up in that far corner of Ye-U and did so only two and a half hours after starting. From there they proceeded to the river, taking up defensive positions with 'C' on the left of the road and 'B' on the right. Joining them in that position overlooking the wrecked bridge, was the platoon of Manchesters, who dug in on the right of 'B' Company to protect the southern flank. Across the river and half a mile due east, along what had now become the

Shwebo road, was the village of Thayetpinzu. Our arrival at the river and the firing by our gunners of a few rounds, on and around that village, stirred up the Jap artillery who then shelled us.

'D' Company having moved through the town behind 'B', established themselves in and around the converged roads, a situation which at home would have attracted commercial buildings and traffic lights. In Ye-U, according to the map, they more sensibly had a pagoda and trees.

Our HQ companies also moved in with 'D', who were asked to send one of their platoons to the assistance of 'A' Company, whose progress along the railway could be followed from the sounds of intermittent small-arms fire. John Bowles was moving with caution up that north-west flank of the town and it was later, at 1205 hrs, that they were close to the station, there to be fired on from the buildings and from Japs who were said to have been dodging about within the cover of railway wagons. A platoon attack was put in and the Japs withdrew, taking up sniping positions further along the line, which continued for nearly half a mile to its junction with the main north road. There the open country commenced, but for the villages of Ye-u-gon to the immediate left of the north road and Kyauksigon, a few hundred yards away on the right.

John continued to the end of the line where he met up with the platoon from 'D' Company, who had travelled up the north road. By then we had pretty well "combed" the town and had done so with very light casualties, which could only be described as amazing and suggested that those Japs were a poor lot, they having had ideal conditions for close and accurate shooting.

Any locals who had been caught up amongst all this activity had been sensible enough to have 'gone to ground' and stayed there. It was therefore a matter of surprise when I received two callers, the first of whom was an obese Burman and wife, or whatever, in an undersized cart drawn by a pony to match. He was very ready to give us all the information he had about the Japs, and confirmed and enlarged on our knowledge of those opposite to us across the river. I was able to identify a modern anti-tank gun, sited to fire down the road and cover the ford by the ruined bridge. When we reached Thayetpinzu I found the evidence of that 47mm gun, for on the ground, where expected, were shells. He also spoke of there being 100 Japs and further guns.

My second visitor was a Burman with a long tale of woe about British troops entering his home and stealing his blankets and cooking utensils. 'C' Company were the culprits and the items were soon returned and we heard no more of the matter. Generally there was very little pilfering, possibly due to there seldom being an opportunity. Anyway, in a town that appeared abandoned by its inhabitants, it was easy to assume that anything found was Japanese. We were concerned that the Burmese should perceive us to be their allies in the removal of a hated invader and that, in the future, life would be infinitely better. That was our conviction and, as much as anything, provided the incentive to keep going.

With the coming of night we settled in where we were, thankful that things had gone so well and ready to prepare for the next uncertain days, for which we had completed an incredibly easy introduction.

But with the coming of darkness the 70 and 75mm guns across the river sited within a group of trees to the north of Thayetpinzu, which we designated 'Gun Copse', fired into 'B' and 'C' Companies' positions and, with the Manchesters' platoon returning the fire, a somewhat uneven engagement ensued. *Spasmodic shelling by the Japs continued throughout the night, they lobbing shells into the town and also over and beyond to where we had been the previous night, that place then being our artillery's gun park.

Our two forward companies, with their view of Thayetpinzu and the copse, could see the Jap gun flashes lighting up the girders of the wrecked bridge. Not having top cover to their trenches, their casualties came from air-bursts as shells hit the trees behind them; thus they had bits of trees as well as mud and shell splinters, from those shells that landed more directly.

During the afternoon Battalion HQ moved about 50 yards north to one of a number of pagodas, tucked in behind some rather decrepit brick buildings. It became a reasonable command post, having just enough room inside and the few external apertures were easily 'blacked out'. Geoffry was up late, planning for the next day with Mervyn and Graeme and, long before he finished, he told me to go and get some rest. It had been a tiring day and I was glad to lie down on the patch of paved ground adjoining our headquarters.

3rd January

Although physically weary, my brain was busy in contemplation of the proposals for the day then starting, thoughts that were only broken by the bangs and thumps from the Japs guns. A parked jeep soon sheltered my top half, for I had wriggled under it after contemplation of the brickwork showing dark against the sky, above my head, and which only required a 'near miss' from a '75' to come tumbling down.

While most took such rest as circumstances permitted, Snagger (I need hardly mention) and his platoon were out on a foot patrol with the ambitious task of crossing the Mu and entering the small village of Yadaw, adjoining the river's east bank. It was believed to hold a 75mm gun, which the patrol might spike. They had moved off at 1900 hrs going north up the river bank and, half an hour later, a small recce party crossed but withdrew when sighted by Japs. Continuing as before they reached the large riverside village of Kyabannyo at 0115 hrs. No Japs were showing themselves and they commenced their return, having decided it would be pointless to attempt a second crossing. At 0300 hrs, when between Kyauksigon and the river they bumped three Japs who ran away, the patrol doing its best to shoot them down. This hard-worked patrol returned at 0400 hrs.

*Within this period of shelling, a member of the platoon commanded by Harold Jones was hit in the face by a splinter from a 75, its shell having exploded on an adjacent stone wall. He was to die a few days later of pneumonia. Harold writes - "Until then I had not realised that a person is mainly the face that you know. Take it away and he becomes a non-person."

The contemplation of 'spiking guns' was a never-ending source of pleasure to senior officers, and such was their keenness that even the constant failure by the "spikers", was no deterrent.

We were now about to bring into operation the division of the battalion into the two forces of 'Major' and 'Minor', the former to do the crossing and the latter to hold Ye-U and provide the back-up.

At 0800 hrs our column commenced the march north from Ye-U, with objective Kyabannyo, preparatory to the crossing of the Mu River in the vicinity of that village. We were in the order of march:

'D' Company, less the platoon with 'A'.
Attack HQ.
Pioneer Platoon and mortar detachment.
The three Grant tanks.
FOOs from the 10th & 99th Field Regiment RA.
One Sherman tank, the armoured OP for the 18th Field Regiment RA,
R.A.P.

Soon we had linked up with 'A' Company and the attached platoon (they had dug in for the night near Ue-u-gon) and could call ourselves force Major. Once clear of the town we swung right moving north-east over open ground, with Kyabannyo one and a half miles ahead. However, the dry bed of a fair-sized river or chaung caused us to incline left towards the north. Thus we continued our advance without closing on the Mu, as had been intended; a diversion that was probably a blessing in disguise for, despite the noise of our tanks and their column of dust, we appeared to have escaped the Jap's notice. In this crucial advance, we had to our right that enemy-held east bank and village of Yadaw.

Yadaw, one mile to the north of Thayetpinzu, had to its south what we designated as 'Pagoda Copse' and, south again, 'Gun Copse'. These four were linked by a track, which continued beyond the Shwebo road for another half mile to a further village – Indaign. We were well aware that all were occupied by the Japenase, positioned to block our advance. There could be no direct assault across the river. Thus it was that Geoffry decided to attack from the north and strike south from Yadaw, with Thayetpinzu the final objective. That was the plan of which our march towards the north was the beginning.

We had been promised the support of an air-strike and during our advance on Kyabannyo, the Hurribombers arrived. Using 250 lb bombs, rockets and ground strafing, they struck at Yadaw and Thayetpinzu and suspected enemy positions, in a formidable demonstration of fire-power; one that gave us cheer as we paused to watch the bombs exploding and the planes sweeping, their machine-guns rattling away at a rate that ours could not begin to match.

Proceeding on our way we reached the village in the late morning, having seen nothing of the enemy. We at HQ, our gunners and the tanks, settled into an area of rough ground behind the river bank, where chaungs provided cover. Yadaw, although not far away, was out of sight behind a screen of vegetation and was very much separated from us by the river which, in that section, averaged 6-700 yards in width, between banks. With the river low and water close to the far bank, we had something like 400 yards of mud between our bank and it.

Following the completion of the air-strike, we were informed that the RAF hoped to do a second; we were not therefore to attempt a river crossing until after 1500 hrs. With the onset of darkness in just over three hours, there would be insufficient time for us to establish ourselves, in enemy territory, before dark. It was decided therefore, to do the main crossing the next day before dawn, but one company would cross in the early hours of this night, and provide protection for the main body.

Our continued occupation of Ye-U must have given confirmation in the minds of the Japs that it was our intention to cross the river there, and when the follow-up strike went in, that was interpreted as cover for us so doing. Doubtless, it was for that reason that they reacted by shelling both the east and west banks, in the vicinity of the town.

We were favoured in that our crossing was to be when the water was at so low a level as to be, in places, fordable. That afternoon I was instructed by Geoffry to recce the river for a crossing place and, accordingly, I set off in a carrier, having little idea of how the river looked as it could only be seen by standing on the river bank, in full view of the other side. After proceeding along the chaung, we turned into a branch leading to the river with, ahead of us, a strip of water and a high sandbank beyond. Selby was the driver, one of our trusted veterans, and we charged through the water and up onto the sandbank for a brief check, seeing in that moment the whole river as far as Ye-U. Then we were speeding down and across an expanse of dry mud to the water's edge, the wet and the dry parts being very much as on our maps. Without more than a slight reduction in our speed we cruised down-river close to the water, going some distance towards the town before retracing our route so that, should we be under observation, it would not be apparent that we were interested in any particular place. Early on we had crossed wheel marks to the water's edge, suggesting an ideal spot at which to cross and one, with luck, that was not too deep for the tanks. I was able to fix them with a visual bearing.

Back at base much had been happening in a short time, for not only was just about everybody settling-in for a rest, but they were enjoying gifts of fruit and eggs from the villagers and other locals. As might be expected, our HQ was strategically sited in the village centre (the better to liaise with the populace) and doing really well, as dozens of locals arrived with produce to demonstrate their delight at our presence. Even the Phongyis – the Buddhist monks – were there. One can imagine that the aerial bombardments had been seen from far and wide, and that they, together with those fearsome rockets adding to the exploding bombs, had demonstrated a destructive power far beyond anything previously seen or imagined in so remote a place.

Here was a very different British Army, and one that was back to stay.

Our reception was in the hands of an English speaking villager, a man of some standing for, before our enforced departure, he had been a Sanitary Inspector. Now he was full of the expectation of getting his job again and was only too delighted to be able to fuss around and air his English. At long last everybody was really pleased to see us and we revelled in it.

But we could not forget the Japs for long. We had been unable to contact Main HQ, something I had mentioned to the FOO of the 18th Field Regiment – he of the Sherman Tank. They too had a problem in that they and the Japs were on the same wave-length. At his suggestion I climbed up to the turret and put on a wireless headset – to be immediately saturated with the babble of Japanese conversation, which was so loud and clear that I felt that I was amongst them. A profoundly sobering experience.

In the late afternoon, as a preliminary for the night, we moved HQ to a large shed at the south end of the village, a handy and better place for the preparation and initiation of the crossing.

It fell to Clive Chettle and his men to be the first to cross and, as darkness came, I guided them down to the water and saw them away. They were across without trouble and formed a bridgehead where they landed, 500 yards to the west of Yadaw.

These were the concluding hours of a day during which we had been unexpectedly free of contact with the Japs and Joe Chamberlin must have been wanting to be in two places at once. Unlike us, 'Minor' force at Ye-U had continued to be at the receiving end of desultory artillery fire, of which 'B' Company suffered the worst and received most injuries. And so peaceful was it that the Kyabannyo headman invited Geoffry and John Bowles to supper. With John being killed soon after, one likes to think of it was a very happy interlude. Even in the midst of battle it could have been so, for Geoffry – so much the extrovert – had the gift of excelling at such times and host and guests would have sat down in celebration of a successful and momentous day, ready to enjoy their curried duck as never before.

Exactly a year earlier, Geoffry, Dick Castle and I had dined in an hotel in Belgaum City, certainly under very different circumstances but ones which, thanks to Geoffry's personality, had been lifted out of the rut and it had been a joyous occasion. The humour had centred on the Indian bearer serving us, and whose unpronounceable name was converted by Geoffry to "Odoedeodo". I doubt that he had experienced such a situation before in those staid surroundings, and it was all a bit much, so that he found it just about the funniest thing that had ever happened and became so swamped by laughter as to be almost incapable of serving us. We didn't have the soup in our laps, but nearly so.

We laughed easily in those days of close-knit comradeship. It is said that the British are partial to operating and doing combat in small and isolated groups, as was our situation at that time. They probably brought out the best in us and by developing a personality, they encouraged a greater confidence, so that we had that indefinable happiness to which I have often referred. In that remote place, after three days, on each of which we were expecting battle, followed by a fourth, on which it was a near certainty, it was the best of all antidotes to prolonged mental and physical stress.

At the extreme end of that long day, to be precise at 2359 hrs, a platoon of 'B' Company led by Lieutenant Dicky Boyle was crossing the river opposite Ye-U.

4th January

The patrol had the intial task of reconnoitring Thayetpinzu, which they approached along the north side of the main road until, when on its outskirts, they spotted a listening patrol of five Japs. This, in order that surprise might not be lost, they by-passed and moved north so that they would be on the side that was of most interest to us. At 0300 hrs, Dicky sent forward a recce patrol under Corporal Crawford, who led them to within ten yards of an enemy position before being challenged. The Japs, by then alerted, opened fire which killed Crawford, but the others succeeded in filtering away under the cover of a smoke grenade. The main patrol then made its way further north so that they might approach the village from that side, doing so to the sound of the Japs firing bursts of light machine-gun fire, happily not directed at them.

Important information on the physical features, of which we could see little other than that the ground appeared thick with trees and vegetation, was to have been wirelessed back but, as so often happened, due to screening by the vegetation and the inevitable harsh treatment of the sets, contact was not obtained. With the approach of daylight, they abandoned all but their prime task, the forming of a bridgehead at the river end of the track leading from 'Gun Copse'. There they were to remain, so that casualties suffered by 'Major' might be evacuated through them and across the river.

The early part of the night had been spent by me and our signallers in fruitless endeavours to contact Main HQ. After failure on our set, I tried again on the gunner's set and also on that of the tanks but with no success. Our clash of frequencies with the Japs, who seemed to be monopolizing the air-waves, was an insurmountable problem. And how we wished that we had someone who understood their language!

Soon after midnight I returned to HQ to join the others in their endeavours to sleep on the very hard and bumpy earth floor of the shed, getting little or no real rest – one wanted to be up and doing. Geoffry, despite his supper, was in a sombre mood and tense with contemplation of the day and his awesome responsibilities. My mind was too full of the crossing and of all that was to follow for sleep to be possible; doubtless the others were the same.

With the Japs so clearly defending the far shore, we could so easily have been going into a trap. Certainly we were not going to have the superiority considered necessary to attack defended positions. It is now known that the Japs opposing the Mu River crossing were two battalions of their 124th Infantry Regiment (old opponents at Kohima) to a total strength of less than 1,000. Of that number only a portion were opposite Ye-U, but as we were crossing with two below-strength companies, we faced the possibility of being outnumbered.

We were up well before 0400 hrs, the time that 'A' Company, followed by our HQ, commenced the river crossing and in the pre-dawn brightening sky the last of the column, Joe and his team, waded ashore. We dug temporary trenches in the sand below the high river bank and waited for a report from Clive on the outcome of a patrol to Yadaw. Downriver the Japs were busy laying down defensive fire, and we wondered how long it would be before they switched their guns to us.

A lot of thought had been given to getting our tanks across the river and, when 'D' Company found the water to be no more than about two feet deep, the Troop Commander decided that they could cross if towed by the Sherman and this had been arranged. Tragically the Sherman 'ditched' itself in the chaung and the tanks and our other vehicles had to be left, guarded by our Pioneer Platoon who also helped in the 'unditching'. This was a profound loss, for the presence of just one tank would have lightened our load and our casualties.

The patrol reported the village clear and we advanced to it, 'D' Company occupying the southern face – our front – and 'A' Company the north, with HQ and the R.A.P. tucked inside. Very few buildings remained, for fires started as a result of the rocket and bombing attacks had swept through the timber houses. But there was one in the north west corner and, after climbing to the elevated floor and pushing a 'pole' aerial up as high as we could, the signaller made contact with Main HQ. Something of an historic moment!

The C.O. then held his 'O' Group for the advance south on Thayetpinzu. Subsequently, while Clive was holding his company 'O' Group, a number of Japs led by an officer and estimated at 60, were spotted by them walking towards the village through a banana plantation immediately to their front. This was at 0830 hrs. Fire was opened up and they deployed in the plantation and returned the fire. We heard this going on before receiving a message as to what was actually happening, and it was not long before the Japanese 50mm Grenade Discharger bombs were dropping around our end of the village. We took what shelter we could, HQ taking advantage of the air-raid shelter trench dug by the owner of the adjoining house. As the trench bottom was so far down as to prevent me from seeing out, I sat on the edge, ready to drop back in again if things became too hot.

While there I watched John Bowles sauntering along his company's front, checking up on their positions, smoking a cigarette and looking very cool and collected. This was the last time I was to see John and the memory is thus much valued – it depicts him so very well.

We had with us Captain Thom, the F.O.O. for the 3.7 howitzers, whose forward planning had included ranging his guns on Yadaw and who could therefore, with the assistance of Clive in his front row seat, bring down a heavy and accurate concentration of fire on the Japs – to within 50 yards of ourselves.

We were then informed by Clive that parties of Japs were moving off to our flanks, one group being armed with a medium machine-gun. To counter them John sent out similar patrols on each side, to act as stops. In addition, Dicky Boyle and his platoon were ordered to move to a position on our right, 300 yards south west of our village, for outer flank protection.

It was to our disadvantage that we were in a well cultivated area for, what with banana groves and the like, we could not see any distance. Our situation was also made difficult in that, although Yadaw was only small, we had insufficient men in the two companies to form a ring around it; there was a big gap on each flank.

However the Japs were contained to our front and, after a somewhat scrappy engagement of about two hours, they withdrew south. That they did so was very much due to the heavy concentration of shelling they received, from the 3.7's and the 25-pounders.

As the Japs withdrew so 'D' Company sent out small parties, searching the ground to their fronts. At the same time, we were able to close on 'D' and form a tight perimeter in the front half of the village.

During all this activity reports on the situation had been transmitted to Main HQ, who did likewise to Brigade. This brought the reply from Brigadier Mike West that Geoffry must let him know by 1100 hrs whether or not he could deal with the situation unaided by the two other battalions, who were moving south on their long right hook. A little before the deadline Geoffry wirelessed that he could see the battle through, but asked permission to bring our two remaining rifle companies forward, leaving Ye-U under the protection of HQ Company. To this the brigadier could not agree; he did however allow the force in Ye-U to be reduced to one rifle company.

Thus it was that Tommy Tucker and his 'C' Company, together with their attached Glosters, were ordered to join us, bringing with them all the ammunition that they could carry, to make good our wastage, also food and water.

In a remarkably short time they had not only disengaged themselves from their positions but, aided by HQ Company and Admin., had gathered together all available transport and set out from Ye-U at 1200 hrs. Following our route they were able to join up with us at 1600 hrs.

In the meantime we had discovered a supply of water in a well, so their noble effort of carrying many gallons to us was wasted, but, having lived off haversack rations for 13 hours, we were glad to see the food.

During the period of waiting for Tommy and company, I had whiled away some spare time by examining the contents of three large packs, found on Japanese dead. As usual they contained nothing of particular interest, and I only mention them because Jones and I had the foresight to transfer to our packs a number of candles and solid fuel stoves, which were to be invaluable that night.

Jones also produced the leather document case which had formed part of the uniform of the Japanese officer who by then was one of their dead. It has proved to be a most useful satchel, often filling the more mundane role of sandwich container.

As usual I was firmly anchored to the wireless set and had no opportunity to look around, in what must have been a very productive horticultural area. One can understand the failure of the Japs to spot us once we were ashore, but it is inexplicable that they failed to observe our crossing. That they pulled back their outpost at Yadaw in order to conserve their forces at night is understandable, particularly as they would have been influenced by our wide-ranging artillery fire and our air-strikes. But their return to Yadaw in so unguarded a manner, without scouts or being dispersed, cost them dearly.

At 1400 hrs a patrol from 'D' Company found Pagoda Copse clear and, it being our next objective, a platoon was moved forward to occupy it.

It was then that the C.O. decided to attack and occupy Gun Copse before last light. This objective was thickly wooded and was in every way different to the small and open Pagoda Copse. It was of sufficient size to completely mask our view of Thayetpinzu, with which it was rightly believed to be linked by the Japs as one defensive position, and we were confident that we would have to fight for it.

With the arrival of Tommy Tucker and his strong Dorset-cum-Gloster company, the strengthening of our numbers made possible an attack on a wide two-company front, and still have a company in reserve. Geoffry therefore chivvied the weary Tommy and company forward to Pagoda Copse. Our reinforcements had every reason to be tired after their fast march for, besides carrying extra bandoliers of 200 x .303 ammo, packs of food or cans of water, men had paired to carry boxes of grenades and, of course, they had waded the river, some going through deeper water than that which we had found.

'C' Company were to attack on the right in a direct advance over some 400 yards of open grass, between their start line and the north face of the copse. On their left 'A' Company were to advance over similar ground in a dog-legged approach to the shorter east face.

An artillery concentration from our 3.7 hows and 25-pounders was arranged to come down on the north edge of the copse, for two minutes from 1654hrs, and on its completion our companies were to attack. Attack HQ was then forward of Yadaw and we watched this ineffective shelling, much of which tragically came down into open ground. 'A' and 'C' Companies commenced their attack and we moved down the track to Pagoda Copse, together with the two remaining platoons of 'D' Company.

The attack by 'C' Company has been graphically recorded by Harry Newcombe:

> We emerged into open ground beyond which was Gun Copse, a long thickly wooded area and, as we stood in extended order, there was no sign of life. I remember how quiet – almost peaceful – it seemed in those few moments, then we were ordered to fix bayonets and the whistle sounded for us to advance. As our double line passed the half-way point the woods suddenly erupted with machine-gun fire and everybody dropped to the ground and as there was no cover all we could do was hug the ground. Sergeant Alec Nott recalls: 'It was so sudden, one minute deathly silence, then all hell breaking loose. It was like a hailstorm with bullets cracking overhead in a continuous stream and bouncing off the ground ahead.' Tommy Thomas lay next to me and I could see the shock on his face and read his thoughts, 'This is it!' I heard a cry behind and turned to see the chap flip over on his back, obviously hit, one hand weakly waving; but no one could move under the intense fire. I heard Lieutenant Jock Given's voice calling for smoke, and then the sound of our 2-inch mortars beginning to fire and the first smoke bombs falling in front of the line of trees. Then Major Tucker and Jock Given began shouting as they stood above us – telling us to get up and attack. Both were taking a great risk, standing there, as they exhorted us to action. And Alec again recalls: 'I heard them shout, jumped to my feet, bayonet out and feeling very alone began to charge, I was struck a sudden blow on my left hip and the machine-gun bullet passed through and exited from my buttock, before I fell'.

Then the impetus generated by our two leaders was taken up by the Company; in a wave of sound the cries – 'Up the Dorsets!' and 'Up the Glosters!' were heard above the shooting and soon were echoing through the wood as we entered and the battle became close combat. I saw one of our chaps and a Jap fighting with bayonets and, through the smoke, fired twice at two Japs carrying something between them. But I lost them in the smoke and it is difficult to shoot accurately on the run with a bayonetted rifle. Just ahead was a covered trench with a slope cut in the ground to a small doorway and, as I was almost on top of it, I caught a glimpse of a steel helmet and the bottom half of a face. I lunged at it with my bayonet and as I did, a voice shouted almost in my ear – 'Grenade! cover!' and I glimpsed a 36 grenade whizzing down the slope and the chap who threw it nearly fell on me. As we went down I felt pain in both ears as the grenade lifted the dug-out roof six inches and smoke and dust poured out of the doorway. The chap was on his hands and knees, holding up two fingers and shouting. I could only hear bells. He gesticulated that there had been two Japs, but I had only seen one. As I carried on I passed a dead Jap in a praying position; he keeled over when my boot touched him. And then we were converging on the far edge of the wood, with more shouting than gunfire, and were just in time to see the Jap survivors running for the village of Thayetpinzu. Someone was calling out that we were not to continue in pursuit.

The company was spread out throughout the wood, sitting smoking, drinking from water bottles or checking weapons, all looked tired, their faces streaked with sweat and grime. I stood with another chap trying to light cigarettes, laughing because our hands were not steady enough from excitement, exhilaration and fear and an overdose of adrenalin. The team of medical orderlies under Corporal Jesty patched up minor wounds and stretcher-bearers carried or helped the more seriously wounded back to Pagoda Copse. One orderly was applying a large dressing to someone who was smoking and grinning, obviously happy to be alive. I saw a lad standing over the body of a Jap, his bayonet pointed at his chest while another, kneeling beside him, unfolded a small Japanese flag – the red sun on a pure white background stood out against the drab surroundings. It had been tucked inside the Jap's tunic.

Neither before nor after did I use a bayonet in action; the memory will stay for ever.

There is no doubt in my mind that our success was largely due to Major Tucker and Lieutenant Given, who transmitted their courage to the Dorsets and the Glosters of 'C' Company.

On the left, 'A' Company had been moving forward over 6-700 yards, for they had to go south to within half that distance from the enemy, before swinging right to attack that east flank. While this was in progress, a small party of Japs ran out on the flank of 7 Platoon, the left of the two leading platoons, but did not interfere with the advance. During this long approach the enemy fire had followed the pattern of that opposing 'C' Company, but had been spasmodic, probably due to an excellent smoke screen laid by 'A' Company and few casualties were suffered. But when their Company HQ and the artillery F.O.O. (the Captain Thom to whom I have referred) were at the turning point, some heavy grenade discharger fire came down on them and 9 Platoon, during which John Bowles was killed. 9 Platoon was under the command of one of our new officers who had not been in action before and who found the strain too great. Command of the HQ and 9 Platoon was taken by Captain Thom, who took them forward to the copse where they linked up with their leading platoons. Those platoons had come under fire from several light machine-guns on their right flank, between them and 'C' Company, at the moment when both were entering Gun Copse, with its entrenched Japs and had commenced hand-to-hand fighting. 7 and 8 Platoons had a number of casualties, including both platoon commanders, John O'Donnel, fortunately for us soon to return, and Colin Beale who was shot through the thigh and whose life with the battalion was ended. Roger Johnson, the company 2 I/C, who was up with the leading platoons, proceeded to 'draw' their half of the copse with the aid of some of 'C' Company. As with that company, when they too reached the southern edge, they were in time to see Japs trying to escape and some they shot down. There the three platoons and the HQ linked up and Roger was able to reorganise and take command. This coincided with the approach of dusk.

Behind all this activity we had moved down to Pagoda Copse, doing so in single file along the track which, in that part, was very similar to one of the smaller English lanes, being just about wide enough to take a farm wagon and enclosed on both sides by high hedges. Just short of the Copse, two adjoining openings gave access to fields east of the track. As we passed them fire from a light machine-gun was directed at us by Japs who had concealed themselves at the back of the fields. These could have been the Japs who appeared on the flank of 7 Platoon. We ran with giant steps as bullets kicked up the dust. During this high speed run I became separated from Geoffry when our aerial fouled a tree and it was not until we had repaired it with the aid of replacements from a gunner set, that I was able to proceed. Arriving in the copse I spotted Geoffry by a fallen palm tree at the southern edge and rejoined him. He had been lucky, for when in a firing position over the trunk a bullet had struck the stock of his American carbine, doing no damage other than a splinter in his forehead.

Dicky Boyle had arrived on the scene and he and his platoon were given the job of covering our east flank. Geoffry had decided that both copses could be held with the forces then in them, and we started to dig in. But almost immediately Tommy came on the set to say that he had insufficient troops for his area, whereupon the C.O. ordered Clive to go forward with two platoons, accompanied by Dicky. With 'A' and 'C' retaining their respective left and right forward positions, the new arrivals closed the rear, thus achieving an all-round defence with great difficulty in the waning light.

We in our small group were, like the others, doing our utmost to establish some degree of order in the fast gathering darkness, and were only too happy to be able to settle down within that east flank of Gun Copse. There, within a defensive perimeter of sorts, a state of blessed and absolute quietness descended, so much so, with the Japs having forsaken their desultory gun fire, that the place might have been almost uninhabited. Thayetpinzu and the surviving Japs could wait for tomorrow. Yet then and throughout the hours of darkness there were jobs to be done and our HQ signallers were 'netting-in' the other sets. That immediate routine took place at each new location, so that we had communication throughout the battalion. We failed however, despite their closeness, to get a response from 'A' Company. Knowing our utter weariness after four days and three nights of, at best, little sleep, it was easy to appreciate how intensified that exhaustion would be in them after their battle and casualties. This gave me a welcome excuse to visit my old Company and, finding Bert Jones 'dead to the world', I set off alone. There they were, crouched by their set and asleep as suspected, but they were soon aroused and with communication established I set off on my return only to find that I had wandered off to the east and well off course out in the open on the Jap side; as was apparent when a break in the clouds enabled me to see our copse away to my rear. Reversing course and progressing with determined strides and loudly repeating – 'It's all right, it's only me,' I was profoundly relieved to make it back to base. But having done so I was very aware of how vulnerable we were to the enemy, who could have eliminated us had he mounted an attack of the type we had experienced at Kohima.

Since our arrival our Defence Group had been busy enlarging and roofing a Burmese air-raid shelter trench; making it about eight feet long, three wide and about four from floor to underside of roof. To this they added a stepped entrance in the centre of one side. In this confined space was Geoffry, all six feet of him, and one and sometimes two signallers complete with wireless set, on listening watch throughout the night and much of the time transmitting messages and receiving them, all of which had to be accurately recorded on paper. I too was there much of the time as was Bert Jones, who busied himself brewing innumerable mugs of 'char' on the Japanese cookers. All this by the light of those candles found with the stoves. This crowding had the advantage of producing a warm fug, for outside it was quite cold, as I soon discovered when I lay down and tried to sleep and failed. We had no blankets and I envied the so much tougher troops, deep in slumber and oblivious to a trivial drop in temperature.

We had lost touch with Joe and, having some casualties, decided to send them by the direct route to the river as had been planned beforehand. Being again desperately short of ammunition, an ammunition carrying party accompanied them and was able to fill a dual role in providing protection. They moved off on a compass bearing and, on informing Main HQ of the situation, they too arranged an ammunition party who crossed the river and assisted with the injured, who were ferried across in canvas assault boats.

While speaking to Graeme I was able to advise him of our belief that the R.A.P. might be making for our original crossing place, and acting on this Mervyn Jones set off with a number of men and ambulances, making for the same place.

The story of the R.A.P. that night, is told by Joe Chamberlin as follows:

> We had some 15 casualties gathered at Pagoda Copse, where we were under the protection of 'Fish' Mullet's platoon. It soon became very dark and one of the injured was an 'A' Company stretcher-bearer, wounded in the testicles and needing to have them put back in place urgently. This we did by torch light under cover of a blanket. I had to chloroform him first, as the morphine hadn't touched him. It was the first and only time that I used this archaic, but very portable, anaesthetic during

the campaign. He looked me up a few years after the war, to show me his two children as evidence of the success of the procedure.

Fish and I were uncertain whether Dicky was still at the water's edge, as he had been gathered into the main enclave around the copse. In any case we were not optimistic about finding him in the dark across a No Man's Land we had not seen. If we didn't find him there would be no means of getting the casualties across. We knew where we could cross on foot, and we knew the route there, and it seemed less likely that we would run into Japs if we went back the way we had come. There were several stretcher cases, with which Fish's men helped us. I elected to carry Pte. Hole, because he was light and was able to hang on a pick-a-back. He had a bullet through his foot. The river where we recrossed it seemed a lot more than two feet deep. As we neared the other side someone called out from the bank. To our joy it was Mervyn and not a Jap.

Later Joe was to describe his meeting with Mervyn as a real 'Stanley and Livingstone' affair.

When the ammunition party returned they had only a fraction of our requirements and I arranged with Main HQ for further supplies. As a result, a carrying party from 'B' Company set off, reaching us at 0100hrs with all that we needed.

Soon after the casualties set off for the river I briefed a recce patrol from Dicky's long suffering platoon, to spy out the land at and around Thayetpinzu. On their return they were able to report having heard voices.

In between these comings and goings, Tommy Tucker and I searched through the document case of a Japanese officer who had been killed. Next day I was able to send off a large parcel of documents to Brigade.

5th January

We decided to make no detailed plans for the attack on Thayetpinzu until knowing more of the situation there and, with this objective, a patrol under Gerry Overman went out before first light. He was to return with the wonderful news that they had entered the village and found it clear.

Our whole force then went forward and occupied the place without opposition. Abandoned clothing and equipment pointed to a very hasty evacuation; but it was not so hurried as to prevent them removing their guns, for none remained. From the condition of their clothing and equipment it was obvious that our old adversaries had been newly equipped and the dead were young men, new to the harsh conditions of Burma.

During the day the remainder of the battalion crossed the river and joined up with us, for the two days of rest that we had been allocated.

That afternoon Clive Chettle showed me an atrocity found in his Company's position. A Burmese youth lay outstretched upon the ground, his body showing the effects of scalding and bayonetting. Captain Thom photographed the body which we then buried. Later I forwarded the negatives and a report to those whose responsibility it was to collate such things. It was common knowledge that the Japanese delighted in tying prisoners to trees and torturing them with the bayonet, one such had been found on Garrison Hill. Here we had confirmation of such behaviour and of a mentality that was beyond our comprehension.

Thinking back to that battle, which remains unique in that it was 'ours' and one with a well defined beginning and an ending, I clearly remember the exhilaration of that final morning when, suddenly, it was all over and we had won. Fate had been kind to us, for with our depleted companies and, once across the river, an absence of armoured support, we had been very thin on the ground. Had the Japs mounted just one determined counter-attack, the outcome could have been so very different.

For many of our reinforcements it was the first time they had been in action and they, and our attached Glosters had acquitted themselves so well – no praise could be too high. We had suffered the loss of ten killed; John Bowles of course, but of the others, seven were our gunner reinforcements. No number of Japanese dead could compensate for them or for the suffering of the many who had been wounded. But as we had to go on fighting into a future to which we could see no end, some satisfaction resulted from a search of the ground back to Yadaw which disclosed 27 enemy dead, of which two were officers. Knowing how the Japanese endeavoured to carry off their dead, that total was probably very incomplete.

On that morning it was clear that strangers had been creeping around in the dark, for someone had removed John Bowles' boots.

We had fulfilled our task and the Camerons, coming up towards Thayetpinzu to our assistance, could be halted.

That afternoon General Nicholson came to see and congratulate us and was duly shown something of Gun Copse and Thayetpinzu.

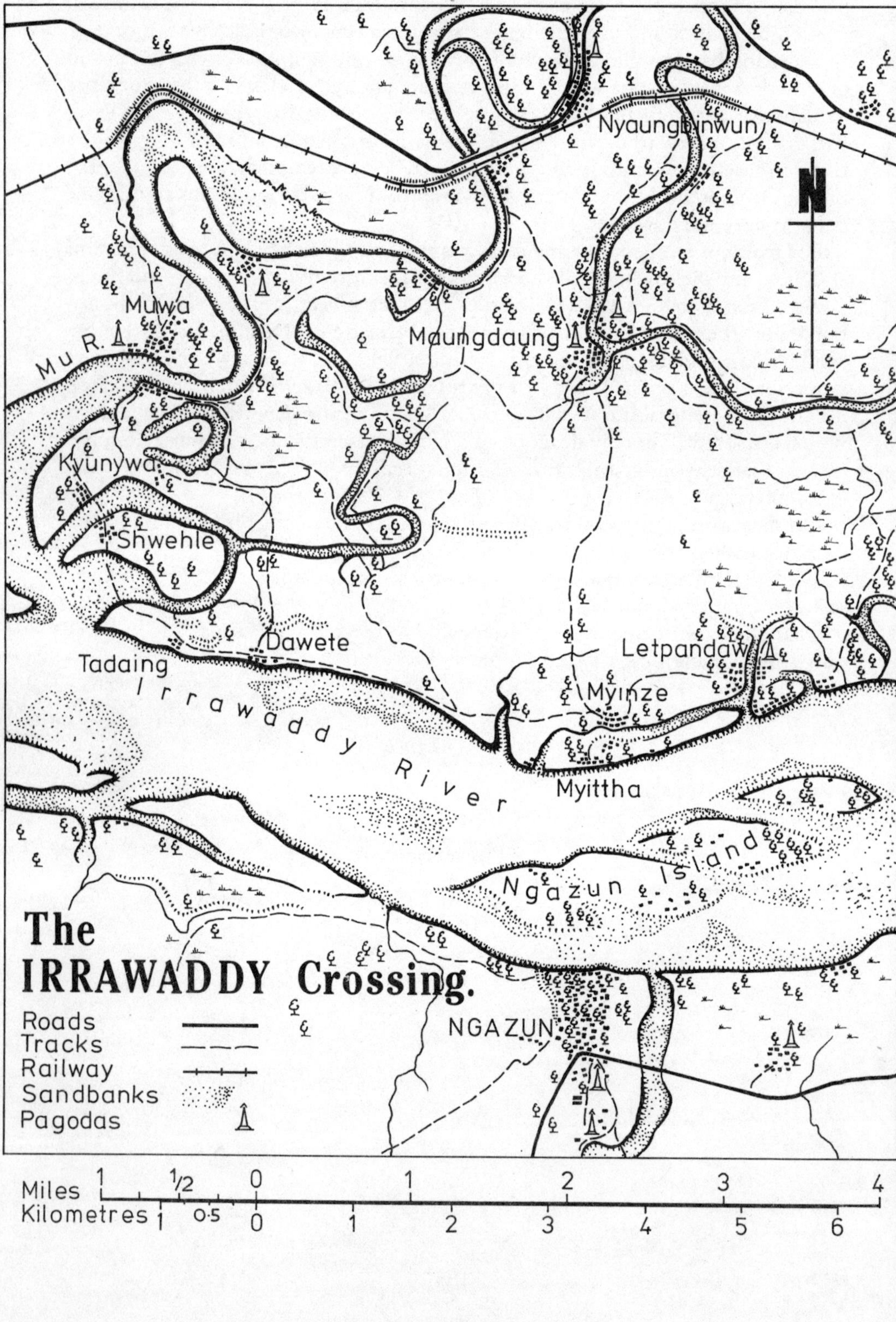

Nyaungbinwun
N
Muwa
Mu R.
Maungdaung
Kyunywa
Shwehle
Dawete
Tadaing
Irrawaddy River
Letpandaw
Myinze
Myittha
Ngazun Island
NGAZUN
The IRRAWADDY Crossing.
Roads
Tracks
Railway
Sandbanks
Pagodas
Miles 1 1/2 0 1 2 3 4
Kilometres 1 0·5 0 1 2 3 4 5 6

CHAPTER TEN

To the Irrawaddy

6th, 7th and 8th January

During that night, the 5th/6th of January, most of us managed to get our first real sleep for three or more nights, and how good it was!

Our two-day rest resulted from necessity as much as reward for our exertions, for the sappers had to bridge the Mu. That they had done by early on the 7th and, soon afterwards, we were reunited with our vehicles and our mules. So on that morning, at 0830 hrs, we set off on another stage of our pilgrimage, making for the village of Kanthit, a distance of about nine miles which we reached in four hours. Just short of the village we arrived at the eastern equivalent of the main canal which had checked us on our approach to Ye-U. But we had no problems and a recce patrol, dispatched along it to the north, made no contact with the Japs.

That night, however, we could hear firing from the area of the town of Kin-U, four miles to the east, where our road crossed the main north/south railway and where 98 Brigade of 19 Division were operating.

We were then well across the Shwebo Plain which terminated only 15 miles further east, at a tongue of hills extending south from the great hill mass of north east Burma. Those terminal hills, rising only 200 feet above our level of just 400 feet above the sea, were covered with fairly dense deciduous forest and bamboo. We were to be fortunate and remain in the plain; a rice growing area with a scattering of small villages, one or two miles apart. A land not unlike the 'Deccan' of India and our memories are of a dry and dusty landscape, in which there was some scrub; a place of bright sunshine, unbroken but for a little rain while at Thayetpinzu, and that sunshine – thankfully – still temperate.

The objective of 2 Div. was Shwebo, only 14 miles south and which was to be attacked on a two-brigade front; with 4 Brigade on the right and advancing from the south and west and our Brigade on the left, moving down from the north.

On the 8th we set off again at 0830 hrs and, as before, we were the rear battalion, and able to leave to others the dispersal of opposition. On halting for the day, at mid-day, we were just under six miles from Shwebo, having left the road that had served us so well from as far back as the Chindwin and moved south. Our old road after passing through Kin-U, terminated after a dozen miles on the fringe of the hills, at the village of Kongyi. A place that could boast of an Inspection Bungalow, possibly much used in the past, for running north for many miles was one of those tracks described as 'jeepable in dry season'. Also an even more difficult track continued east and north over the hills to reach the Irrawaddy. That track, after crossing the highest ground, split, the right half leading to the small village and steamer station of Kabwet, on our near bank. There 98 Brigade were to meet fanatical Japanese, fighting to the last man, and with whom they were to be engaged throughout the month. The left half, after going north for seven miles, arrived at the Irrawaddy opposite the east bank town of Thabeikkyin, reached by ferry, which was to be the most northerly of 19 Division's crossing points.

At that mid-day halt we completed an easy march along a good track on the west side of the canal, then known as the Shwebo Canal. There we established ourselves for the night, with 'C' Company forward to hold a canal bridge and important track crossing.

It was fortunate for us that, when 'C' reached the bridge, the Japs had vacated a row of one man fox-holes in the adjoining east bank. Crossing the canal, they took over this enemy position and open ground bordered on the far flank by a grove of trees, which became shelter for our mules. Trees were also to the west of the canal, with houses within a white picket fence forming an avenue and a touch of civilisation. Had the Japs remained, they could have caught us under close-range fire. At dusk, there being no signs of them apart from a dead one in the canal, the company, less those on guard in the Jap positions, settled down for the night wrapped in their blankets, with kit and weapons beside them.

9th January

Private Frank (Chindit) Hudson tells of how, when on guard duty in the small hours, he and the guard sergeant were surprised by a loud noise which they thought to be the mules stampeding. They then saw it was two or three Japs who were making a racket and scaring the animals as they and another four charged through our lines. During some hectic moments it was Corporal Taffy Beynon who, having sat up, suffered worst, receiving a bayonet wound to the hand and mouth.

On this day we arrived at Shwebo, the entry of our division having been partly forestalled by a brigade of 19 Div., by then further south to block the road and catch retreating Japs. No attempt had been made to hold the town with anything more than a delaying force and we, at the tail, moved in at 1645 hrs, occupying a near corner inside the wall and moat, recently cleared by the Worcesters.

Shwebo is only dimly remembered, although it must have been of considerable interest. The map shows the enclosing wall and moat as an almost perfect square, with sides just over two miles in length. The built-up area adjoined the east wall throughout its length, but extended for only a third or so along the north and south walls. Thus buildings filled the eastern end of the enclosed area, the remainder being mainly an open space – a maidan for parades and public enjoyment. A north to south road ran through the town (away to the east of ours), forming a high street while within it. The north to south railway, having crossed the north moat and breached the wall, then turned diagonally to make an exit through the east wall.

The map also shows a cantonment of well spaced gridded streets, one mile to the north and east and on slightly higher ground. A rifle range, and further east a landing ground, added to the facilities of this self-contained place.

Early in February, when we had reached the Irrawaddy, two Dakotas landed there, bringing a relief party of Glosters to switch with those who had served us so well. It consisted of Major Dick Wilkins and Lieutenant Peter Collister together with a platoon and a mortar detachment, again to a total of 50.

Photographs of the battalion are very rare, but there is one taken in Shwebo. It shows us in our action dress of steel helmets, shirt sleeves and battledress trousers, advancing in columns of sections along an open road. On the near side are empty slit trenches with, beyond and also lining the road, some sadly battered buildings. They are a mix of one or two floors, of which some have arcaded fronts and roofs enclosed by fretted parapets, of classical proportions. Town premises far removed from the familiar timber huts.

At 1600 hrs a patrol, under Snagger, departed in carriers to make contact with 19 Div. and returned with information on their dispositions and intentions.

An evening of peace and quiet was disrupted when five Japs were discovered outside 'B' Company's perimeter by two of their men, one of whom, Private Roche, was killed. As the enemy ran off under fire, two were shot down.

10th January

A static day of washing and bathing, something to be tackled with a determined enthusiasm whenever water was freely available. In that camp we were not only near water but a railway station, a particular attraction for those who had missed out at Ye-U. Regrettably there are no lasting memories of Shwebo's station, which would have been of a size that would make the one at Hornsea (of happy memory) seem positively metropolitan. But Hornsea had no pagoda and Shwebo could boast of having one of the largest in Burma, which many of us visited. It was approached by a flight of stone steps rising to an enclosed courtyard. There the base supporting the tapering structure could be closely viewed and the numerous enclosures, or shrines, housing figures of Buddha, from a few feet in height to 12 or more, fully appreciated. In normal times that elevated paving would have been a busy meeting place for a charming and friendly population, many being devotees there to make offerings, or for meditation. A Phongyi showed us the wooden platforms, erected by the Japanese in the tops of the trees within the pagoda precincts, as observation posts. One more example of the indifference to the feelings of others that so characterized the Japanese.

Reports were coming in of fanatical behaviour by the enemy, desperate to check our relentless advance over this open country. That the Worcesters had been attacked by a platoon led by a sword-brandishing officer, was not exceptional. But another such officer had leapt on to a tank and decapitated its commander and, still with sword in hand, had entered the interior where he was shot, before he could do likewise to the crew. Japs were squatting in holes dug in the roads or ground likely to be used by tanks. There they held aerial bombs nose uppermost, ready for detonation by striking the cap as a tank rolled over.

No unit commander likes to pass a day without an entry in the War Diary which, to some degree, may have accounted for ours: 'A patrol into the centre of the town found no enemy'. No one could criticise such a patrol in that situation. For those concerned it was a cushy one, and probably interesting as an excursion into the heart of a Burmese town having at least some buildings of a character associated with built-up areas.

11th January

In preparation for an 0800 hrs departure we were out and about early and soon forming up on the exit road. We Dorsets were back in the lead and, with the support of a troop of Grants and also some 'Priests',* we had the makings of an impressive column. All this was an aid to another advance south, one of about ten miles to a road and canal crossing near the large village of Moksogyon, the next place with a railway station.

While waiting to start we had the rare sight of some 30 Japanese Oscar fighters circling overhead, planes that were similar to the American Mohawk, and with which they were often confused. We were glad of the cover afforded by trees and buildings and kept out of sight until they departed. We were to learn that they shot down three of the Dakotas bringing our supplies, the three crashing in flames near the town.

When about half way we bumped into 19 div.; they had got to our objective first so, sending our supporting armour back, we continued on our own. This was to be very much one of the better days, one when soldiering could be really enjoyed. Not only was our route very agreeable, in that the road continued to be bordered by a small canal, but we were passing hospitable villages. There was much bartering for eggs and chicken, and what better way can there be for shortening a march for the keen-on-a-bargain and ever-hungry foot soldier!

On reaching Moksogyon I pushed on for a mile to another village, and was able to experience all the advantages that come from being first. An Indian land-owner invited me and the Burma Intelligence Corps sergeant, then acting as our interpreter, into the courtyard of his house. While we were being made welcome with cups of tea and fruit, a couple of ducks were caught and eggs collected. Those ducks provided our mess supper, which was good timing, for we had a visitor in the person of Sam Symes; he whom I had tried to contact when we were back at ms.82.

I enjoyed an evening in the mess of the 10th Field Regiment, missing, therefore, an exchange of views with one who, as C.O. of the 2nd Worcesters in 19 Div., could have told us quite a lot about that division which so often stole our thunder, and continued doing so.

33 Corps, having found the opposition less than expected, right from the time of our leaving the Chindwin, (that decisive battle within the Shwebo Plain had not materialised), was now slowing down 2 Div., in such a way as not to be

* 105mm self propelled gun howitzers of American origin.

apparent to the enemy. With 400 miles between us and the railhead at Dimapur, we were stretching our supply line beyond even its capabilities, excellent as they were. Ammunition in particular was a problem; much had been expended at Ye-U and the gunners were hard pressed to meet our needs. 5 and 6 Brigades were due for a rest and were to be given one, during which an advance south would be kept in motion by 4 Brigade.

12th – 17th January

We were intrigued at being allocated a rest area in the vicinity of hot springs. They were a few miles away to the east, thus our departure at 0830 hrs saw us away in ample time. 19 Div. had not been able to advise us of the presence, or otherwise, of Japs, so we moved with companies deployed and ready to fight.

As those up front approached our objective, a message came down the column that the locals were saying: "There are no Japs." Geoffry reacted by sending me forward with all possible speed, in order that I might reach the Travellers Rest Bungalow, shown on our map, ahead of the others. The whole of the local population seemed to have turned out, and one can well imagine that that was probably so. Most lined the road leading to the village centre and it was quite something to be driving between them. There was no difficulty in finding the bungalow, for it was a large timber building standing within a compound. Gathered there were the local notabilities, one of whom was fluent in English. Making himself their spokesman, he formally welcomed me and said how delighted they were that the Japanese had gone. He continued by offering, on behalf of the community, to provide as much in the way of meat, fowl and eggs as they could spare. Geoffry and the battalion were soon on the scene and, after further expressions of goodwill we, at HQ, installed ourselves in comparative comfort. It is not difficult to imagine the caustic remarks that would have flowed within the companies, at our having bagged all the luxury. A roof over one's head was indeed luxury, as was a level floor. Here was a place in which we could properly set up the typewriter and those things needed for the production of Standing Orders. An Orderly Room that was not a hole in the ground or, at best, a minuscule tent, refreshed our admin. staff, who for so long had performed wonders under impossible conditions.

Our village was known to us as Halin Twinma, although more correctly it was Halin Taungngu, a variation for which I have no explanation. It and the surroundings and its people were delightful, all being made more so due to their semi-isolation from the war. A place unchanged and free of the debris and destruction with which we were invariably associated.

Every effort had been made to supplement the troops' rations through local purchases and for some days everybody did very well. Then our hosts found themselves unable to cope, we were just too many, and we returned to the familiar bully and dehydrated potatoes. Almost certainly we also had the much maligned, soya-link sausage; that mix of soya bean seeds, edible oils and flour (or whatever). Many would say that any resemblance to a decent sausage was confined purely to shape. It was always rated lowly perhaps unfairly for there were some prepared to tolerate it, I being one. The dehydrated potato and the sweet one were frequently on the menu and were criticised by those who yearned longingly, for the sheer bulk of the familiar spud.

For the first time we were meeting educated Burmese and were freely conversing with them. Once, when at the home of our first English speaking acquaintance (our mess being in need of a brace of chicken), I remained for coffee and met his wife, an ex-schoolmistress from Rangoon. She was worried about a missing relative, and was not at all easily convinced that it was quite beyond our abilities to put her in touch with him.

As might be expected the Japs had used the springs as a rest centre, and had improved bathing by erecting timber pavilions. Those ponds of hot salty water were just the thing for easing weary muscles, and warm sunshine intensified their enjoyment.

But some soldiering continued. At 0800 hrs, on our first morning, Snagger was away with a carrier patrol to what was designated Point 316. Probably a hill at the southern tip of the high ground to our east, a place from which one could look for Japs. They were back at 1415 hrs reporting 'No contact'. A foot patrol from 'B' Company, to the village of Gwegon, learned from the locals that no Japs had been in their locality for several days.

The 14th of January was a day of considerable interest, despite it not fulfilling its main objective. After breakfast 'Fish' Mullet and I, travelling in my jeep and with three truck-loads of his platoon, set off for the village of Mingom, some three or four miles distant. There we divided, for I was to remain, while Fish continued in the jeep, accompanied by two of the 15-cwt trucks as a patrol to the distant village of Thitseingyi, on the near bank of the Irrawaddy.

They were to be the first 'Dorsets' to see the river since the involvement of the regiment in a very different Burma War, just over 100 years earlier, a distinction to which that patrol would have been indifferent, had they been made aware of it. Thitseingyi had a military importance at that time and could have been full of Japs, for it was at the end of a road running west to the town of Wetlet, to our south, and was thus a possible base from which to attack our flank.

My small party were at Mingom to receive the surrender of ten members of the Burma National Army. They had previously made known their desire to give themselves up at this rendezvous, and an intermediary had gone by bullock cart the day before to fetch them.

When the Japanese invaded Burma, there were many Burmese very ready to fight for independence from our rule, and they were encouraged to join a Japanese sponsored force – the Burma Independence Army. In that January, three years later and after many vicissitudes, it was known as the Burma National Army, and its members were as ready to see the last of the Japs (and one hopes even more so) as they had been of us.

While we awaited their arrival and spent the morning wandering around the village, a special meal was being prepared for us by the headman. At mid-day, in the company of our host, we sat at tables in his compound, to enjoy the rare privilege of being the guests of a Burmese family. After a multitude of curries of differing degrees of excellence which I have eaten since, the chicken curry we consumed that day, with all the trimmings, is remembered as very possibly the best. What other could match its unique atmosphere and location? Towards the end of the meal my thoughts were on how I might, through a small gift, demonstrate our thanks. When we were outside our 'defended positions' we wore full equipment and thus I had my pack and, searching through it, found a tablet of Lux toilet soap. It was a sorry sight, for the wrapping although unbroken, was discoloured and shabby from being in close contact with my second pair of boots and other hard objects. I handed it to our host with expressions of appreciation, he obviously wondering what on earth it was that he was receiving as he put it down unopened. It would have been much welcomed by his family and, who knows, it might well have subsequently boosted the sale of Lux soaps in Burma.

Fish Mullet and his men returned in mid-afternoon after an uneventful patrol and, the B.N.A. deserters having got cold feet, we arrived back well satisfied although empty-handed.

After four days in our delightful village we were preparing to move on to Wetlet. At 0800 hrs an advance party representing each company departed, to be followed by a recce party under Mervyn at 1700 hrs the next day – the 17th.

One of my letters home that day, referred to as having been written by the light of a hurricane lamp whilst standing up, mentions a pause in my writing as a result of one of the Buddhist monks having called to say good-bye. Understandably, if only because of our differing philosophies and codes of behaviour, it was they who were the least inclined to show pleasure at our presence. That visit well illustrated the genuine welcome we had received.

Circumstances were to prevent us having the opportunity of similar fraternising in the future.

18th – 24th January

On the 18th, the first away, at the early (even for us) hour of 0530 hrs, was the M.T. who were taking the longer route by road. Half an hour later the rest of us set off across country, I part riding and part leading Judy. By 0925 hrs Battalion HQ was moving into the abandoned police lines at their headquarters at Wetlet and taking up residence in another bungalow. There we were to complete our couple of weeks rest in what was virtually an empty town, as a result of considerable damage from bombing and strafing from the air.

For once the whole battalion was able to get into a building of some sort and this included the 'I' Section, which for the first time ever, established its office within brick walls.

Adding to the air of decay was the town's all-important railway, which the Japs had stripped of its rails and sleepers.

Of greatest interest to us at HQ and to me in particular, for I became a sort of unofficial commandant, was the gaol – standing in splendid undamaged isolation within the police compound. This exceptional building, about 30 feet square for the height of its low walls, below a steeply pitched roof, was entered through a door, placed centrally in its east side. That door gave access to a passageway inside the four walls, between them and the cage, which occupied the whole of the remaining floor area. The cage, in keeping with the structure, was of heavy timbers. There were no windows and with the door closed, light and ventilation was restricted to what was obtained through vertical slits, provided for that purpose. To pass prisoners into the cage, or to extract them from it, there was a cunning arrangement in one corner, so constructed that the gaoler could not be overwhelmed by a rush of inmates at that critical moment. The in-going prisoner was passed through a small vertically sliding trap door, into a space sufficient for one, formed of the heavy timber bars of the cage. The gaoler, still in the passageway, then operated a similar trap giving access to the main cage. I have no recollection of any provision for a wash and brush up and as we only obtained a "client" just before our departure, that was something with which we were not involved.

There was an increasing concern at Government level, about the many weapons available in the country for anyone who chose to look for them. We in our retreat in 1942, had lost or had abandoned thousands and the Japs were now doing likewise. As a result orders were going out that all unauthorised weapons were to be surrendered.

One of our companies had occasion to search one of the few occupied houses and discovered weapons concealed under the floor boards. I can only imagine that we had received a tip-off, perhaps from a disgruntled or fearful neighbour, for no dwelling would have been entered without reason. This followed an order issued by us to the locals that they were to hand in weapons to us and the householder, an extremely angry Sikh, was brought to me and I shoved him into gaol, whereupon he became furious. It could be said that he took a very poor view of these proceedings, so much so that he counter-attacked, claiming that our soldiers had stolen all his valuables, including jewellery. An unlikely story, and as we thought him a very shifty specimen, he got no sympathy. We were then departing and he was left to be collected by the civil police.

At about that time I was instructed to search a village suspected of having a hoard of weapons. Taking the Section with me we called on the Headman, advising him that we had arrived to collect all the military weapons that he and his villagers were known to have. And what an amazing pile we received!

Handed to us, with a lack of restraint that causes one to question how many more were stacked away was, amongst the rifles, carbines and light machine-guns, a Japanese copy of the Bren, of which we had heard but not seen and which was thus an item of considerable interest. Most unexpectedly there was a Mauser machine-pistol, its wooden holster designed for use also as a butt.

During those days Geoffry, Mervyn and I would ride into the surrounding country which, being flat and open with sandy tracks, was ideal for a gallop and we made the most of it. Possibly it was this that gave Geoffry the bright idea of holding a race meeting. Here was an opportunity to do something for sheer enjoyment and, under John Main's direction, willing hands cleared scrub and a track was formed. A superficial authenticity was achieved over a 200 yards length at the winning post end, which was fenced off with whitewashed posts (even in central Burma we had our whitewash), between which we strung white tracing tapes. Tapes that were to be next used for their proper purpose – the night crossing of the Irrawaddy.

This unexpected sporting event, was advertised throughout the brigade and entries flowed in from most of the units with ponies, but of all it was the Indian mule companies who were prepared to field the greatest number. On the day, they arrived with mules and ponies, races having been arranged for both.

January the 24th was the big day, claimed as the first British Race Meeting in Burma since the withdrawal. And it very probably was.

At home, pre-war, Alan Cobham and other pioneers of flying used race-courses for their displays. It was therefore appropriate that the day should start with the landing of an American L5 plane, the pilot having been under the impression that he had come down on a forward landing strip. He flew out after half an hour, somewhat bemused but carrying a Japanese rifle, that being the next best thing that we could let him have to the sword he was keen on finding.

The meeting commenced after lunch, with just about everybody present who could find a reason, genuine or otherwise, for visiting the Dorsets. Our race-goers were headed by General Nicholson and Brigadier Mike West. In contrast, and adding colour and a civilian element, was an ENSA concert party. As might be expected a tote had been set up and a number of bookmakers had been 'licensed'. By the end of the afternoon the tote had taken something in the region of 20,000 rupees, roughly £1,500; goodness knows what the bookies made! However, some of the profits were dispatched to the RSPCA (India) and a donation went to the Regimental Old Comrades Association.

The races were ridden in a dare-devil personal and unit rivalry, producing close and exciting finishes. Of all who rode that day, it was the Indian muleteers whom we rated as the most impressive with their bare-back riding, professionals with family riding skills that had been implanted almost from birth.

If only we could have had some of our Burmese friends there too, sharing our uninhibited enjoyment !

The prizes consisted of cash and a number of remarkable trophies that had been made by Sergeant Smith, one of our M.T. fitters. They were presented, with due ceremony, by Colonel Mitford Slade, the then Second-in-Command of 5 Brigade.

Thinking back to those prizes and the skill of their making out of ration tins, I wonder if any survive? And what names they had – The Mandalay Bowl and the Wetlet Stakes; the Plassey Gold Cup and the Sarah Sands Gallop. Should any exist they deserve an honoured place in an army museum, for they typify the unquenchable spirit of that time.

25th – 31st January

During our time at Wetlet, that great morale raiser, our mobile cinema, had caught up with us and for an evening we had been transported by a Hollywood fantasy, and were the better for it. Then, in the final days, we had the ENSA theatrical party, whose company we had enjoyed at our races. Reality was, nevertheless, about to reimpose itself.

The Divisional Intelligence report for the 26th included news of sightings by the local Burmese of Japanese patrols, which were operating on our side of the Irrawaddy and to our rear. Shwebo and Wetlet were but some 14 miles from that river, the east side of which was not only enemy territory, but the very centre of their operations in upper Burma. As we progressed south so we became increasingly vulnerable with our lengthening tail – extending north and parallel to that north/south river frontier.

19 Div., whose task it was to attack Mandalay from the north had, by the 16th, established a first bridgehead on the east bank near Thabeikkyin. Subsequent crossings were made to the south, against increasing opposition which included artillery and the, to be expected, savage counter-attacks. They were then 40 or more miles north of the city, and so hard was to be the going and so severe the enemy resistance, that those miles were not to be covered before early March.

The obvious interpretation of this activity from across the river, was that it aimed to cut our lines of communication and those of General Rees and his vulnerable division. A ground attack on the, also vulnerable, Shwebo air-strip, then more than ever busy with planes landing supplies and bringing in and flying out personnel, was a probability.

A warning came through from brigade that we would have to do something about it and, at 1630 hrs on that same day – the 26th, 'B' Company was ordered to stand by ready to move. Two hours later they departed in trucks for the air-strip; following which, as a result of reports of enemy in the area of Gwegon, 'C' Company received similar orders. They departed at 1030 hrs the next day, heading for a specific area near the village of Noapi-O, about three miles to the north of Halin Twinma. They found it to be a place of undulating ground where scrub was intersected by a network of foot and cattle paths. There they were to lie in wait for the Japs and three ambushes were set up in ideal conditions, for the scrub was so dense that it confined movement to the paths. The furthermost, which was close to the village of Gwegon, was under Dick Castle. Dick, at last recovered from his injuries received when leading 'C' at Kohima, had rejoined us on the day following our occupation of Thayetpinzu and was 2 I/C to Tommy Tucker. On the map Gwegon is just over seven miles from the Irrawaddy. However, those few miles traversed the tongue of hills previously mentioned. Another change of situation sprung upon us necessitated their hasty recall, but not before they had patrolled that broken ground and had seen the distinctive Japanese footprints.

Wireless communication, even within the battalion, could be very tricky and when companies were at a distance, non-existent. 'C' Company having sited themselves within scrub to be screened from the Japs, were also screened from us and contact had been lost. Geoffry decided that he must visit them to see how they were and rather than travel to Halin Twinma by road, a roundabout journey, we would go on horseback across country. So he and I, with Corporal Churchill on Goggles as escort, set off after breakfast, galloping and cantering the eight miles. We passed through a countryside devoid of life until, as we approached the village, we saw a local hoeing a field away to our right. While the others waited I rode over to him, hoping to discover whether there were Japs in the village, which although close was screened from view by uncared-for hedges and trees. My clumsy attempts at interrogation, mainly the word 'Japani?', which I repeated while pointing towards the village, produced nothing but vacant stares and deciding it was hopeless, I rejoined the others. Loosening my revolver in its holster, ready for that 'fast draw' in accordance with the traditions of the Wild West as seen at the cinema, I led the way into Halin Twinma. A changed place from how we had first seen it when it was alive with people, for it was silent and seemingly empty as we rode through to the traveller's bungalow, and there, under a couple of trees, were two of our 15cwt. trucks.

They were 'C' Company's, for Tommy was leaving his vehicles where they would not disclose his positions. They would go forward when they had essentials to deliver, such as water and rations. With those trucks was a ration party awaiting such a delivery.

I can clearly visualise that peaceful scene of the two trucks and half a dozen chaps lounging in the sunshine, which filtered through to them from the branches high above. We were glad to dismount and sit with them and hear of their doings, while puffing away at a cigarette. After a time the rations arrived and leaving our ponies and the mule, we completed the journey by truck which, in addition to the rations, carried a wireless set, a more powerful one than ours, having come from brigade.

It was no surprise to find that Tommy had taken full advantage of the thick scrub to establish some deadly ambush positions, and it was while we were admiring them and discussing their potential, that a message came through on the new set. It was from our Brigadier, ordering the battalion to reassemble at Wetlet, in preparation for an immediate move south. So no ambush, which was a disappointment and the reason for the recall of the platoon patrol in the hills. We three were off in a great hurry, to return as we had come and to do so at an exhilarating gallop.

Incidentally, the Japs had been in Halin Twinma a day or two earlier. Hence the different atmosphere. Our friends must have been shattered at finding themselves again exposed to those whom they believed had gone for good.

Before our departure from Wetlet there are two incidents that are worthy of mention.

Geoffry had been called to brigade during one of the last evenings and Graeme, Mervyn, Snagger and I settled down to the enjoyment of an evening's bridge, being better able to do so within the confines of our headquarters, in the absence of the non-playing C.O. On his return Geoffry produced the more than somewhat disturbing news that it was 5 Brigade who had been chosen to lead the division in the assault crossing of the Irrawaddy, a crossing that would be made in the vicinity of the meeting of the Mu with the Irrawaddy.

Snagger, we were told, would be taking a patrol across the river two days in advance of the main crossing, and Mervyn had been chosen to follow him so that he might guide the crossing from the far bank, using a screened lamp – the job of a Beach Master. Fortunately, the jobs did not materialise, but they were sufficiently probable to encourage an early departure for 'bed'.

The all too obvious dangers associated with our inevitable crossing of that formidable river, occupied our thoughts much as does impending surgery, and one longed for it to be over and done with. For us it was like going down a long and increasingly steep hill on a bike with inadequate brakes; one was committed and there was nothing one could do but hang on and pray and see it through.

The second incident concerned leave. Back at Yazagyo (where home leave started) a party of about a dozen had departed and we were now, at Wetlet, informed that we had an officer vacancy. Names were put in a hat and one was drawn by Geoffry – mine. At first he said that I could not go but Mervyn, who was with him, made clear his feelings were I to be deprived of this opportunity. At about mid-morning I was told by Geoffry to hand over my job to Jimmy Hodder and start packing, as I would be catching a plane for India tomorrow, the first stage of the flight home. However, that afternoon we were informed that there had been an error, the allotment being for one officer from 5 Brigade and not from each of the three battalions. There would be a further draw from the chosen three. Later I learned that luck went to a Cameron.

In February we were advised that there would be no further home leaves, as those with over two and a half years overseas service were no longer eligible. The administrators had decided that, as those going home for 28 days were away from their units for up to four months, it brought the returning man too close to his repat. to make it worthwhile.

During our last days in Wetlet, the Camerons and the Worcesters had been busy chasing Japs eastwards towards the Irrawaddy. When at 0930hrs on the 29th, we moved off in response to that urgent call it was to go south and away from them, for we were to act as a rear-guard to 4 Brigade.

That journey, in trucks, was more agreeable than most for, after an initial move of six miles to the west, we were on the main Shwebo to Sagaing road; one that was not the customary gravel but tarmacadam and not ruined by our heavy vehicles. Our destination was Ondaw, a village only six miles from the Irrawaddy which, having flowed past Mandalay, was running west for 30 miles, before again turning south on its long journey to the sea. At 1400 hrs we were establishing ourselves in a defensive position a little to the north of Ondaw, just clear of the road and within a hollow in very open country. Our only cover, other than that afforded by a few scattered and sorry looking trees, was that of the familiar unkempt hedges.

This land was not irrigated, the canal system having ceased a few miles south of Wetlet, now 25 miles away. In such an area of poor soil, made worse by outcrops of rock, what vegetation there was had wilted after weeks without rain and under a sun that was daily becoming hotter. This was the northern fringe of the 'dry belt', an extensive semi-desert south of Mandalay and Myingyan – our future territory.

We were at last quite close to Mandalay and in the same latitude, for it was about 16 miles to our east. Of more immediate interest was the town of Sagaing, 15 miles down the road and at the north end of the Ava Bridge, the only one across the Irrawaddy. That enduring example of British engineering, almost a mile in length, had been partially wrecked in 1942 when two of many spans had been blown and they remained resting on the river bed. Sagaing, a place of pagodas, was for one short time the capital, but with a population of only 12,000 its importance centred on its location north of that all-important bridge. Looking at it on the map, with so many pagodas and Buddhist monasteries within the hills to the north east, and suburbs bordering the river to the west, it exerts a fascination in the same manner as does Ye-U.

The task of 4 Brigade was not only to engage the enemy north of the river, but to encourage him to believe that 2 Div. would continue to drive down the road to the town, preparatory to crossing the river there. When we arrived 4 Brigade was but a few miles away to our front, having a continuing series of unpleasant skirmishes in and around villages.

Twelve days earlier we had welcomed back Paget Fretts, recovered from the typhus he had contracted at milestone 82. After the death of John Bowles, 'A' Company had been temporarily commanded by Major Heath of the Glosters. In Paget we had an ideal commander for them and on this night (the 29th) it was he who, at 2200 hrs, took them and one Section of the Defence Platoon to occupy an un-named village, one mile south east of Ondaw. There the Section remained after it had been searched by 'A', who then went into two villages – Ywathit, close to the road, and Aungtha further south and two miles forward of Ondaw, but away from the road, which runs south east. They were occupied without incident, but for some rifle fire and grenading in the vicinity of Ywathit, when that place was being searched, but no actual contact was made.

That night a Japanese 70 or 75mm gun, probably the former, dropped a few rounds into our lines, something of a shock after so much peace and quiet. The first woke me and hoping that there would be no repetition I made no attempt to get up but, with the arrival of the second, I made my way to the office trailer and the 'phone, where Graeme and I awaited developments. However, the shelling did not long continue and, after reporting to Brigade, we returned to sleep. No damage was done.

This minor incident is an interesting example of how well the Japs followed our movements even when, as then, we were miles behind our front. And if we were correct in believing it to have been a 70mm Battalion Gun, with its range of 3,000 yards, as against the 7,000 yards of the 75mm Regimental Gun, they were quite close.

The office trailer had been made by our fitters on an 8cwt. chassis, and provided us with a table flanked by bench seats, and was above price. A tubular frame supported a canvas roof and sides which, when closed at night, enabled us to use a light, and many late hours were spent there. Within that light-tight canvas we would sweat in the light and heat of the pressure-lamp, often Geoffry, Graeme and I, writing and studying maps and aerial photographs in preparation for the coming day, in oven-like conditions.

Dorsets moving into Ywathit.

During the morning of the 30th, 'C' Company dispatched two of its Sections to man a road block on the Sagaing road, close to Ywathit at milestone 25 – the road distance to Mandalay.

On the final morning of January 1945, we were 85 miles further into Burma than we were on the first, when we had looked east across the plain to Ye-U. Now with that plain behind us, we were commencing a change of direction to the south west, which would take us to an as yet undesignated place from which we would cross the Irrawaddy.

This move commenced at 1330 hrs when 'D' Company left the perimeter to form an outer screen on our west flank, taking up platoon positions at two railway stations on the Ye-U line which, having branched west from the main line through Sagaing, ran between us and the Irrawaddy. One platoon established itself three and a half miles to our south, where the road from Ondaw to Ngatayaw crossed the railway and a second was sited three miles to their right, where the Ondaw to Ywathitgyi road also crossed the line. Their station had the name Natkayaing. Behind and between, at Tawdwin village, the third platoon and Company HQ dug themselves in. There was no contact with the enemy.

Ywathitgyi was a 'pukka' town on the north bank of the Irrawaddy, with a Steamer Station and a ferry link with the south shore, and therefore a very potential base for Japanese attacks on us. However, our policy was not to look for trouble and when practicable such places were by-passed, as I believe this was.

Some indication of the size of the Irrawaddy and its peace-time importance to the life of the country, is gained from the fact that passenger- and freight-carrying steamers provided a service from the delta up to Bhamo, in the dry season, a distance of 800 miles. After the rains that service continued on to Myitkyina. Throughout those voyages there were ports of call, as at Ywathitgyi.

Back at Ondaw the departure of 'D' Company was made good by the return of 'A' and the section from the Defence Platoon.

1st – 7th February

In spite of the proximity of the Japs our placid life at Ondaw continued almost uninterrupted, as is indicated by a note that Dicky Boyle on Shamus and I on Judy were out one day galloping for long distances over the open country to the north.

Our life was now to be geared to preparation for the assault crossing, and we moved on the 4th as a battalion, going due west for nine miles, but taking a circuitous route to the north for concealment. We then turned south to another place on the railway, the large village of Nyaungbinwun and from there we crossed the railway to complete our hike in the vicinity of the village of Maungdaung, three miles north of the river. This was close to the headquarters of 5 Brigade, to whom we had returned. Which, with all due respect to 4 and 6 Brigades, was where we preferred to be, particularly at such a time.

And we were to be the reserve battalion for the crossing, which also suited us!

We were again in a pleasant and fertile land, one which was well watered, being bounded on the south by the Irrawaddy and to the west by the Mu which, in this expanse of level ground, progressed like a crazy snake up to its junction with the larger river. Numerous chaungs played their part in the distribution of water, but by February these were dry and could be used for concealed movement, making this an excellent area for our purpose. Both rivers were well below their banks and the Irrawaddy was said to be dropping by about three inches a day. As with all such fertile places there were many villages, those that had flourished had pride of place on river banks. Here the Irrawaddy averaged a mile in width between banks and with the water so low, only half that width, there were wide expanses of sand. Across the river the land was very similar and was most difficult to distinguish even when studied through binoculars, using the observation posts that had been established for that purpose in vacated huts on the river bank.

The three battalions had been allocated positions on the ground suited to those they would occupy in the crossing, which were – Worcesters on the right, Camerons left and Dorsets centre rear. Perched on the edge of the high Irrawaddy bank were two hamlets (if such a word can be used to describe collections of Burmese huts); the first and nearest to the mouth of the Mu river was Tadaing and half a mile further east was Dawete, they being Worcester territory. East again and a mile or more away were the Camerons, astride a chaung and their left was at the village of Myittha. We were behind the Worcesters to the west of Maungdaung and Brigade HQ, something over two miles back from the forward battalions.

The plan was that the Worcesters and Camerons would make a night crossing forward of their respective positions and, when they were established, we would cross, doing so behind the Worcesters. Once ashore we would strike left and form one large bridgehead by linking up with the Camerons.

Aiding the brigade would be the Welch Fusiliers, who would occupy a large island in the Irrawaddy, to the immediate left of the Camerons. Massed artillery would be augmented by tanks, taking station on the river bank and firing across the water and, finally, there would be support from the air. It promised to be quite a party.

As part of the deception plan, designed to encourage the enemy in the belief that we were building up our forces outside Sagaing, we spent a day marching towards Ondaw, doing so on a west to east track that was reasonably visible from south of the river. To give the impression of heavy M.T. movement, the trucks dragged bundles of branches to produce, it was hoped, convincing clouds of dust. I was fortunate in being able to avoid this charade.

We were nearing the end of our pony riding, as our animals, including those of our Indian Mule Company, were not to cross the river. This was a bitter blow, for they had become so much a part of our lives and it was an intensely sad time for John Main and his muleteers, who had done so much for us. It was ironic, but a worthy ending, that they were to be particularly busy prior to the crossing, bringing up stores in a special effort to conserve precious petrol.

Burma had to be occupied right down to Rangoon by the start of the monsoon, which could be expected by the middle of May. Without that port it would not be possible to maintain our armies. To defeat the enemy and cover such a distance in so short a time, necessitated an army moving at speeds that only motorised transport could achieve.

For reasons of security we had been given no indication of the date on which we would cross the river; but it was generally understood that the build-up of supplies could not be completed under about four weeks. Accordingly we expected to have that time in our comfortable location which, being out of sight of the river, enabled us to relax. In fact, this was to be abruptly shattered after only four days.

8th February

During the night of 7/8 February a force of some 60 or so Japs crossed the river, at or near Dawete, completely surprising the company of Worcesters in that village, which they abandoned. Fortunately the Japs were contented with their success and did not attempt to exploit it.

We awoke to the sounds of battle drifting back from the river, destroying the peace of our early morning. The 'I' Section had established an observation platform high in a tree and I, and as many of my chaps as it could accommodate, were soon up there observing the smoke of exploding mortar bombs and the like.

No one imagined that we would be involved and the battalion settled into the planned routine, so much so that Geoffry departed for a conference at Div. HQ

12 miles north of Ondaw, on the Shwebo road. Also there was Brigadier Mike West, he having left the brigade in the charge of his Second-in-Command. The absence of the Worcesters' C.O. was accepted as due to their local 'fracas'.

During the middle of the morning, Brigade HQ instructed us to get our Mortar Platoon ready to go to the support of the Worcesters and, not long after, we were warned that the whole battalion might be wanted. Mervyn, as acting C.O., was called to brigade and I accompanied him, but was not present at what was a privy meeting. As we returned Mervyn told me that the Worcesters were being withdrawn from battle and that we were to take their place. We had to be ready to move in about an hour's time and, from 1200 hrs, our companies were to go forward as soon as vehicles were available.

Trucks carried us to a point about 1,200 yards from the Irrawaddy, where the track petered out in a chaung winding its way back from behind Tadaing. There we formed up along the east bank of the chaung, out of sight and able to go forward as in a communication trench. There Mervyn met the Worcesters' new Commanding Officer, his predecessor having been killed, and together they worked out how the change-over would take place. The rifle companies moved off individually, guided by Worcesters from the respective companies being relieved. Contrary to expectations, the change-over proceeded without hostility from the Japs.

Geoffry must have returned to us at about this time, with the battalion establishing itself in a semi-circle around Dawete and towards Tadaing, our headquarters siting itself in an offshoot of the chaung, which gave a covered approach to a point half-way between the villages and to the north. We were thus able to contain the Japs, should they have ideas of proceeding inland.

While we had waited in the chaung, preparatory to going forward, the remnants of the company which had been surprised by the Japs passed on their way to the rear, keeping close to the east bank and thus being in close proximity. Their state of dress, or rather undress, told only too clearly that they had been caught off-guard and unprepared; few had weapons, equipment or steel helmets and many had bare or stockinged feet. It was a sombre and thankfully unparallelled event, one that had none of the chit-chat or wise-cracking so customary between units.

During the next 48 hours we learned the sorry story of how the Japs had crossed the Irrawaddy and, probably by chance, had attacked the company that was at Dawete. That they had succeeded probably resulted from the inducement of a building as a comfortable headquarters, for there were found the bodies of the Company Commander and those who were with him. During the morning the Worcesters, led by their Commanding Officer, had counter-attacked. He and his Intelligence Officer were killed and the attack failed, the battalion withdrawing leaving the bodies in enemy hands. With unknown documents on them, but on the assumption that all our code-names and the like were now in the possession of the Japs, these were changed forthwith. To fill the gap in command our Brigadier promoted the Second-in-Command of the Camerons, Major Tom Irvine, and it was he we had met when taking over.

Initially it was intended that we would counter-attack that evening, but Mike West would not commit us without the assistance of an air-strike. To give time for this to be arranged, our attack was postponed to soon after first light the next morning – providing the Japs were still there.

9th – 23rd February

It was hoped that if we left the Japs alone they might withdraw during the night, and that they did, 'B' Company heard movement on the river in the early hours, and a pre-dawn patrol found Dawete empty. 'D' Company then moved forward and occupied this shattered and partly burnt group of huts, and there they remained until the night of our crossing, as did 'B' Company, who moved into Tadaing. 'A' Company was dispatched to the village of Shwehle, a little to the north west of Tadaing and half a mile inland. 'C' Company was to the rear by another mile, in a copse, together with Battalion Headquarters, our mules and Admin. Company and possibly HQ company, though of the last I am uncertain. So, but for the two forward companies, we had done pretty well out of this shift of territory. Our location was very agreeable, having plenty of greenery from growing crops and a liberal sprinkling of trees. Our copse consisted mainly of mango and palm trees (which was a change) and was reputed to be the burial ground for the area.

We lived in a semi-dug-in life as protection against shelling, and so that we could deal with enemy patrols. One of my more interesting letters home is dated the 23rd, our last whole day in that place. It describes and illustrates by means of a cross-section how we lived. The drawing shows a stepped slit trench, with bedding on the step and over the whole a 'bivvy tent'. It details how, when in the forward areas but not in contact with the enemy, we had bivouac tents, the size of which was improved by excavation. After a description of the merits of the arrangements it ends – 'At night the tent is closed up, the oil lamp lit, and I can get down to a spot of reading in pretty fair comfort'. That was my home, to which at the end of the day I could return as keenly as to any brick or stone walled building. There one regained one's identity.

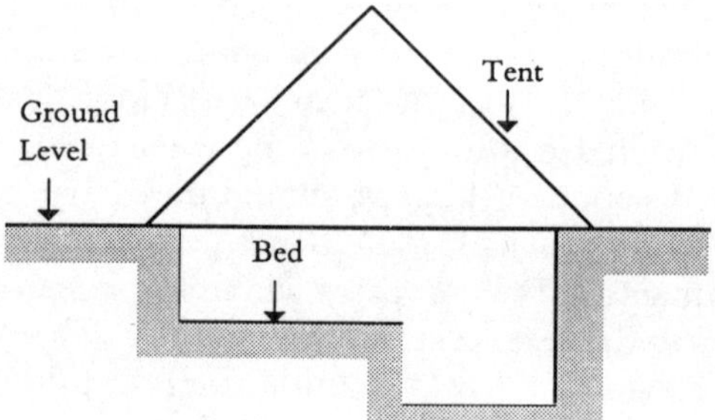

Cross Section

For those who had not experienced active service life, it cannot be easy to appreciate that there were long periods with no week-ends, in fact the individual days had no meaning. We were not living 'over the shop', but in it. At that time we could see no end to our campaign; after Burma, Malaya and Singapore loomed ahead, and much, much more beyond.

The letter ends – 'Our tempers are becoming frayed, for life in Battalion HQ is at times anything but pleasant'.

I am sure that my thoughts were of how nearly I had missed this fearful river crossing. Fears that were general, and due as much as anything to the inadequacy of the boats, designed for use on rivers where the Thames and Severn were exceptional in size, and not that vast expanse of water which was the Irrawaddy. However, we kept busy and our jaded spirits received a boost when it was announced that there would be no change to the planned crossing. The Worcesters would pass through us and we would follow, once they had landed.

Bridge flourished and we received another bottle of whisky during the final days, an increase on the normal officer issue of one per month and which (not surprisingly) often failed to arrive. My letter also reports that we were eating corn on the cob, grown locally, together with vegetables and tomatoes much as at home.

I had an observation post operating at the east end of Tadaing, situated in two rooms of the living quarters of an abandoned monastery, a building of the simple timber construction common to all the dwellings. They overlooked the river, and being on stilts we had an elevated and uninterrupted view across the water. It was manned continually by a part of the Section, observing all that there was to see through holes we had made in the wall. We later had another in Dawete, so that we could make ourselves familiar with that part of the distant shore on which we expected to land. From time to time individual Japs were seen on that far side and dust clouds were noted as rising in the background. Those clouds would have been from vehicles on the gravel roads then, in the increasing heat, deep in dust. So that such clouds would not betray our movements, we manned a check-point by our headquarters and only those with the necessary priority were allowed to proceed, doing so with caution.

Those distant clouds can be linked with the assault crossing of 20 Division, launched by them on 12th February, at a point a dozen miles away to our right. That was where the river changed direction so that it continued to flow south. Thus, once across, 20 Div. could advance eastwards on a line to the south of the one that we would take.

We knew little more than that they had been establishing a bridgehead against determined counter-attacks, the Japs fighting with the spirit shown at Kohima. There were also reports of enemy tanks being involved and that our aircraft had attacked them.

Prior to that crossing, 'A' Company had been patrolling across the Mu to link up with the left flank of 20 Div., which happened to be the 1st Devons.

It was only later that we learned that 4 Corps had carried out a long march south from Kalewa and were completing a crossing much down river, near Pakokku, which they had started on the 14th. From there they were to drive east to Meiktila, and thus sever the main line of communication between the Japs in the south of Burma and those in the north. 20 Div. were to do much the same, but over a shorter distance, their objective being Kyaukse, a town on the same road and railway, but much nearer Mandalay.

Our task was that once across the river we would turn sharp left, and moving east and parallel to the Irrawaddy, we would strike at Mandalay from the south, while 19 Division did likewise from the north.

In preparation, we assault battalions were given the opportunity for flights, in order that key officers might have a preview of where they would soon be fighting. Early on 16th February, our party had consisted of the C.O., the rifle company commanders and myself. We set off for the light air-strip which had been set up at Ondaw, where the American two-seater liaison aircraft, the L.5.'s, were operating and, after waiting for some hours and finding that not everyone would be able to fly, I did not expect to be fortunate. However, eventually Geoffry sent me up. We flew south to the river, passing over where 4 Brigade had been fighting and, turning right, continued slowly downriver almost over the enemy bank but rather too high for accurate observation. A height that was determined by an order on low flying, after two of our fighters had been shot down by machine-gun fire in this area. It was thrilling in the extreme, as well as fascinating to be up there looking down on enemy-held territory. In the brilliant tropical sunshine every feature was visible, but despite this and the comparatively open nature of the region I saw no living thing, neither Jap nor moving vehicle. I did observe a line of the Japanese circular fox-holes dug into the sandy shore, near the water's edge opposite Tadaing, where the bank was well back from the water and providing an excellent beach for our landing. A belt of elephant grass along the bank made the spotting of positions within it impossible. After circling over those fox-holes we retraced our route, I doing my utmost to soak in every relevant detail and landing, as I thought, all too soon. But as we were preparing to leave, four Jap fighters flew over going south at tree-top level. We were glad to be down.

Also taking an interest in the river were members of a Sea Reconnaissance Unit, more generally known as 'cloak and dagger boys'. They were operating in the river at night, which they would enter upstream of us and cross to the far side on a raft which enabled them to float with only their heads above water, or they wore 'frogmen' kit of rubber suit and flippers. Having completed their observation they would land at Tadaing, usually in the pre-dawn or earlier hours.

My specialist job in those last days was the preparation of our photo cover, for the crossing and after, a job that intensified in the final nights, for we received a later issue. These superb overlapping, but individual, photographs not only showed the ground to a much larger scale than that of the One Inch map but they did, of course, also show particular trees, hedges, scrub and huts, ignored by the maps. Small items, but ones vital to us and which could be seen as they actually were. When lucky one picked out enemy trenches, something the maps could not cover. Those pictures overlapped by 60%, so that any one point appeared on at least two photos and, when examined through a stereoscope, a third dimension was obtained, causing trees and buildings to appear to rise above the surface.

Only a few were as fortunate as I, and long periods of idleness were hard to endure when the many hours passed in an endless repetition of discomfort, little sleep and boredom, and there seemed no redeeming feature in the present or the future. One of our lance-corporals deserted, despite an excellent record at

Kohima; he found it all too much. Probably he was the only one to do so when we had penetrated so far into Burma. Then the chance of reaching any sort of haven was so slight as to be almost non-existent. Somehow, and against all the odds, he covered the great distance to Calcutta where, following a fight with an Indian, he was arrested by the military police. Later he was court-martialled and sentenced to nine years' imprisonment, part to be served in the U.K. There must have been many such tragic happenings in Europe; it was good for us that we were spared all but a few.

I was getting in a last batch of riding, often accompanying Geoffry when he rode over to Brigade; and there were evenings devoted to bridge, played in the Command Post, which was an 80-pounder tent erected over a four-feet-deep hole. Amongst those rides was one on an afternoon when Mervyn and I set out on chargers borrowed from the Indian officers commanding the mule company. Mervyn led the way down the track and I was soon finding great difficulty in keeping up with him, for his pace increased to a fast gallop which took no notice of anything, including blind corners round which we skidded. Leaping gullies and with stones flying, we covered the ground in a headlong charge for a mile or more on those large and immensely powerful animals, coming eventually and thankfully to a slithering stop in a cul-de-sac at the far end of a village, through which we had thundered to the consternation of its inhabitants. A somewhat pale Mervyn was able to gasp out that his horse had bolted. Deciding that discretion was the better part of valour, we returned at a walk, stopping now and then to look for my wallet which had jumped out of my pocket. I was worried, for inside that wallet was my identity card, something much desired by the Japs and the loss of which was a serious offence. Happily, it was found next day by an Indian sepoy and still inside was the precious card.

24th – 25th February

Our D-Day. On such days it is leadership that counts and, as always, our success and even survival was determined by the four rifle companies and their leaders, from the Section Commanders upwards. The Company Commanders were those familiar and battle-hardened characters: –

'A' Company Major Paget Fretts.
'B' Company Major Peter Feeney.
'C' Company Major Tommy Tucker.
'D' Company Major Clive Chettle.

With 'A' Company was the recently arrived platoon of Glosters under Lieutenant Peter Collister. Peter was probably the only person in the battalion who had been in the 1942 retreat, for these Glosters, unlike some of their predecessors, were new to Burma. Then, as a 20-year-old platoon commander in another 'A' Company, he experienced the trauma of a fighting retreat amongst the 1st Glosters, during which he was wounded. Now he and his platoon and the mortar detachment were very much 'Dorsets' and, like the battalion as a whole, were ready to go. All were quietly waiting, reading letters from home or writing last ones, much of the time just dozing in the sunshine – with ammunition issued and weapons ready, there was time for thoughts to wander to loved ones and loved places.

> In December '39, when home for Christmas and still awaiting my call to military service, so long in coming, I took my favourite walk; one that I repeated now in my imagination. To be in Dorset and climb again the hill from Swanage to the short grass of Ballard Down, behind 'Old Harry' and, wheeling left, descend on Studland and its Norman church, St Nicholas. A church I bracket with St Martin's at Wareham for delight and fascination, their characters so little changed through many centuries. Then an easy but absorbing stroll along the wide sands of Studland Bay to and across Poole Harbour mouth, not on the car ferry, but in a real boat steered by a blue-jerseyed salt. Working one's way along the cluttered shore on the harbour side of Sandbanks, boats could be examined and admired, and I remembered the time when mine was one of them. A walk in the bright sunshine and cooling salty breezes of early spring – before the summer crowds. On the December walk I had looked down from the great height of Ballard Down, on a Polish three-masted schooner, caught on the rocks and abandoned. Her masts and rigging stood undamaged above her lowered sails, which were awash in the sea which flooded over the port bulwarks. The disaster of Poland was much in our thoughts at that time and one felt for the crew, who had lost their country and now their ship.

Throughout the long wait, the only hostile attention we had from the Japs across the river was from their artillery; Dawete taking the brunt of this shelling which, almost always, occurred just before dark. It was in anticipation that the crossing of the Worcesters and the Camerons would invoke an artillery response, that Battalion HQ was able to boast of a substantial dug-out, constructed by our Pioneers and sited behind 'D' Company.

In the late afternoon of the 24th, Battalion HQ and the rear rifle companies closed up on the river, moving to positions similar to those that they had occupied after relieving the Worcesters. We moved to our dug-out at 1800 hrs (approximately last light), in anticipation that it would be our operations room until we were afloat.

A little later we were joined in our bunker by two war correspondents, one Irish and the other Chinese, a combination surely stranger than fiction. The Irishman was from Reuters and, although not carrying Guinness, actually did even better – producing four bottles of beer and one of Scotch* and all unbroached. We knew that the Chinese were operating in the north and east of Burma, but had seen none. To have one among us so completely unexpectedly and at such a moment of high tension, and accompanied by an Irishman who was carrying alcohol, was incredible!.

It took little time to decide that it would be highly dangerous to take glass bottles into action, they must therefore be emptied and without delay. Our

* The whisky was from our old QM, 'Teddy' Edwards, at Corps HQ.

Chinese friend, who was from Chungking, soon became the life and soul of what I can only describe as a party. Thus the waiting hours passed in a haze of tobacco smoke, alcohol and laughter. Again that precious laughter; which in this instance could, probably rightly so, be proclaimed as evidence of hysteria. For myself, the tears of unrestrained laughter flowed copiously, my reaction to the fun generated in that confined and over-charged space.

It did us all a world of good and well before 2200 hrs we were our customary selves, ready to react as circumstances required. By that hour the other battalions were to be on the move and about to launch themselves upon the river, so that they might achieve their scheduled touch-down on the far shore at 2230 hrs. Clive Chettle and his men at Dawete had been given the job of helping the Worcesters with their boats and their launching. It was therefore from him that we expected to have the first news.

With the approach of that critical time when the Worcesters would be afloat and on their way, Geoffry asked me to go outside and report back on what I had seen or heard. Our bunker was sited in a saucer-shaped hollow, so I scrambled up its earth covered roof to the apex. Seeing was easy, for a brilliant moon illuminated our world with a most shocking clarity. At first all seemed so splendidly quiet and then, from the direction of that out-of-sight river, the soft night air brought the distant sound of small-arms fire, so faint as to seem innocuous; but it was only too sufficient to make clear that the surprise crossing, on which our plans had been calculated, had not been achieved.

My grim news was received in a silence that continued as we waited, tense in the expectancy of a 'phone call from Clive. When it came, it was for him to inform us that the Worcesters were back on our shore, in wet confusion and desperate disorder – their operation a disaster. We learned that they had lost most of their boats, some having been holed by machine-gun fire directed at them when they were barely half-way. Of the remainder most were, by then, sunk or sinking. With automatic weapons in those fox-holes that I had seen at the water's edge, there was precious little chance of survival for men in lightweight folding boats, which I can only imagine were considered suitable because, being low in the water, they would be difficult to see. Similarly one assumes that the fox-holes had not been bombed out of existence in order to maintain that essential element of surprise, which probably had been lost weeks ago, when the Japs raided Dawete. Clive went on to say that the Worcester I.O. was hysterical and that he was sending him back to Brigade immediately, as he was fearful of the effect that he would have on his men. For the moment we were reduced to two battalions, for the long-suffering Worcesters would have to be refitted.

A little later, Brigade HQ 'phoned, instructing us to remain as we were until further notice. My thoughts and doubtless those of the others were would we be expected to succeed where the Worcesters had failed? Great was our relief when, following a call from Mike West to Geoffry, we learned that we were to join the Camerons and be ready to cross behind them, once they had completed their landing. So there, at least, there was a modicum of success.

Orders went out and we closed up on one another, with companies pointing east and so placed that they could take their designated positions in the column of march. We started our hike by first skirting the back of Dawete, where we got entangled in the barbed wire defences, then we proceeded in single file along the footpath bordering the river. By then the moon had gone and it was just about as black a night as before it had been a bright one. As always on such occasions in the dark, we moved in a succession of spurts, all thoughts on maintaining touch with that elusive and shadowy figure ahead. Then there would be an inexplicable halt when nothing seemed to be happening and the problem was to remain awake. We were thankful to have turned our backs on the bloody shambles that could have reduced us to the same state as that of the wretched Worcesters. Briefly, we could close our minds to contemplation of the fast approaching day.

On reaching the Camerons we were directed to a place inland of them, there to dig in on either side of the chaung that they were using to approach the river. We watched loaded DUKWs moving down it and looking vastly superior to the British infantry's assault boats. Actually their amphibious wheeled trucks were not as superior as they appeared, for their size and draught made them difficult to handle in so much shallow water. Their peculiar name was their manufacturer's code, which remained in use; they were generally known as 'ducks'. It became apparent, before dawn, that the Camerons would not complete their crossing for some time and, to get out of their way, we moved further up the chaung and settled down to wait.

Going into battle was inevitably preceded by periods of 'deferred action' and, by then, we had become adept at making the most of such waits, be they long or short. We had the right weather for reclining on the ground, which is what most did that morning. We could see very little of anything by the river and were very content to leave to the Camerons whatever it was that had to be done. There was entertainment in the skies from frequent sorties by our aircraft, attacking not only the enemy across the river, but those away to the south.

Not much news was coming back from the Camerons, but by late morning we knew that earlier crossings had been difficult and costly; by then they were proceeding steadily. And then at mid-day they were across, and we were standing-by to follow.

The moment is well caught in this photograph – of five of 'A' Company. Not yet on their feet but awaiting the order to move, for they are not only wearing their steel helmets but 'Mae West's' – inflatable life-belts. They are in shirt-sleeve order, with sleeves rolled up above sunburned forearms and they wear their big packs; trousers are tucked into short putties over 'ammunition' boots that are white with dust. That dust, and the sun-bleached stony ground, are indicative of our arid world which, from then on, was to become even more so.

What is so striking is that their faces are as relaxed as they would be were this an exercise at home. For them, the crossing of the 'Waddy' was one segment in our journey for which they were amply sustained by their comrades. That spirit surfaces in a letter written in 1988 by Cliff Leech, one of our anti-aircraft gunner reinforcements at ms.82. He mentions his pride at being an old 2 Dorset and how good it was to know that 'some of us are still around and never forget the days

Dorsets waiting for the Irrawaddy crossing.

when we truly found our true selves and our limits'. He continues, 'I managed to go through all the action up to Mt. Popa, thank God I never got more than being blasted a number of times and having my equipment shot off, ie. Bren pouches and small pack, while charging at Ye-U'. Cliff was a Lancashire lad and served us well. I marvel at the thought of someone having his equipment shot off and living to tell the tale!

Moving down the chaung we were soon at the river, looking with interest at the arrangements for our embarkation and at the craft we would be boarding. For once Attack HQ was in the lead. This was so that Geoffry could, on landing, do a quick liaise with the Cameron's C.O., Angus McAlester, and expand the bridgehead in accordance with the situation on the ground.

We were loaded into a craft that was new to us; known as an F.B.E., it was some 20 feet in length and had the appearance of an overgrown rowing boat. Rowing would have been preferable to the arrangement made for its propulsion, by an unreliable and under-powered outboard engine, bracketed out from the starboard bow. Above it and thus also outside the hull, was a car-type steering wheel, an arrangement that could not have been better devised to make steering with any degree of accuracy an impossibility and, when under fire, suicidal.

As a lover of boats and one who until then had believed that anything that floated and could be propelled had a special magic, I was to be very disillusioned.

We were with 'B' Company who, in common with the remainder of the battalion, were using both F.B.E.s and DUKWs. The latter with their greater size and carrying capacity and thus draught, had to take a longer route downstream, where there was a greater depth of water. Ahead of us, in midstream, there was a large sand-bank which prevented us from seeing the far shore. It is shown on an aerial photograph dated 15 January, a date when the river was higher, but even then its length was half a mile.

Just upstream was the western end of a three-mile-long-island, much of which was cultivated, and there, on that morning and after a stormy crossing, were our old comrades of Garrison Hill – the Welch Fusiliers.

We were packed so tightly in our boat that we could have been described as being like sardines in a tin, but for the fact that some of us, and I for one, were kneeling. And what a lousy way to make an assault crossing, damnably uncomfortable and physically inhibiting and demeaning. Had I known, I could have drawn comfort from the fact that the Chindit leader, Major Bernard Fergusson, had crossed the same river on all fours.

We set off and, as I expected, the sapper helmsman was barely able to steer our much over-laden craft across the current, so that we progressed in a series of irregular circles which only ceased when we hit the sand-bank, a moment when my heart really reached my boots. Fortunately we were pointing upstream, the direction in which we wanted to go and we then progressed by literally screwing ourselves along the sandy bottom by use of the propeller. Small props are normally held by shear pins, so designed to break under such conditions and I was therefore expecting this, and for us to drift away downstream. There were already stories of this having happened and of the dire consequences to those concerned. Good fortune was on our side, and we were able to work our way around the up-river end of the bank and into slack water, below Ngazun Island 300 yards to our left. This was the island to which the Welch had crossed, in order to protect our left flank. We then progressed through quiet waters towards the shore that we were seeing for the first time, with feelings of astonishment at having crossed without having been under fire.

I have vivid memories of landing on a tiny beach below a high bank, under conditions resembling a medieval hell. Above us on that bank was a raging fire, the flame and billowing black smoke of which masked all else, but for Camerons issuing from it carrying their blood-covered dead to the safety of the beach, out of reach of the flames. On climbing the bank we found the Camerons, not fighting Japs but the flames, which threatened to sweep across their bridgehead. The elephant grass that I had seen from the air was burning, the fire having started a quarter of a mile away downstream, where we had been shelling a Jap position and the flames had come downwind to us. Those Japs had a bunker, sited with that skill so often shown by them, inside the face of the river bank. It contained a machine-gun with which they shot at our DUKWs. From first light it had been subjected to all the bombing and artillery fire that we could muster. It operated spasmodically and irrationally; we were amazed that it operated at all and, while cursing them for the casualties they inflicted, we had to admire the courage of those who manned it.

Geoffry had dashed off on his recce, going left so that the area we would occupy would be on the side from which we were to advance tomorrow. During that time I had to stand and watch a DUKW under fire, initially seeing the splashes of shots falling short, then closer and then ceasing, to be immediately followed by the cries of men being hit. Later Geoffry joined me and, standing together on the river bank, we again were spectators of one of these craft under fire. During that period one or two hit the sand-bank in or near the danger zone and it was harrowing to stand helpless while they reversed and manoeuvred in a desperate struggle to get clear. In theory these 'ducks' should have been ideal for the operation, but with the sand too soft for the wheels to be effective they became, with their maximum in water of 6mph, no more than slow and unwieldy boats.

Joe Chamberlin, Gus Claxton and the R.A.P. had crossed in one of the DUKWs that had not been fired on. They were to land at the feet of the Cameron's medical sergeant, Jock McEvoy, described by Joe as redoubtable, having learned in Glasgow's Gorbals how to cope with anything. From him they heard that the Cameron's M.O., Peter Barkley, earlier referred to by Joe as a 'gentle dreamy Edinburgh man', had been killed in the crossing, news that caused faces to harden. But his ability to cope enabled Jock to take over and continue in the role of medical officer.

Standing there, on that narrow shore, they had to watch our Mortar Platoon's DUKW getting badly shot-up and in it Michael Newte*, who had succeeded Jock Murrills as their commander, shouting for stretcher-bearers. Jock McEvoy was heard to mutter that, 'Jesus Christ was the only one who could reach them across that strip of water.' It was Gus who, when they had landed, took upon himself the job of conveying the dead and wounded back across that uninviting stretch of river and continued to do so, until they were all on the north bank.

As our chaps came over we fitted them into the extending perimeter, doing so without opposition, Clive being the only one to see a Jap, and he ran away through the long grass. By dusk, we were all over and settling down for the night in trenches dug into soft sand; doing so with a profound thankfulness that we had not suffered the expected casualties. We had been lucky to have made our crossing after those further downstream (of which 20 Div. had been the nearest), for it had been those landings that absorbed the fierce resistance.

Those relaxed faces, caught in the photos and all the others like them, masked mental stress and many had to struggle manfully against the increasing burden of demands caused by ventures such as this; ones that, although completed successfully and relatively lightly, took us ever deeper into an increasingly hostile world, from which there seemed to be no escape or ending. Small wonder that for some it all became too much. One such was a Kohima veteran, with a couple of stripes who, being a little 'bomb happy', went out sniping while 'shouting his head off'. His pals were able to bring him in and he was eased away for rest and recuperation.

* Captain Michael Newte was one of our long-serving Dorsets. Of all our junior officers, it was he with the ready smile and wit, who had the keenest brain.

There was a price to pay for those easily dug trenches. In the early hours, following a shell burst, Corporal Reynel was suffocated when his collapsed on him. He was one of the last of our Channel Islanders, and belonged to Dorset by way of Weymouth.

In conclusion – Cliff Leech tells us how, when the DUKW that he and his pal Lou Adaire were in was approaching the far bank, Lou's Lee-Enfield went overboard. Lou, one of our veterans, also went overboard, although in full marching order, and returned complete with rifle.

Greater Asia

RANGOON: TUESDAY, MARCH 6, 1945 Registered No. R-10.

Nippon Bombers in Burma Score Record Results

ENEMY AIRFIELDS IN BURMA AND INDIA HEAVILY POUNDED

One of the biggest and most effective raids ever made by Burma-based Nippon aircraft was carried out early on the morning of March 4, when a strong force of a Nippon night bomber unit swept over enemy advanced air bases throughout Burma and in the Bay of Bengal.

Intrepid Nippon bombardiers launched dawn attacks against enemy airfields at Cox's Bazar, Akyab, Kyaukpyu, on Ramree Island, all in the Bay of Bengal, Shwebo, Tamadaw and Kalemyo in central and upper Burma.

Composite war results achieved by our unit are as follow: set ablaze more than 27 grounded enemy planes, destroyed more than 15 others and shot down one. Also destroyed 10 motor vehicles, in addition to causing considerable damage to ground installations in the vicinity of the airfields where at one place a huge explosion took place.

Our loss includes one plane which has not yet returned to its base.

FIERCE BATTLES RAGE ON BURMA FRONTS

ENEMY ATTEMPTS TO ADVANCE BEING CHECKED

On the long Burma front, extending from Yunnan in the north to the Ramree Island in the west, fierce battle is raging continuously day and night. The Nippon Army are attacking the invading enemy forces and are fighting furiously on all fronts.

On the Northern Burma Front the newly formed 1st Army is advancing from the direction of Yunnan. The Nippon forces have withdrawn from Hsenwi for strategic reasons. The enemy forces have crossed the Namit River and are planning to advance in the direction of Lashio, trailing on both sides of the Burma-China route. In unison with the newly formed 1st Army are planning to advance in the direction of Bawdwin Mines. The Nippon forces are now engaged in a fierce battle with the advancing enemy forces. Even the enemy is admitting in his radio broadcast the fierce and stiff counter-attacks which his forces are receiving from the Nippon forces. The enemy's 36th division which met with a severe setback by the fierce counter-attacks of the Nippon forces are now frantically rebuilding their forces and position.

CENTRAL IRRAWADDY FRONT

The enemy's 19th division which have built their bridgehead in the Singu sector are getting impatient in trying to break through the strong Nippon position, but the Nippon forces are not moving an inch and are firmly checking all enemy attempts to advance southward. The British 2nd division in the Sagaing sector which from the latter part of February have been showing signs of little active movements are now carrying on futile underground activities in that district.

The enemy forces after crossing the river in the Myinmu front, in unison with the enemy forces in a small island in the middle of the river, on February 25, landed a section of their force in Ngazun located on the east bank of Myinmu. But our garrison forces immediately attacked the enemy forces on the water's edge and fierce battle is now raging between our forces and those of the enemy.

CHAPTER ELEVEN

Our rough road to Mandalay.

26th February

To our profound relief we had seen nothing of the Japs, during a night when they should have counter-attacked and driven us back into the water. That they had not attempted to do so was a good omen.

That morning the Worcesters were being ferried across unmolested. They were to join with us in a two-battalion attack on the large village of Ngazun and, in preparation, we moved forward to where we could form up opposite the near end of Ngazun Island. Our left was then where 'A' Company had spent the night as a forward detachment; from there they would advance as our left leading company. Attack HQ moved to a temporary position behind them and near the top of the river bank. There we could see the curve of the sand bordering the water, between river bank and island, together with that part of the village fringing the river.

In considering the Irrawaddy one has to think big. That overgrown sand-bank, Ngazun Island, was two and a half miles in length, even when the river was high, and contained a number of dwellings. An aerial photograph shows north to south strip cultivation, and there are wooded and scrub covered areas. Then with the water level low its size was increased by sand-banks, particularly at the far end, where it was possible to wade to it through shallow water.

Ngazun extended back from the river for about 1,000 yards, something over twice its width. It was approached from the south and east by unmetalled motorable (all weather) roads and, being the largest of the many villages in that area, had a post office, police station and inspection bungalow. Trees along the west side prevented us from seeing more than a glimpse of timber buildings.

Between us and that near side, a distance of a mile or so, was an expanse of flat, almost featureless ground, mainly a patchwork of irregular cultivated squares, most devoid of vegetation.

An advance over such ground would have been suicidal without air and artillery support, and that we were to receive in abundance. In preparation, Tactical Brigade HQ had crossed to the island, on which were gathering a company of the Manchesters with their machine-guns, a troop of tanks, ferried over so that they might use their guns against tanks and bunkers, and the commanders of our artillery, their guns lined up along the river bank. All were sited at right angles to our attack, no set-piece on Salisbury Plain could have been better staged.

Geoffry and Tom Irvine, the newly appointed Worcester C.O., agreed that we would take the north sector for the greater part of the village to our front, leaving the Worcesters to deal with the remainder and, by swinging north, also attack the southern flank.

Not long after we had taken up our preliminary position a villager arrived, at some risk to his life and in the same strange manner as had happened at Ye-U. He was warmly welcomed, for he was able to warn us of infantry positions along the Worcesters' and our fronts including an unsuspected, outer line of one-man 'fox-holes'. He told us, also, of a 75mm gun and five bunkers within a copse to our left, just short of the river bank. All this was passed to Brigade who, in turn, conveyed it to our air support and gunners.

At 1300 hrs we sat down to watch a remarkable 30-minute display of aerial bombing and ground strafing. Twenty-eight Hurribombers shallow dived on their targets to deliver their pair of 250 lb. bombs. The bombing run completed, a number of runs with their guns followed. At 1330 hrs the gunners commenced their bombardment of 2,000 rounds, some of which were air-bursts exploding above the enemy positions to our front. Our advance was synchronized with this intense barrage so that we, and the Worcesters on our right, had protection while we moved from the Start Line to the Artillery Concentration Line, a distance of about 600 yards. Once we were there the Manchesters took over, enabling us to have very close support, for the final yards. We considered ourselves fortunate not to have been at the receiving end.

As at Ye-U, this was an attack with fixed bayonets. An impressive sight for us in the third row, seeing our rifle companies, led by 'A' and 'C' and with 'B' and 'D' in the second row, moving steadily forward in extended order. In that advance against the enemy, we had been seeing our leading troops appear to double-up and recover, although maintaining their steady progress. We were unable to comprehend the cause until we too passed through that patch of dwarf tomatoes. By then the best had gone!

That bombardment served its purpose but there were, as always, some determined Japs firing at us; including snipers in the trees to which they would tie themselves. Cliff Leech, who was carrying a Bren, let off a blast from the hip at one, his pal Lou who was a step in front got air-blasted and did some verbal blasting in reply. By then the companies were going forward in the charge, as is shown in an unique photo taken by Sergeant Watson of 'C' Company. Of the nine steel-helmeted charging figures, the most prominent is the hefty Bren-gun carrying 'Tiny' Lewis, who cradles the Bren in his right arm as if it were a shot-gun. To his right, where he should be, is his Number 2 – 'Douggie' Slack, another Liverpudlian. To the left, in the same front line, is the smaller but no less determined figure of Tommy Thomas. At that time the Jap machine-guns were chattering away as the remainder of the company went through the trees and into the village. Jock Given was one of a mercifully small number of casualties. Drifting smoke plus the shade of the trees, made it difficult to see the Japs until you were right on top of them: as Harry Newcombe found when he caught a glimpse of a 'pot' helmet and a raised arm in the act of throwing a grenade. Then a second figure. He got off two bursts with his Sten-gun before jumping behind a tree, which was not the best place to be when the grenade exploded behind him. Unable to raise his right arm, he was thankful that the Japs seemed dead. Stumbling away, he remembers stepping over a dead one with ruddy cheeks and whose red collar tabs showed brightly; then he was at the R.A.P. and Alan

'C' Company enter Ngazun.

Critchley was pulling slivers of grenade out of his back and saying, 'You'll live.'

Joe Chamberlin comments briefly: 'The battle of Ngazun was a pie in which everyone had a finger. The list of casualties passing through our R.A.P. included Dorsets, Glosters, Worcesters, Manchesters and Welch Fusiliers. The numbers were mercifully light. When I saw the gunner's ferocious air-bursts over the village, so close to our forward companies, I thought a lot of people were going to get hurt.'

As our companies advanced into the village, so the Japs pulled back and, on reaching the far side, we were in time to see them moving away east. Ngazun presented a grim and tragic picture of wrecked and burning houses, dimly seen through the smoke which hung in the air. At 1500 hrs, when the place was declared free of the enemy (some Japs held out on the southern fringe until next day), we were relieved to be able to pull back out of it and take up a position to the west. The houses were the familiar ones on stilts and, crouching amongst the clutter within one such open floor, was a distraught and weeping woman who, after enduring the past hour and more, had every reason to be so. I tried to persuade her that it was safe to come out and that were she hurt, she would be cared for; but she only crouched the lower and I decided it better that I should leave. One of the good things of our war was that civilians were seldom involved. But there, a few days later, we were to see a slow-moving column of refugees, making their way to the island as a safe temporary refuge.

There followed days of rest and relaxation, for the enjoyment of which our

HQ sited itself within a clump of trees, fifty yards from the river. Of the individually located companies around us, 'C' had the distinction of a zariba, but it was at best only large enough for a platoon. That this was no romantic defensive position but a thorn enclosure for cattle, was of no surprise.

4 Brigade was by then also across the river and getting ready to advance with us, away on our right flank. It would clear the hills and villages, a mile and more to the south of the Irrawaddy. As the remainder of the division made the crossing, 6 Brigade joined with 4, thus the hinterland was covered up to the left flank of 20 Div.

27th February – 9th March

The general opinion of the battalion was that Ngazun was something of a let-down. I doubt that anyone hoped for a cinema, but this was found to be a place without roads, for no more than paths criss-crossed among the dwellings and there was both horror and disgust that the only brick building was the police station. Just one large building remained standing – a corrugated-iron clad store. An open door disclosed bolts of cloth in a variety of colours, stacked to the roof, and littering the floor was the worthless Japanese paper currency, contemptuously known as 'Mickey Mouse' money.

I was in Ngazun a couple of times making the customary searches for enemy documents, but although I had little success I did find a fine fat goose in a Jap one-man fox-hole, and which was well received by our cooks.

Another visit was as guide to a group of American pilots, who had come to see the results of aerial bombing at the receiving end. Most had cameras, which for us were a rarity, being something else to carry and care for, and they were soon busy with them. One unpleasant subject that caught their attention was the head of a man killed by a bomb. All but the head, which remained upright, was buried in the ground. Before leaving they deposited an armful of cigarette cartons, containing 1,000 or more cigarettes for distribution by me. A very typical example of American generosity and more than welcome at a time when our supplies were limited. One departed minus his gaiters which had been coveted by Geoffry. Perhaps he left with a pair of our short puttees in exchange. Anyway the gaiters were not wasted, for Geoffry wore them for ever afterwards and they suited his long legs. They may have added a touch of glamour but, for practical purposes, the puttee was far superior, being comfortable and giving ankle support. They also kept grit and at least some water out of our boots, and were an excellent barrier to mosquitoes and leeches.

Those days were fully spent in the enjoyment of the hot sunshine and in bathing and sun-bathing, under near-perfect conditions. They reminded us of summer holidays at the English seaside and my thoughts were of similar Dorset sands and dunes. As Geoffry wrote – 'they resembled a Scandinavian bathing beach and not a front line'. We often swam or waded to the extensive yellow sands bordering the near side of the island, where there was so much space that one had the bliss of solitude and there were no parades. This was far better than the bathing at Juhu, and the other brigades had every reason to be envious.

A jeep track had been developed along the river bank, to link our crossing place with the road to the east of Ngazun. It was busy with much coming and going as other units moved up and our office trailer, which had been sited by it, was like an unpretentious gazebo; for we used it as a place from which to watch the passing show, and where friends would stop and chat or ask directions.

They were days when we could almost forget the Japs, but on one afternoon we watched shell bursts, from what must have been a heavy gun, exploding on an air-strip under construction away to our south. Not for the first time we admired the driver of a bulldozer, who carried on in a brave indifference to danger. Earlier, the sound of these bursts had caused us to jump into our slit-trenches, then we realised that we were hearing the bursting shells that we had just seen, over a distance that was enough to cause a time lag between sight and sound. That strip was for Dakotas to 'bridge' the river barrier and help in the build-up.

During the afternoon of 2nd March, while we were bathing, the 'stand-to' alarm sounded and, wet and sandy, we doubled to our stations. Standing-to was very much the accepted beginning and ending of days when we were in action, and was when all positions were manned for a predetermined period, from pre-dawn or last light. It was so embedded in my subconscious that, for months after it was all over, I would leap from bed shouting 'Stand-to!'

Then, on the 4th, 'B' Company was ordered to take up a position on the island, immediately north of Ngazun. There a sand-filled inlet from the south and scrub were thought to be a likely place for enemy infiltration.

For one or two days we were reduced to living off bully beef and biscuits. Even so the issue was generous but the individual tins, by the time they were handed out, were sufficiently hot for their contents to be semi-liquid, which was a bit off-putting*. And the tooth testing, high-in-fibre army biscuit, a utilitarian version of the digestive biscuit, was not highly regarded by us. But at least they filled voids. And yet, in a letter dated 3rd March, I mentioned eating a bar of Nestlé's chocolate, something that I had not seen for years. We had had an issue of one bar per man in that day's rations.

Another letter, three days later, reported that most of the previous day and that morning had been devoting to angling. We had the pleasure of seeing one of the Section catch a 3 lb. fish, similar to a perch but more grey in colouring. That followed the loss of one that broke his line and when the float, attached to that part of the line with the fish, bobbed up 50 yards out, Sergeant Brown stripped and swam for it, only for it to disappear after a 200 yard chase.

Those good days ended on 7th of March when we regrouped on the far side of Ngazun, doing so in and around a wide dry nullah, containing the remains of a Hurricane fighter-bomber, believed to have crashed in our battle.

* At about this time, Private Feldman of 8 Platoon had a lucky escape, for a piece of shrapnel lodged in his tin of bully and not his back.

We were in Brigade reserve and ahead were the Camerons, progressing along the side of the river, they on that day occupying the small village of Letpantabin, two miles east. The Worcesters were to their right and to the right of the road between Ngazun and the riverside town of Kyauktalon, five miles from Ngazun. They were up against stiff opposition from Jap held hills which covered our line of advance. Kyauktalon, like Ywathitgyi across the river (the place we had by-passed after Ondaw) had a Steamer Station and with their ferry, their approach roads, quays and deep water, were logical places for a crossing. That this was so obviously an ideal place for the river crossing, was probably our reason for having gone elsewhere. It was almost certainly why, as we progressed into that area, we were finding more Japs.

At Ngazun one had to go two miles and more to find rising ground. There, hills extended from the south right up to the Irrawaddy at Kyauktalon and continued so for six miles to the east. With their steep sides of 100 feet or more and intervening south to north nullahs, this was a real geographical barrier. Even the road ceased and passage through was done on footpaths. It was all made worse by a liberal covering of thorny scrub, and trees were a rarity. This was splendid country for defence, rotten for attack and pretty hopeless for armour. In all it was nasty country in which to find Japs.

When a couple of miles from Kyauktalon the Worcesters had been halted by a strongly held hill immediately south of the road, and at the west end of which they dug in. Our Brigadier decided that this was an objective that required clearing by the Dorsets, in that most frightening of all operations – a night attack.

Thus on the 9th of March we moved forward until we were a good half mile to the rear of the Worcesters and roughly south of the village of Payadu, there to group ourselves in open ground astride the road. We of the 'O' Group moved ahead in carriers (our beloved carriers had been ferried across) up to the Worcesters, to be given a daylight 'dekko' of our objective. Guides took us into an unusually extensive trench system, east of the hill, where the non-stop cracking of bullets whipping across, caused us (and me in particular) to keep our heads lower than was good for observation. Every bullet seemed meant for me and I soon decided that the excursion was pointless. What we sought, was a long hard look and that we did not get. We returned little wiser about this hill of 1,500 yards in length, but only one third that in width at our end and tapering away to a point at the other. In longitudinal section it rose 100 feet at each end, between which was a long saddle. Information obtained from our maps.

Earlier that morning, our mortars had been detached, so that they might support the Worcesters and then ourselves.

10th March

My memory of the early hours of that night is of lying on a sun-baked gravel of an extreme hardness and of sleeping indifferently. We had our customary confidence in our ability to cope when, at 0200 hrs, the battalion less the HQ companies advanced along the road at the start of what we came to know as The Battle of Dirty Pagoda, so called from the small weather-beaten pagoda on the near apex of our objective.

When parallel with the Worcesters we left the road and moving half right, changed to an open formation led by 'B' and 'C' Companies, 'B' to the right and 'C' left. Then came Attack HQ and the Defence Platoon, together with 'A' Company on the right and 'D' on the left. We were making for our start line, a dry south to north nullah at the foot of our objective and which, in effect, formed a barrier between the Worcesters and ourselves on the west side and the Japs on the east. This was a no-man's-land, immediately below the enemy and was to have been reported on by the Worcesters; that they did not do so was to prove damned unfortunate. So that there might be the element of surprise, our advance and ascent of the hill was done without supporting fire.

That nullah became a nightmare and our passage through it a long, exhausting and noisy operation. We found it to be steep-sided, about 12 feet in depth and with sides and a bottom that were thick with scrub; forcing us to 'crocodile' across in the few places where it was not impassable. Knowing that once on the hill, we would have to be below ground by first light, some men were carrying picks and shovels. Add these to equipment, steel helmets and weapons, there were men so burdened as to make it impossible, in such a place, to avoid the clash of steel on steel. And that was what happened as we literally forced a way down, across and up, in darkness – the racket made worse by the quietness of a night without gunfire. Added to our chronic disorder, was the belief that we had trapped ourselves where we were most vulnerable to the Japs above, and thus we were

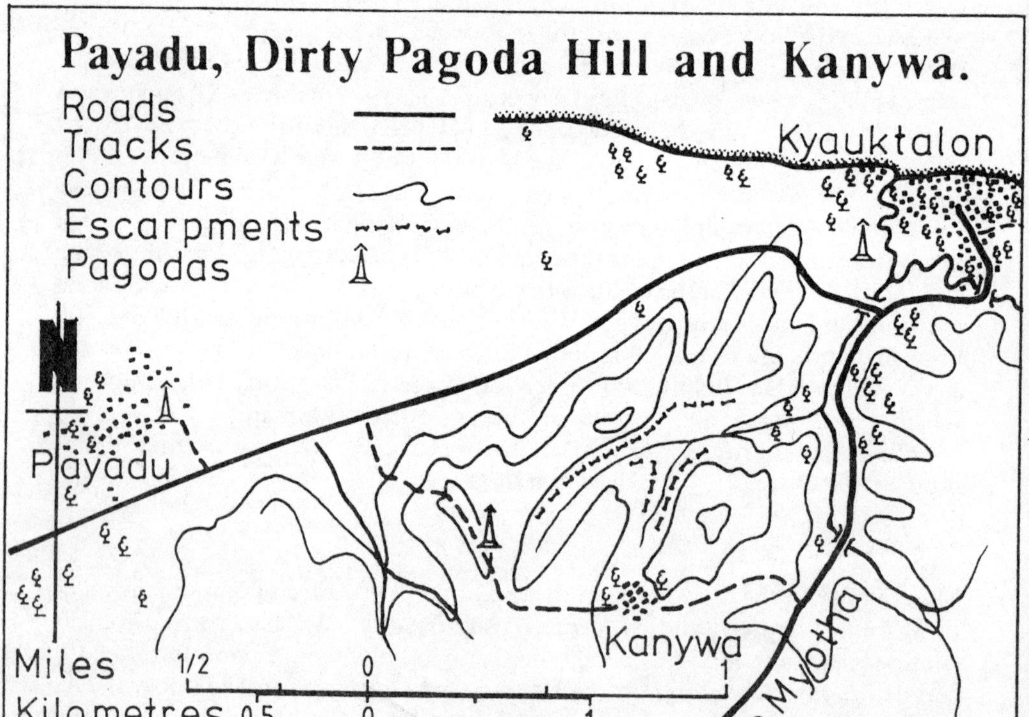

tense in the expectation of imminent slaughter. But we survived. Perhaps the Good Lord believed that ditch to be no place for the final moments of 2 Dorset and, after the loss of 60 or so very valuable minutes, we were through and fanning out and commencing the climb. Up we went, feeling our way through more scrub, on what seemed like a near-vertical slope. And still there was no reaction from the Japs. Then, at the higher levels, we were finding the hot embers of cooking fires, placed in hollows, pointers to a hurried evacuation. This was strange and not what we had expected. Could our hubbub, we wondered, have been so great as to frighten them, as in so different a way, it had frightened us?

At last we were at the top and, as planned, 'B' and 'C' continued across the saddle to the far high point. We at the west end, grouped ourselves with 'A' Company and their Glosters on the right flank, beyond and near the pagoda. Attack HQ and the Defence Platoon settled down between the two companies, close to 'D'. All save 'A', who were interested in the south side, took positions over a minor crest so that they might fire to the east and the north.

Traversing our west position was a gravel track of the farm cart variety; starting at the road, it passed the pagoda, before dropping and continuing south east to the village of Kanywa.

Bert Jones and I decided on a shallow hollow, behind the crest, and knowing that I was starting a very busy day I lay down for a quick snooze, while Bert made a start on the digging of our slit trench. Everywhere the ground was found to be rock hard and, what with that and the lost time at the nullah, we not only failed to be below ground at dawn, but our trenches were, at best, a foot or so in depth.

In the half light, I was awakened by the screams of those of Clive's company whose positions were on the north and east facing slope, a few feet away. They were being shot at by a machine-gun below them, where there was a re-entrant on the north side of the saddle. Soon, that gun or perhaps another, similarly fired on the Defence Platoon. Geoffry, realising that we were in untenable positions, hurried off to recce another locality and having done so, sent his gunman back to fetch us. Our guide, perhaps disorientated by the kerfuffle, lost his way. So we lay down along the track which, although on the ridge, was secure from fire as it was a foot or so below the adjoining ground. By then it was light and I can still see myself and those I was with, lying across the track facing east, our heads and shoulders in the gutter. To our front the ground fell steeply before levelling out in the saddle; not so far to our right stood the forlorn pagoda. A few final members of 'D' were coming up that steep slope, having evacuated their most forward positions. I heard one of the last say, "Bill is still down there." Whereupon, someone behind got up and ran back down the slope and out of sight; soon to reappear with 'Bill' on his back and, as he passed, I could see that the man making the rescue was a sergeant.

Soon Geoffry was found and our HQ was re-established in a wide depression, on the slope up which we had climbed. There and a little lower, was Joe, he and his team busy with our injured and then those of 'A' Company and their Glosters. Paget and his chaps had come under fire from the most westerly of three enemy strong points which, by their firing, had disclosed themselves along the length of that rising ground to the east.

A certain amount of mortaring was in progress and shrapnel wounded Hoffman, fortunately he was with us again in a week or two. One had only to go a short distance down hill to be at the R.A.P., where the full horrors of war were brought home by the visual impact of blood. Joe superb as usual and covered in blood, which included his back from a casualty he had carried, was working among his orderlies, saving lives and repairing and consoling the lesser wounded, the first of many.

> Everyone had their own First Field Dressing, for which a special trouser pocket was provided. Within a khaki outer cover were two dressings, protected by waterproof covers, each consisting of a gauze pad stitched to a bandage and complete with safety pin. Printed instructions advised on their use, including under respirators.

Joe remembers noticing, 'a section of the Defence Platoon, all young soldiers who had joined us at ms.82, stoutly returning the fire with Brens, and I was glad to belong to them.'

The machine-gunning of 'D' is recorded as having started at 0500 hrs, that which was directed at 'A' was probably a little later, when visibility had improved and long-range fire was possible from across the valley, to the south. It has been said that many shots, early on, were bouncing off the pagoda. That is indicative of fire on fixed lines, from the formidable medium machine-guns. At that time the Glosters were forward of 'A' Company. As the light increased many Japs could be seen on the high ground to the east, and it was about then that an enemy mortar opened fire. By 0830 hrs, under cover of smoke, Paget Fretts had his chaps where they were less vulnerable, many being tucked away to the rear of the pagoda.

With dawn and a target, our gunners were firing in support and many remember the 10th Field Regiment's battery commander Major 'Barney' Brook Fox directing his guns. Joe has written: 'I was intrigued by the sight of Barney Brook Fox, sitting on a shooting-stick in a very unsheltered place, observing the Japs through his glasses as if he were at a point-to-point. That he had a bad limp from an old injury did not seem to interfere with his cross-country walks'. Cliff Leach similarly wrote and of his relief when, 'the RA major who limped, aimed his guns at the Japs who were spraying me with bullets and mortar bombs'.

During the morning, some of the enemy from opposite 'A' Company, tried to get around our rear between the Worcesters and ourselves. We drove them back the way they had come, aided by the gunners, who were terrific in answering all calls for help. It did us good to see them scampering through the scrub, for their lives. Those who started the day by shooting at 'D' Company, seemed to have removed themselves and by mid-morning the battle was over.

For Joe and his team and also for Gus, their unrelenting tasks continued and quoting Joe yet again: 'The extent of the disaster soon showed as the casualties came back with the 'A' and 'D' stretcher-bearers (less Ronnie Easter and steady old Carpenter, who had been killed). Among them I remember Percy Basham, hit in the spine and paralysed. He had been wounded at Kohima and struggled against the odds to get back to the battalion. So many had done this, and I came to wish so much that they had taken honourable retirement, instead of coming back for more. Roger Johnson I thought was certain to die, a bullet having gone right through the front of his brain. He recovered, but as it later turned out, I think he would have preferred not to.'

While we had fought our battle, 'B' and 'C' Companies had been involved in a similar one, of which we learned later, having lost wireless contact, partly due to 'C' Company's set having been hit.

At the crossing of the nullah, 'B' had been in the lead, with 11 Platoon under Harold Jones* their forward platoon. Thus it was Harold who found a way through that choked ditch and led up the hill face, his platoon extended in an arrow formation. Moving on a compass bearing he was relieved to arrive at the pagoda as planned. Again by compass he pushed on across the saddle, surprising a group of Japs to his right, and whose haste to douche their fire was such that one caused a great clatter in falling over a bucket. Continuing on his bearing, he reached their objective and halted behind a hedge, beyond which he sensed that the ground fell away eastward. Peter Feeney allotted platoon positions with 10 left and 12 right rear; all started to peck away at the hard ground with their entrenching tools.

By then 'C' Company had arrived on Peter's left and halted short of a gulley behind their objective – the far high point. The high ground must be denied to the enemy and, to that end, Tommy Tucker ordered his 13 and 14 Platoons forward. They were soon on ground that inclined downwards, mainly to the east and within a vaguely sensed perimeter, beyond which the land fell into blackness. 13 Platoon to the right and thus to the south of 14, found itself where the rounded top fell to the south as well as to the east. They were above an escarpment, of which they became aware with the dawn. Distributing themselves within this hard-packed rock-like earth, and believing that they were pausing in an overnight advance, these platoons did not dig in.

As the sky lightened and probably coinciding with the pre-dawn events at our end, 13 Platoon was swept by fire from a medium machine-gun, sited to their south. This was the platoon of Lieutenant Robin Cuthbertson and was forward of Harold Jones and 11 Platoon, who were sheltered by the hedge and a reverse slope. In 13 Platoon was Gunner Cole, one of our newcomers from Maram who, being nearly 40, was known as 'Old Man' Cole. He and Harry Newcombe were pals and were together on that vulnerable right flank and were repeatedly shot at. In such a situation one hugs the ground, moulding one's body into every hollow and scrape, one's head turned so that it too is as flat as can be. All thoughts are on the need to remain still, yet one must get to cover, but how and where? Much that was happening was sensed rather than seen. Trying to hit back with a Lee-Enfield in such a situation is almost laughable, but both let off a few rounds.

* Harold 'Jonah' Jones, tallish and slight of build, was one of the best of our younger officers. Being brave and tough he was much admired and his inquiring mind, which concerned itself with the abilities of those senior to himself, delighted his friends.

Bravely returning the fire was a Bren to which, until it fell silent, they were able to chuck a supply of loaded magazines. Fire raked that exposed slope and men cried in agony. Then, after more of the same, Harry sensed a scuffle and realised that Cole was on his knees firing as he shrieked, "You Bastards! You Bloody Bastards!" amid shouts of "Get down!" The imperturbable George Foot, the company runner, was seen helping to carry a stretcher at a run up the slope with bullets clipping the ground behind him. Others helped the wounded as best they could but most had to remain where they were. George Foot was then wounded as was Private Newell, just behind Harry, who had bullets through his rolled cape and tin of bully beef.

At about then Tommy Tucker set off to report to Geoffry, on his two platoons caught in the open and in need of assistance. The outcome was the promise, from Brigadier Mike West, of a couple of tanks from those supporting the Camerons, who would advance that morning along the north flank of our hill, en route for Kyauktalon.

With the coming of daylight, a gunner F.O.O. with 'B' Company concentrated on the need to give 13 and 14 Platoons the protection of smoke and then to eliminate the enemy position. The difficulty was in spotting it and Andrew MacKenzie, having had his command of HQ Company swapped for that of 2 I/C to Peter, speaks of a tell-tale wisp of smoke, betraying the gun's position within a dug-out. To their joy, a shell was deposited onto the aperture through which the gun was operating.

Amongst those who died on that sorry hill was the young Robin Cuthbertson, who sacrificed his life in efforts to protect and save his wounded men.

With the aid of smoke the survivors scrambled back to the gulley and there they and the wounded gathered. 13 Platoon had taken the worst of the machine-gunning; for 14 Platoon it was the 50mm grenade discharger bomb that caused their losses. Again the stretcher-bearers had done all and more than could be expected of them and two who died were from 'B' Company.

There Harry found Cole, a wide bandage showing under his shirt. Harry writes: "It hit me hard, he didn't speak but his eyes were fixed on my face, I could tell that he knew he was going to die and he knew that I knew". Moistening his neck cloth he wiped Cole's lips, removing dust from them and around his mouth, which drew on a cigarette. Harry found that he resisted when he tried to get him to lie down, it was as if he knew that were he to do so, he would never sit again. People were calling and there was much to do; he had to leave. Harry again: "I stood up and slung my rifle and stepped back. His eyes never left my face. Then I turned and walked away. I didn't look back, had I done so I could not have left him".

In that confined space Tommy Tucker was talking to an officer or senior NCO and Harry caught the words, "I will try and get through and make contact." Then two volunteers were asked for. Thus it was that Major Tucker, accompanied by Tommy Thomas and Harry Newcombe set off; angling towards the north they crossed the rocky waste, their eyes skinned for Japs. Then they entered a defile with high banks, a place in which to be ambushed at a bend or from above, so they proceeded with caution. Harry describes their progress: 'Every so often the Major would stop, raise his hand and we would crouch until he was satisfied. He would point with his forefinger – forward. Not a word was spoken. Eventually the ground opened out and we were on the plain through which ran the Kyauktalon road. And to our left a wonderful sight, a double line of Camerons and about seven Grant tanks. As the tanks swung their guns round towards us we waved and ran to them. There was a brief conversation and Major Tucker indicated that Tommy and I should climb aboard a tank each; we detached from the others and reached our beleaguered companions. With the tanks and the artillery supporting us, the battle was virtually over'.

As soon as the situation at our end permitted, Joe and Gus crossed the saddle. They were nearly lost to us when a 25-pounder shell fell short and (so I heard) landed in the dixie of tea they were brewing.

During the day Basil Chichester-Constable and his Pioneers brought up water and stores in our carriers and took out casualties. That was to be the last we were to see of that doughty warrior, for his carrier was blown up on a mine and he joined the evacuated wounded. Despite the mined roads and tracks, we were also visited by General Nicholson.

At the end of this one-sided battle in which we had been outwitted by the enemy, we were only too aware that we had suffered grievously.

Our casualties were recorded as:

	Killed	Wounded
HQ Coy.	1	10
'A' ,,	3	13
'B' ,,	2	
'C' ,,	8	21
'D' ,,	1	8
Total	15	52

Joe has written:

"My book showed 47 wounded and 13 killed. This did not include some like the indestructible Sergeant Seale, who picked bits of mortar bomb out of themselves and soldiered on. Many of the casualties, like Robin Cuthbertson, were the result of trying to get at wounded comrades. The armoured ambulance came up very close to our position and was again invaluable, as were the carriers. There was no time to stop and grieve. Gus and a burial party were left to bury the dead while we moved on. I did not envy them that lonely task. There was no knowing what stray Japs were around in that desolate place".

At such times the dead were sewn up in their blankets, recognisable through the one identity disc, left by Gus, with the body. Later, after the war, they and the other Dorsets killed in Burma, were interred by the Commonwealth War Graves Commission in Taukkyan War Cemetery, Rangoon.

This was a skirmish that will not feature in any history book, being simply one of many such. We remember it because of brave deeds and we think of those lost and irreplaceable Dorsets, some so young that they had barely started to live – yet they had proved themselves.

11th – 13th March

We moved forward about one mile, finding a pleasantly wooded area astride the road running south from Kyauktalon to Myotha, where 20 Div. was having a battle. While *en route*, having swung south and into the valley across which we and the Japs had exchanged fire, we found their HQ. Staying behind with some of the 'I' Section and one or two chaps to keep watch, I searched it, finding no more than the usual meaningless papers and some, presumably, unwanted flags. It was well sited within a clump of trees at the east end of three positions, from which we had been shot and mortared, and was evidence of a defensive screen to the hills we were about to cross.

We had a day's rest, but for a patrol by 'A' Company along the Myotha road to ms.3 where they were shot at by a sniper.

On the last of these days we continued the advance east, in that best of all positions, Brigade reserve. Kyauktalon had been captured by the Camerons and by-passing it we moved along a cart track, passing two small collections of dwellings, until near the riverside village of Letpanzin, four miles from our start point. We remained there for a second undisturbed night, although we were on the northern fringe of those hills to which I referred as a geographical barrier and which extend southwards for many miles, in fact they disappear off the map.

We were starting a period of marching under a fierce sun in the manner of our predecessors, those of the 39th and 54th Regiments of Foot and British Infantry generally, throughout the centuries. Progressing towards the next battle and those that would follow in single file, each man concentrating on his need to conserve energy. Thus there was little attention to anything but the roughness of the track which, being bent forward to achieve a balance against the backward pull of pack and equipment, was what one saw most easily. When possible, thumbs were hooked behind pack straps, which was a good way in which to ease that dead weight which sagged too low on a sweat-soaked back for comfort and for equilibrium. We had marched for years and took a fierce pride in our ability to keep going in that scorched land and enjoyed feelings of superiority over lesser mortals, such as gunners, who would pass us in their 'Quads', those gun-towing vehicles of the field artillery.

14th March

Too many years have passed for me to be able to recollect just when we knew, officially, that the 2nd Division was making for Mandalay; there to mount an attack from the south in conjunction with 19 Div., coming down from the north. Knowing, as we did, the treatment to which prisoners of the Japanese were subjected to make them talk, it was sound policy not to disclose future plans. But on that day, when we were to make a fast move forward, with the Division as a whole doing likewise, the objective of Mandalay would have been obvious to all, including the enemy. From then onwards the emphasis was on progress, regardless of pockets of enemy on our flanks. They were to be ignored, in the expectation that our overwhelming strength would encourage them to go away. And if they didn't, then someone else could sort them out.

That day's objective was the village of Sinde, only seven miles distant for a crow, and a mere six miles further would take one to the south end of the Ava Bridge, from which Mandalay was ten miles by road. Sinde would be our most easterly point yet, so at the day's end we would be well on our way, again within level ground.

That march was both long and wearisome, a right hook through dry, eroded scrub land, initially hilly, with rock outcrops where the sole variations to the scrub were thin scatterings of trees, around two or three small villages. It was only when we were nearing the end of our hike that we left difficult country for the cultivated plain, where we could move with greater freedom within those sorry fields, scorched to an all-prevailing dun colour; their existence dependent on the monsoon rains and a flooding Irrawaddy, which inundates those plains in the period June to October.

The effect of the mid-day sun was such that anyone foolish enough to sit on a rock would leap up in anguish, much as if it had been a kitchen hotplate. When we were in the open, as we invariably were, the heat assailed us from all sides – there was no escape from it, for all things were hot.

Aiding us that day was a battery of 16 mortars of the Gordons, an element of the 100th Light Anti-Aircraft/Anti-Tank Regiment RA, of the divisional artillery. That powerful unit was able to take the place of our own mortars, which were to have travelled in our carriers, so ours were unloaded and made available for Snagger Highett and his men, to operate as a carrier platoon and screen our column.

Only a few excel in action and one who did just that was Snagger. Those who were not there may well envisage a fearsome giant of a man. Nothing could be further from the slight and unpretentious figure that is the actual person. Not given to exercise unless forced upon him, I found it surprising that, post-war, he played tennis sufficiently well as to be captain of tennis at Cambridge. In the unsettled nomadic existence of our campaign, small familiar things attained an exceptional importance, such as the oval cigarette named Passing Clouds that Snagger favoured, and generously shared with his friends, and playing bridge – both memories associated with him.

Whilst on the subject of cigarettes, I must mention a battered tin, now a home for brass screws, which is a relic of those days and which proclaims that it was the product of ACROPOLO & CO, and held their 'high class' cigarettes of warranted selected Virginia tobacco, produced in their Parel, Bombay, factory, the oldest establishment in India. I thought them pretty good at the time – certainly better than the issue – Victory Vs.

Following our recent descent into the plain, I was approached by a native who was anxious to tell me that Japs were massing in a nullah just off our route, and sure enough, there they were, a pack of about 30 only a quarter of a mile away to our right. Reluctantly, for they presented an easy target, we pretended not to see them and pressed on.

Sinde, as indicated on the map, was one of the larger villages, and having expected to fall foul of the Japs there, and not having done so, it was all the more a surprise when quite strong opposition was encountered a mile beyond, where the map shows a pagoda and a couple of buildings.

We were then on the road to Kadozeik and were advancing prepared for trouble, having two companies deployed, 'A' right and 'D' left, but were hampered by most unwelcome thick hedges, so that visibility was no more than the width of a small field. When the shooting started, we at Attack HQ moved up to behind 'D', and turned left to the cover of a copse. Geoffry and I then went into it, anticipating that we might be able to see forward to where we presumed the Japs to be. We found a grassy centre within the trees amongst which were a few buildings. In all it was much larger than we had imagined, and with its tall trees and general greenery, it was an oasis in a brown world. We lay looking across the clearing which appeared devoid of Japs, and probably was, for the mortar bombs they were firing at our companies were also landing in the copse. For what seemed to be an age we watched the exploding bombs, some close enough to be highly unpleasant, but this was no place from which to see forward, so we returned the way we had come.

It was then about 1600 hrs, and Geoffry wisely decided that it was too late in the day to risk becoming heavily embroiled at a time of fading light, and almost inevitably to be still fighting at dusk. Far better to disengage while we could and restart tomorrow, at a time suited to us. It was no casual engagement, for we had been at the receiving end of fire from machine-guns, grenade dischargers and 81mm mortars, causing five casualties.

We pulled back 400 yards into open ground and settled into a tight perimeter for the night, managing to do so without any follow-up by the Japs. Soon all was peace and quiet. In that stillness of early evening, and a blessed coolness, men set about their routine tasks, the most important of which was digging-in.

My job was to prepare the intelligence report on the day, and get it off to Brigade. We had been on the move for seven or more hot, dusty, and physically and mentally exhausting hours, ever on the watch for the enemy. During those long hours, we had obeyed the order that water-bottles were to remain full and my thoughts after casting off my equipment (the first step to recovery) were to refresh myself, not by drinking, but by washing away the dust-encrusted sweat. Stripping everything off, boots and all, I poured the contents of my water-bottle into my mess tin and, using a face flannel and soap, I had a complete and wonderful 'bath'. When once more dressed, I was ready for anything. . .

15th March

I had smiled to myself yesterday when Geoffry announced that we would resume the battle at 0800 hrs today. Those at that meeting solemnly noted the hour, much as they would at home record an early business meeting. But then, of course, battles were our business.

We were up and breakfasted and ready to go at the appointed hour, setting off again along what was a very minor road towards the village of Kadozeik, a

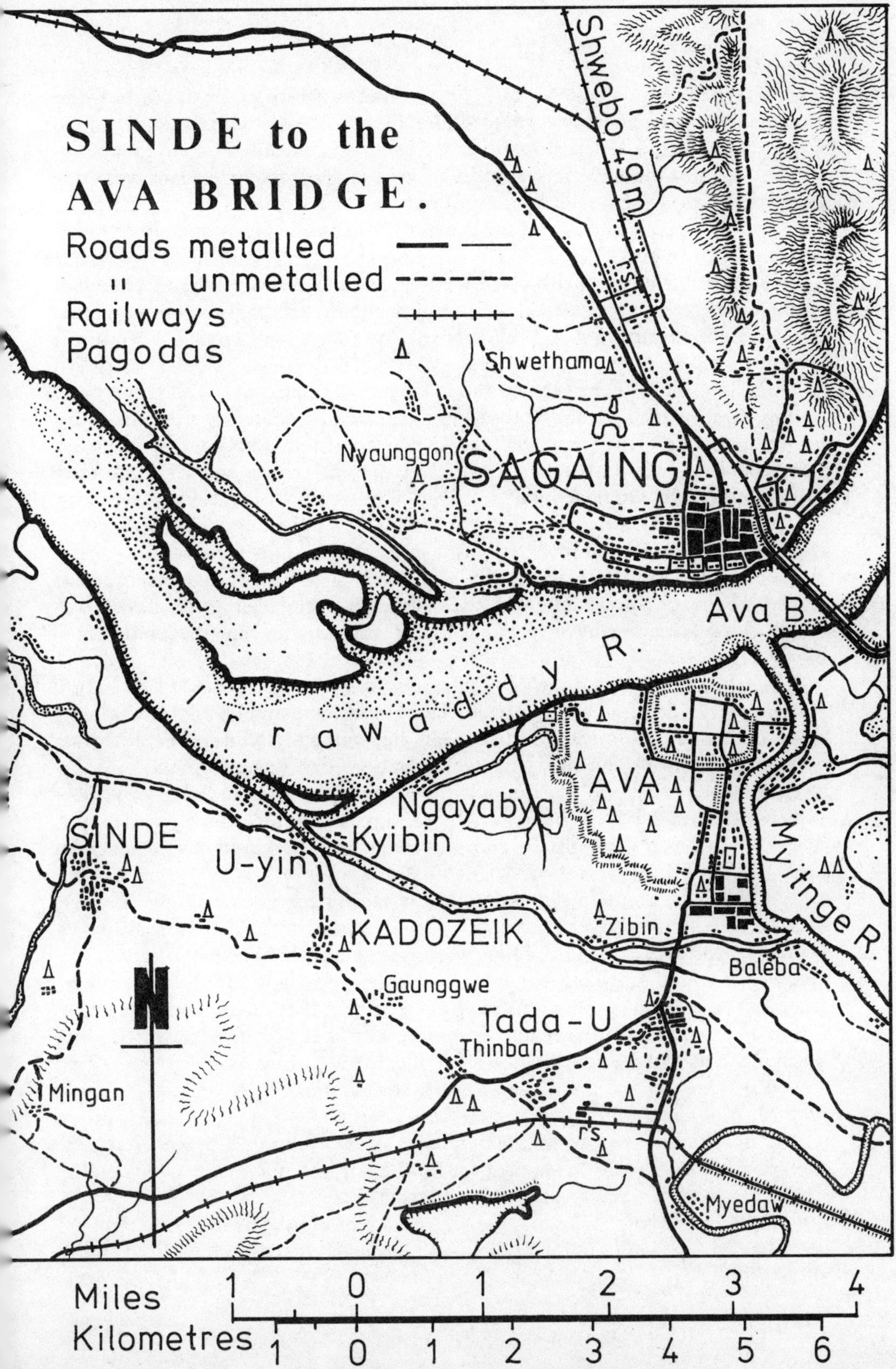
SINDE to the AVA BRIDGE.
Roads metalled
" unmetalled
Railways
Pagodas
Shwebo 49m
rs.
Shwethama
Nyaunggon
SAGAING
Ava B
Irrawaddy R.
AVA
Ngayabya
Kyibin
SINDE
U-yin
KADOZEIK
Zibin
Myitnge R.
Baleba
Gaunggwe
Tada-U
Thinban
Mingan
rs.
Myedaw
N
Miles
1 0 1 2 3 4
Kilometres
1 0 1 2 3 4 5 6

distance of just over a mile.

When we had progressed a little beyond the previous point of contact, the expected happened and we came under fire. We were advancing with 'C' Company right and 'B' left, both preceded by a troop of tanks on their right flank, and an escort of three carriers. It soon became obvious that these Japs were not going to be easily removed and a request was made for air support. This was accepted by Brigade and we settled down to contain the Japs, expecting a delay of an hour or two.

The natural features of this place were almost identical to those of yesterday and again there was a copse, this however contained a small pagoda. The Japs were in well chosen positions in a good defensive location, giving cover for them and not much for us.

Our three tanks were Grants, those formidable machines with their great hulking, gun-carrying solidity; to us, out in the open, under no more than the doubtful shelter of our steel helmets, they seemed so impregnable as to be unstoppable in such a situation. Yet, before they had come under fire one had turned back with engine trouble, leaving the other two to continue. Then one was struck by an armour-piercing projectile which penetrated its stored ammo and, in a matter of moments, it was a mass of crackling flame and its crew condemned to a hideous death. The third then withdrew, as was the correct procedure in such a predicament. This left us shocked and feeling very naked, but the disaster was ignored by Snagger and his carriers, and they remained undaunted in the field.

The day was to be one on which difficulties and set-backs abounded. Even our planning was hampered by a shortage of air photos, our supply literally stopping short of the copse. Good as our maps were, they only showed areas of cultivation by yellow colouring, when what we so much needed was information on the trees and hedges beyond our immediate vicinity.

When mid-day arrived and no planes, an enquiry of Brigade brought the reply that the planes were flying from a strip in India, and we would have to sit tight until they arrived.

In such a situation of stalemate, with the Japs sitting in their holes, and we making do with such cover as existed, or could be improved on, there was always a certain amount of grenading. There was an accepted principle that, if they threw grenades at you, then you threw grenades at them and this tended to apply to the machine-gun; acts that were justified by a belief that they encouraged the other side to desist. One lull, in the early afternoon, prompted Geoffry to dispatch John Joslin on a patrol of the copse, to see what information that would produce. After a careful approach and good use of a generous amount of cover they entered without hindrance; only to find themselves inside a Japanese trench position whose occupants, like the remainder of us, were resting. A decidedly dicey moment, but having the advantage of surprise and mobility, they were able to shoot their way out and return without loss.

John Joslin had come to us in October '44, and must have been a good platoon commander deserving of high praise, and I hope he looked back on his months with us with a proud satisfaction.

Eventually, at around 1600 hrs, when we had just decided that the planes were not coming and that if they did they would be too late, a squadron of Hurribombers commenced circling above our heads. This was the moment for our gunners to put down cannisters of yellow smoke on the enemy positions, as markers for bombing. To our alarm some fell short, so that our forward companies were bracketed by them, and further rounds fired to correct the error only added to it. Our alarm was well founded when some of the planes peeled off and dived in succession upon us, their leader dropping two bombs on 'D' Company, before they zoomed up and recommenced their circling. Those bombs mercifully and inexplicably did not explode. By then, all who could be were out in the open waving to the planes to go away, and it was another shattering moment when we saw them coming down again. By then they had realised that something was very wrong, and were losing height in order to have a close look. Having confirmed who we were and seen that the operation had degenerated into a shambles, they reformed and made tracks for India.

During the latter part of this debacle, the subaltern directing the guns firing the markers, casually strolled across our lines to view the smoke. That easy-going walk conformed to the teaching that at times of stress you always walked and never ran, but for me it was the last straw and I shrieked that they should take their bloody fingers out, and quickly! His glance of contempt made clear his opinion that I was panicky, and I realised that indeed I was, to my lasting shame.

Within eight hours our rifle companies, our mortars and carriers, the latter fulfilling their role of flank protection, had been so much in contact with the Japs that we ended the day again sadly diminished in numbers, having had eight killed and 12 wounded, one of the latter being Harold 'Jonah' Jones. Joe Chamberlin, in his inimitable manner, writes: "Kadozeik was a very confusing affair, obscured by tall grass and scrub. Among the wounded was again Sgt. Seale. This time he had no choice but to go back, with shrapnel in his foot. Harold Jones was a memorable casualty here, with an open chest wound exposing his lung and a near-death appearance. The stretcher party, which included Gus, were much relieved when they stumbled and barged his arm against a carrier and a voice operating strongly on one lung said, 'Be careful of my bloody arm!' It was necessary to sew up the vent in his chest there and then – a rough and unsterile procedure for which he forgave me".

One who also saw the injured Harold was Andrew MacKenzie, to whom he managed to say, "Cheerio Mac, I've had it." That was an excess of pessimism, for after post-war air-borne soldiering and a desk among the Mandarins in Whitehall, he is a living tribute to our medical services. Once clear of us and our shambles, he was whipped away to an air-strip, an L.5 and a flight to the north, of which he is understandably vague. He remembers being 'trimmed-up' and reaching a tented camp with a penicillin-drip, also having his lung aspirated, in his case a long and tedious business, the M.O. having no more than a 10cc syringe. (See Appendix C.)

I have mentioned the Mills Bomb or, as it was often known, the 36 grenade. We also used the No. 77 grenade which, with its Bakelite cap and tin can body, was representative of our conflict, just as the Mills grenade, with a sectionised cast-iron body casing, was typical of our fathers' war. The 77 had the virtue of weighing only 13.5 oz. as against the 25 oz. of the 36 and it was also supplied as a smoke grenade. Prior to throwing the 77, with an overarm action as in cricket, the cap was removed and the end of a tape, whose purpose was to activate the fuse, was retained in the throwing hand. For those who revel in details, I can mention that we had the Mk. 2.

16th – 18th March

Following the abortive air-strike, Brigadier Mike West advised Geoffry to step back once more and disengage, but this time we were to make life so impossible for the Japs that they would clear right out and leave us. Having the extra 16 mortars and gunner support, we were able to give them as continuous a bombing and shelling as generous supplies allowed and the hours of darkness became a welter of noise. By dawn we were pretty confident that we had succeeded. To make sure, Geoffry told me to go and have a look, and this I and half a dozen chaps did. My profound respect for our patrol leaders was not diminished by this venture into Jap territory; a place of level ground and scrub, where you were lucky to see 50 yards. Our return in one piece, at much the same time, 0530 hrs, as a patrol of carriers into Kadozeik found it to be clear, was the confirmation we needed.

Much was happening at that time when Mandalay was just behind the horizon. To our right 6 Brigade was approaching Tada-U, a one-and-a-half-mile conurbation of town, pagodas, monasteries, official bungalows, railway station and, most strangely – a vineyard. To our left the Worcesters were on their way north to the village of U-yin, and the Camerons were pointing north east for Ava. At last a place of some consequence and one we could pronounce.

When our carriers entered Kadozeik, the villagers had reported the departure of large numbers of Japs. So we could also swing north and, again in Brigade reserve, we crossed the Tayok Chaung between U-yin and the adjacent village of Kyibin, doing so at 1140 hrs. We then made our way along the bank of the Irrawaddy to the sizeable village of Ngayabya, there to wash and bathe ad lib.

At mid-day on the 17th, having continued eastward, we entered the walled city of Ava, or to be more exact its remains, for it had been sufficiently damaged by an earthquake in 1837 as to be abandoned four years later.

Before we could reach the Ava Bridge, our immediate objective – second only to Mandalay in importance – we had to cross the Myitnge River. Rising in the mountains of the Northern Shan States, it runs well to the east of Maymyo and changing direction from south to west, it finally turns north to meet the Irrawaddy half a mile downstream of the bridge. West of it and on its bank and the bank also of the 'Waddy, is historic Ava, founded in 1364 and the capital of

Burma, on and off through chequered years, until the 19th century. When we were there it was little more than a place of temples within the enclosing walls, but one regrets the lack of opportunity to stop and stare.

We were still in Brigade reserve when, at 0630 hrs on the 18th, the Battalion 'O' Group was boated across the Myitnge; to be followed by the main body making the crossing in a somewhat inadequate flotilla of DUKWs. For three days we had had no opposition, and in this river crossing we had surmounted what could have been a formidable defensive line, had the enemy chosen to make it so. One that was 300 yards in width and deep enough for river steamers. For the 30 miles width of the central plain, where it twisted and turned and was crossed only by the bridge carrying the main road and rail to Rangoon, it could have been a deadly obstacle.

Ahead of us, the Worcesters, following no more than a skirmish, had reached the Ava Bridge. Our orders were to take up a position at that southern end, which we did at 1145 hrs.

By the end of that morning we were the focus of attention from an enthusiastic press. A photograph taken that day with the bridge in the background is of what Geoffry liked to consider as his carrier, on its side is the word Ava, a cherished battle honour from that previous visit during the Burma War of 1824-6, when we were involved as the 54th Regiment. The carrier also has the white painted five-pointed star, introduced by the Americans for the recognition of all Allied vehicles.

Scrub was growing in the approach roadway to the unrepaired and rusting

The Ava Bridge from the south bank, March 1945

bridge. With skill and cunning the Japs had constructed a walk-way through the two demolished spans. Not having been spotted it was not bombed, and they had a vital footbridge without our knowing – no wonder they made no attempt at restoration. It was soon in use, as those to the north came across to see what it was like at our end.

Clive Chettle was about the only one of us with the energy to make a reverse crossing. In so doing he made contact with 268 Brigade, whose task of filling the gap between the 2nd and 19th Divisions, had commenced back at the Chindwin.

19th March

Our world of unmetalled roads, extending back three months to when we crossed the Chindwin, had changed back to one that was, at least partially, tarmacadam, admittedly pot-holed and in dire straits, but representative of another world, the one we had left behind, and we looked at it and stamped our boots on it with some satisfaction. It was on such a surface that, at 0630 hrs, we commenced that almost mythological march – On the road to Mandalay.

But this was to be no triumphant entry into a great city. Our war certainly lacked glamour, and we advanced in the expectation of becoming embroiled in more skirmishes. With our tenuous supply line having the additional complication of the Myitnge River, we were without artillery, and no more than a collection of depleted infantry battalions. Furthermore, in order that we would not become entangled with 19 Div., by then well into the city and fighting in and around Fort Dufferin, where their battle was nearly concluded, we were to halt in the southern fringes.

We were now to lead the Brigade and our order of march was:

Carriers,
'D' Company followed by 'A',
'O' Group and Main HQ,
'B' Company and finally 'C'.

For the first mile, road and railway ran together, the rails to our left and thus between us and the Irrawaddy, soon to become lost to us as it turned north and we inclined towards the east. Rail and road were elevated above low-lying ground, in which to our left were some scattered buildings and to the right, semi-dry lakes and ponds. Then the railway departed for the river bank and still elevated, we approached Amarapura. This had been the capital city after Ava and preceding Mandalay but then, in our eyes, was thought of as an outer suburb of no distinction. Flanked by watery ground (soon to our right would be Taungthaman Lake), we were thankful to pass this untrodden area, with a significant absence of Burmese and its lack of cover, without incident. After five miles we had Amarapura behind us and approached the ruined Hmandan Fort. Our road, forsaking the railway, which had returned and was to our right, passed through the north west corner of walls that were a mile in length and we continued north, increasingly vigilant in this vacated 'suburbia'.

It was a little later when we had our first contact, 'D' flushing out half a dozen

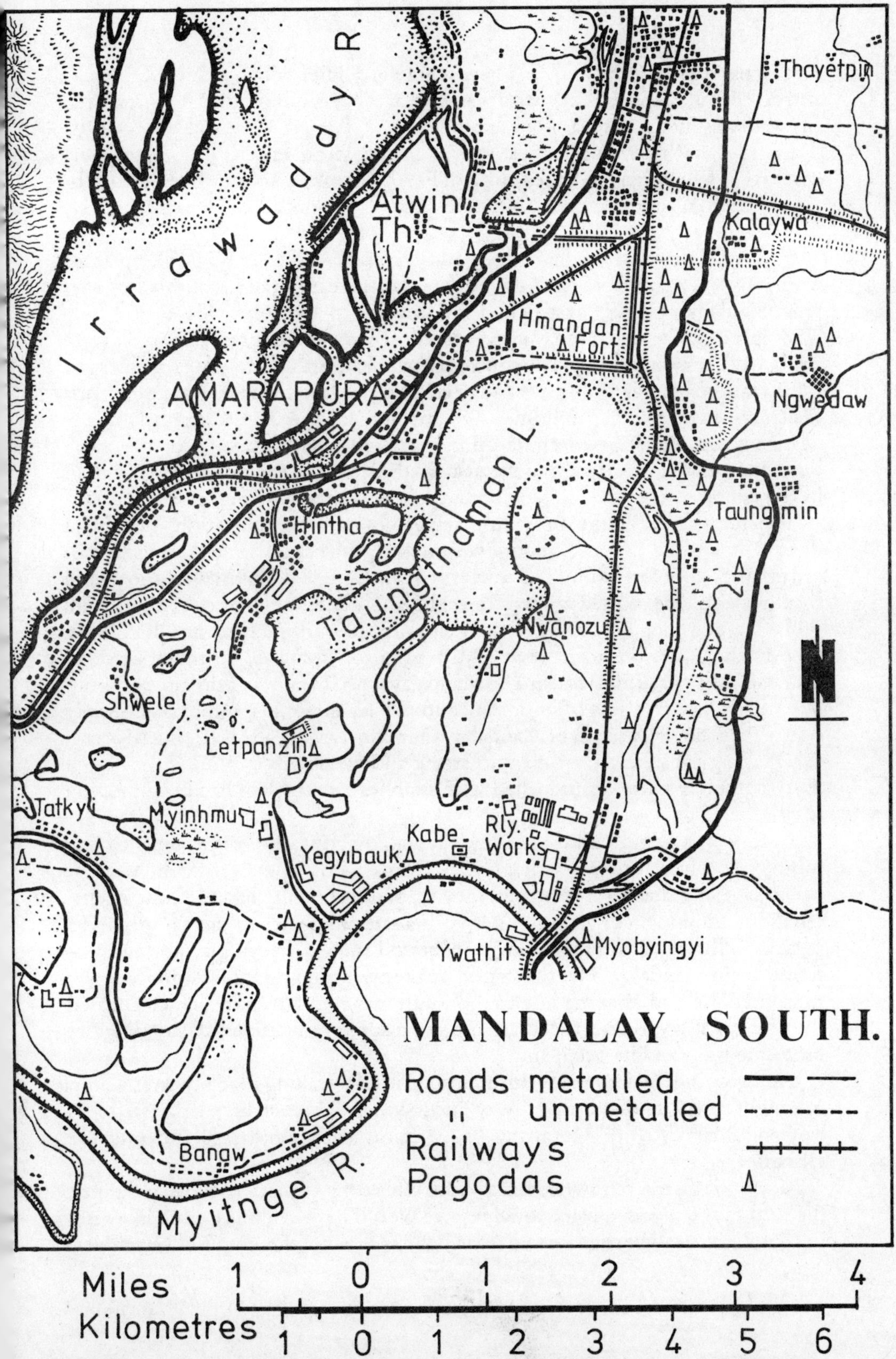

MANDALAY SOUTH.

Japs from pagodas along the road beyond the fort, after which a Gerry Overman patrol fell foul of more. The patrol was soon at the receiving end of 81mm mortar fire and was lucky to return unscathed.

In order that we would not become entangled within the city proper, we were ordered to halt when five miles south of Fort Dufferin. This was the home of the royal palace and administrative buildings, a small city outside of which Mandalay had developed.

In our progression we had edged away from the Irrawaddy, until separated from it by over a mile of wetlands. To deter Japanese infiltration southwards over that left flank, Geoffry dispatched a company to the lone village of Atwin Thayagon, an island in those watery flatlands. To cover our more vulnerable right flank, 'A' Company took occupation of Hmandan Fort's north east corner. It was there that the branch railway we had been following made its exit, joining Burma Railways' main north/south line. Accompanying Paget was a company of the Manchesters and their machine-guns, ready to take advantage of the fort's domination of the level plain to the east. With Clive's company establishing itself in the centre, we formed a wide screen to the Worcesters, to our rear.

The railway, although providing vital lines of communication over great distances, was the narrow (in our eyes) metre-gauge and was seldom fenced. It did not therefore form a physical barrier as in the UK. So different were the tracks, that they could be crossed without restraint, and sometimes without being aware of having done so. To our right was that north to south railway line and, half a mile further east, the main road to the town of Kyaukse, 25 miles south of Mandalay. Both rail and road linked Mandalay with Rangoon, a distance of about 400 miles. Kyaukse was of importance to the Japanese, being the main supply centre for their army south of Mandalay. Our 20 Division, after clearing Myotha, was making for it, and they were to attack and eventually capture it on March 30th, complete with a train loaded with supplies that the Japs had been moving south.

A story was being enthusiastically circulated about one of the units to our south, possibly a leading element of 4 Corps who, in early March, were at Meiktila. On reaching the railway they tapped its telephone and found themselves listening to a conversation between a station-master to their north and a Japanese official, regarding a Rangoon-bound train conveying important personnel from Mandalay. This the station-master was holding at his station as it was rumoured, he said, that the line to the south was cut. This intelligence enabled the unit's artillery to direct accurate and, we assumed and hoped, devastating fire on to the train and its occupants.

That evening 'D' Company distinguished itself by taking a Jap prisoner. Later, in a night patrol up that main railway line to where a branch line departed to the east and Maymyo, 'A' Company had a fracas with some Japs and inflicted casualties.

Maymyo was the renowned hill station, where the servants of the Raj escaped the heat of the plains, a place to which we would have willingly done likewise. In March the strawberries are said to be delicious, as are the 'English' vegetables.

Had we gone there, there could have been a rush for the YMCA or the renowned Candacraig. The latter, built in 1906 in the manner of an English country house, had been noted for the quality of its accommodation and food. Sadly, it could not be. And sadly also, we Dorsets, far from leading our division in a memorable advance, had gone into a dead-end. Ahead of us 19 Division, under its dynamic leader Major-General Reese whose small figure, as often as not, would be seen at the head of his leading troops, was capturing Mandalay. Behind us, other formations were striking east in bold thrusts to cut off the retreating Japs and, in so doing, were retaking large areas of Burma.

We had no liking for our position. Generally, it was only by reference to a map that we could tell what was behind the buildings that restricted our vision. The central plain, in which we had been after Kadozeik, extends for ten miles to the hills of the Shan States, an open space that was lost to us by the multitude of dwellings and pagodas, between road and railway. Were they to be held, we could see ourselves making use of that village fighting drill, performed so well so long ago in Yorkshire. To our left, parallel with the road and behind a scattering of buildings, the Shweta Chaung confined us. It was a place ideal for defence.

It seems barely credible and certainly it was not then appreciated, that we were on the Number 8 Bus Route. Alas – no buses. Thankfully, there were no Burmese either. How they must have longed to see the back of us! Had it been possible to take a bus, a five- or six-minute journey north would have seen the random housing replaced by a formal grid of numbered roads, running east and west and numbered streets doing likewise to the north and south. Those streets or roads occur every 200 yards or so, town planning associated with places such as New York, a formality quite unexpected in a country where formality is rare; and in a city said to be the most Burmese of any. Not large as cities go and with a population of 150,000, it was less than half that of the capital, Rangoon. It had been the capital as recently as the nineteenth century; then, in 1892, not surprisingly in so hot and dry a place, it was largely destroyed by fire.

When we were there, whole blocks of that grid of roads and streets were gone, having been reduced to a wasteland by bombing and the inevitable fires. Outside the city centre, one and two storey timber buildings, closely set in small gardens with mature trees and timber fencing, also had no chance of survival when the bombs fell and, yet again, fire swept them away. We were in an area which was relatively unharmed and which would have remained so.

20th March

We had had a quiet night and morning, until the sudden and sustained firing of the Manchesters' guns indicated that something was happening. And there they were, when we walked across to them, sitting behind their tripods, set in line along the wide raised terrace abutting the outer face of the east flank of Hmandan Fort. From that well chosen viewpoint they looked over a multitude of small, brown coloured pagodas, set higgledy-piggledy in an otherwise desolate landscape. These stood above the scrub like Christian tombstones, in an abandoned city graveyard which, even in its prime, had been ill-favoured. But they were incidental to the road to Kyaukse and the south, of which perhaps half a mile could be seen and on it – the tail end of a Jap convoy going 'hell for leather' away from Mandalay. To our dismay, all but three vehicles kept going, those three swinging left off the road into the shelter of a copse. Then, most dramatically, in the manner of the star in a theatrical production, a lone staff car appeared, going even faster in a suicidal dash for freedom. We watched spellbound, sure of a spectacular crash, but, to our disbelief, the impossible happened – it went on and on down that long road, until it also disappeared.

Thankfully for 2 Div.'s pride, this was not seen by our distinguished visitor, our C-in-C, Lieutenant-General Sir Oliver Leese who later stood on that same terrace and observed the view. He had come to see how the Dorsets were and to tell us of the need to be in Rangoon before the onset of the monsoon.

During the afternoon we learned that Mandalay had fallen to the 19th Division. A magnificent achievement for, almost alone, they had fought their way south from their crossings of the Irrawaddy, opposite Ye-U and Shwebo, doing so at about the time we were relaxing in Halin Twinma. They had captured the strongly held Mandalay Hill, just north of the city, and finally the great Fort Dufferin. That place, with its mile-and-a-half-long moated enclosing walls, had resisted everything that 'Pete' Rees could devise, including skip-bombing by low-flying planes dropping 2,000 lb. bombs. It proved to be more enduring than the Japs who, eventually, could take no more and cleared out. Their retreat from Mandalay was a defeat of the first magnitude, and made clear to the Burmese that it was only a matter of time before the war in their country would be over.

That night 'D' Company sent a patrol north to the Arakan Pagoda*, on the fringe of the gridded roads and streets; there they clashed with Japs and received casualties, one being Private Acourt who was killed. As might be expected, when there was a wholesale exodus of Japs doing their utmost to escape, we had a number of contacts and in one, 'C' Company machine-gunned a group in which there were two trucks towing 75mm guns that, next morning, they found abandoned. And a patrol from 'B' took prisoner four wounded Japs, identified as from 15 Div.

21st March

At the end of the preceding day, Geoffry had moved Battalion HQ into a more agreeable area than the one we had occupied rather casually. There, I was one whose 'patch' was within a stone paved courtyard to a large and beautiful pagoda, elaborately carved and painted white, but for a gilded apex. Waxing lyrical, I wrote – 'The brilliant sun, throwing deep shadows on one side and with the blue sky beyond, made it a wonderful and refreshing sight. The whole enhanced by the sound of miniature bells encircling its pinnacle, set ringing during occasional puffs of wind and noticed most at night'. However, in the middle of the night,

* Also known as the Mahamuni Pagoda. A place of pilgrimage and venerated by Buddhists since the 18th century. A centre for stone masons, wood carvers and gold-leaf makers.

the tinkling of those bells was to be lost in the sound of bursting shells, for we had come under artillery fire. Like the others, I was rudely awakened and abandoning my paving slab, I did a hasty crawl to the nearest trench, there thankfully to tumble in on to its two occupants. We were the target of a Jap medium gun battery, firing off stored ammunition prior to abandoning their guns. Later our gunners identified them as the 105mm, which fired a 35 lb. shell, and they were located at the Government Farm, three miles away to the north east. It was assumed that we had been seen milling about during the day and that General Leese could well have been spotted. No great achievement, for that gangling figure, red tabs and all, lacked the green of our battledress. We were to suffer two more deaths and others injured, in the short but concentrated bombardment. Gus came near to being permanently lost to us when a shell blew his trench in on him, so that little more than his head was above ground. He remained sufficiently conscious to be able to hear one of a couple of passing stretcher-bearers say, "That bugger's nearly had it." Fair comment and one that was, as Gus well knew, in no way personal.

We fully realised that we were getting off lightly in that tangled suburb, but every death was a disaster and every wounded man depleted our weary ranks which, in response, closed in yet again upon themselves.

Joe Chamberlin again: "It was a great relief to reach the Ava Bridge and then the Hunan Pagoda outside Mandalay. The numerous shrines around it housed brightly painted Buddhist figures smiling at something we did not know. No doubt it was the bombardment we received that night, in which we were lucky to sustain only six casualties. The stretcher-bearers were very saddened by the death of 'Lofty' Burden*, a large and gentle countryman who was unnecessarily killed when conducting someone to the R.A.P., who proved to be suffering from panic".

In the morning it was learned that General Slim would re-hoist the Union Flag over Fort Dufferin, an event to be enjoyed by anyone who could get there. As C.O. of 2 Div.'s leading battalion it was only right that Geoffry should have the opportunity to be present. To his delight he was able to link up with 'Mike' West and make the journey, with the formality of a tank and carrier escort. There was no room for me, but I was put in touch with a sapper officer, who was going into the city to check the weight-carrying capabilities of the bridges, from culverts upwards, crossed by the main road. (We were concerned at the weight of our tanks.) I joined him and his armoured-car and sitting on top enjoyed a journey of frequent pauses, while he disappeared below to inspect bridge soffits and abutments along our route.

While on that almost deserted road, a small convoy of open civilian trucks passed us, going south from out of the city centre, in the backs of which and standing packed together were Anglo-Burmese women; presumably just released from internment, for they were in a high state of euphoria. We returned their waving and cheering, thus for one brief moment we enjoyed what our troops,

* Private Burden was a long-serving and treasured member of 8 Platoon.

who were advancing into European cities, were experiencing almost daily.

We continued on our way with feelings of self-satisfaction, arriving in time to join the large informal crowd of servicemen gathered in the maidan, within the fort; there to watch our Army Commander, Lieutenant-General Sir William Slim, hoist our flag where it had last flown in April 1942. This was a no nonsense ceremony, in which the symbolic act was all-important, performed in a typically British, low-key manner, and was soon over. The crowd then slowly dispersed, aware no doubt that there was still the hell of a lot to do.

At 'home', the one remaining excitement of that day was the return of Snagger, back from one of his perpetual patrols and towing a Jap armoured-car of a new and revolutionary design, in its low-slung body. It was soon the centre of a vociferous crowd – like boys with a long awaited toy. That the engine had been 'spiked' was a considerable disappointment, for we would have loved to have taken it with us, and Geoffry as always had to suppress thoughts of having it at Dorchester.

As might be expected, almost nothing reached Dorchester, to our great regret for they would have had an increasing interest. In the early phase of optimism, sufficient to blind those concerned to the plain reality of logistics, a couple of Jap guns, one a 70 and the other a 75mm, were labelled for such a delivery never, of course, to be seen again.

The 22nd and 23rd March were rest days, during which we were told we were moving back to Ava.

CHAPTER TWELVE

The Final Trek.

24th – 27th March

Two factors were now determining our future, of which our distance from India, the source of almost all our supplies, was one.

The overland route from Dimapur, on reaching Kalewa, divided into part road and part river; for from there many of our needs were being transported down the Chindwin to the Irrawaddy on river craft, in an operation of far-sighted and brilliant improvisation, many of the craft having been built on the banks of the Chindwin, from the forest timbers. A fleet that became known as 'The Chindwin Navy'. Supplementing this divided tail was the more direct air route, but that was one of nearly 500 miles from the bases around Calcutta, or at its shortest, 300 from Chittagong.

The second and more critical was our wasting numerical strength, which by then was dangerously low throughout the 2nd Division. In addition to the battle casualties, there was a steady erosion of men reporting sick and we British, unlike the Indians, were receiving few if any reinforcements. Thus within the Indian Army, the British battalions were being superseded by Indian ones, and our treasured division was becoming a spent force.

With all planning concentrated on the capture of Rangoon before the monsoon in May, it made sense to shunt 2 Div. into a backwater and then fly it out to India. From there, rested and rejuvenated, it could be brought back into the fray in its specialist role of an assault division, and arrive at Rangoon from the sea. Such high level planning was beyond our ken, at least for the next week or two, so we continued to accept our role as one of ever moving southward even if, at times, we went off at a tangent.

Within all the movement of thousands of men and their machines, and the daily provision of their essentials for survival and for battle, other miracles were performed in the distribution of letters from home in under two weeks. Geoffry would not have been alone in getting his air mail edition of the Daily Telegraph in about one week from publication. It was eagerly read by all who could get their hands on it.

At last, in our letters home, we were permitted to say that we were part of the 2nd Division (something not known to everybody), and we were also able to recount our route from Tamu to Ngazun – a sure sign of confidence in high places. And I was writing, 'It is only a matter of time before Burma is clear'.

Despite our toughness and the great work done by Joe Chamberlin and his colleagues, tropical diseases and the constant exposure to a tropical climate, from which there was very little escape, were drastically debilitating to all but a remarkable few. Something of that ever-increasing heat is illustrated in one of my letters, when I wrote – 'I have been carrying your letters in my shirt pocket, but unfortunately they have become so soaked in sweat that only the last is legible'.

For most of us, including myself, diarrhoea was a continuously weakening and dehydrating curse. And a serious embarrassment, for life had to revolve around the need to relieve oneself at frequent, and generally difficult to accommodate, intervals.

Septic sores, cuts, abrasions and blisters, to which our life made us very prone, and which refused to heal, were one burden that I avoided, that I attributed to Dettol; a leather covered bottle of which never left my pack, and was used neat on any broken skin.

Joe Chamberlin's observations are specific: "The last phase of the campaign couldn't end too soon for my liking. The Japanese were clearly making for home, and one hoped that they would perish on the way (as we had seen them do in the Kabaw Valley) without a lot of expensive prodding by us. From Dirty Pagoda onwards, the effects of heat and fatigue and dirt, and grief at the loss of old friends, became very difficult to ignore. Most people were by now probably harbouring malarial parasites, though the daily routine dose of Mepacrine largely prevented overt illness. No such umbrella was available for dysentery, but a new sulfa drug had reached us, which greatly reduced the numbers requiring hospital treatment. One took a handful of tablets and hopefully soldiered on. Jungle sores and severe throat infections were common, betokening lowered resistance. In the last six weeks we were sending back an average of 18 sick a week, and about that number of wounded".

On the 24th, in the pre-dawn of 0330 hrs, we turned our backs on Mandalay and commenced an easy ten-mile march on that asphalted road to a camp site south of Ava. A floating Bailey bridge gave us an easy crossing of the Myitnge River and we were soon enjoying our breakfast. Our quartermasters and all who carried the burden of administration, made up for lost time during pauses such as this whilst we awaited orders. The 'I' Section had time to sort and issue a batch of maps, covering a chunk of Burma south of that loop in the Irrawaddy where we had crossed and further to the south west, past where the Chindwin had become a tributary,

An important event was the issue of beer. Having just written about the problem of our ever lengthening 'tail', to get such a heavy and bulky consignment seems beyond belief. For some time I had been making derogatory remarks about beer as a drink, with the result that a number of hopefuls imagined that I would be only too ready to part with my three bottles. Thus my decision to drink them was not well received. Never had I, or would I in the future, enjoy beer so much. It was almost certainly tepid, yet it went down with a tingling freshness which did us a power of good.

It was at 0730 hrs on the 27th, that a fleet of trucks shifted us 60 miles south west to near Myingyan, a place of local importance on the south bank of the Irrawaddy, opposite the mouth of the Chindwin. Initially the road was in the central plain and parallel with a branch line of Burma Railways, both passing through Myotha, the town at the end of the road from Kyauktalon. There and in that country, 20 Div. had carried out a great slaughter of the Japanese and, by so doing, had greatly assisted us.

As can be expected it was a hot and dusty ride that, after 15 miles, made its way into those scrub covered hills through which we had toiled on our way to Sinde and Kadozeik. And it was in such hills that we were to remain.

28th March – 3rd April

Our move had been a part of one by 4 and 5 Brigades, who would advance together along the long road which, after another 80 miles, reached the oil fields of Yenangyaung. Also on the road was the town of Kyaukpadaung, at the latitude of Meiktila, the two linked by an east/west road. Kyaukpadaung and the massif, Mount Popa, between us and it, were reckoned to be bastions of Japanese resistance.

We were briefly to renew our acquaintance with 7 Div., our old allies at Kohima. They had made their assault crossing of the Irrawaddy downriver near Pagan, on the 13th and 14th of February, a horror story of sinking and drifting boats, and of disaster averted by the bravery of the British and Indian troops involved. They had then prepared to move east for Meiktila, south for Chauk (known for its oil fields) and, more importantly for us, north east for Myingyan – strongly held by the Japs, but captured by them ten days prior to our arrival, by which time work was in hand on the repair of wharves, for the town was ideally situated for receiving supplies shipped down the Chindwin. On the 29th we moved back to be much closer and take over the defence of the town from a battalion of 7 Div. On the following day there was a further change and we moved again, for we were to occupy the high ground on which were three villages with the singular names of Thamongaing, Paunggo and Ywathaponywa. We did not grieve when their inhabitants cheerfully reported that the enemy we had arrived to eject, had departed!

That check to our progress ended at 0645 hrs on the 2nd April, when we embussed to be conveyed 35 miles, generally, and I use that word because we moved in a right-handed semi-circle, in the direction that we were required to go. For the last ten miles or so we bumped along on a 'motorable in dry season' track, finally taking up a position to the west of the village of Welaung. We were then 30 miles up the road from Kyaukpadaung, but only 20 from Mount Popa, which was to prove to be our final destination.

After our arrival the Battalion was, as formally as the circumstances allowed, given a Commanding Officer's address; in which Geoffry advised us that 2 Div. would be flying out from the present scene of operations, preparatory to taking up a new role in the support of 14th Army. The order of our going being that 6 Brigade and Divisional HQ would depart first, followed by 4 Brigade and finally our own. We further learned that we would be making for a camp in the Calcutta area. This was news that swamped all else and which made our immediate role seem trivial. Discussion, in which speculation on the matter of repatriation was prominent (it was just three years since we sailed from Liverpool), occupied all minds.

We had been forewarned to expect the arrival of members of the Indian National Army wishing to surrender, and by last light on the 3rd we had received a total of 39, seven of whom 'C' Company had collected and which were found to be members of their 2nd Division.

During the day we had progressed a dozen miles down the road, to within two miles of Legyi, a place around which the road encircled to the east and which was of a size sufficient to warrant a phongyi kyaung, a monastery, and pagoda. However our attention was not directed at its architecture but at the resident Japs, who had resisted a full-blooded attack by the Camerons.

4th and 5th April

At first light a party of 36 members of the I.N.A., one of whom was the adjutant of their 1st Battalion, came marching smartly up the road and into our lines and halted. We had no feeling of hostility and kept them only long enough to organise their onward progress to the rear, to which they were soon on their way.

Ahead the Camerons were still involved and the Worcesters had been put round on a tight right hook, to a position at the Japs' left rear. Mike West then decided to install us astride the road south of the Worcesters and, at 0900 hrs, we set off on a wider hook to a position one and a half miles beyond Legyi.

For the first time for ages I was back in my jeep and enjoying the effortless progress of that remarkable vehicle across difficult country. We considered ourselves accustomed to tough going, but now it was so bad as to defeat our tanks. A world of steep-sided hills, separated by deep ravines, the whole generously covered with scrub and black rock outcrops. Trees and shade were almost non-existent. We found the rock so prevalent, that in some defensive positions digging was impossible, causing us to resort to sangars – 'U' shaped breastworks of stones, as used in Indian hill-fighting along the border with Afghanistan. We lacked the time to do them well, providing only indifferent above-ground protection, and a firing position for two men.

During our 12-mile walk we had steadily crossed contours, widely spaced at first and then closer together, particularly when we crossed a spur from a 1,300 ft. tangled mass of high ground to our left. Then more broken ground, the road dropping at times, but generally climbing. To our right, almost to Legyi, was a major tributary of the Irrawaddy, the Sindewa Chaung, dry, as were the many feeder streams at right angles to our route. As our road progressed deeper into these sun-scorched hills, so it twisted and turned and we had to be ever vigilant.

Legyi sits within a 150 ft. escarpment, facing north east and able to dominate the road to the north. Once having passed around to the south we were on a plateau with hillocks of 50 feet or so, and could observe a reasonably straight and level road for over half a mile. Beyond we could discern rising ground. We were to see no signs of the Japs, either during the move or while we accommodated ourselves astride the road, doing so with 'A' Company on the right of it and

Battalion HQ and HQ Company behind. To the left we had 'C' on one of the hillocks and 'D' similarly placed. Behind was 'B'. Our objective was to prevent the Japs in Legyi from being relieved or reinforced, and should they try and make an exit down the road, we would do our best to stop them. We were fortunate in being on ground that enabled many of us to dig in.

That night there were periods of intense activity in the darkness, from which we were thankful to survive. My version is based on a pencilled letter, started at 0630 hrs, before it became too hot, dated 6th April.

All was quiet until 2215 hrs when five vehicles were observed coming towards us from the south, doing so with every appearance of being oblivious of us. When the leading vehicle was within our lines, Bren-gun fire was directed at it and its occupants killed. Probably the truck was deliberately far ahead of the others, but the trap was sprung too soon and the remaining four were able to escape and report our presence.

Then a party of Japs got into our lines from Legyi and the remainder of the night was punctuated with bangs, mainly exploding grenades, as both sides chucked them where they presumed they would do most good. Added to this was enemy artillery fire, giving its quota of noise. I was not on duty and therefore had no 'phone, but it was very obvious what was happening, during a long night which eventually subsided into a semi-quietness.

This engagement is the one when we were forcibly introduced to the high velocity, low-trajectory anti-tank gun, directed against our forward positions. To be at the receiving end of shells which struck ahead of, or coincidental with, the firing of the gun, so that there was no precious second in which to flatten oneself as with conventional artillery, (where the sound of the gun precedes the explosion), stressed overstrained nerves beyond their limits on that God-forsaken arid slope. Some forward positions became untenable and had to be abandoned and reformed, as could be best managed within the shelter of a rock or slope. Despite these horrors, fortune was again on our side, for we did not have the heavy casualties that could have resulted, had not their artillery been largely firing blind, or had they had the men or the necessary determination to mount an infantry assault.

The following is from a member of one of those forward companies:

> I knew that I was running a temperature and feared a malaria relapse, that and the 'Naga' sores and 'foot-rot' was making life a misery. In the night we were awakened by the sound of trucks, headlamps full-on coming up the road. Everybody opened fire, but at least one truck escaped and many of the troops did also. As the Japs deployed we could hear their feet slipping on the shale as they climbed the ridge. My mate and I decided we would use our '36' and '77' grenades if we could hear several coming, or wait with bayonets if only one, we had to make our grenades last. The ridge we were on was solid rock and there was no chance of digging-in, so it was our only protection. At one time in the night we threw two '77s' and heard them yelling, thankfully we did not have to use the bayonets. Towards dawn we heard a series of explosions down the road. It was five Japs, of whom one was an officer and one a sergeant, committing seppuko suicide. We went down to look at them lying in a culvert.

Back on the ridge they were having breakfast but I wasn't hungry but, oh! that hot sweet tea was a Godsend and, as the heat came up from the rocks, I found that I was getting double vision. Suddenly there was a terrific explosion and lumps of rock (as large as bricks) came down and we were showered with dust. We had no warning of the coming shell. everybody scattered and sought what little protection there was from further shelling and we received casualties. The concussion was tremendous and we had to stay ten feet, at least, below the crest for protection.

Coming up from the rear were two officers, Captain Main and Lieutenant Overman who was leading and who said, "Why are you not up there?" I explained the situation and that we were checking every now and then, that all was well. He casually strode up to the top of the ridge in full view and deliberately walked around the top – the gesture was obvious. As he came down he jerked his thumb and said, "Get back up." His voice was full of contempt. I was feeling pretty awful by then and had had enough. I said we are not going up there to become bloody Aunt-Sallys. He looked at me, then without a word turned and walked away. John Main had said nothing.

Despite the heat, I had started to shiver and the double vision was increasing, with a bad headache. Some time later a sergeant came up to me and said, "The C.O. wants you." I thought, now I'm for it. I don't remember reaching the Colonel's tent but the sergeant bade me enter. I thought – what no left-right, left-right, caps off. As I entered the C.O. was sitting at a small table by which were two folding chairs, with his head in both hands, looking at some papers. He looked up and I was surprised to see how tired he looked. There was no anger in his face or that stern look he could give – just tired.

I remember he asked me how I felt, but I do not remember the conversation, only that he kept on having two faces. Eventually I stood up but could not feel my legs. I thought I was going to fall over the table. he put his hand out and said, "Stand still!" Calling the sergeant he said, "Take him to Joe!" I remember sitting in Joe's tent and he taking my temperature and rolling up my eyelids and then travelling in a truck with others being hospitalised.

They gave me seven days 'twilight sleep' and treated me with quinine, silver nitrate for my feet, sulphanilamide tablets and powder for the sores, plus a drip for dehydration. I was said to be suffering from war neurosis and was downgraded to B.1. Permanent. It was only then that I realised that I had not been charged with disobeying an order.

The shrewd and understanding judgment of Geoffry White, was a side of the Colonel that most people did not see. I'm glad I did!

Back at Legyi the Japs remained encircled by the Worcesters and the Camerons, and it was to be four more days before the Camerons were able to put in an attack and clear the village.

Unknown to us, 6 Brigade and Divisional HQ had flown out to India. And I was reading Angela Thirkell's 'The Headmistress', and also escaping to a very different world.

For some days we had been aware that ahead was Mount Popa*, the apex of which, at 4,801 ft., was about three miles east of the road, when we had travelled

* Now, 45 years or so later, how strange it is that this extinct volcano is one of the few areas of Burma to which tourists go, encouraged no doubt by its description as the 'Olympus' of Burma, a holy place and a centre for spirit worship.

a further six miles or so. Our maps showed large areas of green (for jungle) over the lower slopes, a combination that reminded us of the road south of Kohima, as did the warning that it was thickly populated by Japs. But, unlike those Naga Hills, a scattering of pagodas was also shown within the wider contours and on minor peaks.

On that morning we received orders to explore along the road used by the Jap trucks, and to do so to the cultivated ground west of the village of Myauktaw, situated half a mile to the east of the road, at a distance to our front of three miles. At the same time we were to cover a further mile on the west flank of the road, halting at a phongyi kyaung. Accordingly, 'A' and 'D' Companies advanced on their respective sides, doing so over very difficult going which typified the place – hillocks, rocks and scrub. This was movement over open ground on a line of advance that must have been so anticipated by our opponents, as to make them doubt that we would take it. But to have left that road would have added to the mileage without providing better cover and, to get forward by the easiest route, made sense when facing into that fierce sun. And it paid off, for we had covered most of the distance when, at 1230 hrs, 'A' reported enemy positions on a hillock that was of sufficient size to warrant a ring contour, further movement at a pagoda beyond, and more movement to the east of the road. Paget dispatched a patrol to the ring contour, only to find that two enemy sections were endeavouring to outflank them and, rather than engage in a scrappy shooting match, they returned to report. Artillery fire was provided and the Japs reacted to the shelling, as we had hoped they might, by running away. On the left 'D' Company moved steadily forward and found their objective clear.

6th – 11th April

We passed these days in not doing anything of great consequence, other than patrolling. We had to endure the heat from a sun that, after early morning, blazed down with an increasing intensity, made worse by the Biblical wilderness around. During the evening of the 6th, two 105mm guns and one '75 fired on us and the Worcesters, continuing to do so up to last light, fire that was erratic and did no harm. The shelling was repeated for a second evening, and 'A' Company suffered casualties, one of whom was Private Oscroft who was killed. At the same time the attached company of Manchesters had one of their guns knocked out and its crew of four wounded. Our artillery replied, but the thick country ahead and around the village of Popa, where the enemy guns were believed to be, made their pin-pointing impossible.

A platoon of 'C' Company was detached away to our right for half a mile and, on the 8th, the company as a whole was established there. On that day, Gerry Overman took a patrol to the village of Gwedaukkon, two miles to the west of our road, finding it clear of Japs, although a recce patrol during the morning had 'bumped' six Japs in that area. While at the village, Gerry was told that Japs were in the habit of going there to fill their water-bottles.

Just before last light, on the other side of the road, 'Fish' Mullet and his platoon from 'D' Company set out to establish an ambush where a track ran south from Legyi, providing the Japs in that place with an escape route; a move that preceded a successful, early morning assault on Legyi by the Camerons, during which our mortars assisted with the covering fire. That clearance opened our road to traffic, of which the most important was the tanks. The ambush, like so many, was not put to the test.

Away to the west Gerry Overman continued his activities and later on that day when Legyi was taken, he started out with a second patrol to Gwedaukkon and set up an ambush. Having done so he took four men and moved south of the village to where the ground rose to a pagoda area and, when only a few yards away, realised that Japs were freely moving about within the group of buildings. By then he must have been bitterly regretting that he had only four lightly armed men for, there in front of them, sitting beneath a raised building and out of the sun, were 50 or 60 Japs. And, as they watched, they could see that other Japs were passing to and from a small basha, obviously in use as a cook-house. Amongst all these they identified three officers. This once-in-a-lifetime opportunity was not to be missed, notwithstanding their inadequate numbers, and they opened fire with one Tommy-gun, three Stens and a rifle, doing so directly into the enemy, some of whom were at a distance of only a few yards. Many, including an officer, were seen to fall. Then two Jap sentries, on high ground to the east, opened fire on them, but Gerry was able to throw a grenade into the basha, in which he believed were five Japs. Then he and his party pulled out at high speed, having emptied their magazines.

Later they were able to interrogate some locals, who said there were 600 Japs in their stretch of country to the south, and that they were in the habit of eating their meals and drawing water at that group of building. The patrol claimed 25 enemy killed or wounded.

The area in which the Japs were said to be was subjected to artillery fire.

Next morning, the 10th, Snagger Highett and his Defence Platoon set off at 0530 hrs, guided by a local so that they might reach the area of suspected enemy occupation south of Gwedaukkon. There they met up with Japs and exchanged fire, claiming ten casualties. During a lull, two of the patrol spotted four Japs sitting with their backs to them; they succeeded in crawling up on them and killing all four. The patrol returned at 0820 hrs.

The following day, at the earlier hour of 0445, John O'Donnel set out with an 'A' Company patrol to the high point on our map of 1,481 ft., a distance of one and a half miles to the north west. Passing over and dropping down from a 50 foot contour, they then climbed something over 100 feet to that isolated high point, to the west of which the ground fell 300 feet into a major nullah, which had a source at the apex of Mount Popa. As on previous days the locals were plentiful and very willing to give information, saying that our shelling of yesterday had inflicted casualties as had been intended. No Japs were found, although a group was said to be not far away to the north.

12th and 13th April

We had received orders that on the 12th, the Battalion was to advance from the general level of the plateau, of which Legyi was at the northern fringe, to the steeply rising and very broken ground preceding the much higher plateau, in which are the villages of Popalon and Popa.

Initially it was a closing up of our 'tail' on the forward companies, but the Battalion was to advance along the most hazardous section of the route, for which we had the support of a troop of tanks, a troop of the 10th Field Regt. and the 498 Battery with 6-inch howitzers, big guns at last. 'A' and 'D' Companies moved off at 0600 hrs and 'B' and 'C' 30 minutes later. We were then at and forward of milestone 412; with ahead an immediate rise in the road of 150 feet, a levelling out before a further 200 feet of climb, another pause and a final 300 feet or so. That last climb was on a snake-like section of road, for it crossed the water courses and intervening spurs of the north west fringe of the mountain, rising high into the sky above our left shoulders. This was something not seen since Tamu, and with our preference for progressing on level, or near-level, ground, we were not terribly keen on it.

Since Welaung we had been on a road with those all-important milestones, Welaung being near milestone 430, which was the distance to Rangoon. On roads so lacking in road junctions, traversing country so lacking in distinctive features, they provided an indisputable reference point.

We were soon passing through the roadside village of Kyauktaga, with its phongyi kyaung, and another mile and a quarter took us to the village of Gyaingywa, our objective and just short of milestone 410. This was one of a group of villages sheltering under the flank of the Popa massif.

It had been fully appreciated that this rising ground would be defended, hence the tanks and guns. During the latter stages of our approach we had seen both defences and enemy to the east of Gyaingywa, which our artillery had shelled. Then 'B' Company observed further movement and bunkers, on to which they directed tank fire, as a result of which they were approached by the occupants of the bunkers – an I.N.A. officer, who surrendered himself and his company of 33 other ranks.

That high ground was the western extremity of a steep-sided detached hill, in the nature of an outpost to Mount Popa, rising 500 feet above us. A place of importance to the Burmese for, within the upper contour were phongyi kyaungs, doubtless so placed that they would only be visited by devotees. We at HQ settled for the night on a low spur running north from the hill and terminating close to the road. With us was 'D' Company.

After a quiet but damp night, for our arrival had coincided with a tropical storm, we had our breakfast and continued our advance with 'A' and 'C' leading, their objective being the high plateau. 'B' Company was doing a shorter move to the village of Ngayangon, just south of Gyaingywa, which they found to be clear but destroyed by shelling. 'A' and 'C' reached the top and there 'A' came under fire from two machine-guns. On the road the tanks were progressing, covered by 'D' and when nearly half-way up the final hill they reported an enemy road-block, sited at a culvert over a water-course. With the ground rising steeply on the left of the road and similarly falling on the right, and the block covered by fire, it was the type of barrier we had been anticipating. Then one of the tanks ran over a 250 kilo aerial bomb, buried in the road 300 yards forward of the block, and was destroyed; thankfully the crew escaped.

Clive and his company soon came under fire and suffered a couple of casualties. 'C' Company were by then on high ground above the road-block, and reported it as held by between 20 and 30 Japs. With the road now doubly blocked we were in danger of becoming embroiled with well sited and defended positions, and just prior to our departure, Brigadier Mike West ordered us to pull back our leading companies and sit tight.

When Geoffry and I, our signallers and our escort, moved forward that morning we did so through thinly wooded and pleasant countryside. The sun was shining, but within the trees and before the fierce heat of the day our progress, after a climb, was easy and agreeable over level ground and all was quiet. Suddenly, that quietness was broken by the sound of our guns away to our rear, opening rapid fire. That was followed by the scream of the shells passing above our heads and their muffled crumps as they exploded ahead out of sight. Possibly because that was to be the last time that I was to be in such a situation, it remains clear in my memory; the tingling of my blood as it coursed through my veins, the thrill of that moment. Those guns, on which above all of our supporting arms we depended the most, were traditionally objects of esteem and affection. It was they that epitomized the British Army in its glory. One thinks, in particular, of the 25-pounders and their crews, often stripped to the waist and enveloped in smoke and dust, they had a grim and unmatched splendour.

This was a time when we could leave it to the gunners to maintain the pressure. Another 13 I.N.A. surrendered.

14th – 22nd April

On the 14th, at the uncivilised hour of 0020, four 105mm guns commenced firing into our brigade area and after one and a half hours were estimated to have off-loaded 150 rounds. Our casualties were one, although 'C' Company had many near misses, some being close enough to destroy a number of packs.

By then 4 Brigade had departed for India and we were preparing an advance party under Mervyn, whose job was to have a camp ready for us at an as yet undesignated place near Calcutta, and they left on the 17th for their fly-out.

Next day Mike West addressed us, making it clear that 5 Brigade would only go when we had opened the road through to Popa. It is never easy to regenerate a forward motion once halted, under any conditions, and he had checked us at the road-block. Then, when so near the end of our 'road' and in a place where we were enjoying shade, we were very ready to sit back and 'let the world go by', knowing that we were the lucky ones, the privileged survivors, and we desired to remain so.

Later that day, Geoffry went off to have a look at the high plateau from a light plane, and I think that it was that afternoon when the office trailer had its last session of bridge.

For once the Japs were well provided with artillery, but as they were trapped, they naturally wished to use up their ammunition. We were well into our game when Jap shells started passing overhead, doing so with a peculiar sound as if they were being lobbed and were turning end over end in flight. This was big stuff and their explosions on landing were impressive in their dark red flame and black smoke. Having my back to the guns, I had only to raise my eyes from my 'hand' to see the flame and smoke. This was a frustrating occasion when we were trying so very hard to finish the rubber, which we had begun before the shelling started. Eventually Graeme said, "I cannot, as Adjutant, continue playing bridge while the Battalion is under fire." And that was the end of that. At the time we had believed that the shells were landing just beyond our lines, but we did have casualties of whom, I believe, Dicky Boyle was one.

While we were finishing our war (although we did not know so at the time), much was happening elsewhere, for bold moves were taking the Indian Army forward in their drive on Rangoon. By mid-April, the 5th, 17th and 19th Divisions were advancing south, along that main road and railway we had seen at Mandalay, and were approaching the town of Toungoo, less that 200 miles north of Rangoon. The 7th and the 20th Divisions were to our south, 7 Div. being at Padan and 20 Div. further east, both making for Prome, on the Irrawaddy. Thus the Japs were facing a two-pronged onslaught.

But, of more immediate interest to us, was the fact that 268 Brigade was coming up towards Popa from the south.

During those static days, we had been planning operations against the Japs in the villages of Popalon and Popa, (there was talk of popping along to Popalon), to take place on the 22nd. We were to be in the lead and have the Camerons in support. Consequently, we were delighted when, on the 20th, the Headman of Popa arrived. Very obviously dressed for the occasion in a newly laundered longyi, he handed Geoffry a note, one we assumed had been written for him. It commenced with the news that all the Japs had run away and ended with the warm welcome: "We are wondering your troops to come". In between was the dire warning: "All roads have with explosive take carre".

Thus we were able to set off on that last advance, without having to battle our way forward. However, precautions had to be taken, and Gerry Overman departed on a last patrol to what we knew as 'Black Rocks', a prominent feature above and to the east of the Japs' road-block. Its many trenches were sited to cover the road and it was thought desirable that Tommy Tucker should follow, taking with him one of his platoons and our Glosters. A second 'C' platoon joined 'B' Company as tank escort as they moved up the road, behind sappers who were searching for mines. As they closed on the road-block, they located and removed a further six bombs buried in the road. An accompanying bulldozer set about removing the large rocks that blocked the road, and the column continued, warily, on to the plateau. 'B' Company pressed on and reached Popalon and then covered the further mile to Popa, where the Battalion congregated and set about digging a defensible position.

Our arrival was soon followed by that of a battalion of 268 Brigade, and the road was declared to be open. 5 Brigade had completed its task.

We were soon examining the first of many abandoned vehicles from staff cars to trucks, and weapons which included three Vickers machine-guns. This was some of the jetsam in and around two villages, grievously damaged by our shelling and by air-strikes.

All this and the abandonment of well prepared and maintained positions, made it clear that these Japs had indeed had enough. And, of course, their reluctant henchmen the I.N.A., were only too ready to surrender when circumstances permitted. Retreats and surrenders that our artillery was encouraging to the limit of its capability. Good work in which a troop of 6-inch howitzers, behind my trench, joined in a display of rapid fire, which really did deafen, and the blast from those barrels caused the loose stony ground to fly like shrapnel.

Next morning, well before breakfast, the 'I' Section was en route to where locals said that Japanese guns had operated. In a deep-sided chaung, tucked into the south west flank of the mountain and secure against anything but a direct hit, were four guns, two of which were 150mm – their largest field guns, and probably those that ended our rubber of bridge. Also there were vehicles which included half a dozen British and American cars, all thoroughly immobilized. Such booty was of no interest for, prior to our departure, we had to shed all but those things that were legitimately ours, and which had been included in the manifest; thus most, if not all, of our vehicles were about to be eagerly snapped up by Indian units.

There was time to wander and I did so, going east of the villages to look up at one of the four Buddhist shrines, sited in splendid isolation on the peaks of small editions of the mountain, steep pinnacle hills hundreds of feet in height. There, against the sky and just visible was a pagoda, approached by a flight of steps, which for its unbroken length and steepness was unlike anything I had seen. I gazed upwards, being fascinated and intrigued by this example of a culture of which I knew nothing; deterred from the ascent, in part because of the physical effort, but more from a reluctance to intrude into a place seemingly undefiled.

During our last day, the 22nd, a final Battalion memorial service was held, enabling us to give thanks for the miracle of our survival.

Inclusive of Lance-Corporal Nursaw, the first to die in that so distant an April a year ago, and Private Elford who had died two weeks before, 155 died on the battlefields, or in hospital of wounds or disease. A few of the injured, of whom Roger Johnson was one, were to reach Blighty, for which we all had so great a hunger, and then succumb.

23rd – 25th April

We had finished our breakfast when trucks appeared and, in the same way that we had paraded and packed ourselves into trucks at Dimapur, so we embussed at Popa, then to speed north to an assembly area at Myingyan, retracing our route along that dusty road over which we had made such slow progress. Our eyes opened wide at the sight of Churchill tanks going south and I thought how very typical – the modern machinery of war, of which we had been deprived, was arriving as we departed.

A day of waiting followed, but on the 25th we moved to the air-strip and were directed to the emplaning bays. The sight of General Stopford looking, as always, so reassuringly British, there to say farewell with a smile and a thank you, was an unexpected bonus at this moment of departure from the Burma soil with which we had been so much in contact.

Soon our stores had been loaded into the planes allocated for that purpose, and we were climbing into familiar Dakotas. Then we were air-borne and seeing, far below, what was to be our last view of Burma, as we made our way to Hathazari, north of Chittagong.

Joe Chamberlin writes:

Happily it was the turn of fresher troops to take over the mopping up of the Japanese, and we did not resent exchanging the spectacular beauty of Mount Popa and its Buddhist eyrie, for a Dakota view of the Irrawaddy and the Chindwin, vanishing behind us.

EPILOGUE

Hathazari was followed by Bandel, to the north of Calcutta, reached after two days by boat and by train. There we commenced our rehabilitation. In early June the division moved to basha camps near Kamareddi, 60 miles to the north of Secunderabad and it was there that we who were due for repatriation lived until our departure from India.

Following the Japanese surrender, a reformed 5 Brigade was chosen as the British element within the occupational force; a brigade in which the Worcesters were replaced by the 2nd Royal Welch Fusiliers.* However, 150 Worcester reinforcements became Dorsets, as did 400 from the 10th Glosters. Thus there became two Dorsets, one under Colonel White destined for Japan and a second, comprising those awaiting their return to civilian life. We, those repats., embarked at Bombay on October 29, and disembarked at Southampton on November 15, 1945, doing so to the music of the Regimental Band. A day that was concluded at the Regimental Depot, from where so many had sallied forth.

It was not until April 23, 1946, that 5 Brigade under Brigadier Jock McNaught arrived at Kurie, Japan. There to commence duties that lasted until February 1947. Service in Malaya followed and it was only on January 3, 1948, that 2 Dorset arrived at Dorchester. Three days later, the 54th Regiment of Foot marched with bayonets fixed and colours flying to a final parade on the Depot square.

For ten years the Dorsets continued in being, through the 1st Battalion, and the 250th aniversary of the raising of the 39th Regiment was celebrated in Vienna, where they then were. Service in Hong Kong and Korea followed, before a final return to Europe, in 1954. It was at Minden in Germany, on May 21, 1958, that they, the 39th Regiment of Foot, amalgamated with the 11th, our neighbours the Devons, to form the Devonshire and Dorset Regiment.

Farewell.

*This battalion was from the 29 Inf. Bde. Gp of 36 Division.

The Dorsets Home from Burma.

APPENDIX A

Albany Barracks

I go back to 1940 and to three months with the Hampshire Regiment on the Isle of Wight. It was 13th June when 200 recruits, of which I was one, arrived at Albany Barracks, near Newport, there to be kitted out, injected for typhoid and typhus (the start of many similar jabs) and then to commence the busy routine of eight parades a day. This ordered state was to last barely three weeks, for it was then that the Luftwaffe, regrouped after their victories in France, opened what became the Battle of Britain, with attacks on our shipping and the southern ports, of which Southampton and Portsmouth were to our north. From then on, aerial battles and bombing became customary and we were outraged at the intrusion over our fair country by the hated Germans, who killed and maimed all whose misfortune it was to get in their way. Their brutality and contempt for the rights of others, and particularly those of Poland, awakened an enmity and an anger of the German war machine not known since that earlier war, which we had believed to be the last. . . .

As a minute cog in the defence forces, we began night sessions (between 2100 hrs and 0600 hrs) in and outside the town of Newport. In pairs, we halted pedestrians, cars and buses, one covering the other with his loaded rifle at the ready. His companion, with rifle slung on his left shoulder so that he could wield his bayonet right-handed, examined the civilian identity cards by the light of a 'red' hurricane lamp – a dicey job at best with only two hands, and more so on the buses, which we had to board, the passengers looking justifiably alarmed at the probability of being shot, impaled on a bayonet or set on fire – perhaps all three! We for our part, were embarrassed at our own obvious incompetence. Duty was in shifts of two hours, operating from bases one of which was a mission hall, and using road barriers to control traffic. All individual without identity cards (and there were always some) were handed over to the police. Some weeks later on a moonless night when invasion seemed imminent and we were doing duty at our Area HQ, I 'waved down' a staff car returning at high speed. I waved my lamp with such enthusiasm that it went out, and ticklish moments followed while I rekindled the wick, after borrowing a cigarette lighter from the car's occupant, an apparently apoplectic Brigadier! He seemed of the opinion (and who can blame him!) that it was not only decent equipment that was lacking for the defence of Britain. Fortunately, he had his identity card with him.

But we were about to return to some 'real soldering', beloved by the regulars – a kit and barrack room inspection. Preparation for this first time ordeal occupied the platoon for five hours of the preceding evening, my part being the scraping and sandpapering of our broom handles which, it would seem, had to appear unused.

A letter dated 13 July refers to three lots of trench digging during the week, for which we marched out in full kit, to dig like blazes in solid chalk which came out like loose rock. The same letter asks my mother if she could post me something to eat every five days, slab cake being one suggestion. . . . We were now confined to barracks because of the flap, and the much enjoyed visits to a café down the road specialising in the feeding of famished soldiers with lavish helpings of fried eggs, bacon and fried bread, all swimming in fat, had ceased, and we suffered accordingly. However, on the 31st we were allowed out again, and continued with the digging – we boasted of doing the two and a half miles from the barracks to trench in 30 minutes. A Sunday canteen at Newport Drill Hall provided teas for soldiers for the nominal sum of 4d – one could eat as much as one wished.

The transition from the freedoms of the civilian world to the rigid régime of our training centre was only made tolerable by getting back to the former whenever we could, mainly Newport and West Cowes, towns to which we were restricted. Not places rich in temptation, but certainly we in our platoon of potential officers were more concerned with recharging our batteries for the testing days that lay ahead than chancing anything that might impair our reaching OCTU. Our prime objectives when funds permitted were the self-indulgence of a restaurant with the luxury of service and peace and quiet in a world of tablecloths and upholstered chairs; and the wonderful cinema which provided three hours of escape from reality even with the possibility of an all too familiar notice flashing on the screen recalling troops to barracks. . . .

From noon on Saturday weekends were free of parades, other than those to church, which only started when we were considered sufficiently smart, four weeks after our arrival. But we could be confined to barracks on duties such as fire picket, or fatigues. One Sunday cook house fatigue lasted from 0900 to 1500 hrs, during which we cut up hundreds of cabbages, scrubbed the floors and tables, worked the potato peeler and finally laid tables for tea. Interesting! Although we did not think so at the time.

Commissioned officers played no part in our day-to-day routine, which was governed by the Platoon Sergeants, of whom I remember Jones and Prescott – how excellent they were. They guided, cajoled, inspired and, when necessary, bullied us into a competence in the basic infantry skills. So different from the NCOs portrayed in print and on film.

At noon on 12th August while on a 24-hour exercise, we had a not too close view of the dive-bombing of the radar masts on St Catherine's Point, called wireless masts, radar being unknown other than to those who were directly involved. The angry red of exploding 500 kilo bombs with which the JU88s were bombing our airfields and radar stations brought the conflict closer than anything had done previously. Later we were to take our turn at manning the Bren-gun anti-aircraft defences of those tall lattice structures. Standing among their bases, we were aware that they were different from anything we had seen before and we wondered if, as rumoured, they really did emit 'death rays'.

Three days later at about noon, following a warning, we were interrupted from our map reading study by a plane skimming the roof as it machine-gunned the barracks.

Then there was another, and we dashed to the air raid shelters, where we sensed the bullets striking their turf covering.

We had seven air-raid warnings in 24 hours, a reflection of the intensity of the battle, then at its peak. In that desperate week 134 of our fighter planes were lost in combat, the German losses in fighters and bombers as recorded by them being 261.

Next day, the 16th, we were again in our hut in the late morning during a raid warning, when the platoon sergeant put his head around the door and shouted – "Get your ammo and get outside!" That we did in quick time and made for our shelter, by then crowded. Soon some of us made our way back to the entrance and joined a group that had gathered within the enclosing earth walls and, to ease the crush, three of us were directed to a similar sheltered hollow behind the barracks. There, in a stunned silence, we watched a raid over Gosport, where the air seemed full of planes. Shell bursts from our anti-aircraft guns intermingled with flaming barrage balloons descending into clouds of smoke rising from the ground. Planes manoeuvring and in conflict above our heads, their engines roaring, at times to a high pitched shriek as they twisted and dived, linked us to the awesome scene; as did the acrid smell and the louder sounds of battle. This had slowly waned when there was a shout of, "Here they come!" and three enemy fighters, hugging the ground in a dash for the Channel and home, approached a little to our right, giving me just time to swivel round, rest my rifle on a sandbag wall and fire one aimed shot a little ahead of the last plane. I later described this as 'like shooting at the side of a house', so close were they. And in those split seconds, all our Brens on their anti-aircraft mountings, waiting for such a moment, opened up, before the Germans were lost to view behind adjacent buildings. Later, we heard that one of the three, a Messerschmitt 109, crashed a mile or two to the south. The firing of that shot gave me immense satisfaction, being a positive gesture of my fierce hatred for those desecrators of our country.

That was not the first time that we had been below planes in combat, hearing the chilling rattle of machine-guns as they fought, both for their lives and also for ours.

Two mornings later I was awakened at 0445 hrs and told to be ready to move, in fighting order, at 0600 hrs. I found myself to be one of 12 taken by truck to a subterranean magazine, there to load 800 anti-aircraft shells into lorries. They were two to a case, each handled by a pair of us up 23 steps, which we took at a run and then slung our load into the vehicles at as fast a rate as space and strength allowed. Some, at least, of these cases weighed 125 lbs., presumably containing the 55 lb. 4.5-inch shells of the naval guns used for the protection of naval ports, and surprisingly different from the 28 lb. shell of the more general 3.7-inch gun. This was done to a background of gun fire, which gave an urgency to the task, making us feel that we were part of the battle. Departing lorries took one of us as an armed escort.

The following night we were on a 24-hour guard to a crashed German fighter.

Then we were in the country felling trees, ready for road-blocks.

The identification from aerial photographs of 3,000 self-propelled barges gathered along the Dutch, Belgian and French coasts, combined with favourable moon and tide conditions caused the Chiefs of Staff to conclude that there was a strong possibility of invasion before the onset of the equinoctial gales. By 4th September attack was considered as probably within three days. During that time increased activity was observed and on the 7th, at 2000 hrs, the code word CROMWELL – invasion imminent, was issued as an order to the Southern and Eastern Commands for the manning of their action stations in coastal area. It was repeated elsewhere for information only.

Some over-zealous Home Guard commanders called out their men by ringing church bells, an action that must have given them a thrill and a feeling of self-importance, but by so doing they had used an extreme measure which was reserved for use only when parachutists had been seen landing. As can be imagined they produced considerable confusion, many people being convinced that the enemy had landed.

We knew nothing of this when called from our beds at 2215 hrs and ordered to dress and be ready to move. Some, thinking it was a stunt to see how quickly we could parade, just but their battledress over pyjamas. We paraded in full kit and were rushed off, by coach, to our trench system which was designated a 'forward defence locality' despite it being just east of Carisbrooke Castle and thus well back from the coast, but being on high ground it provided a fine view of the Channel. Any German up above would have had a fine view of us, for our trench with a parapet and parados, in the tradition of World War I, had no top cover or camouflage nets and would have been like a white gash within the grass. We returned to barracks at mid-morning and then marched out again that evening, manning the trench for nine consecutive nights. After a few days we were given a couple of tents, having until then obtained shelter and some flat ground to lie on within an open-fronted cattle shed. Part of the time I was an acting Section Commander, a job I also had during some of our guard duties. I remember having coffee and a cake one evening, in a house where a young couple with a child were displaying a brave face in a very worrying situation. It was as well that they had no idea how inadequately we were armed. We had our rifles which we had fired on the range and we each had 50 rounds of ammunition. We also had an anti-tank rifle, from which we each fired one round. This was the Boys anti-tank weapon, a typically useless British product of the parsimonious 30's, used by the unfortunate Abyssinians with some success against the third rate Italian armoured cars, but not something with which to face a German tank. I have no recollection of us having a Bren-gun, or of firing one on the range. We did have a 2-inch mortar but no bombs, neither had we seen any. One should not forget that we had our bayonets, the long bladed variety with which we had attacked dummies, learning not to drive them into Germans above the belt because of their tendency to become wedged between ribs. Our deficiencies in weapons would have been worse than the average, being recruits of low priority when so much was needed to make good the losses in France, and to equip the expanding services.

A rumour was circulating that the bodies of German soldiers were being washed up on our beaches and from this, it became a general belief that a landing had been foiled by the Royal Navy.

> Subsequently, this period has been described as probably the time of most acute danger faced by our country throughout history. But through it all we remained cheerfully optimistic and in that way reflected the high morale of the British people in that, 'Their Finest Hour'.

My earlier reference to pyjamas might suggest that they were commonplace as night attire, when generally men slept in their khaki shirts. Being potential officers enabled us to be different. However, on the parade ground and when on exercises, that difference was extra chivvying and a very proper insistence on excellence.

In 1983 I returned to the Isle of Wight confident that I could find, at the very least, some depression in the ground identifying that trench, but it and the cattle shed had gone for ever.

Three days after that nightly manning of our trench, I appeared before an OCTU Selection Board in the early afternoon and was seen by our C.O. at 1600 hrs and a Brigadier (not the apopletic one) at 1800 hrs. All was well and I was informed that I would be leaving for an OCTU in seven days. A great moment! On the 26th September at 0830 hrs, I was one of nine paraded on the Barracks' Square for our C.O. to wish us success and we were then away by truck to Newport Station, there to take the train to Cowes; soon after its start, we opened the compartment window and cast out our haversack rations. We were on our way to better things.

The ceremony of departure epitomized the high standard of that training centre of The Hampshire Regiment, a place where we were extremely well treated at a time of crisis and where we were well and systematically trained during those busy weeks, all within the battle developing around us.

At Cowes we took the Southampton boat and then the Salisbury train, our destination being the OCTU at The Gordon Barracks, Bulford, Wilts. The army had not coarsened us, for at Salisbury we lunched at the Cadena, shopped and looked in at the cathedral, before catching the Bulford train.

I was pleased with our new home – brick bungalows, about one year old. There we had the luxury of a spring bed, mattress, pillow (not one filled with straw as before), a pair of sheets and three blankets, later increased to four. A steel cabinet accommodated our clothes. We lived in a barrack room with a coal fire, sash windows in each side wall (all had to be fully opened each morning) and a hardwood floor. Fireplace and floor had to be polished to perfection daily. Soon I was able to advice my mother that the food was good and that I no longer required food parcels.

Life was a continuation of the earlier training but of a higher intensity, as busy days of parades and instruction extended into evenings devoted to study and we seldom went out, passes being limited to 10% of cadets at any one time. But we did have a weekend at home. Sessions in the gym, the study of maps and mapping, together with more drill parades and inspections of us and our work, took the place of tactical exercises. Lectures on non-military and military subjects extended our curriculum and improved self-confidence, as did our increased efficiency on the parade ground under the critical eyes of our Grenadier Guards instructors. We experienced being at the receiving end of what I would describe as unreasonable punishment. Two examples – for being late on parade the platoon spent a wet Saturday afternoon in November, digging in chalk, and the remainder of the weekend in removing the same from our clothing. For being on parade with two buttons undone, I was charged with 'Gross breach of discipline while on Active Service and failure to obey Standing Orders' – result three evening parades. I trust that, as was intended, we learned the virtue of tolerance. Presumably we were much needed elsewhere, for what was a four month course was reduced to three, and those of us not being 'returned to Units' were seeing reps from Austin Reed, and having our final parades. The splendid perfection of our Guardsman C.O. with bulldog to heel as he took our salute on the parade ground remains clear in my memory. One does not need to be a sociologist to appreciate the significant of our choice of that famous Salisbury hostelry the Haunch of Venison for our departing luncheon, a most happy, beer-swilling one, rather than the Cadena as on our arrival. . . .

Happy days – and I was going on to the Regiment of my choice.

APPENDIX B

2 Div. Exercise No: 3.

No: 225/933.

Outline Orders

1.
INFORMATION: On 24th Feb. 41 German forces attempted a full-scale invasion of Great Britain. Enemy forces estimated at 1 inf. div. and 1 armd. div. landed between ATWICK and BRIDLINGTON.

Our defences in this area were over-run. A.F.V.s reached by nightfall the line of the RIVER DERWENT.

In the afternoon of 24 Feb. Comd. 2 Div. ordered a counter-attack by reserve Bns. of the 201st Bde. to re-establish the coastline as far north as BARMSTON 6378. By nightfall this attack had reached the line BARMSTON DRAIN TO GT. DRIFFIELD.

At 1600 hrs. 24.2.41 2 Dorset were ordered to prolong the line of the RIVER HULL defences Northwards, and to cover GT. DRIFFIELD.

Div. Recce. Bn and 13 A/Tk Regt. (less 3 Btys) were ordered to block all approaches Southward from LANGTOFT 4886 to SLEDMERE - to FRIDAYTHORPE.

4th and 5th Inf. Bde groups were ordered to be prepared to move after 0700hrs 25 Feb. to area GT. DRIFFIELD to attack and recover BRIDLINGTON in conjunction with 8th Armd. Div.

2. INTENTION. 2 Dorset will take up a defensive position covering GT. DRIFFIELD.

3. METHOD. Phase 1. Bn. will move by march route and debus at 498779. For March Table, see App. "A" attached.

Protection on the move N9: 4 Pl. will move independently and patrol entrances to GT. DRIFFIELD from WANSFORD to NAFFERTON to WOLD HOUSE to rd. junc. 511818 to KILHAM WESTFIELD from 0715hrs. 25.2.41, and will cover the deployment and recce. of 2 Dorset. 4 Pl. will withdraw to FIELD HOUSE 4978 at 1000hrs.

R.V. for recce parties WANSFORD Bridge 539757 at 0730 hrs.25.2.41

Phase II The Bn. will be dispersed on a three Coy. front with DB Right from WANSFORD - rd. GT. DRIFFIELD to NAFFERTON (excl.) DC Centre from rd. GT. DRIFFIELD to NAFFERTON (incl.) - rd. Pt.147 (5181)- Pt.175 (4980) DA Left from rd.Pt.147 - Pt.175 to cross rds.483837. DD in reserve at FIELD HOUSE 4978. "B" Echelon will lie up in area SUNDERLAND-WICK HALL until ordered to proceed to Coys. with mid-day meal.

4. ADMINISTRATION. (a) Breakfast before leaving camp.
(b) A hot meal will be served in the field. All ration lorries will be clear of fwd. Coys. by 1200 hrs. All eating to be completed by 1215 hrs.

5. INTERCOMMUNICATION. Bn. H.Q. and R.A.P. open at LITTLE KENDALE 4979 at 0845 hrs.

A.T. McBridge

HULL.
24.2.41.
JW

Captain,
Adjutant, 2nd Bn The Dorsetshire Regiment

DISTRIBUTION. O.C. "A" "B" "C" "D" "HQ" "R" Coys, "B" Ech.R.S.M. Q.M. I.O. M.T.O., S.O. Umpires (3) Police, 2/Lieut N.Havers, Adjt., C.O. O.C. 4Pl.,. File.

APPENDIX C

Recollections of a Casualty at the Irrawaddy River

by Harold Jones.

On 15th March, 1945 at 0830 hours the battalion advanced on Kadozeik. On the left 'B' Company supported by three Grant tanks of 'C' Squadron of the 3rd Carbiniers, on the right 'C' Company. Only two tanks joined battle, the third was immobilised by a mechanical fault.

To the front of my platoon, number 11, was what looked like an overgrown English hedgerow and when the enemy opened fire my two leading sections took cover behind the hedge to observe. There was nothing else to do, to attempt to force a way through the hedge under fire would have resulted in heavy losses.

A few yards to the left there was a track through the hedge into the next field and on the far side of the field about 100 yards further on was a second hedge which harboured the enemy. The two tanks advanced along the track, firing. As the leading tank approached the second hedge it was hit by an infantry anti-tank projectile and caught fire. Four of the crew were killed. The second tank withdraw safety but Lieutenant Lothian and three of the crew were wounded.

While this was going on I stood up in the hedgerow to observe. Suddenly I felt a blow in my right shoulder. Even at moments of stress the brain is capable of comic comparisons. It seemed as if a powerful cistern in my back had flushed. Fortunately it was beyond comprehension that the sensation and extraordinary noise was caused by the outrush of a torrent of blood and the inrush of air into the lung.

I fell to the ground almost into the arms of Captain A. C. MacKenzie, the Company Second-in-Command who had come forward to observe.

A few minutes later our Medical Officer, Captain J. A. Chamberlin, MC, who was also among the forward companies to see what was happening, joined me. He rolled me over face down, told me to keep still and said he would sew me up on the spot, which he did.

I was placed on a stretcher which was lifted by four bearers, one of whom was the Regimental Padre, the Reverend L. E. M. Claxton, MC, and hurried to the rear. As the party passed through a field gate my right shoulder struck the upright post. The jolt surprised but did not hurt. I had recovered slightly by now and I cried out, "Mind my b....y arm!" to indicate there was still some fighting spirit left and I was not yet a corpse. I regret to say I may even have addressed this remark to our dear Padre personally for he was supporting the right rear handles and was nearest both to my shoulder and the post.

About 300 yards to the rear my stretcher was placed on a Jeep ambulance and in a short time we arrived at a light aircraft strip.

By 1945 three squadrons of the United States Army Air Force Air Commandos, Squadrons numbers 164, 165 and 166 were operating in Burma. Each squadron had 36 L.5. aircraft and four or five Norsemen. The former aircraft could carry one patient lying or sitting, the latter five sitting or two or three lying.

The most used aircraft, the L.5., was able to operate from small air-strips 300 or 400 yards long and 30 yards wide. The aircraft were at the sole disposal of the medical services and were available on an as-required basis for casualty evacuation from the divisions in combat.

On average an L.5. was able to evacuate five casualties a day. A squadron of 30 such aircraft could evacuate a maximum of 180 cases a day for short peak periods. The aircraft, loaded, could not fly more than 50 miles and back without re-fuelling. In March 1945 the total number of casualties evacuated by light aircraft from IV Corps and XXXIII Corps was 8,309.

At the strip my stretcher was immediately lifted into a waiting L.5. and the pilot took off. He flew with the cockpit window open, and the breeze wafting through was a pleasant sensation after the extreme heat at ground level. As a result of a morphine injection and the excitement, I must have fallen asleep for my next memory is of the Corps Medical Centre.

XXXIII Corps Medical Centre, established at Sadaung 15 miles north of the Irrawaddy, comprised:

7 (Ind.) Malaria Forward Treatment Unit
9 (Ind.) Mobile Surgical Units
67 (Ind.) Field Ambulance less one company
A Mobile X-Ray Unit
2 Field Transfusion Unit
44 (Ind.) Sub-depot Medical Stores
One Sub-section of 6 Motor Ambulance Section
One Sub-section, The American Field Service
One platoon 69 (Ind.) Anti-Malaria Unit
Detachment 56 (Ind.) Field Hygiene Section

From 20th February to 31st March 1945 the average weekly strength of XXXIII Corps was 76,813, the total number of soldiers evacuated beyond the Regimental Aid Posts was 14,652 and the number of battle casualties was 4,556. The Corps Medical Centre at Sadaung treated a high percentage of the serious cases.

I do not remember arriving at the Corps Medical Centre but no doubt my wound was inspected and redressed. My next memory is of sitting propped upright in bed in the main surgical reception ward where casualties were prepared for surgery and retained for post-surgical care.

The ward was like a big English barn. The walls were of stone and brick and the large-span roof was supported by wooden beams. It may have been a monastic building or a Court House commandeered for use as a hospital.

There were about 60 stretcher cases there and a purposeful staff of doctors, nurses and orderlies were moving about continually. I saw, in the next bed, Corporal Crane of my platoon who had been wounded shortly after I was shot.

He was comatose with a drip in his nostril and was heavily bandaged about the waist. He died during the night.

Late in the afternoon a surgeon in a white apron visited me and asked how I was feeling. He said, "We shall take you into the theatre tomorrow morning to tidy up your wound and put some new stitches in." This and the air of efficiency inspired confidence but I remember having an uncomfortable night.

Of the next morning I remember nothing. When I became conscious I was in bed in a canvas marquee with about six other officers and it was late afternoon. In the bed opposite me was a big, fine-looking officer who had been hit in the spine. He had no feeling in his legs and was unable to move them and was incontinent.

Two nursing sisters were constantly in attendance at his bed and he kept apologising to them. I remember thinking how good they were in trying to put him at ease and comfort him.

Again I had an uncomfortable night and woke several times. At about midnight I noticed the bed opposite had been screened. When I woke up again at about 0300 hours, both the screens and the bed had been removed.

The following day, the third since I had been wounded, I felt more robust and asked whether I could get up. This was permitted, so I walked about.

The marquee was pitched on sandy soil and some of the guy ropes were secured to trees. There were people to talk to and the surrounding country of central Burma desert was attractive to look at.

In the Second World War the two great life savers were blood transfusion and penicillin. In 1944 I had suffered a gunshot wound in the left leg during a field firing exercise. A blood transfusion had saved my life then. Now I benefitted from penicillin.

When the surgeons tidied up the wound where the bullet went out of my back, they inserted a short plastic tube and secured it with an adhesive dressing. Every day for about a week, an orderly visited me and asked me to sit on the bed while he dripped the prescribed dose of penicillin into the plastic tube.

On the fourth day, the Medical Officer in charge listened to my breathing with a stethoscope and sounded the lung by thumping my chest with his fingers. "I must aspirate that this afternoon," he said, "there is a lot of fluid there."

After luncheon he reappeared, dressed in shorts, a long white butcher's apron with a halter neck, no sleeves and open at the sides. Shortly I was to see the perspiration streaming off him. He was a tall, tough, lithe Scot and very fit, which was just as well.

He explained what he was going to do and asked me to sit on the edge of my bed. He sat on the other side. He pushed the needle of a syringe into my back and into the lung. It was painless except for the initial prick.

He then disconnected the syringe and connected another. Every time the plunger was withdrawn the syringe filled with blood; he then disconnected it, expelled the fluid into a basin and repeated the operation.

This continued for about 20 minutes and he kept asking me whether I was all right. It was very hot and it seemed to me the doctor, who was trying to complete the aspiration as quickly as possible, was near exhaustion. So I said that perhaps I ought to ask whether he was all right.

He then explained that during the supply of medical stores by airlift or air drop, some of the panniers had gone adrift, including one which contained the large syringes normally used for aspirating. He had, therefore, to perform the operation with a small-capacity syringe normally used for injections. Eventually the lung was emptied and it did not have to be done again.

A few days later the dressing and tube were removed and I was evacuated in a Dakota aircraft. This departed from a heavy air-strip near Sadaung and landed at Comilla where the Advanced Base Hospital was.

After about a week in Comilla I was again evacuated by air to Calcutta where convalescent patients stayed before being sent on convalescent leave. This Staging Unit was housed in a splendid town house with marble floors and verandahs. Although my bed was on a first floor balcony which extended along the whole of one side of the house, the climate was oppressive.

From Calcutta a number of patients were sent by train to a convalescent home in Darjeeling. We arrived there in the dark. In the morning when we looked out of the bedroom window we saw the magnificent sight of Kanchenjunga towering over the town.

One morning, with some fellow convalescents, I rose at about 0300 hours and boarded a native omnibus for Tiger Hill where we climbed to the viewing point. We were rewarded for, as dawn broke and the clouds lifted, we saw Mount Everest trailing its plume of vapour about 110 miles away to the north-west.

I rejoined the Battalion at Bandel near Calcutta about the 9th May, 1945, having been absent for about nine weeks.

Reference was made to the War Diaries of 2 Dorset, 2 Division, 33 Corps and the 5th Field Ambulance, the privately published I Serve by Lt Col LE Oatts and HMSO The Army Medical Services, Burma.

Index

Dr. MURAT BOLELLİ

GÜÇ İLE YÖNETİM

abaküs